Andrew Lownie was educated at Magdalene College, Cambridge, where he was Dunster History Prizeman and President of the Union, before taking his Masters and doctorate at Edinburgh University. A Fellow of the Royal Historical Society and former visiting fellow of Churchill College, Cambridge, he has run his own literary agency since 1988. A trustee of the Campaign for Freedom of Information and President of The Biographers Club, he has written for the *Times*, *Telegraph*, *Wall Street Journal*, *Spectator* and *Guardian* and formerly served in the Royal Naval Reserve.

Praise for *Traitor King*:

'Meticulously researched' *Spectator*

'Briskly written and compulsively readable...Does Andrew Lownie persuade me that it is worth telling the story again, and that he has made out the case for his unforgiving title? The answer is an unambiguous yes'
TLS

'Entertaining... convincing... timely. Urgent reading for royals'
Evening Standard

'Darkly compelling...hundreds of eye-popping details...Gripping though it is, this is an unrelentingly damning portrait of the Windsors'
Daily Mail

'Compelling... a devastating portrait of the duke and duchess... a timely point of comparison when set against the ongoing trials and tribulations of the House of Windsor'
The Tablet

'Lownie reveals Edward not as a dupe of the Nazis, but an active and culpable collaborator...The list of individuals interviewed and archives consulted is formidable. The more impressive then, that this is a wonderfully readable and succinct story'
BBC History Magazine

'Thoroughly researched and compelling narrative of one of the most controversial periods in royal history'
Andrew Morton

'Andrew Lownie has a remarkable ability to fashion a compelling narrative from raw archive text and personal reminiscence. His *Traitor King* (Blink, £25), about the Duke and Duchess of Windsor and their questionable cohorts, is every bit as absorbing as his earlier history of the Mountbattens'
Andrew Lycett, *Spectator* Books of the Year 2021

'Definitively answering some of the enduring mysteries ...Lownie fearlessly yet fairly provides the answers. Lownie appears to have read every book ever written about the Windsors and drilled deep into unpublished archives as well...Lownie has dug into the couple's complex love lives just as deeply...The full ghastly truth about them has remained obscure until now, partly thanks to a judicious cover-up by the British Establishment'
History Today

'Meticulously researched and with so much new material on one of the most controversial Royals of the 20th century. Lownie reveals shocking new aspects to the life of Edward, Duke of Windsor, and firmly placed the Duke as a traitor to his country'
Aspects of History

'This "explosive new royal biography" (front-cover blurb) by the highly regarded author of books about Guy Burgess and the Mountbattens... a biographer as serious and scholarly as Andrew Lownie... Lownie gives heft to George Orwell's famous observation that the England of that time was a family, but one "with the wrong members in control"'
Times Book of the Week

'Andrew Lownie's compelling volume... an unflattering portrait of this entitled couple'
Daily Mail Books of the Year 2021

'Through meticulous research Lownie makes a convincing argument for the duke's treachery...Edward is revealed for what he was: a traitor to the British people and an ally to Hitler....Academic in its tone and shocking in its contents Lownie goes where no royal biography has gone before. It sheds new light on British history and during the Second World War and would make for a stellar TV series'
The Lady

'Andrew Lownie has uncovered an array of new sources regarding the Duke and Duchess of Windsor, and he exhibits a sovereign command of the existing biographies. Tackling the most sensitive subjects-the Duke and Duchess' sexuality, their pro-Nazi views, their problematic behavior during the war, and the complicated nature of their relationship - Lownie has painted the most convincing portrait of the couple to date. The results are fascinating, if disconcerting'
Jonathan Petropoulos, author of *Royals and the Reich: The Princes von Hessen in Nazi Germany*

'Compelling and conclusive'
Clive Irving, bestselling author of *The Last Queen*

'Andrew Lownie has done it again'
Kitty Kelley

The Scandalous Exile of the
Duke and Duchess of Windsor

TRAITOR
KING

ANDREW LOWNIE

BLINK
bringing you closer

First published in the UK by Blink Publishing
An imprint of Bonnier Books UK
4th Floor, Victoria House
Bloomsbury Square
London, WC1B 4DA

Owned by Bonnier Books
Sveavägen 56, Stockholm, Sweden

facebook.com/blinkpublishing
twitter.com/blinkpublishing

Hardback: 978-1-78870-481-6
Trade Paperback: 978-1-78870-483-0
Paperback: 978-1-78870-487-8
Ebook: 978-1-78870-485-4
Audiobook: 978-1-78870-486-1

British Library Cataloguing-in-Publication Data:
A catalogue record for this book is available from the British Library.

Design by www.envydesign.co.uk
Printed and bound in Great Britain by Clays Ltd, Elcograf S.p.A.

1 3 5 7 9 10 8 6 4 2

The publisher has made every effort to contact rights holders for permission to use
their material, but in the event of any omission, will happily make amends and update the
publication at the earliest opportunity.

Blink Publishing is an imprint of Bonnier Books UK
www.bonnierbooks.co.uk

Contents

CHAPTER I

The Year of Three Kings

On Friday 11 December 1936, the final vote on the Abdication Bill was passed in Parliament and Edward VIII ceased to be king. He had reigned for 326 days. His father's premonition that within twelve months of his death his son would 'ruin himself' had come true.

The newly created Duke of Windsor spent the afternoon packing and reading letters of support and sympathy at his country house, Fort Belvedere, in Windsor Great Park. A sham Gothic royal folly with battlements, rows of cannons, turrets and a tower, it had been built for William, Duke of Cumberland between 1746 and 1757, then embellished by the Regency architect Sir Jeffry Wyatville in the reign of George IV.

Prince Edward had taken over the grace and favour residence in 1929. He was later to write: 'The Fort had been more than a home; it had been a way of life for me. I had created the Fort just as my grandfather had created Sandringham; I loved it in the same way; it was there that I had passed the happiest days of my life.'[1]

Sir Giles Gilbert Scott had added a guest wing in 1936 and Edward had installed central heating, en-suite bathrooms, a tennis court, swimming pool, and in the basement, a Turkish bath. It

[1] The Duke of Windsor, *A King's Story* (Cassell, 1951), p. 412.

I

was his private retreat where he had entertained most weekends and where his romance had played out with the woman for whom he had given up the throne. Now he was having to leave it and his staff to venture into an uncertain future.

At 4 p.m., Winston Churchill, who had joined him for lunch and to help polish his speech, left the Fort, his eyes filled with tears, muttering a couplet by Andrew Marvell about the beheading of Charles I:

He nothing common did or mean
Upon that memorable scene

Next there was a dinner to say goodbye to his family: his sister Mary and his mother, Queen Mary, widow of George V; his younger brothers, Henry, Duke of Gloucester; George, Duke of Kent; and Bertie, the new King George VI.

At 7 p.m., his faithful chauffeur, George Ladbroke, drove him the five miles to Royal Lodge, where the family had gathered. It was a strained atmosphere. Bertie was coming to terms with the responsibilities and challenges of his new role, whilst the rest of the Royal Family was still reeling from the events of the past few weeks, when David (as Edward was known in the family) had threatened to commit suicide if he could not marry the twice-divorced American, Wallis Simpson.

The new Duke of Windsor, on the other hand, felt liberated. His obsession with Wallis had given him an excuse to renounce the role of king, which he had increasingly not wanted. It had also allowed the government, concerned about his political views, especially towards Germany, and whether he had the qualities needed to be monarch, to force him to abdicate.

At 9.30 p.m., whilst the family was still at dinner, the lawyer Walter Monckton, Edward's trusted adviser and a friend since

Oxford days, arrived to escort him to Windsor Castle, where the former king was due to broadcast to the nation. They drove in silence down the Long Walk – Wallis's cairn terrier, Slipper, on Windsor's lap – turned into the huge Quadrangle and stopped at the Sovereign's Entrance, where Sir John Reith, the Director-General of the BBC, was waiting. Windsor got out of the car holding a cigar in one hand and Slipper in the other and introduced Monckton to Reith.

The broadcast was to be in the king's former living quarters, a small suite in the Augusta Tower; given its size, most of the electrical equipment had to be set up in the corridor. Windsor greeted the technicians affably and went into the sitting room, where the microphones stood on a table with a chair facing them and an evening newspaper beside them. Reith handed him the paper and requested him to read a few lines aloud to test the voice levels – he chose a passage on lawn tennis. He then popped into the loo, returning with words, 'I expect that's the last time I'll use that place.'[2]

Just before 10 p.m., Reith sat down at the microphone, waiting for the red light to flash. As it did so, he began, 'This is Windsor Castle. His Royal Highness the Prince Edward.' As he slid out of the chair to the left, the former king slid in from the right.

'At long last, I am able to say a few words of my own.' He praised his brother Bertie and spoke generously of the Prime Minister, Stanley Baldwin, continuing:

> I have found it impossible to carry the heavy burden of responsibility and to discharge my duties as King as I would wish to do without the help and support of the woman I love . . . I now quit altogether public affairs, and I lay down my burden.

[2] J. Bryan III and C.J.V. Murphy, *The Windsor Story* (Granada, 1979), p. 285.

It may be sometime before I return to my native land, but I shall always follow the fortunes of the British race and Empire with profound interest, and if at any time in the future I can be found of service to His Majesty in a private station I shall not fail. And now we all have a new King. I wish him, and you, his people, happiness and prosperity with all my heart. God bless you all. God Save the King.

After the speech, the National Anthem was played. Monckton had been standing behind the former king throughout the broadcast. As he moved forward to collect the speech, Windsor laid his hand on his shoulder, saying, 'Walter, it's a far better thing that I go.'[3] At Chartwell, Winston Churchill, who had tried so hard to prevent the Abdication, was in tears as he listened.

Wallis Simpson listened to the broadcast in the sitting room at Villa Lou Vei, the home of her friends Herman and Katherine Rogers in Cannes, where she had taken refuge a few weeks earlier.

'I was lying on the sofa with my hands over my eyes, trying to hide my tears,' she later remembered. 'After he finished, the others quietly went away and left me alone. I lay there a long time before I could control myself enough to walk through the house and go upstairs to my room.'[4]

At 10.30 p.m., Windsor returned to Royal Lodge to say good-bye to his family. Dickie Mountbatten, for whom Windsor had been best man in 1922, had driven over from the Fort and remembered: 'Everybody was still in tears when David came in, but David

---

[3] Lord Birkenhead, *Walter Monckton* (Weidenfeld & Nicolson, 1969), p. 152.

[4] The Duchess of Windsor, *The Heart Has Its Reasons* (Michael Joseph, 1956), p. 278. According to a maid interviewed by Wallis biographer Ralph Martin, a grim-faced Wallis muttered, 'The fool, the stupid fool.' Ralph Martin, *The Woman He Loved* (WH Allen, 1974), p. 295.

was jubilant. He was like a schoolboy going off on holiday. "It's all over!" he kept saying. "It's finished, thank God!"[5]

Queen Mary and the Princess Royal left first at 11.30 p.m. The politician and socialite Chips Channon, basing his diary entry on a conversation with Monckton a few days later, wrote that 'Queen Mary, ever magnificent, was mute and immoveable and very royal, and thoughtfully left off her mourning black for the evening so as not to cast more gloom.'[6] Half an hour later, Windsor said his final goodbyes and the four brothers walked to the door. The Duke of Kent, his eyes swollen from crying, sobbed, 'It isn't *possible*! It isn't *happening*!'[7]

George VI later remembered, 'We kissed, parted as Freemasons, and he bowed to me as his King.'[8] Windsor bent over the new king and declared, 'God bless you, sir! I hope you will be happier than your predecessor,' and disappeared into the night, leaving the Royal Family speechless.[9]

Accompanied by Chief Inspector David Storrier, his personal protection officer, Windsor was driven in heavy rain to Portsmouth by Ladbroke. Arriving at 1.30 a.m. at the Main, not Unicorn, Gate, they struggled to find the Royal Jetty. It seemed symbolic. A naval guard with rifles and fixed bayonets had been paraded for hours on the cold, dark and deserted quayside. Also waiting were members of his household: the Keeper of the Privy Purse, Ulick Alexander; his private secretary, Godfrey Thomas; and his equerry since 1919,

[5] Bryan and Murphy, p. 287.

[6] 21 December 1936, Robert Rhodes James (ed.), *Chips: The Diaries of Sir Henry Channon* (Weidenfeld & Nicolson, 1967), p. 103.

[7] Windsor, *King's Story*, p. 414.

[8] Bryan and Murphy, p. 287. Windsor had joined the Household Brigade Lodge No. 2164 in 1919, Bertie the Navy Lodge No. 2612 in the same year.

[9] Rhodes James, *Channon*, p. 103.

Piers Legh, who had volunteered to go with him, after discovering his former master would otherwise go into exile alone.

Windsor crossed the gangway onto HMS *Fury* – the original choice HMS *Enchantress* was not deemed appropriate – with Slipper under his arm. 'I knew now that I was irretrievably on my own,' he later wrote. 'The drawbridges were going up behind me.'[10]

---

[10] Windsor, *King's Story*, pp. 413–15. According to a rating, 'the ex-King was so drunk he was carried onboard', email to the author from the rating's cousin, David Mason, 24 January 2022.

CHAPTER 2

Waiting to Wed

HMS *Fury* left at 2 a.m. but, because the weather was bad, lay off
the Isle of Wight so the Duke could get some sleep. The Captain, Cecil Howe, had hurriedly had to borrow linen, crockery
and glasses from the Royal Yacht, and a Surgeon-Commander had
been brought on board 'in case the ex-King's state of mental stress
should cause him to require any medical attention while at sea'.[1]
Windsor was fine, preferring to sit in the wardroom until 4 a.m.
drinking brandy and going over the events of the past few weeks
with an exhausted Piers Legh and Ulick Alexander, who was also
escorting him across the Channel.

Much of the time was spent sending farewell cables to friends.
When told that the wireless could not be used when the ship
reached territorial waters, the Duke ordered *Fury* back to sea
until he finished his list. 'He later happily confided to another
close associate, Lord Peregrine Brownlow, how much money he
had saved because all those cables were free.'[2] The ship docked at
dawn. Windsor's first act was to telephone Wallis.

[1] Alfred Shaughnessy, *Both Ends of the Candle* (Peter Owen, 1978), pp. 44–6.
[2] Martin, p. 303.

She spent most of the Saturday in bed depressed by events. Her friend Constance Coolidge had told the journalist Helen Worden Erskine, after listening to the broadcast:

> Can you imagine a more terrible fate than to have to live up publicly to the legend of a love you don't feel? To have to face, morning, noon and night, a middle-aged boy with no other purpose in life than a possessive passion for you?[3]

Wallis, who was two years younger than the Prince of Wales, had first been introduced to him at a weekend house party given by Lady Furness in January 1931. Over the next three years she saw him socially and by January 1934 she had become his mistress. Soon the Prince began to talk of marriage – a situation that became more critical when he succeeded as King in January 1936 and when Wallis was granted a divorce in October from her second husband, Ernest Simpson, an executive in his family's shipping company, whom she had married in 1928.

The problem was that Wallis was now twice-divorced – an early marriage at the age of twenty to an American naval aviator, Earl Winfield Spencer, had ended in divorce in 1927 – and the Church of England, of which the monarch was Supreme Governor, would not conduct the marriage of a divorced person if their spouse was still alive. The Prince would have to choose between marriage to Wallis and being King. Although Wallis had suggested they break off their relationship, Edward was determined to go ahead, even if it meant surrendering the throne.

---

[3] Helen Erskine interview, Box 74, Columbia University, and Andrew Morton, *Wallis in Love: The Untold True Passion of the Duchess of Windsor* (Michael O'Mara, 2018), p. 229.

Quite apart from being divorced, there had long been concerns in Establishment circles about Wallis's suitability as a possible Queen – not least her pro-German views, her lovers, and the fact that the Prince had lavished large amounts of money on her, including expensive jewels. She was put under police surveillance.

A June 1935 Special Branch report had noted that Mrs Simpson:

> was regarded as a person as very fond of the company of men and to have had many 'affairs'. She was with different men at these addresses. Although she spends a great deal of time with the POW, it is said she has another secret lover who is kept by her.[4]

The following month Lionel Halsey, the Prince of Wales's treasurer, wrote to George V's private secretary, Clive Wigram, that Wallis: 'was at present receiving a very handsome income . . . I also told HM that in my opinion both Mrs S and her husband were just hand in glove in getting all they could out of HRH.'[5]

It was against this background that over the past few weeks, Wallis had been receiving threats on her life and hate mail.[6] For legal reasons, she and her lover were now living in separate countries until the *decree absolute* came through. On 9 December, an Essex solicitor's clerk, Francis Stephenson, had filed suit at the High Court that the *decree absolute* should not be granted because of collusion and because Wallis had committed adultery with the

---

[4] MEPO 10/35. He was identified as Guy Trundle, a salesman with the Ford Motor Company.

[5] 18 July 1935, RA/PS/PS/GVI/PS/C/019/287, quoted Alexander Larman, *The Crown in Crisis* (Weidenfeld & Nicolson, 2020), p. 24.

[6] Just after Christmas a Canadian, Elmore Lowell Staples, threatened to kill the Duke and was arrested in possession of a knife and gun.

former king in her homes at 5 Bryanston Court and 1 Cumberland Terrace, at Fort Belvedere, and on holiday on board the yacht *Nahlin* in the autumn of 1936. Having given up so much, there was now a danger they could not wed.

In official circles, there were continuing concerns about the Duke's supporters and Wallis's own ambitions. On 10 December, a Scotland Yard official had written to the Commissioner, Sir Philip Game, stating that two personal protection officers needed to remain with her at Cannes as indications were she 'intended to "flit"' to Germany.[7] A few days later, the officers reported a phone conversation where Wallis had told the Duke, attempting to sort out a post-abdication financial settlement, 'If they don't get you this (*sic*) things, I will return to England and fight it out to the bitter end. The coronation will be a flop compared with the story that I shall tell the British press.'[8]

On 10 December, Horace Wilson, a senior civil servant, had written to the Chancellor of the Exchequer, Neville Chamberlain, of his worries that Wallis Simpson intended:

> not only to come back here but (aided by what she expects to be a generous provision from public funds) to set up a 'Court' of her own and – there can be little doubt – do her best to make things uncomfortable for the new occupant of the Throne. It must not be assumed that she has abandoned hope of becoming Queen of England. It is known that she has limitless ambition, including a desire to interfere in politics: she has been in touch with the Nazi movement and has definite ideas as to dictatorship.[9]

---

[7] Notes of telephone conversation with Inspector Evans, 10 December, MEPO 10/35, The National Archives (TNA). Also CAB 21/4100/2, TNA.

[8] MEPO 10/35, TNA

[9] Horace Wilson to Neville Chamberlain, 10 December 1936, PREM 1/453, TNA.

On the night before the Duke's broadcast, 500 pro-Nazi supporters had gathered at Buckingham Palace, chanting, 'We want Edward!' and 'One, two, three, four, five, we want Baldwin, dead or alive!' later converging on Downing Street. The following afternoon, 3,000 people had attended a mass meeting in Stepney, addressed by Sir Oswald Mosley, leader of the British Union of Fascists, in which he demanded that the abdication issue should be put to the people. On 11 December, the Zionist campaigner Blanche Dugdale wrote in her diary that her friend, the historian Jack Wheeler-Bennett, 'is on record that Ribbentrop used Mrs Simpson, but proofs are hard to come by.'[10]

Meanwhile, from Boulogne, the Duke had taken a special Pullman for Austria, where he had been lent the use of Schloss Enzesfeld, the home of Baron Eugene and Kitty Rothschild, just outside Vienna, after it was discovered he had nowhere to go whilst he waited to marry Wallis. His initial euphoria had now vanished as the reality of his position sunk in. On Sunday 13 December, the Archbishop of Canterbury had preached a sermon berating the Duke for seeking:

> happiness in a manner inconsistent with the Christian principles of marriage and within a social circle whose standards and ways of life are alien to the best instincts of his people . . . ruined by his disastrous liking for vulgar society, and by his infatuation for this Mrs Simpson.[11]

The Duke had been sufficiently angry to consult Monckton about a lawsuit.[12]

[10] Blanche Dugdale diary, 11 December 1936, courtesy of Adam Fergusson.

[11] Philip Ziegler, *King Edward VIII* (Collins, 1990), p. 338.

[12] Martin, p. 305.

There was relief in official circles that the Abdication Crisis seemed to have blown over and the couple neutralised. Amongst those who knew the Duke well, he was not missed. Harold Nicolson noted in his diary, after lunching on 14 December with the Duke's former assistant private secretary, Sir Alan 'Tommy' Lascelles, how he:

> is so relieved at the fall of his master that he was almost indiscreet . . . He says that the King was like the child in the fairy story who was given every gift except a soul. There was nothing in him which understood the intellectual or spiritual sides of life, and that all art, poetry, music, etc. were dead to him . . . He had no friends in this country, nobody whom he would ever wish to see again . . . He was without a soul, and this made him a trifle mad . . . he never cared for England or the English. He hated his country since he had no soul and did not like being reminded of his duties.[13]

It was a view shared by the MP Robert Bernays, who had ruminated in his diary a few days earlier:

> He hasn't one real friend to lean upon in this frightful emergency. His case seems to be arrested development. He has never passed the stage from boyhood to manhood. He is the spoiled child of success with the film star mentality. He sees his job only in terms of cheering crowds . . . He has never thought the matter out. He imagined that he could quietly retire into private life, leaving his brother to perform the dreary ceremonial functions, while he spent a tranquil life gardening at Fort Belvedere and holidaying on the Riviera,

[13] 14 December 1936, Nicolson MS, Balliol College.

occasionally emerging to open a hospital or review the Fleet and receive the cheers that mean so much to him. For the first time he has been brought up against the fact that abdication means exile and that for the rest of his life he can serve no useful purpose.[14]

Windsor was not an easy house guest. Kitty Rothschild had brought staff from her home in Paris and made great efforts to ensure the Schloss was welcoming, giving him a suite of rooms, comprising bedroom, drawing room, library, smoking room and bathroom, but he remained depressed and frustrated.

He watched Mickey Mouse movies, went sightseeing, walked, played golf and skittles, skied, and once a week took a Turkish bath in Vienna. There were card games where 'he played for high stakes, and when he won he cheerfully collected his winnings. But when he lost, he did not pay.'[15] He distracted himself, according to Piers Legh, who had remained with him, by 'playing the jazz drums very loud and long to a gramophone record; he also drank quite a lot of brandy, and performed his celebrated imitation of Winston Churchill trying to persuade him not to abdicate.'[16]

When he shopped, he sent the bills to the British Legation, where no one knew what to do with them, until an equerry, probably Legh, paid them out of his own pocket.[17] Eventually the British Government said the purchases were not their responsibility and the bills were sent to the Rothschilds. Lunching with Sir Walford

[14] 9 December 1936, Robert Bernays and Nick Smart (eds.), *The Diaries and Letters of Robert Bernays, 1932–1939: An Insider's Account of the House of Commons* (Edwin Mellen Press, 1996), p. 279.

[15] Stephen Birmingham, *Duchess* (Futura, 1986), p. 166.

[16] Shaughnessy, p. 64.

[17] Iles Brody, *Gone with the Windsors* (John Winston Company, 1953), p. 238, and Birmingham, p. 166.

Selby, the British Ambassador, he asked what the silver rings around the napkins were. Told they were napkin rings, he expressed surprise that there was not 'fresh linen with every meal'.[18]

Much of his time was spent on the phone to Wallis – the bill at the end of his stay coming to £800, which he, too, expected the Rothschilds to cover.

He missed Wallis. Perry Brownlow, his loyal friend who had escorted Wallis to the South of France in December, now joined him and remembered:

> talking to him until three o'clock in the morning . . . all around his bed, propped up on chairs and tables, were pictures of Wallis. I counted sixteen of them. It was as if he were in a crypt. And there he was, fast asleep, hugging a small pillow of hers with the initials WS on it.[19]

Belittled and undermined by Wallis, angered by his family's refusal to acknowledge the woman he loved and the protracted financial negotiations, Windsor became almost paranoid, later admitting: 'It was the sense of powerlessness that brought me close to the breaking point. I could do nothing there but wait and count the days.'[20] The situation was not helped by Wallis's jealousy of Kitty Rothschild and the suspicion that the Duke was having an affair with her.

A further concern was a series of articles that ran from 17 December, syndicated in various American papers, written by Newbold Noyes, the husband of Wallis's second cousin. Noyes, who was part-owner of the *Washington Evening Star*, the city's largest afternoon daily, had offered to write some supportive articles about the couple.

---

[18] Birmingham, p. 168.

[19] Interview, Martin, p. 306.

[20] Bryan and Murphy, p. 318.

The previous November he had come to Britain, where he was given the use of an office at Buckingham Palace, and on the basis of three hours of interviews he had written 14,000 words; but the articles were not now to the couple's taste.

Wallis repudiated them, claiming in a statement she had not invited him to Britain, they were not related and she had not approved the articles. Statements over the authenticity of the articles flew between the parties for the next year and Wallis tried to sue Noyes, using as her lawyer Armand Gregoire, who had acted for her former husband Ernest Simpson's interests in France. He proved to be an unfortunate choice.

Gregoire, whose appearance was enhanced by a duelling scar across his left cheek, was also the lawyer for some of Hitler's most important officials: his Minister of Foreign Affairs, Joachim von Ribbentrop; the Deputy Fuhrer, Rudolf Hess; and Commander-in-Chief of the Luftwaffe, Hermann Goering; as well as the chief contact of Sir Oswald Mosley in Paris, where he was responsible for channelling funds to Mosley's British Union of Fascists from Mussolini. He had also been the founder and director of Marcel Bucard's fanatical Franciste movement, one of the leading Fascist cells in France, and under the pseudonym of Greg Le Franc, he had contributed pro-Hitler articles to *Le Franciste*, the official journal of the movement. According to a 1934 French Sûreté report, he was 'one of the most dangerous of Nazi spies'.[21]

Wallis's appointment of Gregoire as her lawyer only further confirmed concerns in official circles about the sympathies of the couple. Only on 18 December, a week after the Abdication, the diplomat Orme Sargent had recorded a memo on the Duke's association with Ribbentrop, noting that Hitler was 'very distressed at the

[21] 9 April 1934, Charles Higham, *Mrs Simpson: Secret Lives of the Duchess of Windsor* (Sidgwick & Jackson, 1988), p. 103.

turn that affairs had taken in this country, since he looked upon the late King as a man after his own heart, and one who understood the *Führerprinzip*, and was ready to introduce it into this country.'[22]

* * *

The Duke continued to be alternatively short-tempered, sullen, bored and depressed. Kitty Rothschild tried her best, laying on a musical entertainment on Christmas Eve with entertainers and musicians from Paris, but the Duke did not bother to attend. The next morning she had his gift – a set of sapphire studs from Cartier – placed on his breakfast tray. The gift caught him unawares, but he promised her a little something. Later that day he 'presented her with an autographed photograph of himself.'[23] Meanwhile Wallis spent Christmas Day at the Villa Mauresque as the guest of Somerset Maugham, with her friend, the interior designer Sibyl Colefax.

The arrival at the Schloss Enzesfeld of an old friend, Edward 'Fruity' Metcalfe, helped the situation. Three years younger than the Duke, Metcalfe was a tall, handsome cavalry officer, who had won the Military Cross during the First World War. The two men had met on Windsor's tour of India in 1922 and Windsor had quickly appointed him as an ADC, attracted by the Irishman's high-spirits, good-nature, loyalty, knowledge of horses and personal friendships with many of the maharajas.

It was taking time for the Duke to accept the new situation, but there were compensations – an invitation to open the Zorine Springs nudist colony, and to become mayor of Chippewa Falls in Wisconsin – and the Orpheum Theatre in Los Angeles offered him

---

[22] *Führerprinzip* means 'leader principle', Hitler's political ideology of absolute authority as leader of the Nazi party and total obedience of all subordinates. Royal Archives (hereafter RA) PS/PSO/GVI/PS/C/019/378.

[23] Birmingham, p. 166.

and his 'lovely lady' a million dollars and a Hollywood mansion to star in a 'stupendous historical film'.[24]

The Duke continued to ring the new king at all hours. 'Tonight he was told at dinner that HM wanted to talk on phone to him. He said he couldn't take the call, but asked for it to be put through at 10 p.m.,' Fruity Metcalfe wrote on 22 January to his wife Lady Alexandra Metcalfe, generally known as Baba, the sister-in-law and one-time mistress of Oswald Mosley. 'The answer to this was that HM said he would talk at 6.45 tomorrow, as he was too busy to talk at any other time. It was pathetic to see HRH's face. He couldn't believe it! He's been so used to having everything done as he wishes, I'm afraid he's going to have many more shocks like this.'[25] Eventually George VI told the switchboard at Buckingham Palace not to put the calls through at all.

These phone calls, which were bugged by the Austrians, were not only to sort out his own affairs – his possessions had been moved from Fort Belvedere to Frogmore House in Windsor – but also to arrange a financial settlement and press for recognition of Wallis in the family, not least by the family attending their wedding.

Bertie was sympathetic, but his mother Queen Mary was adamant that nothing should give the impression that the Royal Family accepted the relationship and this view was shared by the new Queen and most courtiers. When Lord Queenborough asked Elizabeth when the Duke might return to Britain, she supposedly replied, 'Not until he comes to my funeral.'[26]

The result was diminishing goodwill between the brothers and a resentment that was to last throughout the Duke's life. He was shocked that his younger brother did not have the time for long and

[24] Ziegler, p. 347.

[25] Anne de Courcy, *The Viceroy's Daughters* (Weidenfeld, 2000), pp. 248–9.

[26] Rhodes James, *Channon*, p. 191.

17

frequent phone calls, but the real break in their relationship was over the financial settlement.

At the Abdication, it had been agreed the Duke would receive £25,000 p.a., the annual annuity traditionally voted for a younger brother of a Sovereign, either from the Civil List or, if not approved by Parliament, from his brother. It was quickly discovered that the ex-king had not been open about his financial situation and he was far wealthier than he had claimed or was realised. He had told his brother he had just under £100,000, when, in fact, he had some £800,000 on deposit abroad, much of it controlled by Mrs Simpson; and another £80,000 was shortly to be paid from the Civil List and Duchies of Cornwall and Lancaster, the result of money saved over many years.[27]

The Duke felt his private wealth irrelevant to the compensation for relinquishing his interest in Balmoral and Sandringham, reiterating he was not well provided for 'considering the position I shall have to maintain and what I have given up'.[28] Negotiations over the issue were to continue over the next year.

A few weeks later, his old friend Walter Monckton arrived to try and thrash out a financial settlement after Windsor supposedly threatened not to sell Balmoral and Sandringham, claiming a 'syndicate of Seventh Avenue sportsmen' in New York were prepared to pay sufficient for shooting rights not to have to sell them.[29]

A mock sale of Sandringham, York Cottage, Balmoral, Birkhall and their contents gave a value of £256,000, which put into a trust fund brought an annual income of £5,000 p.a. Rather than open a can of worms by seeking money through the Civil

---

[27] The figures in today's money would be £7.25 million, £58 million and £5.8 million.

[28] 21 February 1937, RA GV EE 13/7, quoted Ziegler, p. 351.

[29] Bryan and Murphy, p. 307.

List, George VI agreed to top this up by £20,000. In return, Windsor agreed to pay £5,000 p.a. of pensions to former members of staff.[30]

'Of course, he's on the line for hours and hours every day to Cannes,' wrote Fruity to his wife on 24 January:

> I somehow don't think these talks go well sometimes . . . She seems to be always picking on him or complaining about something that she thinks he hasn't done and ought to do . . . All he is living for is to be with her on the 27th April.[31] As we come back every night after skiing, he says, 'One more day nearly over.' It's very pathetic. Never have I seen a man more madly in love . . .[32]

The problems continued, relayed in Fruity's daily letters to Baba. 'She is at him every day on the phone. He always seems to be excusing himself for something or other,' wrote Fruity on 27 January. 'I feel so sorry for him, he is never able to do what she considers the right thing.'[33]

'The evenings lately have been dreadful,' he wrote to Baba a week later:

> He won't think of bed before 3 a.m. and now has started playing the accordion and the bagpipes. Last night there was almost a row on the phone. W said she'd read he'd been having an affair with Kitty! This is d–mn funny, but I can tell

[30] Kenneth Rose, Vol. 2, p. 173. In today's money, £256K= £17.8 million, £5K= £350,000 and £20K=£1.4 million.

[31] When the *decree absolute* was expected.

[32] Frances Donaldson, *King Edward VIII* (Weidenfeld & Nicolson, 1974), p. 311, and de Courcy, *Viceroy's Daughters*, p. 250.

[33] de Courcy, p. 250.

you it was no joke last night. He got into a *terrible* state. Their conversation lasted nearly two hours . . .HRH pays for as little as he can when we go anywhere. I don't believe I'll be able to stick it here very much longer. [34]

Kitty Rothschild had had enough and that day she returned to Paris. The Duke was still in bed and as Fruity reported:

<u>Never saw her to say goodbye or thank her!</u> She was frightfully hurt and I don't blame her. He is awfully difficult at times and this is the worst thing he's done yet. I went down to the station with a letter which I got him to write to her, and that made things a bit better. He also never saw the servants to tip them or thank them, etc! (all due to more d–n talking to Cannes. It never stops) . . .[35]

Even with the financial arrangements almost sorted – though they would only be finalised in 1938 – the couple's future remained uncertain. For example, where were they to live? It was clear they were not welcome in Britain for the moment and the decision was not helped by the suggestion the Duke would now have to pay income tax. There were preliminary negotiations to buy Cloisters,

[34] RA EDW/OUT/METCALFE/1/8.

[35] 3 February 1937, Metcalfe papers. 'I feel she will be a dangerous enemy for HRH to have made, especially as he must be in the wrong,' John Aird, one of his equerries confided to his diary, but she maintained a discreet silence about her unexpected house guest. Ziegler, p. 343. 'It is believed that Eugène destroyed much of his first wife's private correspondence after her death, and that his second wife also disposed of papers of the first Baroness Eugène von Rothschild, and also those of her husband after his death in 1976. Little remains to record their involvement in the events of 1936, and their subsequent relationship with the Windsors.' Justin Cavernelis-Frost, archivist, Rothschild Archive to the author, 26 February 2021.

a huge Gothic residence outside Baltimore, built in 1932, but they came to nothing.[36]

On 9 March, Wallis, with her maid Mary Burke and twenty-six pieces of luggage, moved to Château de Candé, a fairytale castle of high towers, pointed turrets and Gothic doorways in the Loire, in preparation for her third wedding.[37] Lying on high ground with views over the countryside, it had originally been built in 1508. In 1927 it had been sold to Charles Bedaux, a multimillionaire Franco-American businessman, and friend of Herman Rogers – Herman's brother, Edmund, was Bedaux's principal financial agent in America – who had made his fortune with a time-and-motion system that increased industrial productivity.

Bedaux, the fifth richest man in America, and his American wife Fern, had set about modernising the Château de Candé, installing state-of-the-art facilities that included central heating, en-suite bathrooms, a $15,000 telephone system with a full-time telephonist, art deco bathrooms, huge refrigerators, a bar in the old kitchen (which still had the hooks for game) and a gym with the latest exercise equipment. An underground passage led to an old hunting lodge, which Bedaux had converted into a billiard room.

Interestingly, Herman Rogers was installed next door to Wallis's bedroom in an adjoining sitting room with day bed. As she later wrote, 'Herman decided to take this for himself. He had slept in a room adjoining mine with a gun under his pillow ever since I had arrived from England, more than three months before. Upstairs

---

[36] Charles Higham, *Mrs Simpson: Secret Lives of the Duchess of Windsor* (Sidgwick & Jackson, revised edition, 2004), p. 215. It is now an event facility owned by the city of Baltimore. https://www.cloisterscastle.com/about/history.

[37] The couple had also been offered houses in Sorrento by the banker Lord Grimthorpe, in Switzerland by the explorer Lincoln Ellsworth, and a shooting-box near Biarritz by the Duke of Westminster. In March, realising he had overstayed his welcome at Schloss Enzesfeld, the Duke moved to a small hotel in the Austrian Tyrol. There was to be no thank-you note to his hosts.

were several other bedrooms, of which Katherine took one.'[38] And there Wallis, who had changed her name by deed poll to Wallis Warfield, waited to learn if the marriage could go ahead.

The answer came on 18 March when Sir Thomas Barnes, the Treasury Solicitor, announced that there had been no evidence of collusion and the marriage could proceed, though he had not interviewed the one servant who might have established the truth, Wallis's maid, Mary Burke, arguing, 'It is not the practice of the King's Proctor to endeavour to get information from such servants.'[39]

It is clear that evidence did exist of collusion (Ernest Simpson had obligingly been caught in bed with his future wife, Mary Raffray, so Wallis could sue him for adultery), payment (it is thought the King had refunded Ernest Simpson's costs) and perjury, but the King's Proctor chose not to use it – not least evidence of Edward's adultery with Wallis in Budapest in 1935, where an unsigned three-page memo confirming it remains on the file.[40]

Francis Stephenson, who had lodged the objection, later claimed he had dropped his objections, 'Because I was told to.'[41]

At the beginning of April, the Duke sent his cairn terrier, Slipper, sometimes called Mr Loo, to Wallis at Candé. The next day, whilst chasing a rabbit, it was bitten by a viper. Though rushed to the local vet in Tours, it died that night. 'My darling – I have just given Herman Mr Loo's rug to wrap his little body in before Herman

---

[38] Windsor, *Heart*, p. 291. Katherine was Herman Rogers' wife.

[39] TS 22/1/A, TNA.

[40] TS 22/1/A, TNA.

[41] *New York Times*, 19 September 1949. Simpson brought an action for slander on 11 June 1937. In the witness box, Ernest stated that he had not received any money or other consideration for not defending his wife's divorce suit; nor had he been promised any money or other consideration for not so defending. He waived damages in return for his costs. The press suspected a deal had been done.

buries him. Even God seems to have forgotten WE,[42] for surely this is an unnecessary sorrow for us,' reported Wallis. 'He was our dog – not yours or mine but us – and he loved us both so. Now the principal guest at the wedding is no more.'[43]

It was not a good portent for their marriage.

---

[42] WE – Wallis and Edward – was how they often referred to each other.

[43] Michael Bloch (ed.), *Wallis & Edward, Letters 1931–1937* (Weidenfeld & Nicolson, 1986), p. 81. The Duke suggested the dog be embalmed and buried at Fort Belvedere. Instead Herman Rogers buried it in the grounds of the chateau watched by a tearful Wallis.

CHAPTER 3

The Wedding

On 3 May 1937, Wallis's *decree absolute* was made public and the Duke left immediately on the Orient Express from Salzburg with a bouquet of edelweiss, a dirndl for Wallis and some seventeen suitcases in his private car. It was there, nine days later, that the couple listened to the Coronation Service, the Duke knitting a blue jersey for Wallis, whilst a heavy rainstorm raged outside . . . and, where, as Wallis later wrote, '. . . the mental image of what might have been and should have been kept forming, disintegrating, and re-forming in my mind.'[1]

It must have been a bittersweet moment, for 12 May was the date originally set for the Coronation of Edward VIII, brought forward from the customary late June date for Coronations to give spectators above street-level along the Coronation route a better view than if the trees had come into full leaf. Present were all the members of the Duke's family – a cross-looking Princess Royal, his two Royal Duchess sisters-in-law, and his mother, who was keen to signify her support for the new reign by breaking with a tradition going back to the Plantagenet kings, whereby the widow of the previous sovereign did not attend the Coronation of his successor.

The Duke had hoped that some members of his family would also be present at the wedding and that either two of his brothers or

---

[1] *Heart*, p. 297.

Dickie Mountbatten would act as his best man, but the Palace was having none of it.

'You will have heard that although I succeeded in fixing a date for your wedding that suited Bertie, George, etc., that other people stepped in and have produced a situation that has made all your friends very unhappy,' wrote Mountbatten to the Duke on 5 May. 'I have made several attempts to get matters put right, but at present I cannot even accept your kind invitation myself. I haven't quite given up all hope yet, though my chances don't look too good. I will write again when I know finally.'[2] Instead Fruity Metcalfe agreed to be best man.

Not only were close members of the Royal Family forbidden from attending the Windsors' nuptials, but friends and former advisers were warned not to go. Perry Brownlow was told that he risked his position as Lord Lieutenant of Lincolnshire, a role taken by his family for eight generations, if he attended. Ulick Alexander was threatened that he would lose his job as Keeper of the Privy Purse if he accepted an invitation.

The Church of England did not recognise the marriage of divorced people and the Royal Family could not be seen to flout its teachings. It had also banned any minister from conducting the service and the couple had resigned themselves to a simple civil service until the Reverend Robert Anderson Jardine, an eccentric 'large-nosed, bulging-eyed, red-faced' minister from Darlington offered his services.[3]

---

[2] RA EDW/PRIV/MAIN/A/ 3206. Mountbatten sent some seventeenth- and eighteenth-century flagons and tankards as a wedding present.

[3] de Courcy, p. 262. Jardine, a former missionary in the Shetland Islands, subsequently exploited his involvement with a US lecture tour and opened the Windsor Cathedral of Los Angeles, until being deported back to the UK in 1942 for overstaying his visa. When his troubles began in July 1939, the Duke offered to send him $1,000 on the understanding that Jardine 'could expect nothing more in the future and that he must desist from publicity and such things as using a card describing himself as "the Duke's Vicar".' George Allen to the Duke, Monckton Trustees, Box 17, Balliol College.

The Wedding

There was to be a further blow. On 26 May, at Baldwin's last Cabinet meeting as Prime Minister, the question of Wallis's status as Her Royal Highness was discussed. The next day Monckton arrived at Candé with a letter that would cause enduring bitterness by the Windsors towards the Royal Family. Under Letter Patent, Wallis would not be granted the title of Her Royal Highness on her marriage.[4] This was against royal practice – the wives of all his brothers had been granted such status on marriage – and British common law.

The Duke's rank of Royal Highness, as the King's son, was an inalienable birthright, already established by Letters Patent of 1917, which had not been revoked and could not therefore be 'restored'. Following on from this, his wife was entitled to the same rank and status as her husband, but it was argued that he had renounced his royal rank and therefore that of his wife. The Abdication had been about her not becoming a member of the Royal Family. She could hardly be made a member now on her marriage, the reason her husband had abdicated in the first place.

Bertie had bowed to pressure from the Dominions, his mother and wife, amidst the concern that the Windsors' marriage would not last and she might then marry again. To the Duke, brought up to regard title and precedence as important, it was a real insult. It meant that whilst all were required to bow to him, Wallis, though his wife, was not entitled to a curtsey. He was being forced to have the very morganatic marriage that he was told was impossible a few months earlier. As if to rub salt into the wound, it was announced that the Duke's nemesis, Baldwin, who had done so much to manoeuvre the Duke towards abdication, had been granted an earldom.

---

[4] Note' Law Officers Department, 9 April 1937, LO 3/1168, TNA. The drafting from file H0 144/22945 can be found at https://www.heraldica.org/topics/britain/drafting_lp1937.htm.

'The bitterness is there all right. He had an outburst to Fruity while dressing for dinner,' Baba recorded in her diary. 'The family he is through with . . . He intends to fight the HRH business as legally the King has no right to stop the courtesy title being assumed by his wife . . . He will be loyal to the crown but not to the man, his brother. He blames him for weakness in everything.'[5]

Meanwhile the wedding preparations continued. It had been decided to wait until after the Coronation, though the couple announced their engagement on its eve, a gesture suspected of being an attempt to upstage the event, and then had rather insensitively picked the date for the wedding day of 3 June, George V's birthday.

As part of a plan to soften her image, Wallis gave an interview to a distant relative, Helena Normanton, for the *New York Times*, saying she had no wish to be Queen, and denying various accusations, such as she had made off with Queen Alexandra's emeralds and had had a love affair with Ribbentrop:

> I cannot recall ever being in Herr von Ribbentrop's company more than twice, once at a party of Lady Cunard before he became ambassador and once at another big reception. I was never alone in his company and I never had more than a few words conversation with him – simply the usual small talk, that is all. I took no interest at all in politics.[6]

The photographer Cecil Beaton, also part of the Windsor PR offensive, stayed for a few days to take some pre-wedding pictures. He was impressed with Wallis, with whom he sat talking until dawn:

[5] 3 June 1937, quoted Donaldson, p. 324.

[6] Helena Normanton, 'Intrigue Is Denied by Mrs Warfield', *New York Times*, 1 June 1937.

I was struck by the clarity and vitality of her mind. When at last I went to bed, I realised that she not only had individuality and personality, but was a very strong force as well. She may have limitations, she may be politically ignorant and aesthetically untutored; but she knows a great deal about life.[7]

That night Baba noticed the wedding couple parting for the night. 'Good night, sir,' Wallis said and shook the hands of her future husband.[8]

Thursday 3 June was a gloriously sunny day. Hundreds of sightseers had flocked to the gates of the chateau in the hope of a glimpse of the couple, and food stands did a roaring trade. Traffic round the local village, Monts, was stopped at 7 a.m. and there was a flight ban over the chateau.

Though no member of his family attended, there were good wishes. 'We are thinking of you with great affection on this your wedding day and send you every wish for your future happiness. Much love Elizabeth & Bertie,' read one telegram.[9] Winston and Clementine Churchill gave a plate and Adolf Hitler supposedly a gold box.[10] A favourite present was a lavatory-paper holder that played 'God Save the King'.

There were only seven British guests: Walter Monckton; the Duke's solicitor George Allen; Randolph Churchill, there in his capacity as a journalist; Hugh Lloyd Thomas, a friend from the British Embassy in Paris; Lady Selby without her husband, Sir Walford, who had been advised not to attend; Fruity and Baba Metcalfe. They were joined by Wallis's Aunt Bessie – the only

---

[7] Cecil Beaton, *The Wandering Years* (Weidenfeld & Nicolson, 1961), p. 305.

[8] Baba Diary, 3 June 1937, Metcalfe Papers.

[9] Monckton Trustees, Box 15, Balliol College.

[10] Higham, *Wallis*, p. 185.

member of her family to attend – Herman and Katherine Rogers, Kitty and Eugene Rothschild and the Bedauxs.

It was a low-key affair. The French government, in deference to the British, had agreed not to broadcast the wedding and attempts to do so by the American networks, NBC and CBS, were blocked by the French. Baba Metcalfe found the event bizarre:

> I had forgotten how unattractive her voice and manner of speaking are. Her looks ensure that in any room of only moderately pretty women she would always be by far the ugliest and her figure is thin, with absolutely no line . . . The rest of the party, Mrs Merriman – Aunt Bessie – harmless old girl who must have had a stroke as half of her face doesn't function and her mouth is squidgways on. Mrs Rogers – common, ordinary large-boned American. Herman, nice quiet, efficient . . . I feel I am passing the weekend in an ugly chateau with people (with the exception of HRH) who are unattractive and completely ignorant of what is happening and who I never want to see again.[11]

At 11.30 a.m., Herman Rogers escorted Wallis down the grand staircase to the salon for the civil service, conducted by the mayor of Monts. Wallis was dressed in a powder-blue – subsequently called Wallis Blue – crepe, box-shouldered, tight-fitting, ankle-length outfit, designed by one of her favourite designers Mainbocher, with a matching jacket, and halo-style hat by Caroline Reboux, all accompanied by a diamond and sapphire brooch (a wedding present from the Duke), bracelet and earrings.

---

[11] de Courcy, p. 260, and Hugo Vickers, *Cecil Beaton* (Weidenfeld & Nicolson, 1985), p. 316.

The Wedding

Half an hour later, they entered the music room to Handel's 'Wedding March' from *Judas Maccabaeus*, played by the composer Marcel Dupré, for the twenty-minute religious service. The room had quickly been adapted as a temporary chapel with a hall chest, covered by a cream silk cloth to hide the plump nude nymphs, serving as an altar.

The Duke, dressed in black morning coat and striped trousers with a white carnation in his buttonhole, looked noticeably nervous. Wallis appeared more relaxed. The couple mingled with their guests and posed for photographs before sitting down to a wedding breakfast in the dining room of lobster, Chicken à la King and strawberries, accompanied by champagne – and for the Duke, a cup of Earl Grey tea.

'It was hard not to cry. In fact, I did,' wrote Baba in her diary:

> Afterwards we shook hands in the salon. I knew I should have kissed her but I just couldn't. In fact I was bad all day: my effort to be charming and to like her broke down. I don't remember wishing her happiness or good luck as though she loved him. If she occasionally showed a glimmer of softness, took his arm, looked at him as though she loved him, one would warm towards her, but her attitude is so correct and hard. The effect is of an older woman unmoved by the infatuated love of a younger man. Let's hope that she lets up in private with him, otherwise it must be grim.[12]

By 3.15 and a press conference, it was all over.[13] After the cake was cut, Monckton and Wallis strolled in the garden. He explained that

[12] 3 June 1937, Donaldson, p. 326 and de Courcy, p. 265.

[13] Amongst the press corps was the future French foreign minister, Maurice Schumann.

he would do all he could to support them, but she would be scrutinised by the public to see how she treated her husband, who had given up so much for her. She replied, 'Walter, don't you think I have thought of all that? I think I can make him happy.'[14]

It was a marriage that could not afford to fail. The price had been too high.

[14] Birkenhead, *Walter Monckton*, p. 162.

CHAPTER 4

Honeymoon

Shortly afterwards, the Duke and his new Duchess left for their honeymoon in a convoy of cars to join the Simplon-Orient Express, which had been kept waiting for them. They were accompanied by Dudley Forwood, an attaché at the British Legation in Vienna, who had been seconded as the Duke's equerry in Austria, two cairn terriers, a pair of Scotland Yard detectives whose brief was as much to spy on as guard the Windsors, and 186 trunks and eighty additional items of luggage.

Their honeymoon location was another borrowed castle, the forty-room, rebuilt mock Gothic Wasserleonburg in the Carinthian mountains, supposedly haunted by the ghost of Anna Neumann, who had murdered six of her husbands on honeymoon.[1]

This was the German home of Count Paul Münster, who had close associations with Mosley's British Union of Fascists, and was to be the Windsors' home for the next three months. It was there that the reality of their position hit home. Wallis harboured a strong sense of guilt at what her husband had surrendered for her, combined with a terror at what she had let herself in for. She was later to tell Gore Vidal:

> I remember like yesterday the morning after we were married and I woke up and there was David standing beside the bed with this innocent smile, saying, 'And now what do we do?'

---

[1] Originally built in the thirteenth century, it is now run as a holiday let.

My heart sank. Here was someone whose every day had been arranged for him all his life and now I was the one who was going to take the place of the entire British government, trying to think up things for him to do.'[2]

She did her best. They entertained friends, relaxed in the castle's heated swimming pool, played golf and tennis, went deer stalking, and the Duke exercised excessively, as he had always done, often climbing a rocky peak behind the castle and signalling his position to Wallis with a small mirror. The *New York Times* reported on how, 'Attired in Tyrolean leather breeches, white hose and short-sleeved shirt, he watered flowers in the garden.'[3]

Walter Monckton was amongst the visitors and he persuaded the Duke to drop his complaints about the Duchess's title – the Duke was threatening to renounce his own royal title – as bad for his public image.

Whilst there, the Duke was approached by the writer Compton Mackenzie, now best known for his novel *Whisky Galore*, keen to write a biography of the former king with his cooperation. The Duke was tempted by both the money – the deal was that he would receive £10,000 and Mackenzie £20,000 – and an opportunity for Wallis to 'challenge the accusations which have been made against you.'[4] Discussions continued throughout the summer until the Duke withdrew from the book in October, realising it best he not be seen to cooperate with any writer. Mackenzie's *The Windsor Tapestry* on the reign and abdication was published the following year.[5]

[2] Gore Vidal, *Palimpsest: A Memoir* (Deutsch, 1995), p. 206.

[3] 6 June 1937, *New York Times.*

[4] George Allen to the Duke, Monckton Trustees, Box 15, Folio 37, Balliol College. The equivalent now of £700K and £1.4 million.

[5] Monckton Trustees, Box 16, Balliol College.

Part of the Windsors' time was also spent at the Hotel Bristol in Vienna. It was on 20 June, whilst at the Brazilian Legation for dinner, that George Messersmith, the American minister to Austria, unwisely passed on the information to the Duke that a train from Germany to Italy had crashed and naval shells, supplied by Germany to Mussolini's navy, had been discovered. This was in breach of League of Nations sanctions. It also showed that the Americans were reading Italian cyphers. The next day Messersmith was shown an intercepted telegram, sent by the Italian ambassador in Vienna to Rome, discussing the discovered shells and revealing his source – the Duke. It was a salutary warning that the ex-king could not be trusted.[6]

Windsor had continued to stay in touch with Charles Bedaux after the two men had built up a friendship over games of golf and late-night glasses of brandy. The Duke was interested in Bedaux's work practices and attracted to his utopian ideas for world peace, whilst Bedaux realised the benefits of cultivating an association with the former king.

What Windsor may not have known was that, since the First World War, Bedaux had been suspected by the Americans of being a German spy.[7] He had extensive business interests in Nazi Germany, working closely with Krups, Mercedes, Opel and IG Farben. He leased a Schloss near to Hitler in Berchtesgaden and was close to Hjalmar Schacht, head of the Reichsbank, and Robert Ley, head of the German Labour Front.

---

[6] 'Conversations with King Edward (Duke of Windsor) after his Abdication', MSS 109 2017-00, Messersmith papers, University of Delaware.

[7] See for example the report on him to Colonel R.H. Van Deman, Chief of Military Intelligence Section of the War Department, US National Archives 10505-27.

Since his companies had been seized in Nazi Germany in 1934, Bedaux had worked hard to ingratiate himself with the Nazi leadership. The Duke of Windsor now gave him that opportunity. He had only been able to reopen his German businesses after bribing the Nazi authorities in July 1937 to the tune of $50,000 and agreeing that they be supervised by the Nazi labour organisation, the *Arbeitsfront.*[8] It was this very organisation that he suggested should host the Windsors for a tour of the country.

*   *   *

In September, the Windsors stayed with the Bedauxs at Borsodi-vánka Castle, a hunting lodge in Hungary, which Bedaux rented from a nephew of the Regent Horthy, and the plans that they had laid over the previous few months were put into action. Such a visit had several benefits. It would raise Windsor's profile on the international stage, it would help promote Bedaux's business interests, and they both believed it would help secure world peace.

On 19 August, Bedaux had seen Howard K. Travers, chargé d'affaires at the American legation in Budapest, saying that he was acting for Windsor, who wished 'to make a complete study of working conditions in various countries', adding, 'with a view to returning to England at a later date as the champion of the working classes'. Travers reported this to the State Department in a 'strictly confidential' memo that day, where it was seen by George Messersmith, now Assistant Secretary of State in charge of the Balkans. The authorities were now on their guard.

In the spring of 1937, Oscar Solbert, an American general and business executive, who had acted as Windsor's attaché during his 1924 American visit, had written to the Duke suggesting he 'head up

---

[8] Almost £1 million today.

and consolidate the many and varied peace movements throughout the world.'[9] He had discussed the matter with the Swedish industrialist Axel Wenner-Gren, who 'was prepared to put a considerable sum of money behind the plan.'[10] In August, Bedaux replied on the Duke's behalf:

> The Duke of Windsor is very much interested in your proposal that he lead a movement so essentially international. We all know that as Prince of Wales and as King, he has always been keenly interested in the lot of the working man and he has not failed to show both his distress and his resolve to alter things whenever he has encountered injustice . . . He is determined to continue, with more time at his disposal, his systematic study of this subject and to devote his time to the betterment of the life of the masses . . . He believes this is the surest way to peace. For himself, he proposes to begin soon with a study of housing and working conditions in many countries.[11]

The Duke's equerry, Dudley Forwood, interviewed for a television documentary in 1994, explains the background:

> The story goes that he got a very great payment from Hitler, though whether this is true or not I really don't know, if he would arrange to get the Duke of Windsor prepared to accept an invitation to go to Germany that took place. At the trip to Germany, Bedaux was never seen, he wasn't to be seen at all,

[9] 27 April 1937, RA EDW/PRIV/MAIN/A/3200, and Michael Bloch, *The Secret File of the Duke of Windsor* (Bantam, 1988), pp. 109–10.

[10] *Ibid*

[11] 23 August 1937, Charles Bedaux to Oscar Solbert, RA EDW/PRIV/MAIN/A/3409.

but there's no doubt about it, he was behind the scenes . . . he was an unpleasant piece of work.[12]

It was a view shared by one of the Duke's protection officers, Philip Attfield:

I distrusted Bedaux and was quite certain he was working hand-in-glove with the Nazis. My international and personal intelligence service had supplied me with many disturbing details about him and I felt sure he was not cultivating the duke for nothing. Although he always went out of his way to give me every comfort and privilege, I watched his every move with suspicion.[13]

The Duke's communications and travels in the region were now being monitored, not least by his personal protection officer, David Storrier, who filed regular reports to Scotland Yard, but also by local diplomats. On 30 August, Sir George Knox, the minister to Hungary, wrote to the permanent under-secretary at the Foreign Office, Sir Robert Vansittart, about a forthcoming visit to Hungary, reporting that the Duke wished 'to present the Duchess to the Regent and Madame Horthy. While Admiral de Horthy entertains considerable sympathy and friendship for the Duke, whom he knows well, he has expressed himself in strong terms regarding the Duchess.'[14]

There were good reasons for the authorities to be suspicious of the couple's loyalties. The Duke was strongly pro-German, indeed

[12] Forwood, p. 52, BREN 2/2/7, Churchill College Archives, Cambridge. The four-part series, *The Windsors: A Dynasty Revealed*, was shown around the world and published as a tie-in book written by Piers Brendon and Philip Whitehead.

[13] *Sunday Mirror*, 31 October 1954.

[14] FO 954/33A/30, TNA.

considered himself almost German, telling Diana Mosley, 'Every drop of blood in my veins is German.'[15] He spoke German fluently and sometimes referred to it as his mother tongue and had spent most of his summers before the First World War visiting German relatives. The murder of his Russian relations in 1918 had had a profound influence on him and he always considered communism as the real threat to Britain's interests and empire.

Though, as heir to the throne, he was prevented from seeing active service during the First World War, several of his friends had been killed, including an equerry and a driver, and he was determined there should never be war again between Germany and Britain. He was also a believer in strong government. The journalist Robert Bruce Lockhart noted in his diary in July 1933:

> The Prince of Wales was quite pro-Hitler and said it was no business of ours to interfere in Germany's internal affairs either re Jews or re anything else, and added that dictators are very popular these days and that we might want one in England before now.[16]

The following year, Chips Channon wrote in his diary: 'Much gossip about the Prince of Wales's alleged Nazi leanings. He is alleged to have been influenced by Emerald [Lady Cunard] (who is rather eprise [*sic*] with Herr Ribbentrop) through Mrs Simpson.'[17]

[15] Diana Mosley, *Duchess of Windsor: A Memoir* (Sidgwick & Jackson, 1980), p. 89. Fourteen of his sixteen great-great-grandparents were born into German royal houses and the other two into minor Hungarian nobility as subjects of the German Habsburg Emperor. His mother was the German princess, Mary of Teck.

[16] 13 July 1933, Kenneth Young (ed.), *The Diaries of Sir Robert Bruce Lockhart 1915–1938*, Vol. 1 (Macmillan, 1973), pp. 262–3.

[17] June 1934, *épris* means enamoured, Rhodes James, *Channon*, p. 35.

There was certainly plenty of evidence of the Duke's sympathies. In 1935 he had made a speech to the British Legion, suggesting a visit of reconciliation to Germany, which may have directly impacted the Anglo-German Naval Agreement that was being negotiated at the time.

The Germans welcomed his succession. The German ambassador, Leopold von Hoesch, wrote in January 1936 to Berlin:

I am convinced that his friendly attitude towards Germany might in time come to exercise a certain amount of influence on the shaping of British foreign policy. At any rate, we should be able to rely upon having on the British throne a ruler who is not lacking in understanding for Germany and in the desire to see good relations established between Germany and Britain.[18]

Edward's cousin, the Duke of Saxe-Coburg, a senior Nazi official, took the opportunity to consolidate the relationship while attending George V's funeral, reporting to Ribbentrop that:

An alliance Germany–Britain is <u>for him</u> an urgent necessity and a guiding principle for British foreign policy . . . would like a confidant of Ribbentrop as Ambassador in London . . . The King is resolved to concentrate government business on himself . . . His sincere resolve to bring Germany and Britain together would be made more difficult if it were made public too early . . . The King asked me to visit him often in order that confidential matters might be more speedily settled in this way.[19]

---

[18] Documents on German Foreign Policy, Series C, Vol. IV, p. 1023.
[19] RA PS/PSO/GVI/C/042a/392-425.

Honeymoon

In March 1936, when Hitler remilitarised the Rhineland, Ribbentrop was sent to London to work through the new king to keep the Government sweet and prevent any reaction. Fritz Hesse, the press attaché at the German embassy, reported how the ambassador 'von Hoesch went to see the King, secretly, one night' to defend Hitler's actions and argue it was not worth going to war over. Edward later called von Hoesch, telling him, with Hesse present, 'I sent for the Prime Minister and gave him a piece of my mind. I told the old so-and-so that I would abdicate if he made war. There was a frightful scene. But you needn't worry. There won't be a war.'[20]

Von Hoesch had reported to Berlin on 11 March:

> I have today been in indirect communication with the Court. The opinion in authoritative quarters is that our proposals could form the basis for the construction of a permanent peace system; in the same quarter in other respects also there is understanding for the German point of view.[21]

Edward is 'going the dictator way, and is pro-German,' wrote Chips Channon in his diary in November 1936. 'I shouldn't be surprised if he aimed at making himself a mild dictator, a difficult enough task for an English King.'[22]

---

[20] Fritz Hesse, *Hitler and the English* (Wingate, 1954), p. 22.

[21] RA PS/PSO/GVl/C/042A/428. On 18 March, Kurt von Stutterheim, the London correspondent of the *Berliner Tageblatt*, similarly had told his editor: 'The King is taking an extraordinarily active part in the whole affair . . . He has completely taken up the standpoint that the "breach of law" must be got over as quickly as possible and practical consideration given to the proposals of the Fuhrer and Chancellor.' RA PS/PSO/GVl/C/042A/429.

[22] November 1936, Rhodes James, *Channon*, p. 84.

Traitor King

Number 10 increasingly saw Edward as a security risk. Suspicious of the expensive gifts he lavished on Wallis, officials feared he was being blackmailed by nefarious foreign agents and worried about his association with known right-wing personalities such as Sir Oswald Mosley.

Surveillance had revealed that the couple were both having affairs elsewhere. The 1935 Special Branch report that had stated that Wallis had a secret lover, later identified as Ford car salesman Guy Trundle, also observed that: 'Mrs Simpson is very jealous of a certain Austrian or Hungarian woman whom POW met on his recent visit to Austria. This woman has since been to London and spent some time with POW.'[23]

Wallis was regarded as indiscreet and too close to Lady Cunard and her friend, Hitler's minister of foreign affairs and ambassador to London, Ribbentrop.

Baldwin's biographers later wrote:

> Mrs Simpson . . . found herself under close scrutiny from Vansittart, and both she and the King would not have been pleased to realise that the Security Services were keeping a watching brief on her and some of her friends . . . The red boxes sent down to Fort Belvedere were carefully screened by the Foreign Office to ensure that nothing highly secret could go astray. Behind the public facade, behind the King's popularity . . . the Government had awakened to a danger that had nothing to do with any question of marriage.[24]

---

[23] 25 June 1935, MEPO 10/35, TNA. Only this report survives, with the other Special Branch reports destroyed about 2000.

[24] Keith Middlemas and John Barnes, *Baldwin: A Biography* (Weidenfeld & Nicolson, 1969), p. 980.

On 4 February 1936, John Davidson, Baldwin's Intelligence coordinator, wrote in a 'Most Secret' memo that: 'Mrs S is very close to Hoech (*sic*) and has, if she likes to read them, access to all Secret and Cabinet Papers.'[25] The same month Ralph Wigram, head of the Central Department at the Foreign Office, recorded in his diary that senior Whitehall officials thought her to be 'in the pocket of the German Ambassador'.[26]

On 25 November 1936, the wife of the King's private secretary, Alec Hardinge, noted that 'one of the factors in the situation was Mrs Simpson's partiality for Nazi Germans'.[27] In the parliamentary debate on the day of the Abdication Bill, the Communist MP Willie Gallagher had stated, 'Mrs Simpson has a social set, and every Member of the Cabinet knows that the social set of Mrs Simpson is closely identified with a certain foreign Government and the Ambassador of that foreign Government.'[28]

Now in 1937, the Duke's activities raised alarm bells in Whitehall and at Buckingham Palace. There had already been discussions on how the couple should be treated by the diplomatic service, but these were given a new impetus with the imminent plans to tour Germany. On 2 September, Alec Hardinge wrote to Sir Robert Vansittart:

> His Royal Highness the Duke of Windsor and the Duchess should not be treated by His Majesty's representatives as having any official status in the countries which they visit. For this reason it seems to the King that, except under special instructions, His Majesty's representatives should not have

---

[25] Davidson papers, Parliamentary Archives.

[26] William Shawcross, *Queen Elizabeth, the Queen Mother* (Macmillan, 2009), p. 366, and Ziegler, p. 273.

[27] Helen Hardinge diary, Hon. Lady Murray Papers, quoted Shawcross, p. 366.

[28] CAB 21/4100/1, TNA, and 10 December 1936, Hansard.

any hand in arranging official interviews for them, or countenance their participation in any official ceremonies.[29]

According to George VI, the couple were not to be invited to stay in any embassy, ministers should not meet them off the train, and any entertainment at an embassy could only be unofficial.

On 17 September, Fritz Wiedemann, Hitler's personal adjutant, saw the Duke to discuss the tour. It was agreed that a German attaché who spoke English would accompany the couple and would meet Fern Bedaux at the Ritz on 30 September to make the final arrangements.[30]

On 20 September, the British Government received their first official warning about the proposed trip to Germany, then only a few weeks away, when the Duke told the British diplomat Sir Nevile Henderson, 'Although our two weeks tour is being organised under the auspices of the Reich, it will naturally be of a purely private nature.'[31] That same day the Duke told Walford Selby that it was 'in order to see what is being done to improve working and living conditions of labouring classes in several of the larger cities.'[32] Few were persuaded by the Duke's statement.

There was consternation in Whitehall and copies of the correspondence from the Windsors were sent to the King at Balmoral. 'Personally I think these tours, prearranged without a word to us, are a bit too much,' Vansittart wrote to Hardinge on 1 October.

[29] Copy of letter FO 800/847, TNA, and FO 954/33A/36, TNA.

[30] Top Secret memo from State Secretary, 17 September 1937, FCO 12/255, TNA. This was Dr Hans Solf (1910–87) later the first German European civil servant in the Council of Europe.

[31] RA DW 3423, quoted Ziegler, p. 389.

[32] FO 954/33A/52, TNA.

'And I hope our missions abroad will be instructed to have as little as possible to do with them.'[33]

The following day, Hardinge replied, 'I entirely agree with what you say about these tours, and I feel strongly that nothing should be done to make them appear other than what they are, i.e., private stunts for publicity purposes – they can obviously bring no benefit to the workers themselves.'[34]

On 4 October, Ralph Wigram described the tour to George VI as a 'dangerous, semi-political move'.[35] The same day Sir Eric Phipps, the British ambassador in Paris, called on the Duke and warned him not to be used for propaganda purposes. The Duke merely gave an assurance he would not make any speeches.

On 8 October, Sir Ronald Lindsay, the British ambassador in Washington, was summoned to Balmoral, where he was joined by the Foreign Secretary, Anthony Eden, amidst concern that the Duke was a pawn in the hands of a scheming and ambitious wife. 'The Palace Secretaries are extremist, the Foreign Office still more so,' Lindsay wrote to his wife. 'All are seeing ghosts and phantoms everywhere and think there are disasters round every corner.'[36]

At Balmoral, Lindsay related to his wife that the King and Queen were in a:

state of extreme nervousness about it or rather about all the Duke's activities – his theatrical appeals to popularity and these visits of inspection – perfunctory and no doubt pretty

[33] FO 954/33/59, TNA.

[34] FO 954/33/61, TNA.

[35] RA KEVIII Ab. Box 5, quoted Ziegler, p. 389.

[36] 17 October 1937, Ronald Lindsay to Elizabeth Lindsay, Acc 9769, 100/1, part 2 of 2, National Library of Scotland, and John Vincent (ed.), *The Crawford Papers: The Journals of David Lindsay 1892–1940* (Manchester University Press, 1984), p. 619.

insincere, but none the less evidence of his readiness to bid for popularity. Hitherto he has been quiet and has shown no desire to study housing conditions in France and Austria.[37]

Lindsay felt that the Duke 'was trying to stage a come-back, and his friends and advisers were semi-Nazis. He was not straight.' He continued with the observation that there was a personal as well as political aspect to the panic:

It interested me to notice that really the King does not yet feel safe on his throne, and up to a point he is like the medieval monarch who has a hated rival claimant living in exile . . . He talks quite well and vigorously – but he is not clever. There are plenty of rather pointless remarks and divagations, and a fair part of those rather heavy jokes which one gets from Royal Princes.[38]

His view of the Queen was equally revealing. 'Too short and thick-set to be beautiful, and someday she will be a fat little lady though she will always be altogether charming . . . she was backing up everything the men said, but protesting against anything that seemed vindictive.' His shrewdest analysis, however, was of Wallis:

Is she really ambitious? Perhaps; and opinion at the Palace has no doubt of it, but is certainly violently prejudicial. On the other hand, in marrying a man she has pulled him down from a very high place. There are lots of women who have done the same thing and who then, without being ambitious

[37] 8 October 1937, Vincent, p. 582.

[38] Ronald Lindsay to Elizabeth Lindsay, 11 October 1937, Acc 9769, 100/1, part 2 of 2, National Library of Scotland and abridged in Vincent, p. 617.

themselves, try hard to stick him up again on as high a stool as can be found.[39]

Concerns were heightened when on 10 October the Duke met Axel Wenner-Gren.[40] The tall, white-haired Swedish industrialist had founded the Electrolux Company in 1919 and made his fortune from the electric vacuum cleaner and solid-state refrigerator. By 1939 he was the largest private employer in Sweden with interests in newspapers, banking, wood pulp – he was the world's leading producer – and a large stake in the arms manufacturers Bofors.

A close friend of Bedaux, in 1937 Wenner-Gren had published a Utopian tract, *An Appeal to Everyman*, calling for international disarmament, the abolition of trade barriers and the need for improvements in education, wages and working and living conditions. However, it was his dealings with Hermann Goering, ostensibly as an honest peace broker, and his anthropological expeditions in areas of strategic interest to the Nazis, which were causing alarm in British and American official circles, now that he was also meeting with the Duke of Windsor.

How fair were the concerns about the proposed trip to Germany? There was certainly a desire for public attention by both Windsor and his wife. He had no inner life to take refuge in. Royal tours and fawning courtiers were all he had known. Having given up his throne, he was looking for a role and was prey to the unscrupulous. Sensing they would not approve, Windsor had told neither his friends nor the authorities about the tour until the last moment.

---

[39] Ronald Lindsay to Elizabeth Lindsay, 11 October 1937, Acc 9769, 100/1, part 2 of 2, National Library of Scotland.

[40] '3 pm at Duke of Windsor . . . very interesting and pleasant chat. Some cooperation should be considered later,' Wenner-Gren diary, courtesy of Mark Hollingsworth. Cf. Ziegler, p. 455.

Feeling rejected by his family and isolated from his country, flattered by German attentions, determined to give his wife the official reception that he felt that she deserved and naively thinking he could make a difference, the Duke went ahead with the tour.

CHAPTER 5

The German Tour

On Monday 11 October, the couple arrived by train in Berlin
at a station festooned with alternating Union Jacks and swasti-
kas, to be met by Robert Ley, the head of the National Labour
Front, the foreign minister Ribbentrop, and representing Britain, a
lowly third secretary, Geoffrey Harrison – the British Ambassador,
Sir Nevile Henderson, had diplomatically taken a leave of absence,
whilst his deputy Sir George Ogilvie-Forbes later visited the couple
privately at their hotel.[1]

For all the protestations that this was a private fact-finding visit, it
quickly became clear there were other agendas, quite apart from Nazi
propaganda. The Windsors had two servants, Rudolph and Mar-
got, assigned to them. Philip Attfield, their protection officer, who
unknown to the servants spoke French and German, quickly discovered they were spies and searching the couple's luggage. In turn, Attfield himself acted as a spy, reporting back to British Intelligence on
visits to locations, such as Peenemünde, the rocket research station.

The Windsors' first visit was to the stock machine works at
Grunewald, an ultra-modern building for 3,000 workers with
extensive gardens, a swimming pool and restaurant. After lunch

---

[1] Sir Geoffrey Harrison (1908–90) later served as the British ambassador to Brazil,
Iran and the Soviet Union, from whence he was recalled in 1960 after he was
caught in a KGB honey trap with a Russian maid.

in the canteen, they enjoyed a concert given for a thousand workers by the Berlin Labour Front Orchestra, with selections from Liszt and Wagner.[2]

The next day there was a visit to the headquarters of the National-Socialist Welfare Organisation, the Osram Electric Bulb Company factory, garden settlements for working men, and then a dinner given at Ley's 37-room house in the Grunewald attended by Ribbentrop, Hess, Himmler and Goebbels. The visit appeared to confirm many of the German assumptions about the former king. Goebbels later wrote in his diary: 'The duke is wonderful – a nice, sympathetic figure who is open and clear and with a healthy understanding of people . . . It's a shame he is no longer king. With him we would have entered into an alliance.'[3]

In turn, Wallis wrote that Goebbels, 'the club-footed mastermind of the Nazi propaganda mills, impressed me as the cleverest of the lot – a tiny, wispy gnome with an enormous skull. His wife was the prettiest woman I saw in Germany, a blonde, with enormous blue eyes and a flair for clothes. Seen together, they reminded me of Beauty and the Beast.'[4]

On 13 October, the Windsors visited the Pomeranian Training School of Hitler's bodyguard, the elite SS Death's Head or SS *Totenkopf*. Here the Duke was seen to give the Nazi salute – Dudley Forwood later described the gesture as 'merely good manners'.[5] After lunch there was an aerial inspection of a Nazi youth camp along the shores of the Baltic sea, whilst Wallis toured the former Imperial Palaces at Potsdam.

[2] FO 954/33A/118, TNA.

[3] Jonathan Petropoulos, *Royals and the Reich: The Princes von Hessen in Nazi Germany* (Oxford University Press, 2006), p. 208.

[4] *Heart*, p. 307.

[5] Forwood, p. 59, BREN 2/2/7, Churchill College Archives.

There were visits to Berlin's museums on 14 October, then tea with Goering at his hunting lodge, Karinhall, forty miles north of Berlin, where he awaited his guests 'with two rows of huntsmen behind him to play a fanfare on their hunting horns.'[6]

Wallis was amused how Goering, in an immaculate white uniform, medal ribbons emblazoned across his tunic, took pleasure in giving a tour of his home, showing off his Rembrandts, demonstrating some of the weight-lifting equipment in his well-equipped gymnasium – including an Elizabeth Arden massage machine in which he forced his generously proportioned body between one of the pairs of rollers – and the playroom provided for children of friends and relations with:

> the most elaborate toy railway I have ever seen – yards and yards of intricately connected tracks, dozens of switches, coal tipples, charming little stations, and any number of locomotives and cars of different sorts. The Field-Marshall, kneeling down in his white uniform, showed us how it worked. The deftness with which he directed the trains up and down the tracks, opening and closing switches, blowing whistles, and averting collisions, suggested that he must have spent a good part of his time in the attic.[7]

Other 'toys' included a wire-controlled model plane that could drop wooden bombs. The Duke was shocked to see a wall map that showed Austria coloured in as already part of Germany.

There were visits to Essen, where they visited a coal mine, industrial works and garden settlements, and they concluded with a

[6] *Sunday Mirror*, 31 October 1954.
[7] *Heart*, p. 306.

visit to the Krupps Armaments Factory. Another day was spent in Dusseldorf for an industrial exhibit, where they toured a miners' hospital and a concentration camp. Forwood later recalled, 'We saw this enormous concrete building which, of course, I now know contained inmates. The duke asked, "What is that?" Our host replied, "It is where they store the cold meat."'[8]

The tour was not enhanced by the antics of the boorish, drunken Ley, who was relieved of his duties halfway through the trip. Wallis later described him as 'if not actually an alcoholic . . . a noisy, chronic drinker'.[9] Partial to schnapps, which he sneaked throughout the day, 'He had bright eyes, a florid complexion, and a squat, bear-like build. To my American eyes, he was a four-flusher.'[10] Ley took particular pleasure in driving extremely fast. Wallis 'was afraid of being blown out of the back seat', whilst 'all the while, above the roar of the wind, a radio blared out German tunes to which Dr Ley kept time by rolling his head from side to side.'[11]

Meanwhile the British Government kept a watching brief, not least on Charles Bedaux, who had arrived in Berlin two weeks before the Windsors' visit. On 17 October, Ogilvie-Forbes reported to Eden:

I dined two nights ago privately with Prentiss Gilbert, the new Counsellor and at present Chargé d'Affaires at the United States Embassy . . . He raised the subject of the Duke of Windsor and of His Royal Highness's intended visit to the United States . . . He also said that as a result of the approaches

---

[8] Forwood, p. 44, BREN 2/2/7, Churchill College Archives.

[9] *Heart*, p. 304.

[10] *Heart*, p. 304. Four-flusher means braggart.

[11] *Heart*, pp. 304–5. Rarely sober, with a penchant for underage girls, Ley committed suicide whilst awaiting trial at Nuremberg for war crimes. His wife, twenty-six years his junior, was driven to suicide in 1942 by his brutal treatment of her.

which Mr Bedaux had made to him, it was clear that this individual was 'running' HRH and probably paying his expenses
for the tour outside Germany . . . Much of the above will I
fear be painful reading, but you ought to know what has been
going on here and that it would be as well to keep an eye on
Mr Bedaux's activities . . . This letter which I have typed
myself will not be put in the Chancery archives.[12]

On 22 October, the couple arrived in Munich for the highlight of
their trip – tea with Hitler at Berchtesgaden.[13] A special train took
them to Hitler's mountain retreat seventy miles away. Arriving early,
they were made to wait whilst the Fuhrer had his nap, but eventually
the meeting began at 2.30 p.m. Though the Duke spoke German,
Hitler insisted on using an interpreter, Paul Schmidt. Wallis was
taken off by Eva Braun and Rudolf Hess, who talked to her about
music, 'which he loved', whilst the detective Philip Attfield was left
to his own devices, though always with a Gestapo man with him.[14]
Reporting the visit, the *New York Times* noted that 'the Duchess
was visibly impressed with the Fuhrer's personality, and he apparently indicated that they had become fast friends by giving her an
affectionate farewell. He took both their hands in his saying a long
goodbye, after which he stiffened to a rigid Nazi salute that the
Duke returned.'[15]

Wallis, always drawn to powerful men, later wrote of Hitler's
'pasty pallor, and under his moustache his lips were fixed in a kind
of mirthless grimace . . . his eyes were truly extraordinary – intense,

[12] Ogilvie-Forbes to Secretary of State, 17 October 1937, 'Bedaux Activities'. FO
954/33A/94, TNA.

[13] 'Report of Consul General in Munich to British Embassy, Berlin', 22 October
1937, FO 954/33A/114, TNA.

[14] *Heart*, p. 308.

[15] *New York Times*, 23 October 1937.

unblinking, magnetic.'[16] Forwood was more direct. He remembered Hitler as 'a funny little man sitting beside the Duke. He didn't impress me as being a great person.'[17]

No record exists of what the Duke and Hitler talked about, though Paul Getty, later a friend of Windsor, was to muse, 'It would not surprise me if one day a musty EYES ONLY file is fished out of some top security vault and new light is thrown on the episode.'[18] The only ostensible drama of the visit, recounted by the Duke's detective, Attfield, was when, 'An English woman schoolteacher got through the guards. I caught her as she was about to embrace the Duke. She had followed the party for ten days.'[19]

The Duke was equally impressed by what he had seen:

> I have travelled the world and my upbringing has made me familiar with the great achievements of mankind, but that which I have seen in Germany, I had hitherto believed to be impossible. It cannot be grasped and is a miracle; one can only begin to understand it when one realises that behind it all is one man and one will.[20]

The Windsors returned to Paris on 24 October. For all the concerns in British Government circles, their visit to Nazi Germany had made little impact. Nigel Law, who had been in Germany on business, reported his impression to the Foreign Office:

---

[16] *Heart*, p. 308.

[17] Forwood, p. 60, BREN 2/2/7, Churchill College Archives.

[18] J. Paul Getty, *As I See It* (WH Allen, 1976), p. 84. Paul Schmidt, the interpreter, claimed there were no minutes. Paul Schmidt, *Hitler's Interpreter* (Macmillan, 1951), p. 75.

[19] *Sunday Mirror*, 31 October 1954.

[20] RA PS/PSO/GVI/C/042/063

The visit of the Duke of Windsor seems to have made a bad impression. His entire journey and expenses were paid by the German Labour Front. He was always with Dr Ley, who is invariably drunk and is of second rate importance among the Nazis. He saw very little of the real leaders and spent but a short time with the Fuhrer. Even the bill for the manicure of his secretary was paid by Dr Ley and no tips were given at the Kaiserhoff where he stayed. Germans say he did not understand half of what he saw or what was said to him. The whole visit is described as lacking in dignity for one who has held such a great position.[21]

The reaction in the United States was similar. Ian G. Walker, responsible for organising the American trip, wrote to the Duke:

The reaction of the American press on your visit to Germany has been anything but favourable . . . The tone of the various newspaper articles implies that your Royal Highness is in complete sympathy with the German National Socialist Movement.[22]

On 24 October, Bedaux, who was financing the trip, writing from the Paris Ritz, sent Lindsay the 'first draft of the complete schedule of visits'.[23]

The visit would start in Washington on 11 November and finish in Los Angeles and San Francisco in mid-December. The Duke would see President Franklin D. Roosevelt at the White House; his wife,

[21] CHAR 2/300, TNA.

[22] Walker to the Duke of Windsor, 22 October 1937, RA EDW/PRIV/ MAIN/A/3464.

[23] FO 954/33A/183, TNA.

Eleanor, would personally show him the housing projects in which she was involved; the Duke would lay a wreath at Arlington Cemetery and broadcast to the nation. A private Pullman train had been hired to take them from the East to the West Coast and General Motors had put at their disposal a fleet of ninety of the latest Buicks.

Three days later, Bedaux and his wife, Fern, set sail for New York in preparation. Also aboard the *Europa* was Ernest Simpson, *en route* to marry Mary Raffray.

The Windsors prepared for their new trip, sending a seven-page memo to the staff of the *Bremen*, the German ship that would take them to New York, outlining their requirements. It included service in the Red Room, a separate dining room set aside for them on the Sun Deck, provision for a special English blend of tea, and a barrel of London drinking water. The memo informed chefs that the Duke liked plain food, steaks and cutlets and chicken for dinner, preferred French dressing without mustard, and only drank mineral water before cocktail time. He also enjoyed canapés of liver paste, Westphalian ham and rarebits. With dinner he liked claret, but not white wines or champagnes, and had an after-dinner brandy with his coffee.[24]

On 2 November, the day after the Bedauxs arrived in New York to finalise arrangements, Sumner Welles, the US Under-Secretary of State, reported his talks with the British Ambassador, Ronald Lindsay:

> The Ambassador said rather significantly that there recently had been a widening of this sentiment of indignation because of the fact that the active supporters of the Duke of Windsor within England were those elements known to have

[24] Martin, p. 353.

inclinations towards fascist dictatorships and that the recent tour of Germany by the Duke of Windsor and his ostentatious reception by Hitler and his regime could only be construed as a willingness on the part of the Duke of Windsor to lend himself to these tendencies.[25]

Trouble was brewing. The media was already sceptical. London columnist Hannen Swaffer wrote, 'It's nothing but a publicity stunt. I travelled with the Duke when he was studying housing in Wales, and if he were there for fifty years he wouldn't know anything more about it than he knows now.'[26] Now the American unions, who were no fans of Bedaux's industrial practices, responded. Ronald Lindsay reported to the Foreign Office:

> Tone of the press and trend of opinion as regards Duke of Windsor's tour has been growing even more unfavourable ... Language about Duchess has been unfriendly. But most of all his prospects have been damaged by association with Bedaux, who is of course anathema to Labour. A culmination was reached today when a manifesto by Baltimore Federation of Labour was issued attacking the tour of the Duchess and especially of Bedaux and fascist tendencies displayed by circumstances of Duke's recent visit to Germany.[27]

Organised Labour had long been critical of Bedaux and took their revenge. The American Federation of Labour and the Congress of

---

[25] Washington Dept of State file FW033.4111, Memorandum of Confidential Conversation, 2 November 1937, National Archives, quoted Greg King, *The Duchess of Windsor* (Aurum, 1999), p. 286.

[26] Martin, p. 354.

[27] Lindsay to Foreign Office, 4 November 1937, FO 954/33A/121, TNA.

Industrial Organization issued statements criticising his companies and their efficiency policies. The Union of New York Longshoremen announced they would picket Windsor's ship and not unload any of his luggage. Shares in Bedaux's American companies fell dramatically and his fellow directors forced him to stand down as president of American Bedaux Associates. A former lover, Louise Booth, presented him with a lawsuit of $250,000 and the Inland Revenue handed him a bill for $202,718.[28]

Bedaux, who took flight to Canada then Europe, realised the game was up and cabled the Duke, copying in the press, 'Because of the mistaken attack upon me here, I am convinced that your proposed tour will be difficult under my auspices . . . I respectfully . . . implore you to relieve me completely of all duties in connection with it.'[29]

The Duke now cancelled the trip. Lindsay's brother, Lord Crawford, noted in his diary:

> So the Duke of Windsor has cancelled his journey to America. Ronald told me he had put himself hopelessly in the wrong by starting his visit with a preliminary tour in Germany, where he was of course photographed fraternising with the Nazi, the Anti-Trade Unionist and the Jewbaiter. Poor little man. He has no sense of his own and no friends with any sense to advise him. I hope this will give him a sharp and salutary lesson.[30]

[28] Jim Christy, *The Price of Power: A Biography of Charles Eugene Bedaux* (Doubleday, 1984), p. 169.

[29] Associated Press, 5 November 1937. Bedaux lost £200,000, control of his US companies, had a nervous breakdown and spent months in a Bavarian sanatorium.

[30] 6–7 November 1937, Vincent, p. 585.

On 8 November, the *Daily Herald* editorial was clear. 'The Duke of Windsor has now announced that he will in future consider himself "no longer a public figure". That is a wise decision.'[31]

But suspicions remained about his ambitions. On 22 November, Robert Bruce Lockhart wrote in his diary, after talking to the diplomat Rex Leeper, 'German view of Edward, Duke of Windsor. Germans still believe he will come back as social-equalising King, will inaugurate English form of Fascism and alliance with Germany.'[32]

A week later, Lindsay wrote to Alec Hardinge that, 'In the greatest confidence I have been shown copies of two letters which were written by Bedaux in August and September about the tour of the Duke of Windsor which was then being planned.'[33] The letters outlined that the Windsor trips were part of 'a worldwide peace movement', in which a manifesto would be issued 'at some moment during the Duke's tour in America. I am told that advance copies of this statement had been given to some newspaper editors, and that these are therefore still in their hands. I am sending a copy of this to Vansittart.'[34]

Then in December a further example of the Duke's views was brought to the attention of the Government. William Tyrrell, staying with his successor as British ambassador to Paris, Sir Eric Phipps, at the end of 1937, was told that a member of the embassy staff had seen the text of an interview that Windsor had given a *Daily Herald* journalist:

> in which it was stated that His Royal Highness said that if
> the Labour Party wished, and were in a position to offer it, he

[31] *Daily Herald,* 8 November 1937.

[32] Bruce Lockhart Diaries, 22 November 1937, Vol. 1, p. 382.

[33] Ronald Lindsay to Alec Hardinge, 29 November 1937, FO 954/33A/183, TNA.

[34] Ronald Lindsay to Alec Hardinge, 29 November 1937, FO 954/33A/183, TNA.

would be prepared to be President of the English Republic. Tyrrell urged Greenwood [the *Daily Herald* journalist] to have this left out of any published account of this interview, as he was so shocked and horrified. This Greenwood promised to do, and, I understand that, so far, the interview has not seen the light of day . . . I am not informing anyone of the above except yourself.[35]

The Duke was clearly on manoeuvres. These would be confirmed by subsequent events.

[35] Eric Phipps to Anthony Eden, 28 December 1937, FO 954/33a/186, TNA, and PHPP 1/19, Churchill College Archives.

CHAPTER 6

Interlude

Since returning from honeymoon, the Windsors had been living in a suite of rooms at the Hotel Meurice, overlooking the Tuileries, where they had agreed a reduced rate of $30 a day, on the basis that they were a good advertisement for the hotel.[1] Given they would not be allowed to return to Britain – their concern was as much taxation, now payable as private citizens, as any stipulations from the Royal Family – and their financial future was secure, they now decided to put down roots in France.

On 26 January 1938, Wallis wrote to her Aunt Bessie:

We have decided not to go to Havana this year as we feel we really *must* have a home before we travel any more. This life of trunks and hotels is very unsatisfactory. I have looked at a number of places in different directions outside of Paris, furnished and unfurnished. The former are hopeless and the unfurnished ones either palaces or too small, the wrong direction or too far from golf, etc, etc, so just to get out of this hotel we have taken a furnished house at Versailles with a small garden and tennis court, belonging to Mrs Paul Depuy. It is comfortable, no charm but dignity, and we have taken it

---

[1] The equivalent today would be about $550.

from February 7 to June 7 – appalling rent as everyone is out
to do the Windsors . . .[2]

This was the Château de La Maye in Versailles, which sat in a large
private garden with swimming pool, tennis court and a nine-hole
private golf course.[3] This was a compromise as Wallis wanted to
be in Paris and the Duke to have a country house, where he could
indulge his love of gardening. One of its advantages was that it was
near the Villa Trianon, the home of their close friends, Sir Charles
and Elsie, Lady Mendl.

Elsie de Wolfe, a tiny woman whose party trick was standing on
her head, was thirty years older than the Windsors. She had single-
handedly invented the profession of interior decorating and with
her lover, Elisabeth Marbury, a literary agent representing Oscar
Wilde and George Bernard Shaw, had come to Paris at the turn of
the century. She and Marbury, who died in 1933, had bought the
eighteenth-century Villa Trianon, which had been built by Louis
XV as a retreat from the main palace but was then a wreck, and
restored it.

In 1926, de Wolfe had surprised her friends by marrying
the bisexual Sir Charles Mendl, the press attaché at the British
Embassy in Paris. It was an arrangement that worked well as
he needed her money and she wanted a title – Mendl had been
knighted in 1924 for reputedly retrieving letters from a gigolo
blackmailing the Duke's brother George, but more likely for his
espionage activities.

---

[2] Michael Bloch, *Secret File*, pp. 124–5.

[3] It is now a luxury private hospital. There had been rumours they would take the
Château de Grosbois, which Napoleon had given to Marshal Berthier, but Wallis
thought it 'too royal'. *New York Times,* 20 February 1938.

Interlude

Constance Coolidge, an old friend of Wallis, often dined at Château de La Maye. On 22 March, she noted in her diary:

Well the dinner was a great success . . . Wallis looked lovely in a blue sequin dress. It wasn't a bit formal and everyone talked all the time. Wallis did interrupt the duke rather but then he stayed in the dining room a long time afterwards and talked politics very well. He said Czechoslovakia was a ridiculous country – just look at it – how could anyone go to war for that. It isn't a country at all, just an idea of the Wilsons.[4]

Coolidge's diary gives a glimpse of a strange episode in the Windsors' life that appears in little other documentation. The next day, Coolidge recorded how she was invited to meet a woman called Maroni at a third-floor flat at 36 Boulevard Emile Augier in the 16th arrondissement:

a butler in white coat opened the door – very queer apartment – white satin sofa & curtains . . . a queer woman, light hair died (*sic*), dark eyes, a long nose – Italian – certainly an adventuress . . . she was the intermediary for a friend . . . also a duchess . . . This woman has papers, letters, photographs . . . proofs of something very harmful to the royal family & the duke. She wants to see the duke alone . . . you can't believe the papers & if he asks her to she will burn the papers but she must see him. She has followed him around Austria . . . She will offer me a very large sum. 'What is your price?' to arrange

---

[4] Constance Coolidge diary, supplied by Andrea Lynn, but available at reel 5, Crowninshield-Magnus papers, Massachusetts Historical Society.

this. There is a man who will buy these papers to print them in America.[5]

Two days later, Coolidge lunched with a police inspector, who told her there was already a dossier on Maroni, that the woman was a former maid of the Duke and 'the papers had to do with the Prince of Hesse'.[6]

The Prince of Hesse was most likely Philipp of Hesse and, like the Duke of Windsor, a great-grandson of Queen Victoria. An architect and bisexual – one of his relationships was with the poet Siegfried Sassoon – he had married Princess Mafalda, daughter of King Victor Emmanuel in 1925. In October 1930, Hesse had joined the Nazi Party and by June 1933 was an *Oberpräsident* or regional party leader in Prussia. He was close to both Goering and Hitler, who was godfather to one of his sons, and, being fluent in English, French and Italian, had served as a special envoy for the Nazis. In that capacity he had had dealings with the Duke and had accompanied him on his October 1937 German tour.

The blackmailer appeared to have incriminating material. According to Charles Higham, the woman:

> had posed as a maid at the home of the duke's cousin, Prince Philipp of Hesse, Hitler's favourite and a frequent emissary to the Italian dictator, in order to steal photographs and documents showing that the duke had a secret and intimate connection with the bisexual Philipp.[7]

---

[5] Constance Coolidge diary, 23 March 1938. This was a different stalker from the one in chapter 5.

[6] Constance Coolidge diary, 26 March 1938.

[7] Charles Higham, *In and Out of Hollywood* (University of Wisconsin Press, 2009) p. 279.

Interlude

The Windsors, who were in the South of France, looking at renting a villa for the summer, immediately rushed back.[8]

'The duke and two chief of police, one English & one French were there and I had to tell them everything before the Duke,' wrote Coolidge in her diary. 'Even that about "a man who renounced a throne & had a mistress in Austria". It was embarrassing very!'[9]

Faced with police involvement, Madame Maroni disappeared and, according to Higham, 'her documents were seized by the Sûreté and . . . sent to Moscow; when they were returned to Paris after World War II, they vanished again.'[10] The hunt was now on for the letters with Hesse, which might reveal a sexual relationship with the Duke, or at least some embarrassing communication relating to politics.

Aside from the Hesse letters, there were numerous issues surrounding the Duke, not least the claims of illegitimate children he had fathered across the world. The question of the Duke's sexuality has long intrigued. Before meeting Wallis, he was known to have had many affairs, including a long-standing one from just after the First World War until 1929 with Freda, the wife of William Dudley Ward, a Liberal Member of Parliament. As with Wallis, there was a certain mother fixation. He called her 'Fredie-Wedie' and their correspondence was marked by lots of baby talk ('vewy angwy', 'your own little David is cwying so hard inside') and dirty jokes.

A petite, elegant, loyal, discreet woman with a good sense of humour, she was seen by the Duke's friends as a good influence

---

[8] It was the chateau, Villa Leopolda, built for King Leopold of the Belgians and then owned by the American architect Ogden Codman. Later owners included Gianni Agnelli and Edmond and Lily Saffra. It is regarded as the most expensive property in the world.

[9] Coolidge diary, 5 April 1938. The inference was that Wallis's suspicions about Kitty Rothschild were true. The Prefect of Police was Roger Langeron.

[10] *In and Out*, p. 279.

on him. Freda only learnt that she had been dropped as a royal favourite when the Buckingham Palace switchboard refused to put calls through, but what most hurt her was the behaviour to her two daughters Penelope and Angela, as he 'had been like a father to them'. As she later told the author Caroline Blackwood:

> They adored him. But once he met the Duchess, they never heard from him again . . . The Duke did something that really shocked me. It was so petty and cruel that it really hurt me . . . He had arranged for one of my daughters who was quite small at the time to receive a pearl from a jeweller every time she had a birthday . . . The idea was that she would have a necklace by the time that she was grown up . . . The moment he met the Duchess he cancelled the order with the jeweller! I thought it was really shocking that the Duke, who had more jewellery than anyone in the world, would take away a tiny pearl necklace from a child.[11]

Ward's position as royal mistress was taken by the former actress Thelma Furness, then married to the shipping magnate Viscount Furness. In 1934, she told her friend Wallis to look after 'the little man' and the rest is history.

Along the way there were many affairs, especially on the world tours he made after the First World War.[12] There have even been claims of illegitimate children, including with a French seamstress Marie-Leonie Graftieaux (Marcelle Dormoy), which produced a

---

[11] Caroline Blackwood, *The Last of the Duchess* (Macmillan, 1995), p. 211.

[12] One was an affair with Pinna Cruger, the actress wife of a New York haberdashery millionaire, on a trip to the United States in 1924, whilst travelling as Lord Renfrew.

son Pierre-Edouard (1916–94).[13] Frederick Evans, born in 1918, claims that his concert pianist mother, Lillian Bartlett, had an affair with the Prince, that his birth was registered as the son of a Welsh miner, James Evans, and that she told the Prince of the boy and he responded with financial support.[14]

According to Peter Macdonald, who heard the story from his grandfather, in 1920, whilst staying at the Dunedin Club on his New Zealand tour, the Prince impregnated a servant who went on to have a son 'who was paid a remittance from London . . . his nick-name in Dunedin was King . . . the King would strut around town and he had a great resemblance to the Prince of Wales's father, as he wore similar clothes and wore the royal beard.'[15]

There are also rumours that Edwina Drummond, born in April 1920, was fathered by the Prince of Wales, her godfather, who was a regular visitor to her family home Pitsford Hall, outside North-ampton, where he rode with the Pytchley Hunt. Wilf Harris, then a choirboy at the village church, recalls the Prince's visits. 'We all knew he was fond of horses and her [Mrs Drummond].' Many in the village, he said, believed the Prince was having an affair with Kathleen Drummond and was the father of her third daughter, Edwina. 'No doubt about it,' said Harris.[16]

Another local, a retired policeman in Northamptonshire, agrees. His mother was an employee at Pitsford Hall and he has been left in no doubt by the stories handed down to him. 'Edwina was the

---

[13] Pierre's son makes the case in *L'homme qui aurait dû être roi: L'incroyable récit du petit-fils caché d'Edouard VIII* by Francois Graftieaux with Jean Siccardi, and Helen Grosso (Cherche Mido, 2016). A British version of the story is *The King's Son: The True Story of the Duke of Windsor's Only Son* by J.J. Barrie (privately published, 2020).

[14] The story was optioned for film by Todd Allen.

[15] Peter Macdonald to the author, 25 February 2021.

[16] *Sunday Times*, 11 July 1999.

prince's daughter,' he said. 'Everyone knew she was different.' Her father George Drummond is supposed to have caught his wife Kathleen with the Prince of Wales in a compromising situation in the stables and said, 'Sir, I will share my wine and horses with any man, but I will share my wife with no man!'

Drummond's second wife, Honora, claimed that whereas Edwina's three sisters inherited their father's aquiline nose, Edwina had a turned up nose like the Prince. In 1937, whilst at finishing school in Germany, she saw the Prince on his visit to Hitler. The links between the two families continued with George VI becoming godfather to Drummond's son George from his second marriage and the Princesses Elizabeth and Margaret learning to ride at Pitsford. Edwina later married Eric Mirville, who had served in the French Foreign Legion, and moved to Ireland where she died in the 1980s.[17]

A more convincing case can be made for the actor Timothy Seely (born 10 June 1935), whose mother, Vera, was the sister of Freda Dudley Ward. The Duke of Windsor, then Prince of Wales, had been best man at Vera's wedding to Jimmy Seely in 1925 and was godfather to Tim's sister Elizma. The Prince and Jimmy Seely had become friends on the hunting field and the Prince often stayed with the Seelys in Nottinghamshire. The Seely family later played down the story, which was first revealed by the author John Parker, and refused to talk to the author about it, but after the Duke's death, Seely was contacted by the Duke's lawyers.[18]

'Over the years various authors/reporters have contacted Tim for interviews/articles, but the response was always the same, he

[17] *Sunday Times*, 11 July 1999.

[18] Anthony Camp, *Royal Mistresses and Bastards: Fact And Fiction 1714–1936* (Society of Genealogists, 2009), p. 398, and John Parker, *King of Fools* (St Martins, 1988), pp. 71–2. Seely contributed a foreword to the latter. Family members have suggested that it was actually Elizma who was the Duke's child.

is not interested,' his wife Camilla said firmly. 'He is immensely discreet . . . We would not wish to be even a small part of yet more unworthy stories concerning The Royal Family.'[19]

* * *

The Windsors continued to be in limbo. Chips Channon wrote in his diary in March 1938:

> Disturbing news of the Windsors; they dine alone night after night, ignored, snubbed by the French, and neglected by the English. The Duke of Windsor is, of course, very pro-German; he maintains that had he been on the throne, the German coup in Austria could never have happened. 'I should have appealed personally to Hitler,' he said pathetically to Kitty Brownlow. He is so lonely, so bored.[20]

The journalist Collin Brooks, running into the couple at the Sporting Club in Monte Carlo that month, provides a portrait of them at the time:

> Leading a little knot of people through the bowing function-aries came a small, tight-lipped, dark-haired woman, very regal in her carriage, followed by two nondescripts and then by a miniature of a man with blond hair, a very red face, and the general demeanour of a happy grocer's boy. It was the Duke of Windsor. To my eye he looked tanned and well and far more composed than when I last saw him. There was no fiddling with the tie, his hands were thrust in his trouser

[19] Camilla Seely to author, 25 August 2020.
[20] 26 March 1938, Simon Heffer, *Henry 'Chips' Channon: The Diaries 1918–38* (Hutchinson, 2021), p. 846.

pockets. She was the focal point of the little party, not he. Her face has become palpably harder – she is the creature of hard lines altogether, the dark hair parted and smoothed down like the painted hair of a Dutch doll, the line of the mouth, hard, the eyes hard, the severe black dress cut in hard lines.[21]

In May 1938, the Windsors found their summer villa, taking a ten-year lease on the Château de la Croë, situated on the Cap d'Antibes peninsula, from the British newspaperman Sir Pomeroy Burton. Built in the early 1930s, it became known as 'Chateau des Rois', as it was successively occupied by the Windsors, King Leopold III of Belgium, and Queen Marie Jose of Italy.[22]

A three-storey, gleaming white villa with green shutters and matching awnings, behind high walls and hedges, it was set in twelve acres of garden and woodland, with fir, pine, yew, eucalyptus and cypress trees, reached by a narrow winding road from the port. It included a tennis court, servants' quarters, greenhouses, garages, and on either side of the entrance gate was a small lodge that provided accommodation for the staff.

The house was built round a huge central hall, dominated by the Duke's red and gold Order of Garter banner, which ran the full depth of the house, off which led large rooms with 25-foot-high ceilings and tall, mirrored doors. On the right of the hall was the

---

[21] 27 March 1938, N.J. Crowson, *Fleet Street, Press Barons & Politics: The Journals of Collin Brooks* (Cambridge University Press, 1998), pp. 202–3.

[22] The Greek shipping magnate Aristotle Onassis owned the chateau from 1950 to 1957, selling it after his wife, Athina Livanos, found him in bed with her friend, the socialite Jeanne Rhinelander. The house was then acquired by Onassis's brother-in-law and business rival Stavros Niarchos, who bought it for his wife, Eugenia Livanos, Athina's sister. Since 2001 it has been owned by the Russian businessman Roman Abramovich, who is believed to have spent £30 million restoring the chateau.

dining room, which could seat twenty-four and where hung Alfred Munnings' *The Prince of Wales on Forest Witch*, whilst on the left was a drawing room and panelled library.

Everything had been decorated by their friend Elsie Mendl in Buckingham Palace colours of white, red and gold. Dining chairs were of red leather with black and gold backs, the red and white library was dominated by a huge portrait of Queen Mary over the marble fireplace, and there was a Steinway grand piano at which the Duke would play – when the Duchess was absent. There were mirrors over the fireplaces and on many doors – a mark of Wallis's style – and glass, china, furniture and linen from Fort Belvedere and York House.

A marble staircase twisted to the first-floor gallery and their bedrooms: Wallis's bedroom decorated with *trompe-l'oeil* images symbolising her past – one was a pack of cards with a king of hearts falling down – in soft pink and apricot, his in scarlet and beige. Wallis's bathroom was in scarlet and black and boasted a stone tub, gilded, and with a swan's neck at each end.

There were two guest rooms – the Rose Room and the Venetian Room in red and gold, with two striking antique beds and a bow-fronted Venetian chest, and then four more guest rooms on the second floor – the Directoire, the Blue Room, the Wedgewood and the Toile de Jouy – each with a pair of antique beds, with rugs, curtains, bed covers, cushions, towels and even stationery in matching colours.

Atop the villa was a penthouse, reached by a lift, which the Duke called 'The Belvedere', a mixture of office, private sitting room and Fleet Admiral's quarters, where a telescope allowed him to look out to sea. It was decorated with a ship's chronometer, which had belonged to George V, ship's brass bell and a barometer, together with golf and hunting trophies, photographs of his parents and about half a dozen pictures of Wallis.

'Two low built-in shelves of unvarnished oak held the Duke's collection of tiny toys and mementos – the result of a life-long hobby,' remembered Dina Hood, who worked as the Duke's secretary in this period:

> Many of the little figures were amusing; some were rather touching, like the little set of doll's house furniture in black and gold, which included a grandfather clock, a screen and a writing desk with a bookcase above it. There was a tiny toy tea service on a tray, a miniature table with a cocktail shaker and glasses on it, and a minute bookcase full of books. One shelf was entirely devoted to toy animals: a dog in a kennel and a dog on a chair, two funny little pigs, a small white frog and a tiny green hedgehog with pink quills.[23]

Outside the house was a crescent-shaped terrace with six columns facing the sea. Steps down the cliff led to the sea where a swimming pool was cut into the rocks and there were two small pavilions for changing, with large red-and-white awnings. Above them flew the Prince of Wales's standard.

The Windsors employed sixteen servants, including two chauffeurs, a butler and a famous French chef, Pinaudier, all dressed in a personal livery designed by the Duke of scarlet coats with gold cuffs for formal occasions and black suits with crimson, white and gold striped waistcoats during the day. There were lightweight dress suits of pale grey alpaca for summer, whilst in Paris they wore black suits with crimson, white and gold striped

---

[23] Dina Wells Hood, *Working for the Windsors* (Wingate, 1957), p. 61.

waistcoats with silver buttons and gold-collared scarlet waistcoats for formal dinners.

WE was entwined with the Duke's coronet on the silver buttons of the grey alpaca livery worn by the butler and footmen and on everything from the uniforms, writing paper, menu cards, bed linen to the lifebuoys hanging by the pool. Most nights they dined out of doors at a W-shaped table on the terrace overlooking the sea with elaborate meals, such as melon with tomato ice, and eggs in crab sauce. A hairdresser came daily, a manicurist twice a week.

Royal protocol was insisted on, with guests bowing or curtseying to both Windsors on first seeing them in the morning, whilst the Duke's secretary had to stand whilst she took dictation. Wallis referred to her husband as 'the Dook' and she was always 'Your Royal Highness'. Everything, in short, was an attempt to recreate the life they had lost.

'I sat next to the Duchess. He sat opposite. They called each other "darling" a great deal. I called him "Your Royal Highness" a great deal and "Sir" the whole time. I called her "Duchess",' wrote Harold Nicolson to his wife, after dining with the Windsors at Somerset Maugham's house in August 1938:

> One cannot get away from his glamour and his charm and his sadness, though, I must say, he seemed gay enough. They have a villa here and a yacht, and go round and round. He digs in the garden. But it is pathetic the way he is sensitive about her. It was quite clear to me from what she said that she hopes to get back to England. When I asked her why she didn't get a house of her own somewhere, she said, 'One never knows what may happen. I don't want to spend all my life in exile.'[24]

---

[24] 5 August 1938, Nigel Nicolson (ed.), *Harold Nicolson: Letters and Diaries 1930–1939* (William Collins, 1966), pp. 351–2.

There were recurrent attempts by the Palace during this period to try and give the Windsors some position. 'Both the King and the Queen have talked to me recently about the Duke and Duchess of Windsor, and have mentioned the feeling of bitterness which they are understood to feel towards their majesties and the other members of the royal family,' Lord Halifax wrote to Sir Eric Phipps, the British ambassador in Paris, on 3 May 1938. 'They suggested it might be a good move, and do something to remove some of this feeling, if the Duke and Duchess were to be asked to dine on some suitable occasion at the embassy.'[25]

But the concern remained that the Windsors might upstage the new king. In July 1938, when George VI and Elizabeth paid a state visit to France, the Windsors diplomatically chartered a 200-ton motor yacht for six weeks and cruised down the west coast of Italy with Herman and Katherine Rogers, though they were dissuaded by the Foreign Office from staying with Wallis's friend, the architect Georges Sebastian, in Italian-dominated Tunisia.

'You will remember how miserable I was when you informed me of your intended marriage and abdication and how I implored you not to do so for our sake and the sake of the country. You did not seem able to take any point of view but your own', wrote Queen Mary to her son in July, adding, 'My feelings for you as your Mother remain the same, and our being parted and the cause of it, grieve me beyond words. After all, all my life I have put my Country before everything else, and I simply cannot change now.'[26]

But relations within the family remained strained, not helped by the mutual antipathy between the new Queen Elizabeth, whom

[25] F0 800/326, TNA.

[26] Queen Mary to Duke of Windsor, 5 July 1938, RA EDW/PRIV/MAIN/A/3681.

Wallis called 'Cookie', and Wallis, whom Elizabeth could never go beyond calling 'That Woman'.

At the end of August, Monckton was summoned to Balmoral, joining Neville Chamberlain, who had succeeded Stanley Baldwin as Prime Minister, to discuss a possible visit of the Duke to Britain in November 1938. Chamberlain wanted him 'to be treated as soon as possible as a younger brother of the King, who could take some of the royal functions off his brother's hands,' recorded Lord Birkenhead in his life of Monckton, which was based on private papers. The King 'was not fundamentally against the Prime Minister's view', but the Queen was against giving him 'any effective sphere of work' on the grounds he was a threat to her husband, who was 'less superficially endowed with the arts and graces that please.'[27]

The discussions rumbled on throughout the autumn, with no change of attitude by the Royal Family and growing concerns that the Duke might become a rallying point for Mosley's fascists and other organisations.[28] 'I have been warned in the most emphatic terms . . . that such a visit . . . would evoke strong protest and controversy,' wrote Chamberlain to the Duke, reporting on public opinion towards a Windsor visit in spring 1938. He had received almost 200 letters and 'of these letters, over 90 per cent, in one way or another, express opinions adverse to the proposal.'[29]

---

[27] Birkenhead, p. 169. The Duke insisted on being provided with a house near Windsor, ideally Royal Lodge, for the visit. Duke to George V1, 29 August 1938, EDW/MAIN/PRIV/A/3722 and Duke to Neville Chamberlain, 29 August 1938, GVI/OUT/MONCKTON/3/10/1.

[28] In June 1938, Henchmen of Honour founded by a retired barrister Robert Elton had unsuccessfully tried to have the Abdication Act repealed and 'Friends of the Duke of Windsor in America' had begun a campaign to 'cut short the oppression against him and restore him to rightful, useful place among the nations.' *Sunday Dispatch*, 8 January 1939.

[29] Monckton Trustees, Box 16, folio 214, Balliol College.

This was supported by a Special Branch report. 'It is openly stated in circles connected with the Press that the Duke of Windsor has been in touch with certain newspaper proprietors with the object of starting a publicity campaign in this country, in order to create an atmosphere favourable to the return of himself and the Duchess of Windsor.'[30]

It was clear the Windsors were to be kept out of Britain.[31]

---

[30] 5 January 1939, RA MEPO 10/35, TNA. A copy is at RA GO42A/111.

[31] The Duke insisted on being provided with a house near Windsor, ideally Royal Lodge, for the visit. Duke to George V1, 29 August 1938, RA EDW/MAIN/ PRIV/A/3722 and Duke to Neville Chamberlain, 29 August 1938, RA GVI/ OUT/MONCKTON/3/10/1.

CHAPTER 7

Countdown to War

In October 1938, the lease having expired at Château de La Maye, the Windsors took on a ten-year lease of a mansion close to the Bois de Boulogne and the Saint-Cloud Golf Club. No. 24 Boulevard Suchet, in the 16th arrondissement, was a four-storey town house on a small corner lot, overlooking a paved square and surrounded by a tall iron fence and thick hedges. The imposing front door led into a pillared entrance hall with a black-and-white Carrara-marble floor and white columns, from which led several rooms used by the secretaries and detectives. At each corner of the hall in a mirrored recess stood a tall white caryatid, bearing on her head a crown of candles.

There was a small lift to their apartments on the left and on the right a curved white marble staircase with green carpet led to four interlocking reception rooms built round a big central landing – a formal drawing room, small salon, dining room, and a lounge known as the banquette room.

There were sixteen servants including: James Hale, the English butler who had previously worked for Charles Bedaux and who was known as 'the butler with the golden voice'; a French chef, Monsieur Dyot, previously chef to the Duke of Alba; an Austrian valet, Rudolf Kopp, and chauffeur, Karl Schafranek; French and

English footmen; two English housemaids; and for Wallis, an English chauffeur, Tony Webster, and a Swiss lady's maid.[1]

Protection remained a big issue, with several British and French police officers always with them, even when the Duke played golf. When the couple lunched or dined in restaurants or with friends, or they paid visits to couturiers, milliners, jewellers or antique shops, an officer always waited outside and a Gendarme always stood guard at the front door of their home.

The new house became their project, a way of demonstrating their love for each other. 'Tirelessly she searched for exactly the right furniture, rugs, materials, lamps and *bibelots*. She came to know intimately every antique shop, large and small, in Paris,' recollected Dina Hood. 'Everything that concerned the house was of absorbing interest to the Duchess. Besides the furniture and bibelots, she collected fine porcelain, glassware, silver and linen.'[2] She thought nothing of paying £8,000 for a single Meissen figure or £30,000 for a pair of canary diamonds – generally bought with cash to avoid tax.[3]

The couple ate little during the day, the Duke preferring to spend the lunch hour on the golf course, knowing that few Frenchmen would venture out at such a time. Instead, Hood remembered, he might have a light brunch, which 'consisted of stewed fruit or open fruit tart served with cream, accompanied by digestive biscuits and weak tea. He was very fond of fruit tarts, especially of Apfelstrudel, which he had learnt to know in Austria.'[4]

Their focus was on the evening, giving two dinner parties each week and out most other nights. 'Never in my life have I worked so

---

[1] On Wallis's Buick, the initials WWS for Wallis Warfield Simpson were etched in small plain gold letters in a tiny diamond-shaped frame on one of the doors.

[2] Hood, *Working for the Windsors*, p. 41.

[3] The equivalent of £550K and just over £2 million.

[4] Hood, p. 41.

hard,' remembered the butler James Hale, who worked at both La
Croë and Boulevard Suchet:

> The Duchess, I soon discovered, graded the villa, not so much
> as a home, but as the stage on which to present an unending
> show of hospitality and entertainment. She was the producer;
> I was her stage manager. On my arrival . . . I found house
> telephones not only in the butler's pantry, not only in my
> bedroom – but in my bathroom and lavatory as well. It was
> clear that when the Duchess insisted on instant communica-
> tion with the staff at all times, she meant, *at all times*.[5]

They were demanding and not always popular employers. 'A
dropped plate, a careless intrusion, or a slip in attentiveness could
be counted upon to bring a swift dressing down, followed often by
peremptory sacking,' remembered Charles Murphy, who worked
for the Windsors. 'The hours were long, praise was scanty. It is
doubtful that any household staff in all Paris was driven as hard as
the one that served the Windsors.'[6]

Each morning Wallis discussed the menus for the day with the
chef. 'She examined these minutely, sometimes approving, sometimes altering or adding to his suggestions,' Hood remembered.[7]

She continued:

> Into every branch of expenditure she enquired exhaustively.
> Household accounts were kept with scrupulous exactness in
> accordance with the cash book and ledger system into which
> Mr Carter had initiated me that day at Buckingham Palace.

[5] *Sunday People*, 29 April 1973, quoted Martin, p. 361.
[6] Bryan and Murphy, p. 394.
[7] Hood, p. 105.

In the ledger, payments were grouped under various headings which were sub-divided in such minute detail that a close watch could be kept on every kind of disbursement.[8]

With little else to occupy them, the devil was in the detail. 'They decided the exact shade and size of their personal notepaper and how it should be engraved,' Hood later wrote. 'The same for their menu cards. Their luggage labels were printed according to their own instructions. Together they chose the designs and colourings of their Christmas cards.'[9]

*   *   *

In October 1938, Valentine Lawford, a young diplomat at the Paris Embassy, wrote to his mother: 'Last night I had quite a historic time, as I was asked to a musical evening at Elsie Mendl's, and found on my arrival (with the dessert) the men of the party sitting around the table being held forth to by the Duke of Windsor.' He continued:

> HRH was in a marvellous mood and made me come and sit beside him and tell him every detail of my (rather humdrum) life . . . After we moved out of the dining room, he told me to come and sit by him on a sofa in a corner of one of the rooms, and there we sat for half-an-hour, while he held forth on politics and pumped me all that time about what the younger generation thought about everything. He's very Nazi in his ideas and seems to have a horror of Bolshevism . . . he was quite charming to talk to and obviously means well, though I think he's very wrong-headed and prejudiced, for all his

[8]   Hood, p. 106.
[9]   Hood, p. 119.

experience. Of course he wanted to know what the FO thought about Chamberlain's foreign policy (of which he entirely approves) . . . Please, keep the Windsor dope to yourselves. People talk so much that it might get back to HRH that a certain 3rd Secretary had said he was a 'Nazi', etc.[10]

Lawford, then in his late twenties, became a regular part of the Windsors' and Mendls' entourage. On 1 February 1939, he described a film viewing that included Somerset Maugham's wife Syrie amongst the guests. 'It was amusing to see HRH watching his great-grandparents gambolling about at Balmoral, and he seemed to enjoy it . . . We went back after, to supper at Elsie's, where the Duke spoke fluent Spanish and became quite jolly . . .'[11]

The next night he dined with them:

The Windsors were very kind and nice and jolly the other night and I had quite a heart-to-heart talk with the Duchess. We dined at Maxim's, where we were joined by Alexandra Metcalfe and the Sacheverell Sitwells . . . The Duke found that the orchestra got in the way of his talking – and he talks a great deal – so we left Maxim's and drove back to their house on the Boulevard Suchet. Incidentally, his French is appalling: he calls it the Bwaa de Boolone. The house is so far only half furnished; but it looks as if it would eventually be extremely pleasant: high rooms with tall windows and, of course, beautiful furniture.

His bedroom is also Empire, darkish red and gold; and he has a passion for little helmets. His chairs have helmets at both corners of the back; and his bedside-clock is enclosed in

[10] Lawford to his mother, 17 October 1938, courtesy of Charles Tilbury.
[11] Lawford to his mother, 1 February 1939, courtesy of Charles Tilbury.

a helmet of metal and mother-of-pearl . . . His bed – on which were laid out the royal pyjamas and dressing-gown – is also Empire, dark red . . . The Duchess has a bedroom of very dark blue, and white . . . I can't help feeling that he is sadly wasted . . . But the Duchess said they were in no hurry to go back to England if they weren't wanted . . . I am dining on Saturday at the Ritz with [Lady] Bertha Michelham, when the Windsors will be her guests of honour. I don't seem to be able to get out of their orbit; but I must admit that I honestly enjoy being with them both. HRH is astonishingly plain-spoken, simple and straightforward; and she is marvellously good company.'[12]

In the spring of 1939, the Duke's blackmailer again popped up, writing to him from the Ritz Hotel:

Davy dear, Last month mother gave me the documents concerning my birth. These documents are now in safety with those concerning my relations with you. They can be produced at your request. Neither has consented to give us the chance to solve our problem by ourselves – thus until the middle of May I shall then rely entirely on her . . . I shall ask a solicitor to manage an interview between you and I or with your entourage, unless you should prefer to give me an answer either by letter or by telephone . . . Alexandra.[13]

'I know Walter Monckton has communicated with you regarding the files of the woman named Moroni (*sic*), and I enclose one of two supplicate letters she has written under the signature "Alexandra"

[12] Lawford to his mother, 1 February 1939, courtesy of Charles Tilbury.
[13] 12 April 1939, Monckton Trustees, Box 17, Balliol College.

from the Ritz Hotel in Paris,' wrote the Duke to his solicitor George Allen a few days later:

> You will remember that she was expelled from France about a year ago and this is the first notification that I and <u>even the French police</u> have had of her return to France. I had our detective, Attfield, communicate with Monsieur Perrier of the Sûreté Nationale, informing him of Moroni's (*sic*)presence in Paris, and he has reported to me this evening that he understands that the woman is getting one month's imprisonment for entering the country while being the subject of an expulsion order and will then be deported again.[14]

There were also rumours that Wallis was having an affair. 'That lunatic Mrs Corey (Mabelle Gillman Corey) was next to me, and she kept repeating tactless observations, "Mr Bullitt – you know, Chips, the American Ambassador in Paris – is madly in love with the Duchess of Windsor,"' noted the diarist Chips Channon on 31 May.[15]

The story is backed up by Eleanor Tydings Ditzen, the daughter of close friends of the Windsors, Joseph Davies, the US ambassador to Russia during the 1930s, and his wife, Marjorie Merriweather Post:

> The Duke would escort his wife to one of the dress designers for fittings and return for her after an hour or two. Wallis would slip out the back door for a rendezvous with the ambassador. As the British Secret Service was guarding both

[14] 15 April 1939, Monckton Trustees, Box 17, Folio 64, Balliol College.
[15] Channon, Vol. 2, p. 133

Windsors, this affair was reported to their government. The British were afraid that the Prince might find out, and there would be a great scandal again. So the Secret Service was protecting Wallis's transgressions from the Duke![16]

There was to be a further embarrassment the following month with perceptions of the Duke upstaging his brother and interfering in politics. 'I see on the news bulletin today that David is going to broadcast to America this evening,' wrote Queen Elizabeth to Queen Mary. '. . . how troublesome of him to choose such a moment.'[17] At the invitation of a friend, Fred Bate of NBC, the Duke had agreed to make an appeal for peace from Verdun, in the belief only American intervention could prevent war. Attempts by friends, such as Lord Beaverbrook, not to go ahead were ignored:

> For two and a half years I have deliberately kept out of pub-
> lic affairs and I still propose to do so. I speak for no one but
> myself, without the previous knowledge of any government.
> I speak simply as a soldier of the last war, whose most earnest
> prayer is that such a cruel and destructive madness shall never
> again overtake mankind.[18]

It was unfortunate timing, as the King and Queen had just left on a goodwill tour to the United States, where there were strong

[16] Eleanor Davies Tydings Ditzen, *My Golden Spoon: Memoirs of a Capital Lady* (Madison Books, 1997), p. 177. 'Lady Williams-Taylor told me this story, and Marjorie corroborated it.' *Ibid.* The draft manuscript can be found in her papers at *Special Collections and University Archives, University of Maryland Libraries,* Box 6: Series 5.

[17] RA QM/PRIV/CC12/93, quoted William Shawcross, *Queen Elizabeth, the Queen Mother* (Macmillan, 2009), p. 453.

[18] *New York Times*, 9 May 1939.

isolationist sentiments, and Canada, whose unity was threatened by the French Canadian separatist movement and the Abdication.

The BBC refused to broadcast the talk, but it made a huge impact in America, with a copy of the text inserted into the proceedings of Congress, and the Duke received hundreds of letters of support from amongst others Marie Stopes, John Foster Dulles and Lord Alfred Douglas; although his position was slightly undermined when it was revealed he had dined earlier that week with Count Johannes von Welczeck, the German ambassador to France and a longstanding friend.[19] At the very least, it was seen as yet another attempt to upstage his younger brother.

'What a fool he is and how badly advised; and everyone is furious he should have done it just after you left,' wrote the Duke of Kent to George VI. 'If he had mentioned you in it, it wouldn't have been so bad, and why he broadcast such a peace talk only to America, when they have no intention of fighting, I don't know.'[20]

As international tensions increased and war became more likely, the Windsors retreated to La Croë, where their first house guest was Philip Guedalla with proofs of his book on the Abdication, on which the Duke had assisted. This was to be one of several books in which the Duke attempted to control the narrative of his life – an attempt in November 1938 for Robert Bruce Lockhart to ghost a book or articles for Beaverbrook had come to nothing, whilst legal action had been taken against Geoffrey Dennis's *Coronation Commentary* for suggesting the Windsors had slept together before marriage.[21]

---

[19] Martin, p. 364; Morton *Wallis in Love*, p. 262, suggests the date was 22 June 1939.

[20] RA GVI 342, 6 May 1939, quoted Ziegler, p. 399.

[21] 21 November 1938, Bruce Lockhart, Vol. 1, p. 410. It was true, but the Duke still won his case.

Amongst the guests that summer were Noël Coward, Somerset Maugham, Lords Beaverbrook and Rothermere, Maurice Chevalier, and a party of a dozen Highland pipers and dancers, who were invited to give a display led by the Duke in his full Highland kit.

The Duke still felt that war could be averted and on 27 August he sent a personal telegram to Hitler: 'Remembering your courtesy and our meeting two years ago, I address to you my entirely personal, simple though very earnest appeal for your utmost influence towards a peaceful solution of the present problems.'[22]

Six days later, Hitler replied: 'Assure you that attitude towards England remains the same and my wish to avoid a new war between our two countries remains. It depends however on England whether relations between the Germans and English can find the correct channel.'[23]

Throughout August, amidst concerns they might be kidnapped, Walter Monckton liaised with Sir Horace Wilson about arrangements for the couple's return to Britain, which included sending a plane to bring them back. On 2 September, Fruity Metcalfe, who had spent the summer at La Croë with his wife and son David – who was the Duke's godson – arranged for the Windsors' staff to take the train to Paris.

The same day Monckton reported to Alec Hardinge and Horace Wilson, after speaking to the Duke on the phone:

He then said that unless his brother was ready to have him and his wife to one of their houses they would not return to England ... Great pity the difficult arrangements on which we have all worked so hard should have broken down. They

[22] Monckton Trustees, Box 17, Folio 93, Balliol College.
[23] *Ibid.*

will be difficult to rearrange when all are desperately busy on war preparations. In my case I had given up chance of seeing my son today before he leaves.[24]

The next day, war was declared. The Duke's reaction, on learning the news from a call from the British Embassy in Paris, was to remark to his wife, 'Great Britain has just declared war on Germany. I'm afraid in the end, this may open the way for world communism.'[25] He then returned to the swimming pool and dived in.

[24] Monckton Trustees, Box 17, Folios 116–17, Balliol College.
[25] *Heart*, p. 330.

Above: The Duke of
Windsor making his
abdication speech,
11 December 1936.

Right: Wallis Simpson
with Lord Brownlow and
her friends Herman
and Katherine Rogers
at the Villa Lou Viei,
10 December 1936.

Schloss Enzesfeld near Vienna where the Duke stayed December 1936 to March 1937 while waiting to marry Wallis. © *AP/Shutterstock*

Chateau de Candé in the Loire Valley, the venue for the Duke and Duchess of Windsor's wedding, 3 June, 1937. © *Hemis/Alamy Stock Photo*

The Duke and Duchess in a moment of reflection on their wedding day.

Above: With Charles and Fern Bedaux in Hungary, September 1937, where plans for the German trip were made. © *AP/Shutterstock*

Right: The Duke on his German visit with Dr Robert Ley, head of the German Labour Front.

© *Hulton-Deutsch Collection/*

CORBIS/Corbis via Getty Images

Above: The Duke of Windsor in conversation with Joseph Goebbels, 12 October 1937.
© *Popperfoto via Getty Images/Getty Images*

Below left: The Windsors meeting Hitler, 22 October 1937. © *Popperfoto via Getty Images/ Getty Images*

Below right: The Duke with Dr Robert Ley, 11 October 1937. © *FPG Archive Photos/Getty Images*

Above: La Croë, on the Cap d'Antibes peninsula, the Windsors' summer home 1938–49.
© Leslie Priest/AP/Shutterstock

Below: The Windsors at La Croë, 2 January 1939. © Len Putnam/AP/Shutterstock

Above: 24 Boulevard Suchet, the Windsors' Paris home, 1938–38. © *AD075PH_ARC0658, Paris Archives*

Below left: Wallis at her circular writing table, 28 July 1939. © *AP/ Shutterstock*

Below right: The dining room at Boulevard Suchet, 28 July 1939. © *AP/Shutterstock*

Fruity Metcalfe and the
Duke at La Croë, just
before the war.

© With permission from the Metcalfe family

CHAPTER 8

Phoney War

Fruity was furious to discover that the offer of the plane to Britain had been withdrawn after the Duke had insisted he would only return if the couple were invited to stay at Windsor Castle, the Duke was given some wartime job and Wallis awarded the status the former king believed his wife was entitled to.

'I just sat still, held my head & listened for about 20 minutes & then I started,' he wrote to Baba:

> 'You have just behaved as two spoiled children. You *only* think of yourselves. You don't realise that there is at this moment a war going on that women & children are being bombed & killed while you talk of your PRIDE. God it makes me sick. You forget everything in only thinking of yourselves, your property, your money and your stupid pride . . . You are just nuts! . . . Now if this plane is sent out to fetch you, which I doubt very much, then get into it and be b–y grateful . . .'
>
> Every ½ hour it is 'I won't go by plane! We will motor to Paris,' or to Boulogne, etc. I point out the impossibility of doing that – roads blocked with troops, no hotels, etc, etc. Today there is talk of a destroyer being sent out.[1]

---

[1] Fruity Metcalfe to Baba Metcalfe, 3 September 1939, quoted Donaldson, p. 346, and de Courcy, p. 302.

Instead, Monckton arrived by plane but the rescue was rejected, because Wallis had a fear of flying and there was insufficient room for their luggage. As the Duke had told Mr Mack at the British Embassy in Paris, 'They could not be expected to arrive in England for a war with only a grip.'[2] Monckton returned alone. The Duke told Churchill, who had just been appointed First Lord of the Admiralty:

> It would greatly facilitate the Duchess and my return to England if you would send a destroyer or other naval vessel to any French Channel port Monday or Tuesday that you designate. This would enable us to bring our whole party of five and our small amount of luggage in one journey.[3]

Two days later, on 8 September, the party set off in a convoy of three cars for the Channel ports, where on 12 September they were collected at Cherbourg by Lord Louis Mountbatten in his first command, the destroyer HMS *Kelly*. Zigzagging across the Channel, to avoid enemy submarines, they landed later that day at the same quay from which the Duke had left almost three years earlier.

There was no member of the family to meet them, no message, no offer of a car or office. Instead, and only after Churchill intervened, they were met by a Royal Marine band and the C-in-C Portsmouth, Admiral Sir William James, who put them up for the night at Admiralty House. The next day Baba drove them to the Metcalfe home in Ashdown Forest, which was to be their base in Britain along with the Metcalfe's London home.

---

[2] John Mack to Walter Monckton, Monckton Trustees, Box 17, Folios 122–3, Balliol College.

[3] 6 September 1939, Duke of Windsor to Winston Churchill, CHAR 19/2A/14-15, Churchill College Archives.

Phoney War

On 14 September, the Duke saw the King, their first meeting since the Abdication. It was not a success. 'He seemed to be thinking only of himself, and had quite forgotten what he had done to his country in 1936,' George VI wrote in his diary that night.[4] Two days later he noted in his diary that commanding officers 'must not tell D or show him anything really secret.'[5]

Lord Crawford was even more critical:

The Duke and Duchess of Windsor are back in England – it is announced that he is about to take up a public appointment; but a stray field marshal is not easily placed, nor a superfluous admiral of the fleet, and he can't do the work allotted to his younger brothers Kent and roly-poly Gloucester. He is too irresponsible as a chatterbox to be trusted with confidential information, which will all be passed on to Wally at the dinner table. That is where the danger lies – namely that after nearly three years of complete obscurity, the temptation to show that he knows, that he is again at the centres of information will prove irresistible, and that he will blab and babble our state secrets without realising the danger.

I dined with Howe at the Club. He is working at the Admiralty, and to his consternation saw the door of the Secret Room open – the basement apartment where the position of our fleet and the enemy is marked out by hour – and Lo! out came Churchill and the Duke of Windsor. Howe . . . was horrified.[6]

---

[4] 14 September 1939, RA GVI/PRIV/DIARY. Chips Channon wrote in his diary on 20 September, 'Their visit has been a flop; due I fear to the hardness of the old Queen, who is quite unforgiving,' Channon, Vol. 2, pp. 207–8.

[5] George VI's War Diary, 16 September 1939, quoted Deborah Cadbury, *Princes at War: The British Royal Family's Private Battle in the Second World War* (Bloomsbury, 2015), p. 106.

[6] Vincent, p. 604.

What to do with the Duke was to prove a problem. He had originally been offered a choice of posts – Deputy Civil Defence Commissioner for Wales or liaison with the British Military Mission in France – and picked the first; but when he saw the Secretary of State for War, Leslie Hore-Belisha, the next day, he was told the King had vetoed the appointment on the grounds that he did not want the former king in Britain.

Instead the Duke was forced to accept the liaison role with the French, relinquishing his rank of field marshal and reverting to the honorary rank of major general so that he could report to Major General Sir Richard Howard-Vyse.

'I see endless trouble ahead with the job in France as I don't think he will think it big enough and I doubt his getting on with the "Wombat" (Howard-Vyse, because of his large ears and Australian service),' noted Baba Metcalfe in her diary:

I do think the family might have done something, he might not even exist but for one short visit to the King. Wallis said they realised there was no place ever for him in this country and she saw no reason ever to return. I didn't deny it or do any pressing. They are incapable of truly trusting anybody, therefore one feels one's loyalty is misplaced. Their selfishness & self-concentration is terrifying. What I am finding it difficult to put into words is the reason for his only having so few friends. One is so perpetually disappointed.[7]

The views of the Royal Family were clear. 'I haven't heard a word about Mrs Simpson – I trust that she will soon return to France and STAY THERE,' wrote the Queen to Queen Mary. 'I am sure that

[7] 25 September 1939, quoted Donaldson, p. 349.

she hates this dear country, and therefore she should not be here in war time.'[8]

On 29 September, the couple returned to France, the Duke to the British Military Mission near Vincennes with Fruity, who was acting as an unpaid ADC. What, however, was meant to be a sinecure with the intention of giving the Duke something to do out of harm's way was to prove to be an opportunity for the British. Hitherto, they had not seen the French lines and defences, to evaluate their strengths and weaknesses. Now they had their chance.

* * *

The Windsors had renewed contact with Charles Bedaux at the beginning of the war and the two met regularly through the early months of the Phoney War, with Bedaux commuting between his offices in the Hague and Paris. One of Bedaux's companies now had a contract with the French Ministry of Armaments, responsible for the inspection and control of armament production.

'Last night I fixed a dinner in a private room here (the Ritz) for Charles B to meet them,' wrote Fruity to Baba on 4 October. 'He, Charles had much to say. He knows *too* much – about *every* country in Europe & also our Colonies. It is *terrifying* and he is right a great deal. He has left at dawn for an unknown destination this morning. He hinted at Berlin being one of those places . . .'[9]

There were already concerns about the Duke being a security leak. On 16 September, George VI had noted in his diary the Chief of the Imperial General Staff, Edmund Ironside's concern that the Duke was seeing the secret plans of the French, that Wallis also knew about them, and she was not to be trusted.[10]

---

[8] RA QM/PRIV/CC12/113, quoted Shawcross, p. 494.
[9] 4 October 1939, Donaldson, p. 353.
[10] Ziegler, p. 403.

The 2nd Lord Ironside in 1987 told the author Charles Higham:

> My father determined that the Duke was a serious security leak.
> He was giving the Duchess a great deal of information that was
> classified in the matter of the defences of France and Belgium.
> She in turn was passing this information on to extremely dan-
> gerous enemy-connected people over dinner tables in Paris. As
> a result, the information made its way into German hands.[11]

The historian Gerhard Weinberg has argued 'there seems to have
been a German agent in the Duke's immediate entourage, with or
without the Duke's knowledge, and during the first months of the
war important information passed from his blabbering through that
agent to the Germans.'[12]

Martin Allen argues that several of Bedaux's staff now worked
for the Windsors and may have reported back to Bedaux, writing, 'Indeed it is known that one of the Duchess's maids had the
German code name "Miss Fox". In the summer of 1940 she would
travel back to occupied Paris and report to Otto Abetz, Bedaux's
long-term friend, Gauleiter of Paris, and former Paris representative
of Dienststelle Ribbentrop.'[13]

On 6 October, the Duke set off on the first of his tours of the French
defences, a two-day visit to the French First Army on the right flank

---

[11] Higham, *Mrs Simpson*, revised edition, p. 305.

[12] Gerhard Weinberg, *A World at Arms* (Cambridge University Press, 2005), pp.
143–4. 'Relevant documents are either still closed or have been destroyed, but
please look at the documents from the German archives published and cited in
my book, *A World at Arms,* on p. 144, n. 82. The second one of the documents
referred to contains information that would have been top secret at the time.'
Weinberg email to the author, 20 July 2020.

[13] Martin Allen, *Hidden Agenda* (Macmillan, 2000), p. 124. This is presumably
Jeanne-Marguerite Moulichon, but Allen is a discredited source and it seems
unlikely.

of the British Expeditionary Force facing Belgium, and the French Ninth Army on its right flank between Fourmies and Charleville, covering the last stretch of the Belgian frontier to the Ardennes. He was accompanied by Captain John de Salis, 8th Count de Salis, a last-minute substitute to act as his translator and help write up the report. Salis had known Wallis whilst attached to the Washington Embassy during the 1920s, but it was his background in intelligence – he later served in MI6 – that accounted for his appointment. His role was to keep an eye on the Duke and report back on him.

'We returned very late last night Sunday. We covered about 800 miles. HRH was all through absolutely delightful company. No one could have been a more interesting or amusing companion,' wrote Fruity to Baba on 9 October. 'The only few minutes I hated & when he was all wrong was when I had to get the hotel bills & get them paid and then he was *frightful*.'[14]

At the end of October, the Duke toured the French Fourth and Fifth Armies on the Vosges, covering some 900 miles in three days. Fruity remained confused that once back with Wallis, the affectionate camaraderie was replaced by iciness. '<u>It always will be the same</u> I believe as long as she is alive, and she makes him the same way.'[15]

The Duke produced four reports on the French defences, pointing out their areas of weakness, the poor morale and discipline in the French army, and questioning the reliance on and effectiveness of the Maginot Line, but they were largely ignored in London – with devastating consequences in May 1940.[16]

[14] Fruity Metcalfe to Baba Metcalfe, 11 October 1939, quoted Donaldson, p. 354, and de Courcy, p. 312.

[15] Fruity Metcalfe to Baba Metcalfe, 30 October 1939, quoted de Courcy, p. 317.

[16] They can be seen at WO 106/1678, TNA.

The Duke found it difficult to come to terms with his changed rank and status and was infuriated with the 'accidental discovery of an order issued by the King behind my back, which in effect, imposes a ban of my entering areas occupied by British troops in France.'[17]

'The Duke of Windsor is on us again,' wrote Henry Pownall, Chief of Staff to Lord Gort, the C-in-C of the British Expeditionary Force, in his diary. 'Behaved charmingly here but badly up forward where he took the salute of all Guards which turned out. C-in-C was there, a full General, and Master W definitely should not have pushed in on that. He's here as a soldier, not as Royalty. C-in-C very annoyed about it and is getting it back to Proper Quarter. If Master W thinks he can stage a come-back he's mighty wrong.'[18]

On 13 November, the Duke wrote to Monckton that he wanted to return to London because, 'The recent exposure of a network of intrigue against me, makes my position here both impossible and intolerable until I have been able to clear the matter up with my brother.'[19]

Churchill replied the same day: 'I see no objection to his coming over by the duty plane in the ordinary way, if the King agrees. An interview with His Majesty will be all to the good if it restores relations.'[20] But the King refused to discuss the situation unless Lord Gort and Major General Howard-Vyse were there.

Windsor was becoming increasingly paranoid. 'I am sending this via the officer flying back today, and the blue paper slip is only a

[17] Duke of Windsor to Winston Churchill, 14 November 1939, CHAR 19/2A/89-90, Churchill College Archives and RA EDW/PRIV/MAIN/A/4388.

[18] Pownall diary, 8 October 1939, Liddell Hart Centre.

[19] Monckton Trustees, Box 17, Folio 179, Balliol College.

[20] Monckton Trustees, Box 17, Folio 189, Balliol College and RA EDW/PRIV/MAIN/A/4386.

precaution against what I suspect as becoming a common practice in official military circles!' he wrote to Monckton on 14 November. A blue piece of paper was enclosed on which was typed in red: 'To whomsoever steams this letter open, I hope you are as edified at the contents of this letter, as I am over having to write them.'[21]

The fact was that the Duke was in a difficult position. If he did his job too well he was accused of upstaging his brother and, if not, he had let down the monarchy. But his visits were not always welcome. Immaculately dressed in riding-breeches and polished riding boots, he insisted on using his own cars and drivers, often with lots of luggage. This was a distraction for the military, who were increasingly concerned about his loose talk.

He had also become discouraged about how useful his contribution was to the war effort, as he was sent off on long tours to obscure French army zones, often in wet and freezing conditions. 'At the start he had reported to his office at 11 a.m. daily, looked at the situation map, chatted with Howard-Vyse for half an hour, then knocked off for the afternoon,' noted the author Charles Murphy. 'But presently he was dropping in only three times a week, then twice, then scarcely ever, except for an occasional luncheon with Gamelin.'[22]

On 9 December, the Duke wrote to Monckton, 'The edge has naturally been taken off my keenness in the job, and I am really only carrying on because it's the one that suits the Duchess and myself the best.'[23]

It was a similar situation for Wallis. She had operated a soup kitchen in the Bal Tabarin nightclub in Montmartre and, after

---

[21] 14 November 1939, Monckton Trustees, Box 17, Balliol College.

[22] Bryan and Murphy, p. 415. Gamelin was the Commander-in-Chief of the French Armed Forces.

[23] Duke of Windsor to Walter Monckton, 9 December 1939, Monckton Trustees, Box 17, Folio 212, Balliol College.

British charities were not interested in her services, became honorary president of the French relief organisation, Colis de Trianon, founded by Elsie, Lady Mendl, distributing socks, gloves, scarves, toiletries and cigarettes to French troops. Supposedly she had 'created a new type of trench mitten with a zipper attachment, permitting a soldier to use his trigger finger in an emergency.'[24] She had also joined the Section Sanitaire of the French Red Cross, taking plasma, bandages and cigarettes to the front, driven by the Countess de Ganay, known as 'Pinky', famous before the war as a French racing driver.

Both the Windsors quickly lost heart, feeling that their efforts were not recognised. By spring 1940 he was often to be found on the golf course at Saint-Cloud, Saint-Germain or Mortefontaine, the two took long weekends at La Croë or Biarritz, and they continued to dine out extensively – often with Bedaux. Their thoughts were only for themselves and what especially annoyed the French was when he started pulling strings in both the French and British armies, at her instigation, to have their chef demobilised and returned to their kitchen.

* * *

On the morning of 10 January 1940, Belgian soldiers on duty at a guard post near Mechelen-sur-Meuse saw an ME108 Taifun (Typhoon) crash landing, supposedly on a routine flight from Munster to Bonn. When the soldiers rushed to the crash site, they were confronted by two Luftwaffe officers desperately trying to burn papers. They appeared to be a complete set of the German attack plans. The Allies couldn't believe their luck. Sixty German divisions

24 Martin, p. 370.

were stood down to await intelligence reports at the knowledge that the Allies now knew the German plans of attack.

On 18 January, the Duke flew secretly to London, ostensibly to see Churchill and Edmund Ironside in the hope of lifting the ban on him visiting British troops. But he had another purpose – to try and persuade the Government to negotiate with the Nazis to bring the war to a swift end.

Amongst those he met were Major General J.C.F. Fuller, a retired army officer who had been an active member of the British Union of Fascists – he had been a principal guest at Hitler's fiftieth birthday parade in April 1939.[25] He also saw Lord Beaverbrook, who realised the Duke's 'idea of himself as the leader of an international "Peace Movement" and rival leader to his brother, had never left his mind.' Monckton, at whose home the two men had met, was disturbed by what he heard, and as he told Charles Peake, head of the Foreign Office News Department, that 'both men agreed that the war should be ended by a peace offer to Germany.'[26]

Peake reported the Duke's meeting with Beaverbrook to the diplomat Oliver Harvey on 26 January:

> WM tells me that he was present at a frightful interview between the D of W & the Beaver two days ago. Both found themselves in agreement that the war ought to be ended at once by a peace offer to Germany. The Beaver suggested that the Duke should get out of uniform, come home and after enlisting powerful City support, stump the country, in which case he predicted that the Duke would have a tremendous success. WM contented himself with reminding the Duke

[25] Major General John Fuller date book, 18 January 1940, Fuller 4/4/35, Liddell Hart Centre.

[26] Ziegler, p. 415.

that if he did this he would be liable to UK income tax. This made the little man blanch & he declared with great determination that the whole thing was off.[27]

Further evidence for the Duke's discussions with Beaverbrook comes from Harold Nicolson's diary:

It seems that when the Duke of Windsor paid his visit here after the war he dined with Walter Monckton and Beaverbrook was there. He spoke about the inevitable collapse of France and said that he would return to England and conduct a movement for peace with Germany. Beaverbrook was delighted. 'Go ahead, Sir,' he beamed, 'and I shall back you.' When Beaverbrook went, Walter explained to the Duke that he had been speaking high treason and that if he really came to live in this country, he would have to pay income tax. The latter thought filled him with such appalling gloom that he gave up all idea of saving England by negotiating with Germany.[28]

By 27 January, Neville Chamberlain was aware of the discussions, writing to his sister Ida, 'I have heard on unimpeachable authority that while the Duke of Windsor was here this week, Beaverbrook tried to induce him to head a peace campaign in this country promising him the full support of his papers.'[29]

The day before, Alec Cadogan, the permanent under-secretary at the Foreign Office, had reported that 'secret documents were

---

[27] BL Ad Ms 56402, British Library, quoted Sarah Bradford, *King George VI* (Weidenfeld & Nicolson, 1989), p. 433.

[28] 1 October 1940, unpublished Nicolson diary, Balliol College, by permission of Juliet Nicolson.

[29] Neville Chamberlain to Ida Chamberlain, 27 January 1940, Chamberlain papers 18/1/1140, University of Birmingham.

communicated . . . to the German Government! I can trust no-one.'[30]
The explanation soon became clear when a communication was
intercepted between the German ambassador to the Hague, Count
Julius von Zech-Burkersroda, to State Secretary Baron Ernst von
Weizsäcker, dated 27 January 1940:

> Through personal relationships I might have the opportunity
> to establish certain lines leading to the Duke of Windsor. As, of
> course you know, W is a member of the British Military Mission
> with the French Army Command. He does not, however, feel
> entirely satisfied with this position and seeks a field of activities
> in which he would not have merely a representative character
> and which would permit him a more active role. In order to
> attain this objective he was recently in London. There, however,
> he achieved nothing and is supposed to be most disgruntled
> over it. He has expressed himself in especially uncomplimentary
> terms about Chamberlain, whom he particularly dislikes and,
> as he thinks, is responsible for his being frozen out. Also there
> seems to be something like the beginning of a Fronde forming
> around W which for the moment of course still has nothing
> to say, but which at some time under favourable circumstances
> might acquire a certain significance . . . W had had especially
> good connections with the Reich Foreign Minister (Ribbentrop)
> in London . . . I had explained to him through an intermediary
> why it is completely utopian for England to effect a change of
> regime in Germany, and the statements of my intermediaries are
> believed to have made a certain impression on him.[31]

[30] Cadogan Papers, diary, 26 January 1940, ACAD /1/15, Churchill College Archives.

[31] Documents German Foreign Policy (hereafter DGFP), Doc. 580, Ref. 122667, Series D, Vol. VIII, p. 713. RA PS/PSO/GVI/042A/433. Ribbentrop added, 'State Secretary please discuss with me.'

Three weeks later on 19 February, Zech-Burkersroda reported again to Weizsäcker:

> The D. of Windsor, about whom I wrote you in my letter of the 27th of last month, has said that the Allied War Council devoted an exhaustive discussion at its last meeting to the situation that would arise if Germany invaded Belgium. On the military side, it was held that the best plan would be to make the main resistance effort in the line behind the Belgian-French border, even at the risk that Belgium should be occupied by us.[32]

The report is interesting, as the Allied plans for the defence of Belgium were not what the Duke allegedly reported and discussion about the change of strategy had been in the War Cabinet whilst the Duke was in London, rather than the Allied War Council. Might it be possible that a spy within the German Embassy at the Hague, Wolfgang zu Putlitz, was reporting back to the British about the Duke, that Churchill had discussed the issue with the Duke in January, and deliberately fed disinformation to test his loyalties?

On 2 March, Weizsäcker wrote to Count Julius von Zech-Burkersroda that the report supplied by the Duke had been of interest to the Fuhrer, adding, 'If you can without inconvenience obtain further information of this nature, I should be grateful if you would pass it on to me: please do so preferably in the form of a report . . . directing it to me personally.'[33]

On 21 February, Major Langford, an MI6 officer in the Hague, sent a message to London that 'a very clever spy' in the German

---

[32] DGFP, Doc. 621, Ref. 12269 and RA PS/PSO/GVI/C/042A/434.
[33] RA PS/GVI/C/042A/435.

embassy, named Walbach, had informed him that the Duke's friend and adviser, Charles Bedaux, was visiting Zech-Burkersroda 'on an almost fortnightly basis'. Bedaux was alleged to bring 'defence material, strengths, weaknesses and so on' of the 'best quality'.[34] Bedaux was already on MI5's radar and the subject of discussion with the French Deuxième Bureau.[35] The source of the leak was now clear.

* * *

At dawn on Friday 10 May, the Germans invaded France and the Low Countries, targeting the Ardennes, which Windsor's reports had revealed were vulnerable. The Windsors waited to see what might happen. On 14 May the Germans breached the French defences near Sedan and by the 16th, Panzer divisions had reached the Oise. The same day the Duke made arrangements for Wallis to leave and sit it out at the Hotel du Palais in Biarritz.

The Duke supposedly spent the days after the invasion 'tearing up secret documents and burning them in the fireplace of the Duke's Embassy office', according to Martin Kinna. His uncle Patrick, always known as Peter, had been sent out in September 1939, nominally as Clerk to the Duke, 'to ensure that the Duke never took a single piece of paper home where it might fall into the hands of the Duchess.'[36] The reason, Kinna had been told, was that the Duchess had been close to Ribbentrop and could not be trusted.[37]

---

[34] DGFP, Doc. 582, Ref. 122669, Series D, Vol. III. Extended source notes for *Blackshirt*, p. 487/3, University of Sheffield.

[35] See for example Guy Liddell's diary, 14 February 1940, Nigel West, *The Guy Liddell Diaries, Vol 1: 1939–1942* (Routledge, 2005), p. 66, where he complains about the Deuxième Bureau leaking information passed to them on Bedaux.

[36] Obituary Patrick Kinna, *Independent*, 23 October 2011.

[37] Interview Martin Kinna, 2 May 2021.

Further evidence for suspicions about the Duke's loyalty comes from a letter on 20 May, with Howard-Vyse reporting to Hardinge that 'No military information is to be given to HRH over the telephone, other than confirmation of what is already common knowledge – and as little of that as possible.' It is clear that Buckingham Palace were being kept closely advised of the Duke's activities.[38]

Chaos reigned during those days in mid-May. 'As you now know, the 9th Army could not "take it". The General and all his staff are now either shot or prisoners of war,' wrote Fruity to Baba on 24 May:

> It has been a terrible shock and surprise. I fear there are bigger shocks to come. HRH came back two days ago. I am *very* uneasy about him. He might do *anything* – anything *except* the right thing. I live from hour to hour fearing to hear the worst. He talks of having done enough! Of course do not repeat <u>any</u> of this . . . I do not know what will happen. W is like a magnet. It is terrible. I have seen a great deal and hear everything. I can't yet work out what Thomas and I will do, or where even try for, if the situation changes much worse (I refer to one's life and also should HRH make his fatal decision).[39]

The day before, Hitler had halted three separate Panzer corps at the Canal du Nord, thereby letting the British Expeditionary Force escape. The question is why? Certainly the supply tail needed to catch up and tanks be maintained, but the Germans could have lasted a few more days. It has been suggested that Goering wanted

[38] RA GVI/C/042A/154.

[39] de Courcy, p. 327. The Thomas referred to here is likely to have been the Duke's batman.

victory to go to the Luftwaffe, not the Panzers, but there is another possibility – that Hitler hoped to sue for peace, with Windsor as a Pétain figure, to allow him to concentrate on his plan for *Lebensraum* ('living space') in Eastern Europe.[40]

Already at Cabinet on 26 May, the foreign secretary Lord Halifax had suggested a negotiated peace in order to save the Empire. It was only when it was realised that the BEF could be evacuated and Britain fight on alone that the idea was dropped.

On the evening of 27 May, Fruity, who had been working without payment, said his usual 'Goodnight, sir. See you tomorrow.' The following morning he put through his usual call at 8.30 a.m. to the Duke, to be told, 'His Royal Highness left for Biarritz at six-thirty this morning.'[41] Fruity had worked for months without pay, sacrificing his own needs for those of the Windsors, and had been abandoned to find his own way home by someone he called his best friend.

'Re my *late* Master, he has run like two rabbits,' he wrote to Baba:

He never made one single mention of what was to happen to me, or his paid Comptroller Phillips. He has taken all cars and left not even a bicycle!! . . . He has denuded the Suchet house of all articles of value and all his clothes, etc. After twenty years I am through – <u>utterly</u> I despise him, I've fought and backed him up (knowing what a swine he was for 20 years), but now it is finished . . . The man is not worth doing <u>anything</u> for. He deserted his job in 1936. Well, he's deserted his

---

[40] Hitler's master plan was to seize large areas of Western Russia and settle the land with German farmers and war veterans, deporting most of the Russians to Siberia and using the remainder as slave labour.

[41] de Courcy, p. 327, and Donaldson, p. 357.

country now, at a time when every office boy and cripple is <u>trying to do what he can</u>. It is the *end*.[42]

The report that Howard-Vyse filed 'on the work of various officers . . . under my command', does not mention the Duke. His only comment was: 'I wish never to be asked about that man again!'[43]

[42] 27 May 1940, Ziegler, p. 417, and de Courcy, p. 328. Gray Phillips eventually got to the South of France by hitching lifts on military lorries and Fruity reached London on 5 June 1940.

[43] Bryan and Murphy, p. 420.

CHAPTER 9

Escape

The Duke had returned to La Croë and it was from there on 19 June, Wallis's 44th birthday, that a convoy of three cars, organised by the British Consulate in Nice, set off for non-belligerent Spain. The Windsors had refused to leave by cargo boat, because they would be allowed only two suitcases, so instead a small lorry, with various possessions, followed their Buick, driven by the faithful Ladbroke and also carrying the cairn terriers and Gray Phillips, the Duke's Comptroller and Private Secretary.

Well over six foot, Phillips had been a brilliant classical scholar at Eton, before going on to Magdalen College, Oxford – the same college the Duke had attended. During the First World War, he had served with the Black Watch, winning an MC, before taking up a career as a barrister and serving as Comptroller to the Duke of Sutherland. Charming, witty, kind, and with impeccable manners and a strong artistic streak, Phillips – a gay man, he was a lifelong bachelor – was to be a loyal servant of the Windsors.

George Wood is an intriguing figure. Born in 1887, he had served in the Intelligence Corps during the First World War before becoming a King's Messenger and going out to Kenya. Married to a Hungarian countess, he had been in Austria at the same time as the Duke in 1936 and 1937 and then found himself in the South of France, where he had a villa, during the summer of 1940.

The writer Charles Higham says he was 'believed to be secret agent'.[1] He was not regarded as necessarily a good influence on the Duke, a minute to Churchill noting:

> I saw in the papers that a certain Captain George Wood – and his wife – had attached themselves to the Duke of Windsor's party. A nasty bit of work, if he is the man I am thinking of: lived for years in Vienna, married to a Hungarian, daughter married a Hohenberg last year, poses as a notch big-game shot, e.g., 'white hunter' . . . I should suspect him of holding utterly defeatist views and being a bad influence.[2]

By 23 June, the Duke's 46th birthday, the party had reached Madrid, from where a flying boat was due to fly them to Lisbon the next day. The British Ambassador, Sam Hoare, had known the Duke since the First World War and often shot at Sandringham. As he later wrote, he was determined the couple should move on quickly and 'prevent any compromising incidents while he was in Madrid.'[3]

Hoare had only just arrived in Spain himself and the Windsors were not put up at the Ambassador's residence, because 'it was badly equipped, and had no facilities for distinguished visitors.'[4] Instead they stayed at the Ritz, which Hoare admitted was 'One of the most active centres of the German secret service, where every word that was spoken could be automatically recorded by the Nazi listening posts.'[5]

---

[1] Higham, *Mrs Simpson*, p. 324.

[2] Minute to John Martin, June 1940, FO 800/326/191A, TNA.

[3] 'A Deep-laid plot', p. 10, XXIII/1–2, Templewood Papers, Cambridge University Library.

[4] 'A Deep-laid plot', p. 10. Hoare had only arrived in post a few weeks earlier.

[5] 'A Deep-laid plot', p. 10.

Escape

Madrid was the greatest concentration of the German intelligence services outside Berlin, and Spain was virtually a German protectorate – General Francisco Franco owed his victory in the Civil War to German support. Some 70–100 intelligence staff were attached to the German embassy sending, as Hoare later wrote, 'worthless reports to Berlin. And worst of all, Hitler believed what they sent him rather than the careful reports from the Abwehr that did not always suit the Fuhrer's wishful thinking.'[6]

On the day the Windsors arrived, Eberhard von Stohrer, the German Ambassador, sent a 'Strictly Confidential' telegram to Ribbentrop reporting the couple's arrival and that 'from certain impressions which General Vigon had received in Germany that we might perhaps be interested in detaining the Duke of Windsor here and eventually establishing contact with him. Please telegraph instructions.'[7]

Vigon, head of the Spanish Supreme Army Defence Council, had met Ribbentrop on 16 June. It was only on that day that the Duke had seen Hugh Dodds, the British consul in Nice, asking what he should do and was told he should make his escape through Spain.[8] So how did the Germans know so quickly about the Spanish plan when there were plenty of other options, including leaving by ship from Cannes or Bordeaux? Though ostensibly it was Dodds's advice, might the Germans have had a hand in directing the Windsors to Spain?[9]

---

[6] 'A Deep-laid plot', pp. 7–8.

[7] DGFP, Series D, AA-B15/B002531, Vol. X, p. 2.

[8] Hugh Dodds report to Halifax, 23 June 1940, Hugh Dodds papers, courtesy of Bel Crewe.

[9] It seems to have been an open secret. David Eccles wrote to his wife from the British Embassy in Spain on 16 June: 'I must get out before Wally Windsor and all her friends arrive. I should not be able to behave well to them, and I long to be at home.' Sybil and David Eccles, *By Safe Hand: Letters of Sybil and David Eccles 1939–42* (Bodley Head, 1983), p. 121. In fact Wallis had telegrammed Selby on 30 May saying the couple intended to come to Lisbon. RA GVI/C/042A/157.

A complication now took place. The Duke of Kent was due in Lisbon the next day as head of the British delegation for the week-long celebrations for the 300th anniversary celebrations of Portugal's independence. It was felt undiplomatic for the two brothers to meet, so the Windsors were to be kept on stand-by in Madrid until 2 July. The family quarrel provided an opportunity for the Germans – and also the Duke.

After the snub in September 1939, the Duke wanted an assurance he was going to be given a proper job on his return, that the Civil List would be used to compensate any extra tax he might have to pay, as he would lose his status as a tax exile, and that his wife would be treated with the respect to which he felt she was entitled. According to Wallis, 'all that he ever specifically asked for was a fairly simple thing: that I be received, just once, by the King, his brother, and the Queen, in order to erase by that single gesture of hospitality the stigma attaching to my never having been received since our marriage by the Royal Family, his family.'[10]

Churchill equivocated and said a job could be discussed on his return, but the Duke was adamant. He wrote to Churchill on 24 June:

> My visits to England since the war have proved my presence there is an embarrassment to all concerned, myself included, and I cannot see how any post offered me there, even at this time, can alter this situation. I therefore suggest that as I am anxious to continue to serve the Empire, some useful employment, with more official backing than I have hitherto received, be found for me elsewhere.[11]

---

[10] *Heart*, pp. 340–1.
[11] The Duke to Churchill, 24 June 1940, CHAR 20/9A–B/7, Churchill College Archives, and FO800/326/197A, TNA and RA EDW/PRIV/MAIN/A/4512.

That evening, Hoare followed up:

> Duke of Windsor is most anxious to have reply to his personal
> wire before leaving here. He does not want to appear to be
> returning as a refugee with nothing to do. I hope you can help
> him with a friendly answer as soon as possible. I have told him
> that if he fails to return to England in a few days, all sorts of
> mischievous rumours will circulate about him.[12]

David Eccles, a young diplomat with an intelligence brief at the
British embassy, wrote to his wife on 25 June:

> I have learned a great deal about the collapse of France, I do
> not think it wise to put it into this letter, but I have made
> some notes, and I will one day tell you the sickening story
> of treachery, weakness and shame. You will have difficulty
> in believing your ears, but sad to say, it is true. Are we quite
> sure we have no similar canker at the heart of our public life?
> I pray so, but we must be vigilant. I distrust the Duke of
> Windsor; he and his Duchess are coming here to stay next
> week. I shall watch him at breakfast, lunch and dinner with
> a critical eye.[13]

He was right to be suspicious. On the same day, the Spanish
foreign minister, Colonel Juan Beigbeder, wrote to General Franco
enclosing information from a secretary of the embassy, relaying a
conversation with Windsor, in which he reported the Duke was
against the war:

[12] Sam Hoare to Winston Churchill, 24 June 1940, CHAR 20/A–B/8, Churchill
College Archives.
[13] Eccles, p. 128.

He throws all the blame on the Jews and the Reds and Eden with his people in the Foreign Office and other politicians, all of whom he would have liked to put up against a wall . . . if (the Germans) bombed England effectively this could bring peace. He (the Duke of Windsor) seemed very much to hope that this would occur. He wants peace at any price.[14]

The report was forwarded to the Germans.

On the same day, the head of the Fifth Department of the NKVD, Pavel Filin, sent the Kremlin a memo, presumably based on reports from his agents:

The former king of England Edward together with his wife Simpson is at present in Madrid, where he is in touch with Hitler. Edward is conducting negotiations with Hitler on the question of the formation of a new English government and the conclusion of peace with Germany contingent on a military alliance against the USSR.[15]

It was clear that the Windsors remaining in Madrid was becoming a problem for the British. On 26 June, Churchill sent a telegram to the Duke asking him to return to Britain as soon as possible.

'Impossible to persuade Duke to leave Madrid before Sunday and Lisbon before Wednesday,' reported Hoare to the prime minister later that day. 'He insists there is no need for such haste unless there is some job for him in England or the Empire. I could

---

[14] Document 56, Fundacion national Francisco Franco, Documentos ineditos para la Historia del generalismo Franco, Vol 11–1, Madrid, 1993, quoted Karina Urbach, *Go-Betweens for Hitler* (Oxford University Press, 2015), pp. 191, 192, 213.

[15] Secret memorandum No. K5/8175, quoted Urbach, p. 202.

not have put more strongly case for immediate departure but with no result.'[16]

The Duke continued to hold out, sending a telegram to Churchill the following day:

> Regret that in view of your reply to my last message I cannot agree to returning until everything has been considered and I know the result. In the light of past experience my wife and myself must not risk finding ourselves once more regarded by the British public as in a different status to other members of my family.[17]

The negotiations continued with the suggestion that the Duke be offered a naval command, or a position on the staff of the C-in-C Middle East, General Wavell, in Egypt.[18] The Duke had now 'dropped the condition of receiving some post, and that it boiled down to both of them being received once only for quite a short meeting by the King and Queen, and notice of the fact appearing in the Court Circular,' reported Hoare.[19] The Duke had also backed down on his tax position, but Hoare was becoming increasingly desperate, as the longer the couple remained in Madrid, the greater the chance of them being kidnapped or used by the Germans.

[16] Hoare to Churchill, 26 June 1940, CHAR 20/9A–B/9, Churchill College Archives.

[17] The Duke to Churchill, 27 June 1940, CHAR 20/9A–B/13, Churchill College Archives, and FO800/326/199B, TNA.

[18] Hoare to Churchill, 27 June 1940, CHAR 20/9A–B/28–9, Churchill College Archives; Templewood Papers X111/16/29, Cambridge University Library, and Alec Hardinge to Winston Churchill, 28 June 1940, CHAR20/9A-B/13–14, Churchill College Archives.

[19] Hoare to Churchill, 28 June 1940, CHAR 20/9A–B/16 and CHAR 20/9A/15, Churchill College Archives, and FO800/326/199c, TNA.

'Can you help me with a friendly message that will get him back to England? Could Monckton also help?' he plaintively telegrammed Churchill late on 28 June.[20]

Churchill's response was swift, threatening the former king with a court martial:

> Your Royal Highness has taken active military rank and refusal to obey direct orders of competent military authority would create a serious situation. I hope it will not be necessary for such orders to be sent. I most strongly urge immediate compliance with wishes of the Government.[21]

Meanwhile the Germans were ingratiating themselves with regard to the Windsors' property in France. On 30 June, Ribbentrop's Secretariat sent a telegram to the Protocol Department:

> the Foreign Minister requests first that Abetz be instructed to undertake unofficially and confidentially an unobtrusive observation of the residence of the Duke. Secondly, Ambassador von Stohrer is to be instructed to have the Duke informed confidentially through a Spanish intermediary that the Foreign Minister is looking out for its protection . . . However, no written statement whatever is to be made.[22]

---

[20] Hoare to Churchill, 28 June 1940, CHAR 20/9A–B/17, Churchill College Archives, and FO800/326/199D, TNA.

[21] Churchill to the Duke, 1 July 1940, CHAR 20/9A–B/22 and CHAR 20/31A/51–2, Churchill College Archives, and FO800/326/201A, TNA and RA EDW/PRIV/MAIN/A/4520. The line 'Already there is a great deal of doubt as to the circumstances in which Your Royal Highness left Paris,' had been struck out.

[22] DGFP, 30 June 1940, AA–B15/B002536, No. 66, pp. 68–9. Copy at RA PS/PSO/GVI/C/G042A/392–435.

The Duke's intentions seem to have been an open secret. Chips Channon wrote in his diary on 1 July: 'Rumours are over-ripe and rife. Diana C(ooper) told me today that the Windsors genuinely believe that they will be restored to the throne under German influence: he will become a sort of Gauleiter and Wallis a queen. Perhaps!'[23]

Two days later, after dining with the Duke of Kent, who had just returned from Portugal, he added: 'The Duke referred to the Duke of Windsor slightingly and said, 'My brother wants to be a Gauleiter! They are hopelessly estranged and the D of Kent pursues the vendetta with all the animosity of one who knows he has been treacherous and has behaved badly.'[24]

These communications were all against the backdrop of a series of German peace initiatives. During the first week of July, Sir David Kelly, the British ambassador to the Vatican, who had already fielded peace feelers from the Papal Nuncio, met in Switzerland with Dr Carl Burckhardt, acting president of the International Red Cross, who passed on a peace proposition from Berlin.

Shortly afterwards Prince Max zu Hohenlohe-Langenburg (later suspected of being a German agent) saw Kelly in Berne, introduced by Spain's minister to Switzerland.[25] In Washington, Lord Lothian had received an approach from the Italians through Assistant Secretary of State Adolf Berle, who claimed to be acting as an intermediary. Berle added that 'a similar communication on the same line' had been received from Don Alfonso, the ex-King of Spain.[26]

Writing to his sister Elizabeth, Alexander Weddell, the American ambassador to Spain, described how he had entertained 'Wally

---

[23] Channon, Vol. 2, p. 357.

[24] Channon, Vol. 2, p. 359.

[25] See KV2/1696, TNA, for more on peace initiatives.

[26] More details of the extensive dealings can be found in FO 371/24407 and FO 371/24408, TNA.

Simpson and her Boy Friend' to mint juleps on Saturday 29 June. 'Wally herself gives every suggestion of extreme acuteness and unlimited ambition; her exterior suggests heavy armour plate or some substance slightly harder than a diamond. But very pleasant, very genial, and very witty.'[27]

A few days later, Weddell reported to the US Secretary of State, Cordell Hull:

> the Duke of Windsor declared that the most important thing now to be done was to end the war before thousands more were killed or maimed to save the faces of a few politicians . . . These observations have their value if any as doubtless reflecting the views of an element in England, possibly a growing one who find in Windsor and his circle a group who are realists in world politics and who hope to come into their own in event of peace.[28]

On 2 July, the Duke of Kent having left Portugal, the Windsors, accompanied by the Woods, set off by car for Lisbon, spending the night as guests of the Spanish Government at Merida.

The German Ambassador, Stohrer, reported later that day to Ribbentrop: 'Windsor has expressed himself to the Foreign Minister and other acquaintances in strong terms against Churchill and against this war. The Foreign Minister supposes that Windsor also is going to Portugal in order to replenish his supply of money.'[29]

---

[27] Alexander Weddell to Elizabeth Weddell, 3 July 1940, Weddell, AW, Ms 1W 4126c FAZ, Virginia Museum of History and Culture.

[28] Alexander Weddell to Cordell Hull, 2 July 1940, Foreign Relations of the United States 1940, Vol. III, 1939/4357, p. 41.

[29] Eberhard von Stohrer to Joachim von Ribbentrop, 2 July 1940, DGFP, AA–B15/B002538, No. 86, Vol X, pp. 96–7.

Escape

The next day, instead of being escorted to the Hotel Palacio at Estoril, which supposedly did not have room for them, they were directed to a large pink stucco house at Cascais, seventeen miles west of Lisbon on the Portuguese coast, which had been made available by a well-known banker, Dr Ricardo de Espiritu Santo e Silva. Ostensibly the suggestion was on the recommendation of the manager. In reality, the direction had come from the German authorities.

Santo was a German agent and a close friend of the German minister in Lisbon, but it was felt that the couple would be there only temporarily – two flying boats of RAF Coastal Command were waiting in the Tagus to take them the next day to Saighton Grange in Cheshire, which the Duke of Westminster had put at their disposal.

The plans were put in disarray when, on the very day they were due to fly back to Britain, Churchill, against the wishes of George VI, Queen Elizabeth and the Colonial Secretary, Lord Lloyd, offered the Duke a job – Governor of the Bahamas. For the former King Emperor, who had ruled over a large part of the world, it was a humiliation. For the Government, a neat solution to the developing situation.

No other member of the British royal family had served as the Governor of a Crown Colony. The Bahamas was regarded as a hardship posting and was so low in the pecking order that the appointment did not even carry a knighthood. The Duke hesitated before agreeing, but it was something.

'He has accepted a job under great pressure from HE and your affectionate DE, you'll see about it in the papers,' wrote David Eccles to his wife that day, after lunching with the Windsors. 'A very cunning solution. It means some recognition at last for her. He's pretty fifth-column, but that's for you only.'[30]

---

[30] Eccles, p. 132.

On the same day, Eccles sent his Foreign Office colleague, Gladwyn Jebb, a 'Most Confidential' telegram. 'I had some conversation today with the Duke and Duchess of Windsor, Mr and Mrs George Wood and Major Phillips. They are very nearly 5th column.'[31]

Churchill now drafted a memo to the prime ministers of Canada, Australia, New Zealand and South Africa, explaining the situation, marked, 'Most secret and personal. Decipher yourself.'

> The activities of the Duke of Windsor on the Continent in recent months have been causing HM and myself grave uneasiness as his inclinations are well known to be pro-Nazi and he may become a centre of intrigue. We regard it as a real danger that he should move freely on the Continent. Even if he were willing to return to this country, his presence here would be most embarrassing both to HM and to the Government.
>
> In all the circumstances it has been felt necessary to try to tie him down in some appointment which might appeal to him and his wife and I have decided with HM's approval to offer him the Governorship of the Bahamas (I do not know yet whether he will accept). Despite the obvious objections to this solution, we feel that it is the least of possible evils. I wished you to have the earliest possible advance information of this. You will appreciate how necessary it is to preserve complete secrecy. We here are of course doing all we can to ensure this.[32]

[31] David Eccles to Gladwyn Jebb, 4 July 1940, FO 1093/23, TNA.

[32] Winston Churchill to Prime Ministers, 4 July 1940, CHAR 20/9A/34, Churchill College Archives. The eventual version was watered down. 'The position of the Duke of Windsor on the Continent in recent months has been causing HM and HMG embarrassment as though his loyalties are unimpeachable there is always a backwash of Nazi intrigue which seeks to make trouble about him.' This would be the future line, not least to Roosevelt in a telegram the same day, FO 371/24249, TNA.

'I did my best with them while they were here and I greatly hoped that you would come to some accommodation over the offer,' wrote Hoare to Churchill the next day. 'I am certain that this is the moment to end the trouble and if it is not ended now, the rift between them and the rest of the Family will become deeper and possibly more dangerous.'[33]

The appointment had been made narrowly in time. Sir Alexander Cadogan, the head of the Foreign Office, had received a memo from Reginald Leeper, Head of the Political Intelligence Department, on 7 July from an intelligence source in Prague, stating:

> Germans expect assistance from Duke and Duchess of Windsor, the latter desiring at any price to become Queen. Germans have been negotiating with her since 27 June. The status quo in England except undertaking to form anti-Russian alliance. The Germans propose to form an opposition government with Duke of Windsor, having first changed public opinion by propaganda. Germans think King George will abdicate during the attack on London.[34]

'The King is grateful to the Prime Minister for letting him see the enclosed,' – presumably an intelligence report on Wallis – Alan Lascelles told Eric Seal, Churchill's principal private secretary, two days later. 'As I told you once before, this is not the first time that little lady has come under suspicion for her anti-British activities. And

---

[33] Hoare to Churchill, 5 July 1940, XIII/16/37, Templewood papers, Cambridge University Library.

[34] Report from Informant in Close Touch with (former foreign minister) Neurath's Entourage', 7 July 1940, RA GVI/C/042A/202 and FO 1093/23, TNA.

as long as we never forget the power that she can exert over him in her efforts to avenge herself on this country, we shall be all right.'[35]

Alec Cadogan, in conversation with the King at a lunch party on 10 July, noted in his diary that George VI was 'amused at C's report of the quisling activities of my brother.'[36]

[35] Alan Lascelles to John Seal, 9 July 1940, CHAR 20/9B/120-122, Churchill College Archives
[36] 10 July 1940, ACAD 1/9, Churchill College Archives. C was the head of MI6.

CHAPTER 10

Operation Willi

Later that day, 10 July, Peter Russell, an Oxford don – later Professor of Spanish Studies at Oxford – who had been working for British Intelligence since the mid-1930s, flew out to Lisbon. He had been on stand-by throughout June and an earlier flight on 30 June had been aborted as a result of mechanical trouble to the flying boat, which suggests the authorities anticipated problems with the Windsors. A fluent Spanish and Portuguese speaker, his role was to monitor the couple and was supposedly 'under orders to shoot them if they threatened to fall into German hands during their nightly visits to the casino at Estoril.'[1]

Russell stayed with the couple until 24 July. 'There is . . . no doubt whatsoever in my mind that he had plenty of personal contact with them during this time,' says his biographer Bruce Taylor. 'He would talk about this quite freely while never giving up any very specific information as to time and place, nor taking any questions!'[2]

The Windsors remained at Santo's country house, near the Boca do Inferno (the Jaws of Hell), whilst arrangements were made for

---

[1] Biographical Memoirs of Fellows X, Proceedings of the British Academy 172, BAA/FEL/10/585, British Academy Archive. Cf. obituary, *Independent*, 5 July 2006.

[2] Bruce Taylor to the author, 27 April 2021.

them to leave for the Bahamas. It was a very comfortable house, set in several acres of walled gardens with a large swimming pool, with a staff of a dozen, including a chef with an international reputation. Wallis played bridge, the Duke golf. There were occasional visits to the British embassy and they were entertained by various friends of the Santos.

But the couple could not relax. Amidst concerns they might be kidnapped or speak indiscreetly to the press, they were virtual prisoners. There were patrols in the garden, they could only leave the compound with permission and an armed guard, and could walk only along the shore road where they could be observed. They were well aware that they were under surveillance from everyone and surrounded by informers. Bored, angry at the way his country had treated him, the Duke began to drink heavily and was vulnerable to any blandishment that might be offered.

On 10 July, Baron Oswald von Hoyningen-Huene, the German ambassador to Portugal, wrote to Ribbentrop:

> As Spaniards from the entourage of the Duke of Windsor have reported in strictest confidence during a visit to the Legation, the appointment of the Duke as Governor of the Bahamas is for the purpose of keeping him away from England since his return would greatly strengthen the position of English friends of peace whereupon his arrest at the instigation of his enemies could be counted on. The Duke intends to postpone his journey to the Bahamas for as long as possible, and at least until the beginning of August, in the hope of an early change in his favour. He is convinced that had he remained on the throne war could have been avoided and describes himself as a firm supporter of a peaceful compromise with Germany. The Duke believes with

certainty that continued heavy bombing will make England ready for peace.[3]

The German foreign minister was determined to lure the couple, perhaps through an invitation from a Spanish friend, from Portugal, where they were heavily guarded, back to Spain, where it would be easier to deal with them. As Ribbentrop told Stohrer in a top-secret telegram dated 11 July:

> At any rate, at a suitable occasion in Spain the Duke must be informed that Germany wants peace with the English people, that the Churchill clique stands in the way of it, and that it would be a good thing if the Duke would hold himself in readiness for further developments. Germany is determined to force England to peace by every means of power and upon this happening would be prepared to accommodate any desire expressed by the Duke, especially with a view to the assumption of the English throne by the Duke and Duchess.[4]

Amongst the friends seen by the Windsors was Don Javier 'Tiger' Bermejillo, who had been a friend of Ernest Simpson whilst serving in the Spanish embassy in the early 1930s and a regular visitor to the Fort. Aristocratic, light-hearted and a romantic, he had been recalled because of a scandal in 1935 and the Duke had been instrumental in a refugee exchange that had saved his life during the Civil War.

[3] DGFP, AA–B15/B002549, Vol. X, p. 152.
[4] Ribbentrop to Stohrer, 11 July 1940, DGFP, AA–B15/B002549–51(GD D/X/152), No. 152, Vol. X, pp. 187–9.

Bermejillo reported back to the Spanish authorities his conversations with the Windsors:

> He said the appointment was offensive but had several advantages. First, official recognition of Her (his wife Wallis). (Second) not having to take part directly in the conflict, to which he had never been party. (Third) to have more freedom to exert his influence in favour of peace.[5]

The Germans now put their plan into action. Using as intermediaries Spanish friends of the Duke, he was invited to stay as a guest of the Spanish Government and offered the Palace of the Moorish Kings at Ronda.

The Duke asked 'the confidential emissary', 'Tiger' Bermejillo, 'if a maid of the Duchess to be permitted to travel to Paris in order to pack up various objects there and transport them by van to Lisbon, as they were required by him and the Duchess for the Bahamas.'[6] The Germans were only too happy to agree 'since if necessary the maid's journey to Paris and above all the return journey to Lisbon can be held up as required in order to postpone further his departure.'[7]

Wallis's maid, Marguerite Moulichon, was given safe passage to Paris to collect various belongings, such as bed linen for the new posting.[8] American diplomats also repatriated Wallis's favourite Nile-green swimsuit, which she had left behind at La Croë, under what came to be called Operation Cleopatra Whim.

---

[5] Document 56, Fundacion national Francisco Franco, Documentos ineditos para la Historia del generalismo Franco, Vol. 11–1, Madrid, 1993, quoted Urbach, p. 214.

[6] Stohrer to Ribbentrop, 16 July 1940, DGFP, B15/B002563.

[7] Stohrer to Ribbentrop, 16 July 1940, DGFP, B15/B002563.

[8] She was held up by the Gestapo as part of a negotiating ploy and finally reached the Bahamas in November.

Alec Cadogan was now briefed by one of his intelligence agents in Lisbon:

> of the exceptional care with which the Germans have fulfilled all of the Duke's desires. Special camions were sent to and fro, and a detailed inventory list was made of all the furniture and personal property of the Duke and Duchess of Windsor, which was shown to the Duchess for approval, to give her an opportunity to say if there was anything missing. Some of the more valuable belongings were transported in limousines and special instructions were given for everything to be in perfect order. The desire of the Germans to please the Duke and Duchess of Windsor was absolutely marked and evident.[9]

A new issue now arose. The Duke wanted to take his chauffeur and valet to the Bahamas, both of whom had been called up for war service. The War Office took the view that this would set an 'unfortunate precedent' and had already refused Lord Athlone in Canada a similar request, but the Duke was adamant. After taking advice from Monckton and Lord Lloyd, the Colonial Secretary, Churchill's assistant private secretary John Peck wrote to Churchill 'that HRH had to be treated as a petulant baby, and that there was a by no means remote possibility that he was prepared to face a break on this subject.'[10] Shortly afterwards permission was given for piper Alastair Fletcher to accompany the couple to the Bahamas.[11]

* * *

[9] 'Most Secret' telegram to Alec Cadogan, 26 September 1940, FO 1093/23, TNA. Parts remain redacted under 3(4) of the Public Records Act.

[10] John Peck to Churchill, 20 July 1940, CHAR 20/9A–B/96, Churchill College Archives.

[11] Churchill to the Duke, 24 July 1940, CHAR 20/9A–B/103, Churchill College Archives.

It was arranged that the couple would leave for the Bahamas on 1 August but, instead of going via New York as was usual and where Wallis wanted to have medical treatment, the British Government insisted they should sail via Bermuda, arguing that the Duke's views and presence in the US might bring 'harmful publicity' before the November presidential elections. They also used the technicality that the Duke was Commander-in-Chief of the Bahamas and his presence would flout American Neutrality Legislation.[12]

The Duke was furious, writing to Churchill on 18 July: 'Have been messed about quite long enough and detect in Colonial Office attitude very same hands at work as in my last job. Strongly urge you to support arrangements I have made as otherwise will have to reconsider my position.'[13]

There were good reasons for concern on the part of the British government. On 19 July, Alec Cadogan had received a 'Most Secret' telegram from the Lisbon Embassy: 'We have now learned from a reliable and well-placed source in Lisbon that Silva and his wife are in close touch with the German Embassy, and that Silva had a three-hour interview with the German Minister on the 15th July 1940.'[14] Herbert Pell, the American minister in Lisbon, sent a telegram to Cordell Hull on 20 July after dining with the Windsors: 'Duke and Duchess of Windsor are indiscreet and outspoken against British government. Consider their presence in the United States might be disturbing and confusing. They say that they intend

---

[12] The cost of diverting a ship via Bermuda was $7,500 at a time when every available cruiser was needed to protect Britain.

[13] The Duke to Churchill, 18 July 1940, CHAR 20/9A–B/87, Churchill College Archives, and CO 967/122, TNA.

[14] Lisbon to Alec Cadogan, 19 July 1940, FO 1093/23, TNA.

remaining in the United States whether Churchill liked it or not and desire apparently to make propaganda for peace.'[15]

Sir Robert Vansittart, former permanent under-secretary at the Foreign Office, reported a similar conversation to Halifax, the Foreign Secretary, three days later:

> A very important and influential friend of mine has informed me that he recently sat next to the Duke of Windsor at dinner. My friend is very much perturbed at the prospect of the Duke's activities. It is evident that he has formed a very low opinion of him. He said that he wished the Duke had been appointed to some post other than the Bahamas, for it was clear that the Duke and Duchess meant to spend a great deal of their time in the United States, where their presence and activities were certain to do our cause considerable harm.[16]

This was set against a backdrop of continuing peace feelers from Germany to Britain. On 19 July, the German chargé d'affaires had approached Philip Lothian, the British ambassador in Washington through Malcolm Lovell, the executive secretary of the Quaker Service Council in New York. The approach was taken sufficiently seriously for Lothian to call Halifax that night and for Halifax to circulate it to the War Cabinet.[17]

---

[15] Herbert Pell to Cordell Hull, 20 July 1940, NA 844 E 001/52, NARA. Sam Hoare told Walford Selby that the Duke had to be 'dissuaded from going to the US because he wants to launch a peace appeal'. Sam Hoare to Walford Selby, 20 July 1940, RA EDW/PRIV/MAINA/4598.

[16] Robert Vansittart to Lord Halifax, 23 July 1940, CO 967/122, TNA.

[17] See John Costello, *Ten Days That Saved the West* (Bantam, 1991), p. 347, and FO371/24408, TNA.

On the same day Hitler, in a speech to the Reichstag, 'A Last Appeal to Reason', had called for a negotiated peace to avert the 'destruction of a great world empire' and appealed 'once more to reason and common sense in Great Britain . . . I can see no reason why this war need go on.'

On 22 July, Eduard Hempel, the German minister in Eire, sent a telegram to the Foreign Ministry in Berlin:

> The impression in the Ministry of External Affairs here about the situation is as follows: A speedy conclusion of peace on reasonably tolerable terms on the basis of conditions brought about by the German success to date would be favored (*sic*) in general by Chamberlain, Halifax, Simon, and Hoare, whose dispatch to Spain was noteworthy from this point of view, also conservative circles (the Astors, Londonderry, etc.), high officialdom (Wilson), the city, the Times. Prospects for continuation of the war are generally regarded with pessimism . . .[18]

Italy's *Gazzetta del Popolo* had reported that day that the Duke wanted a government under Lloyd George and that Ribbentrop had received information from London that he had urged the King to appoint a pro-appeasement Cabinet. 'There are now rumours,' wrote George Orwell, 'that Lloyd George is the potential Pétain of England.'[19]

'Lord Lothian has offered his good offices,' minuted Ernst von Weizsäcker, State Secretary at the German Foreign Ministry, referring back to the approach of Malcolm Lovell, on 23 July. 'If he is a normal British Ambassador, he must have had a high approval. We

[18] Eduard Hempel to Foreign Ministry, 22 July 1940, Telegram 201, B15/ B002577, Vol. X, p. 262.

[19] Stephen Dorrill, *Blackshirt* (Penguin, 2006), p. 517.

may proceed on the assumption that the Quaker is authorised to bring us together.'[20]

And what of the Duke? According to the Portuguese Secret Service surveillance records, the Duke, who asked for his police protection to be removed at one point, was 'an active player in the plot – using his car to ferry the conspirators around, allowing them to meet at his house, engaging in a constant shuttle between the German, Spanish and British embassies in Lisbon – and portrays a man in a state of agitated indecision.'[21]

On 22 July, the Italian minister in Lisbon had radioed that the Duke had no intention of leaving Portugal until October.[22] The next day the Duke rang Bermejillo saying he wanted to discuss an urgent matter with him. On 24 July, the Duke told the Spanish ambassador in Lisbon, General Franco's brother Nicolas, that he was 'ready to return to Spain'.[23] The following day, the Italian minister radioed to Rome that the Duke had applied for a Spanish visa and told a friend that the king had 'demonstrated much feebleness'.[24]

The same day, Max zu Hohenlohe-Langenburg had reported a conversation about a negotiated peace with the Aga Khan to Walther Hewel, Ribbentrop's liaison official with Hitler, that: 'He

[20] Diary note, 23 July 1940, in Weizsäcker Erinnerungen (Freiburg, 1950), p. 294, quoted Costello, *Ten Days*, p. 348.

[21] *Observer*, 12 November 1995; Report of the PVDE on the Visit of the Duke of Windsor to Portugal, PT/TT/AOS/CO/NE-1A/17, Arquivo Nacional, Torre do Tombo, Lisboa.

[22] Bova Scoppa to Count Ciano, 22 July 1940, Italian Foreign Office archives, quoted David Irving, *Churchill's War*, Vol.1 (Veritas, 1987), p. 375.

[23] Stohrer to Joachim Ribbentrop, Nos. 2474 and 2492, both unpublished, *Churchill's War*, p. 375.

[24] Bova Scoppa to Count Ciano, 25 July 1940, Italian Foreign Office archives, *Churchill's War*, p. 375.

had seen Windsor as late as in April and the latter was thinking just as he was and was on close terms with Beaverbrook.'[25]

On 25 July, the German Ambassador, Stohrer, reported to Ribbentrop that Don Miguel Primo de Rivera had returned from Lisbon, where he had had two discussions with the Duke, who claimed: 'Politically he was more and more distant from the King and the present English government . . . The Duke was considering making a public statement and thereby disavowing present English policy and breaking with his brother.'[26]

The next day, the Duke had a two-hour meeting with Nicolas Franco. 'The influence upon the Duke and Duchess exerted by the confidential emissaries is already so effective that a firm intention by the Duke and Duchess to return to Spain can be assumed as in the highest degree probable,' reported Stohrer to the Foreign Ministry.[27] He quoted the Duke calling the war a crime and that he was shocked by Halifax's speech on 22 July, rejecting Hitler's peace offer. He concluded, 'The Duke is said to be delaying departure.'[28]

The Germans now put into operation a new plan, one of the strangest episodes of the Duke's life – Operation Willi.

* * *

Walter Schellenberg was a clever and ambitious intelligence officer, fluent in French and English, who had read medicine and law at the universities of Marburg and Bonn, before joining the SS in 1933 and rising quickly within its ranks. Now the thirty-year-old

[25] DGFP, No. 228, 1504/371063–6, quoted James Graham-Murray, *The Sword and the Umbrella* (Times Press, 1964), pp. 239–241.

[26] Stohrer to Ribbentrop, 25 July 1940, DGFP, B15/B002582–3.

[27] Stohrer to Foreign Ministry, 26 July 1940, DGFP, AA–B15/B002591–3, Telegram 235, pp. 317–18.

[28] Hoyningen-Huene to Berlin, 26 July 1940, DGFP, No. 749, B002597, unpublished, *Churchill's War*, p. 375.

Schellenberg was tasked by Ribbentrop to persuade the Duke to work for the Germans either through persuasion – he was authorised to offer 50 million Swiss francs – or by force.[29]

On Friday 26 July, Schellenberg arrived in Lisbon. That afternoon the Duke saw an Abwehr agent, Ángel Alcázar de Velasco, who operated under the code name 'Viktor'.[30] He brought with him a letter from Don Miguel Primo de Rivera, claiming that unless the couple left for Spain, they would be murdered by British Intelligence, and that they should agree to be escorted to Guarda, a village 150 miles north-east of Estoril on the Spanish border.

The Duke asked to have forty-eight hours to think about it. David Eccles 'flew back to London with despatches furnished by Franco's brother. These confirmed that the Duke was planning to return to Spain'.[31] Eccles later reiterated, 'They were trying to get him to agree and he would sort of play the hand for a peace conference in which the Germans would see that he got the throne.'[32]

The British, who were reading Abwehr codes, now decided to act and the trusty Monckton was despatched to Lisbon. He arrived on 28 July, bringing with him a letter from Churchill:

> It will be necessary for the Governor of the Bahamas to express views about the war and the general situation which are not out of harmony with those of His Majesty's Government . . . Many sharp and unfriendly ears will be pricked up to catch any

---

[29] In 1940, 50 million francs would have been the equivalent of £3 million, almost £172 million today.

[30] De Velasco operated as a German spy in Britain from 1941. See his MI5 file KV2/3535, TNA, and his memoirs, *Memorias de un Agente Secreto*, Ed Plaza & Janés, Barcelona, 1979.

[31] Bloch interview with Eccles, 1983, *Churchill's War*, p. 375. Cf. Stohrer to Ribbentrop, 4 July 1940, RA PS/PSO/GVI/C/G042A/392–435.

[32] Lord Eccles interview, BREN 2/2/5, p. 14, Churchill College Archives.

suggestion that your Royal Highness takes a view about the war, or about the Germans, or about Hitlerism, which is different from that adopted by the British nation and Parliament.[33]

On 29 July, the Italian minister in Lisbon, Renato Bova Scoppa, reported to Ciano that the emissary de Velasco had told a colleague, 'The Prince thinks like us.' The message was sent on to Berlin.[34] It had said that it looked like the Duke was ready to fall in with the plan, but Monckton's efforts had been effective. The next day, Schellenberg wrote in his log: *Willi will nicht* ('Willi says no').

Later that day, Hoyningen-Huene sent a telegram to Ribbentrop stating that, though the Duke was still in favour of peace negotiations, he considered 'the present moment as inopportune for him to manifest himself on the political scene', adding 'that his departure for the Bahamas need not imply a rupture, since he could return with 24 hours' flying time via Florida.'[35]

At noon on 30 July, the Duke gave a press conference at the British embassy to say he was off to the Bahamas. Ribbentrop now decided that there was only one option – to abduct the couple.

The following day the Duke saw Don Nicolas Franco, who reminded him that: 'The moment may come when England will

---

[33] Churchill to the Duke, 27 July 1940, CHAR 20/9A-B, Churchill College Archives, and Monckton Trustees, Box 18, Folio 51, Balliol College. A cryptic telegram, with no enclosure, in the Royal Archives reads, 'I beg to send you, enclosed herewith, a copy of a cable received today from my principles.' C.W. Kalloch to Duke of Windsor, 27 July 1940, RA EDW/PRIV/MAIN/A/4601.

[34] Bova Scoppa to Count Ciano, 29 July 1940, Italian Foreign Office archives, *Churchill's War*, p. 376.

[35] Hoyningen-Huene to Ribbentrop, 30 July 1940, DGFP, AA–B15/B002609 (unpublished), No. 783, marked most urgent. Copy RA PS/PSO/GVl/ O42A/393/27. De Rivera reported the next day exactly the same: 'He could, if the occasion arose, take action even from the Bahamas.' DGFP, B15/ B002619–20, quoted Donaldson, p. 373.

feel the need to have you once more at her head, and therefore you should not be too far away.'[36]

On 31 July, de Rivera reported:

Yet the Duke declared he wanted to proceed to the Bahamas. No prospect of peace existed at the moment. Further statements of the Duke indicate that he has nevertheless already given consideration to the possibility that the role of an intermediary might fall to him. He declared that the situation in England at the moment was still by no means hopeless. Therefore, he should not now, by negotiations carried on contrary to the orders of his government, let loose against himself the propaganda of his English opponents, which might deprive him of all prestige at the period when he might possibly take action. He could, if the occasion arose, take action even from the Bahamas.[37]

Ribbentrop responded later that day by sending a 'Most Urgent Top Secret' telegram to the Legation in Portugal, stating that 'Germany is now determined to force England to make peace by every means of power. It would be a good thing if the Duke were to keep himself prepared for further developments.'

He requested Santo Silva 'make the most earnest effort to prevent his departure tomorrow, since . . . We are convinced that the Duke will be so under surveillance there that he will never again have the chance to come to Europe, even by airplane,' adding:

[36] Neill Lochery, *Lisbon: War in the Shadows of the City of Light 1939–45* (Public Affairs, 2011), p. 82.

[37] de Rivera, 31 July 1940, DGFP, B15/B002619–20.

Should the Duke in spite of everything be determined to depart, there is still the possibility that the Portuguese confidant might remain in touch with him and arrange some other way to transmit communications verbally, whereby we can continue beyond this present contact and, if occasion arises, negotiate . . . Please keep this telegram confidential and under your personal charge.[38]

The British authorities had no illusions about Santo. An intelligence officer, Desmond Morton, had filed a memo to Churchill, based on information from a source in Madrid and Lisbon:

Senhor Esperito Santo, head of the bank of that name in Lisbon, is very pro-German and a centre of peace propaganda. HRH the Duke of Windsor visited him in Lisbon and according to Senhor Espirito Santo, manifested extreme defeatist and pacifist sympathies. I find that Mr Jebb, Foreign Office, has heard similar reports about HRH. Senhor Esperito . . . is a crook. He is handling very large sums in bank notes and dollar securities from Germany via Switzerland to the Americas. These monies are almost certainly German loot from the captive countries.[39]

The psychological stress on the Windsors continued right up to departure. Pressure was put on the Portuguese prime minister, António de Oliveira Salazar, by Don Nicolas Franco to try and keep the couple on the Iberian Peninsula. In the small hours of

[38] Ribbentrop to Portuguese Legation, 31 July 1940, DGFP, AA–B15/B002617–18, Vol. X, No. 265, pp. 378–9.

[39] Desmond Morton to Winston Churchill, 4 August 1940, FO 1093/23, TNA.

Thursday morning, 1 August, Santo Silva was summoned by Hoyningen-Huene and he agreed to ask Salazar to intervene to try and keep the Duke in Portugal. Wallis was sent an anonymous gift of flowers with a greeting card containing a warning. One of their chauffeurs was bribed to refuse to go to the Bahamas, the car taking their luggage to the ship was sabotaged, and the luggage only reached the ship after an hour's delay.

Primo de Rivera was also sent to try and dissuade the couple from leaving and told Stohrer, 'The Duke hesitated right up to the last moment. The ship had to delay its departure on that account.'[40] However, on the evening of 1 August, Schellenberg watched through binoculars from the tower room of the German Embassy as the Windsors steamed out of Lisbon on SS *Excalibur*. The same day, Hitler issued his Directive No. 17 ordering a full-scale attack on Britain.

On 2 August, Hoyningen-Huene sent a 'Most Urgent, Secret' telegram to Ribbentrop that: 'Every effort to detain the Duke and Duchess in Europe (in which connection I refer particularly to Schellenberg's reports) was in vain,' but, 'To the appeal made to him to cooperate at a suitable time in the establishment of peace, he agreed gladly . . . He would remain in continuing communication with his previous host and had agreed with him upon a code word, upon receiving which he would immediately come back over.'[41]

It was clear the Duke had not given up hope of returning to Europe.

---

[40] Stohrer to Ribbentrop, 3 August 1940, DGFP, B15/B002641–2, Vol. X, No. 285, pp. 409–10. Copy RA PS/PSO/GVI/O42A/392-435.

[41] Hoyningen-Huene to Ribbentrop, 2 August 1940, DGFP, B15/B002632-3, Vol. X, No. 276, pp. 397–8. Rudolph Schleier, the consul general at the German Embassy in Paris responsible for implementation of anti-Jewish measures in German-occupied France, reported on 4 August that Wallis's maid had said that 'the Duke of Windsor had no intention of leaving to take up his new post, but would rather wait in Lisbon for further developments in Europe.' RA PS/PSO/GVI/O42A/393/38

CHAPTER II

Exiled

The royal couple, together with the Woods and Gray Phillips, arrived in Bermuda on 9 August and were met by a guard of honour and band at the Yacht Club steps. They spent the next few days at Government House, swimming, shopping and playing golf, whilst they waited to pick up their connection to the Bahamas.

Whilst there, the Duke was appalled to receive a telegram from Lord Lloyd, the Secretary of State for the Colonies, saying that the Duchess was not entitled to a curtsey and should be addressed as 'Your Grace'. He drafted a reply, saying in that case he would 'not proceed to Nassau to take up my appointment'. Eventually he was persuaded not to send it.[1]

He also sent an elliptical telegram to Santo:

> It will be a great help if you are able to effect the transaction that you and I discussed in my cabin in the presence of Gray Phillips before the ship sailed. I shall appreciate your notifying me one way or the other at your earliest convenience as in the event of proving difficult to carry out the plan in the most advantageous way, I shall have to make other arrangements from this side![2]

---

[1] RA DW 4628 and RA W 4627, quoted Ziegler, pp. 440–1.
[2] Duke of Windsor to Espirito, 10 August 1940, RA EDW/PRIV/MAIN/A/4629.

Five days later, at the height of the Battle of Britain when Britain was fighting for its very survival, the Duke sent another coded telegram to Santo, who reported it to the German Ambassador. In turn, Hoyningen-Huene sought instructions from Berlin. 'The confidant has just received a telegram from the Duke from Bermuda, asking him to send a communication as soon as action was advisable. Should any answer be made?'[3]

If genuine, as it almost certainly was, this was communication with a known foreign agent during wartime, which meant that the Duke could have been prosecuted under the 1940 Treachery Act.[4]

The royal couple arrived in the Bahamas on board the Canadian cargo ship MV *Lady* on Saturday 17 August. They inspected a guard of honour in the 95°F heat – the Duke sweating profusely in the heavy khaki uniform of a major-general – before being sworn in by the Chief Justice and driven to Government House, where the Duchess gloomily inspected their new residence and the Duke played nine holes of golf.

Their new home was a Spanish colonial house dating from 1801 of white stone with a tiled roof and large patios, and consisted of seven bedrooms, six bathrooms and twenty-four other rooms. It sat in a ten-acre garden in the heart of Nassau, facing the water and surrounded by hedges of purple bougainvillea, with rubber trees and an avenue of giant royal palms. It had only recently been

[3] Hoyningen-Huene to Berlin, 15 August 1940, GDFP, Series D, Vol. X, B15/ B002641–2. Copy RA PS/PSO/GVl/C/042A/393/40.

[4] Michael Bloch suggests that the telegram was about missing luggage, but that would not have justified a telegram to Berlin. John Costello argues that it was sent by MI6 on grounds that 'a deliberately engineered provocation cabled in the Duke's name to his host Santo Silva would have furthered Britain's interests' as a way of keeping negotiations going and hold off a German invasion whilst Britain prepared, but negotiations had ended. *Ten Days*, p. 374. The spy writer Nigel West believes 'the Duke knew exactly what he was doing and was not a dupe.' Nigel West to the author, 5 November 2020.

renovated at a cost of $7,000, but the couple argued it required rewiring and painting inside and out, and had patches of humidity and termite infestation, with Wallis describing the dining room as looking like a 'ski-hut in Norway'.[5]

There was no laundry room and all washing was carried out in a small stream in the garden and dried on rocks. Within a week the royal couple had moved out to a villa, three miles outside Nassau, loaned to them by Frederick Sigrist, creator of the Hurricane fighter, who had just been appointed Director of British Aircraft Production in America.

The Duke argued that £5,000 was required 'in order that Government House becomes a worthy residence for the King's representative in this Colony,' and 'to ensure some dignity during my term of office.'[6] He continued that it would 'take at least two months to make it habitable' and 'as there can be no official entertaining during that period and the heat is now intense, I propose with your concurrence to take advantage of the hot weather season and go to my Ranch in Canada.'[7]

Officials were appalled that Windsor wanted to leave the island as soon as he had arrived and, when resources were limited, was focused only on his own comforts. Lord Lloyd responded that the request placed him 'in a rather embarrassing position . . . For example, may it not be said that if a sum of £5,000 can be spared from Crown Funds it might have been used to buy a fighter?'[8]

---

[5] Duke of Windsor to Lord Lloyd, 12 October 1940, CO 967/122, TNA. $7,000 would be $133K today.

[6] Duke of Windsor to Lord Lloyd, 26 August 1940, CHAR 20/9B/180–1, Churchill College Archives. £5,000 would be £286K today.

[7] Duke of Windsor to Colonial Office, 24 August 1940, FO 371 24249, TNA.

[8] Lord Lloyd to the Duke of Windsor, 27 August 1940, CHAR 20/9A-B/182–5, Churchill College Archives.

Walter Monckton told the Duke that Churchill was 'very grieved to hear that you were entertaining such an idea' and hoped that, given people were suffering rather greater hardships during the Blitz, that the new Governor 'would be willing to put up with the discomfort and remain at your post until weather conditions made things less unpleasant.'[9]

The Nassau House of Assembly voted a sum of $8,000 for redecoration, but the final cost came to $20,000, which included building a new three-storey west wing to house the Duke's staff.[10] The Windsors paid for much of the internal renovation, redecorating the mansion in a modernistic style with occasional Regency touches, and Wallis furnishing it 'with low, glass-topped cocktail tables, open cupboards that displayed Sèvres porcelain, and she dotted it with bamboo chairs. She filled the house with so many tropical flowers, it seemed like a garden.'[11] As Wallis told the press, 'I must make a home for him. That's why I'm doing this place over; so we can live in it in comfort as a home. All his life he has travelled, and a palace to come back to is not always a home.'[12]

It was not a good start, with press complaints that the couple were undignified and extravagant – Wallis regularly flew in a hairdresser from Saks Fifth Avenue and flowers from Miami. Lord Lothian, the British ambassador in Washington, reported to Cadogan, 'it is most important from the point of view of opinion in this country to avoid the impression that the Duke of Windsor is not taking his duties in the Bahamas entirely seriously.'[13] Enclosing 'copies of

[9] RA DW 4647, quoted Ziegler, p. 463.

[10] $20K is about £380K.

[11] Caroline Blackwood, *The Last of the Duchess* (Macmillan, 1995), p. 144.

[12] Adela Rogers St Johns, *The Honeycomb* (Harper & Row, 1969), p. 533.

[13] Lord Lothian to Alec Cadogan, 4 September 1940, Monckton Trustees, Folio 118, Balliol College, and FO 1093/23, TNA.

correspondence and newspaper cuttings which should illustrate as clearly as anything what I mean,' he added that, 'if we are to maintain a full and due measure of American sympathy in the present ordeal, we must one and all give the impression that we are taking life with befitting seriousness.'[14]

Wallis made no secret of her disgust at the posting, crossing out the Government House heading on official stationery and replacing it with the word Elba. 'The Place is too small for the Duke. I do not mean that in any other way but that a man who has been Prince of Wales and King of England cannot be governor of a tiny place,' she wrote to Walter Monckton shortly after arriving. 'It is not fair to the people here or to him. The spotlight is on an island that cannot itself take it and the appointment is doomed to fail for both concerned.'[15] In return, the locals nicknamed Government House 'in honour of Wallis Windsor's past . . . the red-light district.'[16]

There were numerous suspicions that the Windsors were not fully committed to their new posting. Courtney Letts de Espil, the wife of Wallis's former lover, Felipe de Espil, was a friend of Alice Gordon who, together with her husband George Gordon, formerly American minister in the Hague, had been on the boat to the Bahamas with the Windsors. Alice, an old friend of Wallis, confided to Courtney that the Duke was:

'. . . openly an admirer of the Germans. And we all know she was a great friend of Ribbentrop when he was Ambassador to England. She was even more stupidly outspoken against the

[14] Lord Lothian to Alec Cadogan, 4 September 1940, Monckton Trustees, Folio 118, Balliol College.

[15] Duchess of Windsor to Walter Monckton, 16 September 1940, Monckton Trustees, Box 18, Folio 99, Balliol College.

[16] Michael Pye, *The King Over the Water: The Scandalous Truth About the Windsors' War Years* (Hutchinson, 1981), p. 62.

British government than he . . . They both also openly admit their tenure of Nassau will not be long. And they were furious to have been sent there.' All this Alice told me. There are many who think the Windsors expect to return to England in high capacity – when England makes terms with Germany.[17]

The British authorities remained nervous about the Windsors' proximity to America and the inspiration they might give to Isolationists. 'According to reports from the United States of America, President Roosevelt will try to bring about peace negotiations between Great Britain and the Axis Powers,' claimed one briefing paper sent to Churchill in October. 'The Duke of Windsor may also play a part in this attempt. He is known to have become convinced of the necessity for making peace when he was Liaison Officer in France.'[18] The Foreign Office sent details to Philip Lothian, the British ambassador in Washington, as further evidence that the Windsors and Roosevelt should be kept apart.[19]

Franklin D. Roosevelt had his own concerns about the couple. He now reviewed an FBI report, commissioned at the time of the Duke's appointment. 'It has been asserted for some time the British Government has known that the Duchess of Windsor was exceedingly pro-German in her sympathies and connections and there is strong reason to believe that this is the reason why she was considered so obnoxious to the British government that they refused to permit Edward to marry her and maintain the throne,' ran the memo to Brigadier Edwin Watson, secretary to the President:

[17] 11 September 1940, Courtney Letts de Espil papers, Box 10, Folder 2, Library of Congress.

[18] 7 October 1940, CHAR 20/9A–B/210, Churchill College Archives.

[19] 13 October 1940, Monckton Trustees, Box 18, Folio 122, Balliol College.

Both she and the Duke of Windsor have been repeatedly warned by representatives of the British Government that in the interests of the morale of the British people, they should be exceedingly circumspect in their dealings with the representatives of the German Government. The Duke is in such a state of intoxication most of the time that he is virtually *non compos mentis*. The Duchess has repeatedly ignored these warnings.

Shortly prior to the designation of the Duke to be Governor of the Bahamas the (*redaction*) established conclusively that the Duchess had recently been in direct contact with von Ribbentrop and was maintaining constant contact and communication with him . . . The contacts of the Duchess of Windsor with von Ribbentrop from the villa which they were occupying became so frequent that it became necessary for the British Government to compel them to move.[20]

The fact Wallis sent her clothes to New York for dry cleaning made the FBI suspect that 'the transferring of messages through the clothes may be taking place.'[21]

One of the FBI concerns was 'that the Duchess may align herself with Axel Wenner-Gren, who you will recall has within the past year or so purchased a home at Nassau and apparently intends to maintain a permanent residence there. Lady Williams Taylor (the grandmother of Brenda Frazier) has been entrusted by the British Government with the social side of the problem of keeping the Windsors and the Wenner-Grens apart.'[22]

[20] Edward Tamm to Edwin Watson, 13 September 1940, FBI file HQ 65-31113.
[21] Memo for Clyde Tolson, 19 October 1940, FBI file HQ 65-31113.
[22] Edward Tamm to Edwin Watson, 13 September 1940, FBI file HQ 65-31113.

At the beginning of August, a letter sent to Axel Wenner-Gren from Rio de Janeiro had been intercepted by the FBI. It mentioned the arrival of a 'new and interesting family with which I assume you will at once become friendly. I have met an old acquaintance who ... states that family hold sympathetic understanding for totalitarian ideas ... This should be of great significance for forth-coming development of events.'[23]

Wenner-Gren had been busy pushing for a negotiated peace since meeting the Duke in October 1937. For the previous eighteen months he had been scuttling between Roosevelt, Goering and Chamberlain and had tried to accompany the American under-secretary of state Sumner Welles on his 1940 tour exploring peace feelers. Welles instinctively distrusted him, telling a colleague, 'I have not a shred of evidence, but I have a very strong feeling that this man acts as a spy for the German government.'[24]

On 17 October, Wenner-Gren arrived in the Bahamas from South America, writing in his diary the next day about the Duke, presumably after a telephone call: 'Extremely pleasant and interest-ing conversation ... He has a good memory and remembers very well our conversation in Paris.'[25]

The next day Wenner-Gren called on the Duke and on 25 October, after a day together inspecting projects on Hog Island, Wenner-Gren and his wife dined with the Windsors at Government House. 'Pity that political considerations prevent closer social intercourse. Extremely interesting discussion,' wrote Wenner-Gren in his diary that night.[26]

---

[23] RA GVI 141/35, quoted Ziegler, p. 455, and CHAR 20/31A–B, Churchill College Archives. It was sent to Churchill on 13 January 1941.

[24] 3 July 1946, *Expressen*, p. 53, and FBI report, quoted Ziegler, p. 456. The various peace initiatives can be seen in PREM 1/328, TNA.

[25] 18 October 1940, Wenner-Gren diary, by courtesy of Mark Hollingsworth.

[26] 25 October 1940, Wenner-Gren diary, by courtesy of Mark Hollingsworth.

Within a week the Wenner-Grens were back at Government House for dinner. It was the beginning of a close friendship with benefits for both parties. The Duke saw Wenner-Gren as an ally for the economic development of the island and an important employer, and someone in this backwater with whom he could discuss the state of the world. Wenner-Gren was only too pleased to have this important contact.

Wenner-Gren had first come to the Bahamas in 1938, attracted by no income tax and because it was a useful base for his operations in North and South America. He had already founded the Bank of the Bahamas – affiliated to the Stein Bank of Cologne – and developed a 700-acre estate on Hog Island, which he had named Shangri-La. Here he had entertained Greta Garbo and Marlene Dietrich and had created gardens, modelled on those at Versailles, filled with exotic birds, flowers and trees, employing over a thousand labourers in the process. By the spring and summer of 1941, the Hog Island project employed over 15 per cent of Nassau's total workforce.

But Wenner-Gren's activities caused concern. There were rumours that his role was to develop links with South America on behalf of the Axis powers – in particular Mexico, which apart from its oil and mineral potential, had an important role if the United States, on its border, entered the war – and that Wenner-Gren's new hurricane harbour was to provision German vessels.

In September 1940 an Anglo-American agreement had been signed, exchanging fifty US destroyers in return for bases in Bermuda and the Bahamas. The islands were now taking on an important strategic significance. In November 1940, Leslie Heape, the Colonial Secretary and in effect Deputy Governor, met the US consul John Dye, worried about aerial photographs being taken by Wenner-Gren's architect of Mayaguana, an island earmarked as an American base. It was decided aerial photography should henceforth be banned.

'Axel Wenner-Gren has since November 1, 1939 been constantly steaming in and out of Nassau Harbor on his yacht, equipped with high-powered radio antennae,' noted Department of State official G.A. Gordon to State Department colleague Fletcher Warren on 20 November. 'This yacht is manned by ex-Swedish Navy officers, all of whom, according to my informant, are definitely and professedly pro-Nazi.'[27]

It was on his yacht *Southern Cross* that the Windsors made their first visit to the United States after arriving in the Bahamas. The *Munargo,* the regular passenger boat between Miami and Nassau, had cancelled its sailings and Wenner-Gren offered to transport the couple when Wallis needed dental care for an infected tooth. They left on 9 December, almost exactly four years since the Duke had signed the Instrument of Abdication.

It was the Duke's first visit to the country since 1924, and hers since 1933, and now possible after Roosevelt had romped to victory in the November presidential elections. A crowd of 12,000 awaited them – and their twenty-seven pieces of luggage – on the quayside, with a further 8,000 lining the streets to St Francis Hospital.

But Wenner-Gren was confined to the port as a suspected subversive and the FBI were monitoring their movements. 'Before England and Germany became war enemies, this couple visited Hitler and are known to be the Nazi's friends,' ran an FBI report. 'More recently in the *Boston Transcript*, its foreign correspondent Leland Stowe had a big story of their strong ties with von Ribbentrop and Hitler, especially Mrs Simpson-Windsor.'[28]

[27] Higham, *Mrs Simpson*, p. 354.
[28] Letter to Hoover, 10 December 1940, FBI file HQ 65-31113.

All this was set against continuing German peace moves. In December, Adolf Berle noted in his diary that he had seen an FBI report that 'Sir William Wiseman and Fritz Wiedemann, the German consul general, were cooking up some peace moves together. Wiseman expects to do it through his contacts with Lord Halifax bypassing Lothian.'[29] Also involved as an intermediary was Stephanie Hohenlohe, Wallis's former neighbour in Bryanston Court, a close friend of Bedaux and Goering and described by Berle as 'an old hand at international intrigue.'[30]

Throughout the autumn of 1940, Wiseman had held a series of meetings with James Mooney, the head of General Motors Overseas, to discuss brokering a negotiated peace with Germany. Also involved was the Archbishop of New York, Cardinal Francis Spellman. At the beginning of December, it had even been suggested that the Duke of Windsor be brought in under cover of playing golf at Cat Cay on 6 January.[31]

On 12 December, the British ambassador in Washington died – as a Christian Scientist, Philip Lothian refused simple medical treatment that would have saved his life. The Duke, who had been lobbying London and Washington to succeed him, took the opportunity to hold a press conference. It was a further irritation for the British authorities.

* * *

[29] 5 December 1940, Adolf Berle diary, Cambridge University Library. Wiseman had headed the British intelligence mission in the United States during the First World War and stayed on as a partner in the American investment bank Kuhn, Loeb & Co.

[30] 5 December 1940, Adolf Berle diary, Cambridge University Library.

[31] The full details can be found in Box 1, Folder 22, James D. Mooney papers at Georgetown University.

Back on the island, the Windsors were able to move into the refurbished Government House. Since mid-October they had been living at the twenty-room Westbourne owned by Sir Harry Oakes – the baronetcy had been given for financing the rebuilding of St George's Hospital at Hyde Park Corner in 1939 – the richest resident in the Bahamas. A stocky and bluff man, who had made a fortune from gold mines in Canada, he had arrived in the Bahamas in the early 1930s, attracted by the absence of income tax and a 2 per cent inheritance tax.

Oakes was the greatest property owner on New Providence – at one point it was estimated he owned a third of the island – and had been elected first to the House of Assembly and the Legislative Council.[32] He owned the Moorish pink stucco British Colonial Hotel, where almost all the employees were people of colour, and he had paid for, amongst much else, the airport, a waterworks plant and botanical garden, had developed a bus line to bring workers from Grant's Town, and given over $1 million to local charities.[33] A generous benefactor, he was to be an important ally for the Duke.

A few days after returning, the Duke met Roosevelt – in Bahamian waters on board the *Tuscaloosa* inspecting potential naval bases in the Caribbean, as part of the Lend-Lease Act – to discuss the bases, the economic future of the islands and how the Civilian Conservation Corps, an unemployment relief programme, could be adapted for the Bahamas. It was to be the first of a dozen meetings between the two men during the war.

Almost immediately on his return from the United States, the Duke gave a two-hour interview on 20 December to the editor of

---

[32] He also had homes in Maine, Palm Beach, Sussex and London.

[33] Just under $20 million today.

the popular American weekly magazine *Liberty Magazine,* Fulton Oursler, who was a close friend of Roosevelt and professed isolationist. According to Oursler's son, after the interview, Vyvyan Drury, the Duke's ADC, asked Oursler to take a message back to the President: 'Tell Mr Roosevelt that if he will make an offer of intervention for peace, that before any one in England can oppose it, the Duke of Windsor will instantly issue a statement supporting it and that will start a revolution in England and force peace.'[34]

Three days later, Oursler saw Roosevelt at the White House – White House logs show the meeting took place between 10.50 and 11.40, though no official records of the meeting exist – to pass on the message. Oursler was shocked to discover 'that agents of the Colonial Secretary had been listening to what the Duke had said and to what Drury had said to me, and that this report had been sent to the British Embassy and the embassy had sent it to Roosevelt. Roosevelt knew exactly what I had come to tell him before I opened my mouth.'[35]

The Duke's friendship with Wenner-Gren was causing increasing alarm in both British and American official circles. 'Mr Hopkins mentioned the deplorable effect which the Duke's recent cruise with Mr Wenner-Gren had had in America, and he afterwards told me that he thought Lord Lloyd ought to know that any claim by Mr Wenner-Gren to intimacy or friendship with members of the United States Administration was quite unfounded,' Churchill's private secretary John Colville minuted to Christopher Eastwood, the private secretary of the Secretary of State for Colonial Affairs.

[34] Fulton Oursler Jr, 'Secret Treason', *American Heritage* 42, No. 8 (December 1991).

[35] Fulton Oursler Jr, 'Secret Treason', *American Heritage* 42, No. 8 (December 1991). Oursler dictated a seventeen-page account of the episode to his secretary on 26 December 1940, which was later corroborated by Louis Nichols, a senior FBI official.

'He was considered a dangerous pro-Nazi and all his activities were closely watched.'[36]

The Duke was warned by the Colonial Secretary to keep his distance from 'Goering's Pal' and shown an MI6 report produced in November 1939 for Sir Charles Dundas, the previous Governor, himself alarmed at Wenner-Gren's activities. 'He may not be impressed by it, but he will at least have been given a further warning!'[37] The Duke refused to believe his officials, replying, 'He is a very prominent and important resident of the Bahamas engaged in various development schemes most beneficial to this Colony and giving vast amount of employment. I regard him as deserving of all possible encouragement.'[38]

The Colonial Office began to accumulate large files on Wenner-Gren and his plans. One entitled 'Development and Wenner-Gren Bahamas 1941' stated: 'Material about Mr Wenner-Gren is contained in 13131/39/40 Defence (Secret) from which it will be seen that there are considerable misgivings about Mr W's attachment to our cause and indeed some hints that he may *sub rosa* be engaged in acts of economic warfare directed against the Allied cause.'[39]

Buckingham Palace continued to be kept closely apprised of the Duke's associations. On 9 January, Christopher Eastwood wrote to Alec Hardinge:

---

[36] John Colville to Christopher Eastwood, 13 January 1941, CHAR 20/31A, Churchill College Archives. Colville in his diary for 11 January 1941 reported on a meeting with Harry Hopkins, where the American had expressed concerns 'about HRH's recent yachting trip with a violently pro-Nazi Swede', John Colville, *The Fringes of Power: Downing Street Diaries 1939–1955* (Hodder & Stoughton, 1985), p. 394.

[37] Hopkinson to Robinson, 17 January 1941, FO 1093/23, TNA.

[38] 9 January 1941, report 'from most secret sources (FBI to MI5) attached', CHAR 20/31A–B, Churchill College Archives.

[39] Memo, 26 March 1941, CO 23/750, TNA.

Lord Lloyd thought that the King might care to have, for information, the attached note which summarises what we know about Mr Axel Wenner-Gren. The report is, of course, derived from most secret sources.[40]

Marked secret, it described how Wenner-Gren had been:

in favour of a compromise peace on the basis that a strong Germany is necessary as part of a united front against Bolshevism. At the same time some sources have stated that he had shown definitely pro-German sympathies and it was also reported that he had arranged shipments of oil to Germany in the early part of this year. More recent reports have alleged that he is sponsoring an opposition movement in America for the overthrow of the present Swedish Government, in favour of a National Socialist Government which would collaborate closely with Germany . . . the United States authorities suspect Wenner-Gren of being in close touch with Nazi leaders.[41]

A State Department memo now drew attention to the fact that both Wenner-Gren and the Duke were:

seeing a great deal of prominent and influential American businessmen, particularly from the mid-Western states, where a strictly commercial point of view would appear to prevail in business circles with regard to relations between the United States and Germany. There would appear to be certain indications that Wenner-Gren, as well as the Duke of Windsor, is stressing the need for a negotiated peace at this time on account

[40] RA PS/PSO/GVI/C/042/141/34.
[41] RA PS/PSO/GVI/C/042/141/35.

of the advantages which this would present to American business interests. This angle, I think, should be closely observed.[42]

The MI5 officer Guy Liddell discussed Wenner-Gren with his opposite number in the American embassy in London on 17 January 1941. 'I had a talk with Herschel afterwards about Axel Wenner-Gren. He said that if I would give him a note, he would send it over to Washington DC by bag and made the suggestion that somebody should say something privately to the Duke of Windsor.'[43]

A few days later Christopher Eastwood, Lord Lloyd's private secretary, wrote to Churchill's private secretary, John Martin, in a letter marked 'Secret', 'that the Americans should arrange for a hint to be dropped to the Duke from the American side. They could probably arrange for one of their agents to visit the Bahamas.'[44] Churchill immediately agreed to this, but the friendship continued. 'Long confidential discussions with Windsor; in many respects we share the same opinions,' wrote Wenner-Gren in his diary on 3 February 1941.[45]

One of the concerns was that the brother of the new President of Mexico, General Maximino Ávila Camacho, was due to arrive in Nassau early in February to discuss with Wenner-Gren a huge investment project in Mexico. The State Department were suspicious of the Swede's intentions. 'I think it is highly important that we have more than the customary routine reports of Mr Wenner-Gren's activities,' minuted Sumner Welles to Fletcher Warren.[46]

---

[42] Sumner Welles to Fletcher Warren, January 1941, State Department files, 800.20211/WG/44 ½, NARA.

[43] *The Guy Liddell Diaries*, Vol. 1, p. 125.

[44] Christopher Eastwood to John Martin, 21 January 1941, CHAR 20/31A–B, Churchill College Archives.

[45] Wenner-Gren diary, 3 February 1941, courtesy of Mark Hollingsworth.

[46] Sumner Welles to Fletcher Warren, January 1941, State Department files, 800.20211/WG/44 1/2, NARA.

Camacho, as governor of the province of Puebla, was officially associated with the Mexican government, with whom diplomatic relations had been broken in 1938 over the expropriation of British oil properties. The Duke, as a representative of the British government, should not have met him but, as a favour to Wenner-Gren, he entertained the Mexican for two hours at Government House.

The meeting, which also involved a scheme to circumvent foreign exchange rules by sending monies to Mexico City, was reported to the authorities by Montgomery Hyde, an MI6 officer, who by chance was doing a security audit of Government House. A check revealed that one of those in the sixteen-member Mexican delegation was on an FBI blacklist.[47]

At the end of January 1941, a British Intelligence report stated:

> some sources have stated that he had shown definitely pro-German sympathies and it was also reported that he had arranged shipments of oil to Germany in the early part of this year. More recent reports have alleged that he is preparing an opposition movement in America for the overthrow of the present Swedish Government in favour of a National Socialist government which would collaborate closely with Germany. Wenner-Gren is also said to be attempting to form in America a cartel to control the wood trade . . . It is known that the United States authorities suspect Wenner-Gren of being in close touch with Nazi leaders . . .[48]

[47] H. Montgomery Hyde, *Secret Intelligence Agent* (Constable, 1982), p. 117.

[48] 29 January 1941, Box 71, Departmental correspondence State Dept, PSF, FDR Library. It is also quoted at Charles Higham, *Mrs Simpson*, p. 380. The State Department had built up large files on Wenner-Gren, which included FBI reports and reports from consular officials in Nassau. The FBI had been tasked with planting an agent on *Southern Cross*. See memo 18 April 1941 on Wenner-Gren by Harold Hoskins, Box 71, Departmental correspondence State Dept, PSF, FDR Library.

A further area of concern was the simultaneous arrival in the Bahamas of Alfred P. Sloan, the head of General Motors, and his colleague James D. Mooney.[49] On 5 February, James B. Stewart, the American consul general in Zurich, sent a highly confidential memo to Fletcher Warren headed 'Alleged Nazi Subversive Activities in the US of James D Mooney':

> Mr Eduard Winter, formerly General Motors distributor in Berlin, and at present this company's representative in Paris, acts as courier in delivering communications from Mr James D Mooney, president of the General Motors Overseas Corporation, to high German officials in Paris. Mr Winter has a special passport which enables him to travel freely between occupied and unoccupied France. Mr Mooney is known to be in sympathy with the German government, and the persons who supplied this information believe that the General Motors official is transmitting information of a confidential nature through Mr Winter.[50]

There were business, as well as ideological reasons, behind Mooney's activities. Since Hitler had come to power in 1933, General Motors had invested over $100,000,000[51] in Germany – money that had been diverted from car to tank production – with Sloan arguing 'an international business operating throughout the world should conduct its operations in strictly business terms, without regard to the political beliefs of its management or the political beliefs of the country in which it is operating.'[52]

---

[49] The Windsors were lent Sloan's yacht for a week in April to tour the outer islands.

[50] Higham, *Mrs Simpson,* pp. 361–2.

[51] In today's money almost $2 billion.

[52] Alfred Sloan, 8 August 1941, 862.20211/M/19, NARA.

On 4 March, George Messersmith, now the US ambassador in Cuba, filed a report on Mooney describing him 'as mad as any Nazi and is one of those who nourishes the hope that when the United States may turn fascist he will be our Quisling or our Laval.'[53]

On the same day, John Dye, the US consul in the Bahamas, sent a memo marked 'Confidential' to the State Department saying that, according to Mrs William Leahy, wife of the former Puerto Rican governor, Admiral Leahy, Wallis had been making secret visits to San Juan in Puerto Rico. The Windsors were told by the British embassy in Washington not to travel to the island.

Meanwhile, suspicions continued about the activities of the Windsors. Valentine Lawford wrote in his diary on 19 February, 'Charles Peake has just written to Jim Thomas from Washington to say that the Windsors are hard at work putting out propaganda against AE and working for appeasement.'[54]

In March, the interview given the previous December appeared in *Liberty*. In it, the Duke implied that Britain could not defeat Germany and would have to reach a negotiated settlement with Hitler. 'America will help Britain more by not engaging in actual fighting but remaining a keystone for the new world which must be created when the war is over. There will be a new order in Europe, whether imposed by Germany or Britain.'[55] It threatened to scupper America coming into the war.

Goebbels noted in his diary: 'The Duke of Windsor has given an interview to a magazine in the USA in which he pretty frankly disclaims all chance of a British victory. We decide not to use it for the

---

[53] Higham, *Mrs Simpson*, p. 362.

[54] 19 February 1941, LWFD 2/3 Diary, Churchill College Archives. AE is Anthony Eden. Jim Thomas was a Conservative MP, then PPS to the Secretary of State for War.

[55] Quoted John Parker, *King of Fools* (St Martins, 1988), p. 210.

present, so as to avoid suffocating this tender seedling of reason.'[56] Valentine Vivian, the deputy head of MI6, immediately briefed Kenneth Robinson in the Colonial Office how it 'infuriates heads of news services who have seen advance copy. Article contains useful ammunition for appeasement group.'[57] The article was discussed with the head of MI6, Sir Stewart Menzies, and Sir Alexander Cadogan, Permanent Under-Secretary of State for Foreign Affairs, but it was 'decided that it was too late to act.'[58]

Churchill, who had been passed a press summary and had also briefed the Palace, immediately sent a telegram to the Duke marked 'Personal and Secret':

> Exception is taken also in the United States to Your Royal Highness's interview recently published in *Liberty*, of which it is said that the language, whatever was meant, will certainly be interpreted as defeatist and pro-Nazi, and by implication approving of the isolationist aim to keep America out of the war . . . I must say it seems to me that the views attributed to Your Royal Highness have been unfortunately expressed by the journalist Mr Oursler. I could wish indeed that Your Royal Highness would seek advice before making public statements of this kind. I should always be ready to help as I used to in the past.[59]

[56] Quoted Jim Wilson, *Nazi Princess: Hitler, Lord Rothermere and Princess Stephanie von Hohenlohe* (History Press, 2011), p.115.
[57] Valentine Vivian to Kenneth Robinson, 20 March 1941, CHAR 20/31A/6, Churchill College Archives.
[58] Christopher Eastwood to Eric Seal, 20 March 1941, CHAR 20/31A/45, Churchill College Archives.
[59] Churchill to the Duke, 18 March 1941, FO 954/33A/189, TNA, and CHAR 20/31A, Churchill College Archives.

The Duke, who had seen and approved the article before publication, now attempted to distance himself from it, claiming to Lord Moyne, the new Colonial Secretary, that 'many views and opinions expressed in the Liberty article were words put into my mouth as is so often the case in American journalism.'[60]

He now went on the attack against Churchill:

> The importance you attach to American magazine articles prompts me to tell you that I strongly resent and take great exception to the article in the magazine *Life* of 17th March entitled 'The Queen' in which the latter is quoted as referring to the Duchess as 'that Woman'. I understand that articles about the Royal Family are censored in Britain before release and this remark is a direct insult to my wife and is I can assure you no encouragement in our efforts to uphold the monarchical system in a British colony.

He ended his letter, 'I have both valued and enjoyed your friendship in the past, but after your telegram FO No 458 of the 1st July and the tone of your recent messages to me here, I find it difficult to believe that you are still the friend you used to be.'[61]

Churchill, who had more important priorities, did not answer.

---

[60] The Duke to Lord Moyne, 19 March 1941, FO 954/33A/189, TNA.

[61] The Duke to Churchill, 27 March 1941, FO 954/33A/190, TNA, and CHAR 20/31A/51–2, Churchill College Archives and EDW/PRIV/MAIN/A/4764. The Duke had in fact made one of his regular threats to resign on 18 March. The Duke of Windsor to Lord Moyne, 18 March 1941, EDW/PRIV/MAIN/A/4758.

CHAPTER 12

Under Surveillance

The Windsors, who required permission to visit the United States, were now lobbying to make another visit. The authorities suspected the trip might involve Wenner-Gren. Churchill advised that the trip 'would not be in the public interest nor indeed in your own at the present time' and that Wenner-Gren was 'according to the reports I have received, regarded as a pro-German international financier, with strong leanings towards appeasement and suspected of being in communication with the enemy.'[1]

One of the consequences of the *Liberty* article was that the FBI, under orders from Adolf Berle, Assistant Secretary of State for Latin American Affairs, and Franklin Roosevelt, now put the couple under surveillance whenever they were in the United States. On 16 April, agent Percy Foxworth sent a memo to Hoover that 'this request was predicated upon information which we have had in the past concerning these people'.[2] At the same time Roosevelt wanted agents on *Southern Cross*, because 'it was easily possible that the Wennergren (*sic*) yacht might have evidence of suspicious activities

[1] Churchill to the Duke, 17 March 1941, CO 967/125, TNA, and CHAR 20/31A, Churchill College Archives.
[2] P.E. Foxworth to Hoover, 16 April 1941, FBI file HQ 65-31113.

on board.' He wanted 'greater energy . . . in covering the activities and connections of Mr Axel Wennergren.'[3]

On 18 April, the Windsors arrived in Miami and were driven to Palm Beach, where they were staying at the Everglades Club. The ostensible purpose of their visit was to see Sir Edward Peacock, the Canadian financial adviser who had helped negotiate the Abdication Settlement and was now in the United States as head of the British Purchasing Commission, to discuss their financial affairs – but much of their time was spent playing golf and shopping.

It did not go down well with the locals. An intercepted letter was passed to the Colonial Office. 'What do you think of the very precious Duke and Duchess of Windsor charging up to thirty thousand dollars' worth of knick knacks during their brief stay in Miami, Florida,' wrote M.L. Smith of Encino, California to Mrs Begg in Aberdeen. 'The nerve of them leaving those shopkeepers holding the bag, because dear Edward was unable to take any money out of the Bahamas because of wartime restrictions. Now, these various shopkeepers can only hope that they will be paid when this war is over.'[4]

The FBI had recruited two informers from the Windsors' entourage – Alastair 'Ali' Mackintosh and William Rhinelander Stewart. Mackintosh was a former equerry to the Royal Family, whom the Duke had known for many years. His first marriage had been to the silent screen star Constance Talmadge, when Rhinelander Stewart, another golfing partner of the Duke, had been best man.

Rhinelander told the FBI that 'there was current rumour and gossip in Nassau to the effect that when Hitler defeated England, he would then install the Duke of Windsor as the King' and that the Duke:

> was so embittered against what he thought was the raw deal his people had given to her that such a change might be brought about . . . He also stated he was told that at a dinner at the Government House where the Duke and Duchess were piped in, after being seated the Duchess made some remark to a dinner guest and then turned to the piper and made the statement, 'You can also report that to Downing Street,' which indicated to everyone present that they thought the piper was some kind of a spy for England. Stewart states that the Duke looks upon Nassau as a sort of Elba for himself and that undoubtedly he does have some personal political aspirations.[5]

On 2 May, the FBI agent wrote again to Hoover, claiming that Robert Palmer Huntington, the architect and tennis champion, 'had proof that Goring (*sic*) and the Duke of Windsor had entered into some sort of an agreement, which in substance was to the effect that, after Germany won the war, Goring, through control of the army, was going to overthrow Hitler and then he would install the Duke of Windsor as the King of England.'[6]

Another FBI source, whose name is redacted, told Foxworth 'that her information came from Allen MacIntosh (*sic*) and, 'there was no doubt whatever but that the Duchess of Windsor had had an affair with Ribbentrop, and that of course she had an intense hate for the English since they had kicked them out of England.'[7]

[5] P.E. Foxworth to J. Edgar Hoover, 21 April 1941, FBI file HQ 65-31113.

[6] Foxworth to Hoover, 2 May 1941, FBI file HQ 65-31113.

[7] *Ibid.*

There continued to be numerous reports of the outspoken political views and extravagant spending of the Windsors from postal censorship interceptions. In April, Robert Brand, the head of the British Food Mission to the United States, relayed to the Foreign Office a conversation that he had had with a recent visitor to the Bahamas, Bob Windmill, 'who said the Duke had told him, "It was an absolute tragedy if your country came into the war. The only thing to do is to bring it to an end as soon as possible."'[8]

In May, a letter was forwarded to Churchill, written by the Wall Street stockbroker Frazier Jelke, who had just spent three months in Nassau and had dined at Government House several times, 'amazed . . . to be told by each of them personally and separately that they were opposed to America entering the war, as it was too late to do any good.' The Duke had told him, 'I have always been a great realist and it is too late for America to save Democracy in Europe. She had better save it in America for herself.'[9]

Postal censorship had already picked up a similar letter:

I have talked with a man Jelke this afternoon, lately back from the Bahamas. He met Wenner-Gren and dined with him on his yacht several times with the Windsors . . . Jelke had the feeling that W-G probably has some channel of communication with the higher German authorities. The British Government has apparently forbidden the Windsors to frequent his yacht anymore . . . Several nights later the Duchess told Jelke that if the US entered the war, this country would go down in history

---

[8] Robert Brand to Foreign Office, 7 April 1941, FO 1093/23, TNA.

[9] Reginald Baxter to Churchill, 27 May 1941 of letter of 17 April, CHAR 20/31A/68–70, Churchill College Archives, and CO 967/125, TNA.

as the greatest sucker of all times. Jelke had the impression that they both admire Hitler.[10]

In April a letter from Lady Lawford in Palm Beach to a Mrs Darlington was intercepted after their most recent American trip:

> The Windsors were here for a week . . . they had maids, valets, secretaries, majordomos, etc etc. Special cars, planes and no one knows how much it must have cost. She bought up most of the swank shops – antique furniture, jewellery etc and the British out here almost penniless, it has made everyone very bitter – even their dogs came and had a special vet to attend them. They spent like drunken sailors – the Windsors were given each a 5000-dollar car by a very rich American – one of the Woolworth family.[11]

The following month Sir David Montagu Douglas Scott, an under-secretary at the Foreign Office, exasperated by the *Liberty* article and various reports on the Windsors' activities, minuted:

> The Duke of Windsor is notoriously pro-Nazi. He is also a heavy drinker and what few wits he had have wilted. He shd of course never have received a post like this, where despite his intellectual insignificance, he is capable of much harm as is now clear. I propose that he shd now be told of the harm that he has done, and strictly prohibited from giving any further

---

[10] Norman Whitehouse to 'Darling', 12 April 1941, FO 1093/23, TNA. A copy of Jelke's letter to Baxter dated 7 April is at FO 371/26191. Brand has added a note: 'We have had this story from other source.'

[11] RA PS/PSO/GVI/C/042A/296.

interviews at all without having his texts vetted and authorised at home. This prohibition should be made public.[12]

The Windsors had become increasingly concerned about the safety
of their French properties and paying the caretaker staff. In April
1941, Churchill personally, through the American ambassador in
Paris, William Bullitt, arranged for the 55,000 francs in back rent
on the Paris property to be paid together with 10,000 francs insurance and 15,000 francs due for the strongroom space they rented
at the Banque de France, though the bank was under the control
of Hitler.[13] According to Charles Higham, 'Bedaux acted as a go-
between in the arrangements, since he was close to Bullitt and Nazi
Ambassador Otto Abetz.'[14]

Bedaux's activities continued to be monitored. In April, an MI6
officer in Lisbon had obtained a note from a Madame Dubonnet,
who had 'got it direct from Mrs Bedaux'.[15] The note revealed that
'German authorities recently approached M Bedaux and asked him
to ask the Duke of Windsor whether he would be King of England
in the event of a German victory. M Bedaux refused to do so, as he
was no longer friends with the Duke of Windsor.'[16]

The British and Americans meanwhile also kept watch on Wenner-
Grens. After the Duke 'submitted for approval an ambitious

[12] FO 371/26191, TNA.

[13] Michael Pye, p. 63, 70032L, No. X1937/188/503. Charles Higham, *Mrs
Simpson*, p. 369, quotes Churchill's instruction in full. In August the strongroom
was broken into by the Germans, but it is unclear if anything of the Windsors
was removed. Duke of Windsor to George Allen, 10 August 1941, CO 967/125,
TNA. Further details of the property in Paris can be found in the Chief Clerk's
file, FO 366, 1160, TNA.

[14] Charles Higham, *Trading with the Enemy* (Delacorte, 1983), p. 183.

[15] RA PS/PSO/GVI/C/042A/299–300.

[16] Alan Lascelles to Alec Hardinge, 7 May 1941, RA PS/PSO/GVI/
C/042A/299–300.

proposal for social and agricultural development on the island of Grand Bahamas by Axel Wennergren (*sic*), which would involve transfer to Wennergren of large tracts of land', the Foreign Office contacted Washington seeking views, given the site for the US base in the Bahamas had not yet been chosen. The answer was swift and clear: 'Admiralty and MI5 have been consulted and are not inclined to favour grant to person named on account of his somewhat doubtful political proclivities and strategic position of island.'[17]

In the summer of 1941, the Windsors expressed a desire to visit the Duke's ranch in Canada. Delicate negotiations went on to avoid the Duke crossing with his brother, the Duke of Kent, who was due to visit in September, and to arrange a route that avoided Ottawa, where he might have to be entertained by the Governor General, his uncle, Lord Athlone. There was, also, still the concern of encouraging Isolationists at a time when Britain was anxious to bring America into the war.

At the end of September 1941, the couple flew to Miami – Wallis's eyes bandaged because of her fear of flying – where they inspected 300 RAF cadets training with Pan-American instructors before taking a train to Washington, where there was a reception at the National Press Club and they stayed at the White House. From Washington they continued by train, lent by a friend, the railway magnate Robert Young, through Chicago to the Alberta ranch, where they spent the first week of October.

The Duke had bought the one-storey building during his first visit to Canada in 1919 and had paid short visits in the summers of 1923, 1924 and 1927. He was interested in stock breeding and wanted to introduce practices from the Duchy of Cornwall lands.

[17] Foreign Office to Washington, 15 May 1941, CO 967/125, TNA.

By 1930 he had spent almost $250,000 on it and with the help of W.L. Carlyle, a professor of agriculture, built the finest breeding herd in Canada, but he had not made money and had contemplated selling it several times.

In 1932, the Canadians had gifted him several thousand adjacent acres of Crown land and rights to their mineral resources but, after the Abdication, he realised it would be difficult to return to what was British territory. In 1938, the Duke had sold off the cattle herd but the ranch continued to lose money – $3,000 in 1939 – and attempts to sell it during the early months of the war had come to nothing. At the end of 1940, the American polar explorer Lincoln Ellsworth had offered him $40,000, and the Duke was tempted to accept, but then drilling for oil began in the area. It was this interest that had prompted the 1941 visit.

The Windsors returned via Washington, where a lunch for twenty-two had to be cancelled at the last minute, because the Duchess preferred to send out for food and the Duke to eat fruit in his bedroom, and Dorothy Halifax, wife of the British ambassador Lord Halifax, was 'outraged to be presented with a bill for £7.10 for hire of a lorry to take their luggage to and from station – it did seem a little unnecessary for a 24-hour visit.'[18]

Against advice, the couple stayed at the Waldorf Towers in New York, where they took a whole floor. They saw doctors, lawyers and friends, shopped, saw some shows and ate out, but they also made time for public duties. The Duke saw Mayor LaGuardia to discuss urban housing conditions, whilst the Duchess visited a centre for unmarried mothers and babies. They reviewed mobile hospital units of the British-American Ambulance Corps, lunched with the British War Relief Society, inspected relief agencies, housing projects and armaments factories, and played darts with sailors at

[18] de Courcy, p. 355.

the British Merchant Seamen's Club. Everywhere they went, they attracted large crowds, 'who interfered with traffic, tossed tickertape and shreds of phone books and must inevitably have recalled to the Duke his wild reception here as Prince of Wales.'[19]

At Baltimore, the couple were met at the little station of Timonium in the Dularey Valley by a crowd of 5,000, including General Warfield, Uncle Harry, the nearest relation on Wallis's father's side, and they stayed with him at his 400-acre farmhouse, where Wallis had often stayed as a child. At the official reception, there were crowds of a quarter of a million as they drove with the Mayor in open cars and a police escort from City Hall to the Baltimore Country Club, where 800 people had been invited to meet them. The visit was taking on aspects of a Royal Tour.

They inspected British war relief projects, lunched with the Governor of Maryland and visited two camps of Civilian Conservation Corps. They remained on message in support of the British war effort, but attracted criticism for not returning to the Bahamas, where many properties lived in by Black people had recently been destroyed in a hurricane.

On 14 October, the Duke travelled to Washington to see Lord Halifax, who wrote to Churchill:

> His visit seems to have gone off all right, and not attracted too much publicity, and on the whole the Press, with the exception of one or two rags, have behaved all right. I had a long talk to him a few days ago, in which he opened his heart and talked quite freely. He feels pretty bitter about being marooned in the Bahamas, which he says is a foul climate, and where there is nobody except casual American visitors whom he can

[19] *New York Times*, 23 October 1941.

see anything of as a friend. I must say it certainly sounds pretty grim.[20]

The Windsors inspected the automobile plants of Chrysler in Detroit, had tea with Henry Ford – which led to Ford, an Isolationist, being prepared to supply arms to the Allies – and saw James D. Mooney at General Motors.

Meanwhile the FBI were building their file on the couple. At the end of September, they had interviewed the Reverend Dom Odo, a Benedictine monk, about a suspected Gestapo agent, operating under cover of being a priest. Prior to entering the order, Father Odo had been Duke Carl Alexander of Württemberg, a cousin of Queen Mary, and 'related that he knows Queen Mary and her brother, the Earl of Athlone, the present Governor General of Canada, very well.'

Württemberg had come to America in 1940 from Portugal. Fleeing the Nazi regime in 1934, he had settled in Switzerland where, with financial assistance from Queen Mary, he had set up an organisation called Catholic Help for Refugees to resettle Jews.[21]

The FBI agent had 'casually inquired whether Father Odo had seen the Duke and Duchess of Windsor during their recent visit to Washington', to be told that he had not, but that he had previously met the Duchess of Windsor on numerous occasions and 'that Von Ribbentrop, while in England, sent the then Wallis Simpson seventeen carnations every day. The seventeen supposedly represented the number of times they had slept together.'[22]

---

[20] Halifax to Churchill, 19 October 1941, CHAR 20/31B/161–2, Churchill College Archives.

[21] His file, 'Alien Case File for Charles Württemberg', A4540117, can be found in RG566, National Archives at Kansas City. The Zurich Police had told the State Department that he might be a Nazi agent, but there is no evidence to support that. Lord Halifax was one of his supporters.

[22] Memo, 29 September 1941, FBI file HQ 65-31113.

Further evidence was being gathered of the couple's sympa-thies. In a naval intelligence report from a recent Washington conference, Major Hayne Boyden, a Marine Corps naval and air attaché seconded to George Messersmith in Cuba, reported to both Adolf Berle and J. Edgar Hoover that the German Legation claimed the Duke:

> as no enemy of Germany. (He was) considered to be the only Englishman with whom Hitler would negotiate any peace terms, the logical director of England's destiny after the war. Hitler well knows that Edward at present cannot work in a manner that would appear to be against his country and he does not urge it (a reliable informant on close terms with a Nazi agent reported). But when the proper moment arrives he will be the only one person capable of directing the destiny of England.[23]

As a result of the *Liberty* article, the British authorities recog-nised that the Windsors needed a press spokesman to steer them clear of controversy. An old friend of theirs, Colin Davidson, was approached, but would do so only if promoted from Major to Lieu-tenant-General and, eventually, René MacColl, head of press and radio at the British Information Service, was appointed solely for the US part of the visit, with instructions that 'the Duke must say as little as possible, must hold no press conferences, give no interviews, make no statements.'[24]

He had pressed the Duke on whether he still advocated a nego-tiated peace. No, he was told, that was only during the Phoney

---

[23] Report, 14 October 1941, Higham, *Mrs Simpson*, p. 377. Boyden retired as a Brigadier General.

[24] René MacColl, *Deadline and Dateline* (Oldbourne Press, 1956), p. 122.

War 'before Hitler lost his head'. MacColl felt reassured until the next morning when the Duke approached him. 'I've been thinking about the question about negotiated peace,' Windsor said. 'I've been talking to the Duchess. I think we'll play that one by ear.'[25]

In the end, the visit had been carefully controlled with set speeches and few interviews. When she had been interviewed, Wallis had claimed, 'I'm afraid people credit me with much more interest in clothes than I really have,' adding, 'I care far more about the poor little children of Nassau. It's them, not clothes, I intend to shop for. I want to buy them all Christmas presents.'[26] Her statements were rather contradicted by the numerous packages picked up *en route* from the designer Mainbocher and from Bergdorf Goodman.

Though some press coverage had been favourable, a running media theme was the extent of the Windsors' luggage – estimated to be up to seventy-three pieces and often having to be left in hotel corridors – and questions about how they funded their spending, given currency restrictions. On 18 November, Sir Ronald Campbell sent a 'Personal and Secret' telegram to the Foreign Office. It was a request from the Secretary of the Treasury, Henry Morgenthau, to 'let him know where the Duke and Duchess of Windsor got the dollars which they spent during their visit to this country', because there had 'been a certain amount of criticism in the press in regard to the sums spent on clothes etc. in New York.'[27]

Three weeks later Halifax, in a 'Most Secret' telegram to the Foreign Office, reported 'So far as I can ascertain, the only banking accounts in the United States in the name of the Duke or Duchess of Windsor are two accounts with Chase Bank in the name of the Duchess. One account covers securities to the value of 9,000

[25] Pye, p. 155.

[26] MacColl, p. 132, quoting Helen Worden in *New York World-Telegram*.

[27] Ronald Campbell to Foreign Office, 18 November 1941, FO 954/33A/206, TNA.

dollars, while the other account had a credit balance of 29,931 dollars on 14 June this year as compared with a balance of 1,197 dollars on the same date last year.'[28] The question everyone was asking was where this money was coming from.

According to Charles Higham, 'The surrounding documents are missing from Lord Avon's files at the Public Record Office in London, but it is clear from this memorandum that the gravest suspicions had yet again been aroused of the Windsors' improper use of currency against all the restrictions in force at the time. Documents located in the National Archive in Washington, DC indicate that the couple had obtained even more black market currency through Wenner-Gren.'[29]

A British Press Service Report was blunt: 'The general impression created was that of a rich and carefree couple, travelling with all the pre-war accoutrement of royalty, and with no thought either of the suffering of their own people or of the fact that the world is at war.'[30]

On 24 November, in light of the media coverage, a Labour MP, Alexander Sloan, asked a Parliamentary Question drawing attention to 'the ostentatious display of jewellery and finery at a period when the people of this country are strictly rationed' and suggesting the couple be 'recalled since their visit is evidently doing a certain amount of harm and no good.'[31]

Churchill telegrammed the Duke, expressing regret at the personal attacks.[32] The Duke was not happy with the official response. 'Mr Hall's lame reply did not silence Sloan, and unless I have from

[28] Halifax to Foreign Office, 4 December 1941, FO954/33A/207 and FO 371/26191, TNA. The sums today would be $164K, $550K and $21K.

[29] Higham, *Mrs Simpson*, p. 379.

[30] 24 November 1941, British Press Service Report, 789/1941, NARA.

[31] 24 November 1941, Hansard, CHAR 31B/174, Churchill College Archives.

[32] Churchill to the Duke, 28 November 1941, CHAR 20/45/132, Churchill College Archives.

this distance taken an exaggerated view of the importance of this incident, I wonder if it should be left this way?'[33]

Events were to overtake the criticisms. On 7 December, the Japanese attacked Pearl Harbor and America finally came into the war.[34] Within a week, Wenner-Gren, long suspected of sheltering U-boats on Hog Island, was on the official US economic blacklist. Shangri-La was closed, the staff cut from thirty to seven, the Bank of the Bahamas, in which the Windsors had an interest, was closed, and the exotic birds sold or given away. A search of the property found none of the supposed landing strips or submarine pens.

America's entry into the war may have silenced the Windsors' defeatist sentiments, but fresh controversy was now to follow them.

[33] Duke of Windsor to Lord Moyne, 27 November 1941, FO 967/125, TNA.

[34] Wenner-Gren had supposedly been on his way in *Southern Cross* to take the Windsors to Mexico days before war was declared. *Washington Times Herald*, 31 January 1942, in FBI file 94-8-350-66 and intercepted letter of 8 December 1941. 'He is going to return to the Bahama Isles and will bring back the Duke and Duchess of Windsor, who are thinking of buying a villa and settling down here.' Report, 16 March 1942, FO 837/858, TNA.

CHAPTER 13

Governor

The entry of America into the war ended all talk of a negotiated peace and made protection of the Duke ever more important. At the end of March 1941, Montgomery Hyde, during his security inspection of the Bahamas, had been appalled that there were no proper passport checks, security files were kept in the Governor's private office rather than the Colonial Secretariat, defence was limited to thirty 'coastal watchers', and there were only two guns larger than machine guns.

Now a year later, Churchill, remembering Operation Willi, provided a Personal Minute for the Chiefs of Staff Committee. 'The danger is of a kidnapping party from a submarine. The Germans would be very glad to get hold of the Duke and use him for their own purposes. In my opinion continued protection against an attack by 50 men <u>during darkness</u> should be provided. Very considerable issues are involved.'[1] There was also a concern that occupation of the islands could provide a base for attacks against the United States.

The Americans agreed to set up air and sea reconnaissance stations in New Providence and a string of intelligence posts throughout the islands, and a squadron of bombers and fighters were put on call in Florida. In March, a company of Cameron Highlanders arrived

---

[1] Churchill to COS Committee, 28 February 1942, CHAR 20/63, Churchill College Archives.

for the defence of Nassau and Government House, reinforcing the existing protection of an armed police guard of four NCOs and twelve men.

At the end of April 1942, after long, secret negotiations between London, Washington and Nassau, in which the Duke had played an active part, it was announced a major base would be constructed under Lend-Lease by the Americans on New Providence using local labour. The Bahamas were now to be a staging post for transport command for planes built in California *en route* to service in North Africa, a school of operational training for the RAF, and a base for ocean patrol and air-sea rescue work during the anti-submarine campaign in the Caribbean and West Atlantic. The building programme came to be called 'The Project'. The security and economic problems would be sorted in one go.

The Duke had embarked on his governorship with ambitious plans for reform. John Dye, the American consul in Nassau, thought his opening of the Legislature in October 1940 'one of the most sensible and business like that had been delivered by a local Governor for many years . . . It may be true that he and his Duchess were sent out here to get rid of them, so to speak, but he is taking his job seriously and is showing a keen interest in the welfare of the Bahamas.'[2]

The new Governor made clear his reformist intentions saying that he would appoint an Advisory Board to look at wages and that he wished to encourage local enterprise, improve working conditions and deal with unemployment. However, he soon ran into opposition. Technically the wartime Defence Regulations gave him dictatorial powers, but the island's government was complicated and the Governor's powers limited.

[2] 844E 001/60, NARA.

Governor

Assisting the Governor on the Executive Council was his deputy the Colonial Secretary, Leslie Heape, and the Attorney General, Eric Hallinan. ExCo, as it was more often known, set policy on issues like immigration, but it had no money raising powers. That was the prerogative of the twenty members of the lower chamber, the House of Assembly, who were elected every seven years. This was dominated by local merchants, called the Bay Street Boys, as most of their businesses were located on Bay Street in Nassau.

The Bay Street Boys were corrupt, reactionary and they ruled entirely in their own self-interest rather than for the 90 per cent Black population. As they made most of their money importing food and drink and the House of Assembly earned revenue from import duties, there was no incentive to improve local agriculture. The Bay Street Boys kept non-whites out of public life – they were not even admitted to any of the major hotels – and refused to provide funds for public secondary education, or anything that might improve their social or economic mobility.

'In brief, this body represents nobody but the "merchant princes" of Nassau, is selected in a manner reminiscent of the worst excesses of the unreformed Parliamentary system of this country in the eighteenth century, and in performance shows itself to be irresponsible, crass or malignant,' ran one Colonial Office report about the parliament shortly before the Duke's arrival.

'As things stand, however, the constitution of the Bahamas is more or less in the form in which it was as originally created and we would only have an opportunity to alter it in the event of the House taking some step which was a danger to the external security of the Empire, or in the event of the Colony becoming bankrupt. Neither of these eventualities seem likely at the moment . . .'[3]

---

[3] Monson memo, 12 May 1940, CO 23/712, TNA.

The Duke's predecessor, Sir Charles Dundas, had tried to stimulate agriculture in the Outer Islands by encouraging large farming estates run by farmers from Europe and America, and to weaken the power of the Bay Street Boys by trying to introduce income tax and secret voting, but he had been thwarted.

The advice from the Bay Street Boys to the Duke was clear:

> He will learn . . . that the best way to govern the Bahamas is not to govern the Bahamas at all. If he sticks to golf, he will be a good Governor and they'll put up statues to him. But if he tries to carry out reforms or make any serious decisions or help the niggers, he will just stir up trouble and make himself unpopular.[4]

Wallis had also thrown herself into war work, giving her, hitherto, rather aimless life some purpose. She was automatically President of the Red Cross and of the 'Daughters of the British Empire' and she helped with the YMCA, and the Nassau Garden Club. She arranged for locals to be taught the basics of hygiene, diet and nursing, promoted courses in domestic service and started a class in needlepoint. On her trips to the United States, she lobbied department stores to stock Bahamian jewellery and weaving.

Shocked by the high infant-mortality rate amongst the non-white population, she set up a clinic for the children of mothers with syphilis. She worked closely with Alice Hill Jones, a local Black nurse trying to lower infant-mortality rates, providing a car to save her travelling to outlying areas by public transport. Here, every Wednesday afternoon, the Governor's wife worked, weighing and washing babies, changing diapers, feeding them and rocking them

---

[4] Geoffrey Bocca, *The Life and Death of Harry Oakes* (Weidenfeld, 1959), p. 89.

to sleep. When the House of Assembly refused to grant funds, the Duke signed over income from one of his charitable trusts.

By September 1942, the airbases were completed and there was growing unemployment. The Duke then arranged for 5,000 Bahamians to work in the US, mainly Florida, as agricultural labourers. The new initiative, nicknamed 'The Contract', after the document they had to sign, lasted six to nine months and required the men to remit 25 per cent of their earnings home. Not only did it help the United States, which was short of labour, but it provided employment and taught agricultural skills that the Bahamians were able to use on their return. By July 1944, almost 6,000 people, a twelfth of the population, had been involved in 'The Contract'.

Many of the Duke's attempts to diversify the economy, however, continued to be scuppered, with the House rejecting his plans for a public works programme, income tax, laws on shop workers' hours, trade union rights and workmen's compensation. He was constantly frustrated in his attempts to raise wages in line with the cost of living, which had risen 30 per cent during the war.

Nevertheless, he did set up an Economic Investigation Committee – the first official body in the Bahamas on which non-white men were represented substantially – to develop the islands. When it could not agree on a chairman, he appointed himself to the role. The result was the equivalent of F.D. Roosevelt's Civilian Conservation camps, which came to be known as the Windsor Training Farms.

But an underlying tension with his economic initiatives was Whitehall's lack of confidence in his abilities and concern that he stray into politically contentious areas. In May 1942, the Secretary of State for the Colonies, Lord Cranborne, wrote to Churchill, irritated because Windsor wanted to take a trade delegation to

Washington, arguing that 'the subjects for discussion are of too trivial a nature to justify his personal participation as Head of the delegation, and that especially in the matter of contracts such procedure would be embarrassing to the State Department and might cause resentment.'[5]

More importantly, doubts also remained about his loyalties. In February 1942, an American Naval Intelligence Officer, Commander C.A. Perkins, had reported to US Naval Intelligence that there was reason to believe 'considerable Nazi funds have, during the past year, been cleared through the Bahamas to Mexico', and that the Duke of Windsor may be an 'important Nazi agent'.[6]

According to Perkins, Wenner-Gren had made huge investments in Peru, including building a harbour at Chimbote Bay, and in Mexico, where he was involved in highway construction and setting up an 'Export Control Board'. There were press reports that the Windsors planned to visit the Duke's cousin, ex-King Carol of Romania, who lived in Mexico. 'Carol's consort, as well as the society group at this resort, constantly have been reported pro-Nazi,' Perkins wrote. 'Such associations indicate that there may be something to the reports received by this office that the subject (Duke of Windsor) is pro-Nazi.'[7]

Wallace B. Phillips at the Washington Office of Naval Intelligence replied, accepting that the Duchess was 'bitterly anti-British', that Wenner-Gren was 'up to no good in Mexico' and that the

---

[5] Cranborne to Churchill, 20 May 1942, CHAR 20/63, Churchill College Archives.

[6] Letter from Commander Perkins to US Naval Intelligence, Washington, 11 February 1942. NND 883021/SIS Intelligence Reports/29 November 1941–31 March 1942, NARA.

[7] Letter from Commander Perkins to US Naval Intelligence, Washington, 11 February 1942. NND 883021/SIS Intelligence Reports/29 November 1941–31 March 1942, NARA. In fact, Carol was pro-British and his mistress Magda Lupescu was Jewish.

Duke's former equerry, Frank Budd, now living in Mexico, required investigation. 'We shall have to take some steps to determine his relationships both to the duke as well as to the Nazis.'[8]

* * *

In April 1942, unbeknownst to the Duke, the Duchess wrote to Queen Mary: 'It has always been a source of sorrow and regret to me that I have been the cause of any separation that exists between Mother and Son and I can't help feel that there must be moments, however fleeting they may be, when you wonder how David is.'[9] She suggested that the Queen receive the departing Bishop of Nassau, John Dauglish, who 'can tell you if all the things David gave up are replaced to him in another way and the little details of his daily life, his job, etc., the story of his flight from France leaving all his possessions behind.'[10]

Queen Mary did see Dauglish, a former navy chaplain, and was interested in her son's doings but, when he talked about the Duchess, 'He met with a stone wall of disinterest.' Her only reaction was in a letter to the Duke a few weeks later, in which she added, 'I send a kind message to your wife.'[11]

The family remained suspicious of Wallis's intentions, with the King writing to his mother, 'I wonder what is the real motive behind her having written . . . I must say I do feel a bit suspicious of it!!!'

---

[8] Wallace B. Phillips to C.A. Perkins, 18 February 1942, NND 883021/SIS Intelligence Reports/29 November 1941–31 March 1942, NARA.

[9] *Heart*, p. 356.

[10] *Heart*, p. 356.

[11] *Heart*, p. 356. According to Peter Coats, the Duchess told him that after she wrote to Queen Mary, she received a reply with a brooch. 'At the time of your marriage my heart was too full to think of wedding presents, but I hope that you will accept this now. It belonged to Charles I.' Peter Coats, *Of Generals and Gardens* (Weidenfeld & Nicolson, 1976), p. 273.

adding he'd just seen the prime minister, who had received a letter from the Duke asking for a change of post. 'A coincidence!!'[12]

The Duke was indeed anxious to be moved elsewhere. After a visit from Lord Beaverbrook, he wrote to Churchill in April, '(1) that I cannot contemplate remaining in the Bahamas as Governor for the duration of the war and (2) that I feel confident that I could serve my Country best in some appointment in America, or failing that, in Canada.'[13] The letter was shared with the King, but there were no slots for him.

The suggestion of a roving ambassadorship in Latin America was also dismissed. 'I fear I cannot report to you any advantage in a visit by the Duke of Windsor to South America at this time. It would certainly arouse suspicions in Washington,' minuted Anthony Eden to Churchill, adding that the Duke did not have sufficient 'authority and first-hand knowledge'.[14]

The South African prime minister, Jan Smuts, asked for his views on the offer of the Governorship of Southern Rhodesia, argued against such an appointment on the grounds of the strong republican sympathies in neighbouring South Africa and concerns about the Duke's 'attention and judgement'.[15]

There were discussions about federating the British West Indies – the printed index to the Foreign Office Political Department for 1942 has a reference under the Duke's name of 'Proposed

[12] George VI to Queen Mary, 5 May 1942, RA GV CC 13/12, quoted Ziegler, p. 487.

[13] The Duke to Churchill, 18 April 1942, CHAR 20/63, Churchill College Archives, and CO 967/125, TNA and RA EDW/PRIV/MAIN/A/5040.

[14] Eden to Churchill, 14 May 1942, CHAR 20/63, Churchill College Archives, and FO954/33A/210, TNA.

[15] Smuts to Churchill, 25 May 1942, CHAR 20/63, Churchill College Archives.

Governor-Generalship of British West Indies if raised to Dominion status' – but there was no federation.[16]

On Monday 1 June 1942, the Duke arrived in Washington, partly on a private visit to sort out his business affairs and partly to discuss defence and trade matters. No sooner had he arrived than he received news of demonstrations at the building of the new airbase. What had merely been a strike and march to the Colonial Secretariat, to lobby for an increase in the daily rate of pay, had quickly escalated into something more threatening.

The acting governor, Leslie Heape, and the commissioner of police, Reggie Erskine-Lindop, were slow to respond, by which time several of the demonstrators, many drunk, began looting in Bay Street. Several people were killed and fifty were injured. Some of the long-standing grievances, concerning poverty and racial prejudice, were beginning to come to the surface.

The Duke returned immediately, accompanied by a hundred US Marines sent by Roosevelt, concerned about the security of the airbases. A public emergency was declared and order restored. 'This morning about 1500 workers have returned to work, representing about sixty per cent of workers previously employed,' wrote the Duke to the Colonial Office on 6 June, 'but work cannot yet be said to be normal and workers are being guarded by American soldiers.'[17]

Concerned about the interruption of work on the military project and worried that the Americans might pull out of the project, he immediately began addressing the men's grievances, which included problems with transport for the eight-mile journey from Nassau to the building site, food at lunchtime, the timing of wage payments, and differential pay rates for Americans and local workers.

[16] Knowledge Management Department, FCO to author, 11 November 2020.
[17] Duke of Windsor to Colonial Office, 6 June 1942, FO 371/30644, TNA.

On 8 June, he broadcast to the island, promising free lunches, to raise wages by one shilling a day, and an independent enquiry by a retired colonial judge, Alison Russell. Not only did the Duke face the anger of the Bay Street Boys, who felt law and order had broken down to their detriment, but Whitehall was aghast that an agreement that the Americans employ local labour at the local going rate, rather than the rate paid for imported labour, might be changed. The Duke now had critics on all sides.

The crisis was, however, the making of him. 'The feature which now stands out above all the others is the fact that it was eventually resolved by the dominating personality of one man, His Royal Highness the Governor,' reported the *Nassau Tribune*. 'HRH approached the gigantic problem calmly and efficiently ... he handled a delicate situation with tact and dignity, resolution and authority.'[18]

The Duke resumed his American trip, having a three-hour lunch with Roosevelt on 15 June and then seeing Churchill on 23 June, but Wallis's activities in New York were causing concern at the Colonial Office. It is difficult to establish exactly what happened, as many of the documents are redacted or have been retained, but Wallis appears to have had a series of meetings with Gaston Henry-Hay, until November 1941 the Vichy ambassador to America, and a man closely monitored by the FBI, not least because Nazi agents operated from his embassy.

'As our source in question is a particularly delicate and secret one, may I ask that this letter should be seen by the minimum possible number of people,' wrote Clifford Thornley to the Colonial Office in one of the heavily redacted reports.[19] One of them was the prime minister himself.

---

[18] *Nassau Tribune*, 9 June 1942.

[19] Clifford Thornley report, 9 July 1942, FO 1093/24, TNA.

The Duke was now back on the islands and faced a new challenge – a complete block of buildings between Bay and George Streets had been burnt down, arousing suspicions of further civil unrest. It turned out to be a storekeeper setting his own property on fire to collect the insurance but, again, the Governor earned new respect when he was seen to be personally taking charge of operations.

However, in spite of improved popularity ratings, the Duke remained bored and unhappy with his posting. The writer Patrick Skene Catling, then an eighteen-year-old Pilot Officer, had an unexpected encounter on the golf course:

> The Duke, as usual by tea-time, was drunk. Not very drunk, not yet arrogant and clumsy, but sufficiently soft in the head to have driven his Cadillac convertible along the fairways of Nassau's premier golf club. This was before electric buggies. Evidently, he was not in the mood for long walks between shots; and, after all, he was the Governor . . . He had given me a friendly wave as he drove the car past me on the sixteenth fairway. He finished his game quickly and was well ahead of me in the bar. In the early stages of drinking, he had a charmingly whimsical, some said boyish, slightly tilted smile. Free for the afternoon from the Duchess's surveillance, he was able to indulge in playful informality.[20]

The Duke, dressed in a lime-green shirt and shocking pink doeskin trousers, offered Catling a drink. 'After more than one drink, he became quite chatty, asking some of the questions that strangers ask in casual barroom encounters,' and then suggested 'let's go for a ride.'[21] They headed 'Over the Hill' to the Black ghetto. 'Part-way

[20] Patrick Skene Catling, *Better Than Working* (Liberties Press, 2004), p. 1.
[21] Catling, p. 3.

down the far side of the hill, I was surprised when the Duke produced an Army cap with the scarlet band of superior rank and jammed it jauntily on his well-groomed fair head.'[22]

Turning off the main road, they drove 'along a narrow, unpaved road with a row of dilapidated wooden shacks on each side, and announced his arrival with long blasts on the horn.'[23] Fifteen small boys in shorts ran out carrying rifles. The Duke stood up in the car, his expression stern and 'commanded the boys, in a high-pitched, military shout, to "Fall in"', which they duly did. He 'proceeded to drill them in accordance with the protocol of the Brigade of Guards'.[24] He then tossed them some silver coins. 'How His Excellency laughed! I thought he was an awful shit and a fool, but I was grateful to him, and I am still, for demonstrating so vividly that warfare is absurd.'[25]

* * *

The death of his younger brother, George, Duke of Kent, whom he had not seen since 1937, in an air crash on 25 August, only further brought home the Duke's separation from his family. At the memorial service in Nassau's cathedral, he broke down in tears and a period of depression followed. 'My thoughts go out to you, who are so far away from us all, knowing how devoted you were to him, and how kind you were to him in a difficult moment in his all too short life, kindness I for one shall never forget; he always remembered it, for he was very fond of you,' wrote Queen Mary to him on 31 August. 'I hope you will write often to me now, as you used

---

[22] Catling, p. 4.
[23] Catling, p. 4.
[24] Catling, p. 5.
[25] Catling, p. 5.

Left: The Duke with French troops during the Phoney War, 2 November 1939.

© AP/Shutterstock

Left: : The Duke and Duchess of Windsor arriving at Madrid Airport on 25 July 1940. © Pictorial Press Ltd/ Alamy Stock Photo

Right: The Duke as a Major General, 1940.

© Granger Historical Picture Archive/Alamy Stock Photo

Right: The 18th-century home outside Lisbon of Ricardo Espírito Santo Silva where the Windsors stayed in July 1940.

Below: The Windsors and Santo Silvas in the garden of the house.

© *Centro de História BES, courtesy of the Neill Lochery Photographic Archive*

Above left: Walter Schellenberg, the German intelligence officer, sent by Ribbentrop to bribe or kidnap the Duke to persuade him to become a British Pétain. © *Bettmann/Getty Images*

Above right: Miguel Primo de Rivera, the first 'confidential emissary' and a pre-war friend of the Windsors. © *Photo 12/Alamy Stock Photo*

Below left: Juan Beigbeder, the pro-British Spanish Foreign Minister who thought the Duke might help to end the Second World War. © *Universal History Archive/Getty Images*

Below right: Ángel Alcázar de Velasco, an Abwehr agent and the second emissary.

© *L'immagine appartiene ai rispettivi proprietary*

Above: Government House, Bahamas, which the Windsors requested be redecorated as soon as they arrived. © *Michael Ochs Archives/Getty Images*

Below: The Duke inspecting naval ratings. © *AP/Shutterstock*

Above left: Axel Wenner-Gren, the Swedish industrialist and friend of the Windsors, who was suspected of being a German agent. © *Bettmann/Getty Images*

Above right: The Windsors aboard *Southern Cross*, the yacht Wenner-Gren bought from Howard Hughes. © *Hulton Deutsch/Getty Images*

Below: *Southern Cross* on which the Windsors often cruised. © *Bettmann /Getty Images*

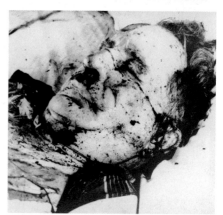

Above: The Duke with Sir Harry Oakes at a polo match, 28 December 1940.
© *Bettmann/Getty Images*

Below left: The bloody and partly burnt bed where Oakes was discovered on the morning of 8 July 1943. © *Pictorial Parade/Getty Images*

Below right: Police photo showing Oakes' battered head. © *Pictorial Parade/Getty Images*

Letf: Harold Christie, the leading real estate developer in the Bahamas, who was suspected of financial irregularities with the Duke of Windsor.
© *AP/Shutterstock*

Below: The Windsors with the Miami detective Eddie Melchen whom the Duke mysteriously asked to investigate the Oakes murder. © *AP/Shutterstock*

Right: The Duchess as President of the Red Cross, a role in which she flourished.

Below: The Duke working at his desk.

to do. Please give a kind message to your wife, she will help you to bear your sorrow.'[26]

The death had brought some thaw in family tensions. 'He was in some ways more like a son to me, and his charm and gaiety brought great happiness to York House those years he lived with me,' replied the Duke. 'Remembering how much you and I hated the last war, I can well imagine how our feelings about this one must be the same – a deep-rooted conviction that it could have been avoided.' He ended by saying he was longing to see her again, 'always hoping that maybe one day things will change and that I shall have the intense pride and pleasure of bringing Wallis to see you . . .'[27]

It was not just the isolation from his family but from the world outside. 'Although our life is a busy one, it seems cramped and isolated so far from the centres of interest and we certainly feel very much out of touch with the people who are directing the momentous events and framing the policies, which will so profoundly influence the future of mankind,' the Duke wrote to Sibyl Colefax, after she had written to him about his brother's death. 'Who knows that maybe someday we shall get a more interesting job and a better opportunity of pulling one's weight!'[28]

It was a feeling shared by Wallis, who wrote to an old friend, Edith Lindsay, 'How I long for the sight and sound of human beings – my mentality is getting very dire after over two years here and only two months leave.'[29]

---

[26] Queen Mary to the Duke of Windsor, 31 August 1942, RA DW Add 1/156, quoted Ziegler, p. 384.

[27] The Duke of Windsor to Queen Mary, 12 September 1942, RA GV EE 3, quoted Ziegler, p. 485, & RA QM/PRIV/CC9, quoted William Shawcross, *Queen Elizabeth, the Queen Mother* (Macmillan, 2009), p. 552.

[28] The Duke of Windsor to Sibyl Colefax, 8 October 1942, Folio 6, MS Eng c3272, Colefax papers, Bodleian.

[29] Duchess of Windsor to Edith Lindsay, 30 August 1942, MHS, 1772, Windsor collection, Maryland Historical Society.

By late summer, the new airbase at Windsor Field was completed and over 3,000 RAF officers and men were stationed on coastal watch duties alongside the US Army Air Force, hunting submarines, supporting convoys, and providing a vital link in the supply chain across the Atlantic. Wallis, realising the colony needed more facilities and organisations for the new troops, founded a canteen for Black members of the Bahamian Defence Force and ensured it was supplied with all it needed from playing cards and ping-pong balls to staff and girls for dances.

She persuaded Frederick Sigrist to lend the Bahamian Club as another canteen for airmen, where her afternoons were spent cooking bacon and egg to feed thousands of British RAF officers, now stationed as part of a Coastal Command training programme. 'My real talent was as a short-order cook,' she later wrote. 'I never kept track of the number of orders of bacon and eggs that I served up, but on the basis of forty an afternoon, and three hundred and sixty-five afternoons a year for nearly three years, I arrived at a rough total of about forty thousand. And that's a lot of eggs.'[30]

'No one has any idea how hard she worked,' recalls one friend from the Bahamas. 'With the Duchess, it wasn't just raising money – she did plenty of that – but she went beyond what other Governors' wives had done. She got in, rolled up her sleeves and worked. I'll never forget her returning to Government House one night. She had been away for twelve hours, first at one hospital, then a school, a clinic, a canteen. Her energy was palpable, contagious. She walked in and immediately began planning what to do the next day.'[31]

'I never worked harder in my life,' she later wrote. 'I never felt better used. I have to keep busy. I couldn't stay here if I didn't.'[32]

[30] *Heart*, p. 355.

[31] Greg King, *The Duchess of Windsor* (Aurum, 1999), p. 371, citing private information.

[32] *New York Post*, 5 June 1943.

But the hard work took its toll on her health. 'I have been having a really bad time with my old ulcer – just dragging myself around, half-doing too many things,' she wrote to a friend. 'I don't seem able to find 3 weeks off to put myself right once again ... Everything gets more difficult every day on the way of supplies, etc. – but I have nothing to really complain of except my stomach and the fact that we are left here so long.'[33]

Her involvement with child-welfare agencies fulfilled her maternal urge, which, hitherto, had had no other outlet. Every Christmas she helped organise a children's party at the airbase for which she paid personally, where the children watched Mickey Mouse movies, were given Coca-Cola, sweets, ice-cream and some pocket money. The war work had given her a new sense of purpose, having previously focused only on the Duke, his needs, their houses and entertaining.

For perhaps the first time in many years, she was thinking of others rather than herself. 'I really admire the way Wallis has thrown herself into all her various jobs,' wrote Rosa Wood to Edith Lindsay. 'She really is wonderful and does work hard. I do hope that people everywhere are realising all the good she is doing. I think she has such charm and is always amusing to be with, I really don't know what I would do without her.'[34]

But the enhanced responsibilities, which could have brought them together, threatened to drive the Windsors apart. Whilst she made a point of getting to know people – the children, mothers, servicemen – and made the most of her situation, the Duke had become increasingly accepting of his exile and political impotence. He was bored by trivial political matters – the duty on an imported

[33] Bryan and Murphy, p. 443.
[34] Rosa Wood to Edith Lindsay, 25 October 1942, Ms 1772, Windsor Collection, Maryland Historical Society.

church bell, the endowment of a public library, or overcrowding in Nassau prison (average number of inmates 146).

He bicycled each day to Cable Beach to swim – a tandem proved not to be a success and was abandoned after the couple fell off before it had left the grounds of Government House – and played golf most afternoons. His ADC, John Pringle, remembered how to lift his spirits he would take his official car out to the airport and 'hurtle it down the darkened runway over and over again'.[35]

Bert Cambridge, a local jazz musician and Black politician, recalled how he was 'summoned to the Governor's residence, not in his political capacity but in his musical one – to accompany the striptease artistes who gave private performances for the Duke. The Duchess . . . took it all in her stride; there was not, perhaps, much other entertainment to be had in the Bahamas.'[36]

Above all, he began to drink heavily. 'He drank, as he had always done, but the effects became more noticeable,' wrote his biographer Michael Pye.[37]

> What had been binges on his great Imperial tours, kept care-
> fully separate from his official appearances, were now ses-
> sions that happened all too publicly. He looked and acted
> drunk. He became loud and indiscreet. The Duchess was
> patient until a fund-raising evening at the Collins mansion
> on Shirley Street, where the Duke was too obviously full of
> whisky to fulfil his duties. She forbade him cocktail parties, cut

[35] James Owen, *A Serpent in Eden: The Greatest Murder Mystery of All Time* (Little, Brown, 2005), p. 62.

[36] Owen, p. 209.

[37] Pye, p. 56.

entertainment except for their American visitors and a handful of politically necessary guests, took control.[38]

In November 1943, submitting names of local candidates for the New Year's Honours List to Churchill, the Duke reiterated his plea that 'after five and a half years, the question of restoring to the Duchess her royal status should be clarified . . . I am now asking you as Prime Minister to submit to the King that he restore the Duchess's royal rank at the coming New Year's, not only as an act of justice and courtesy to his sister-in-law, but also as a gesture in recognition of her two years' public service in the Bahamas.'[39]

The Palace's position was clear. Writing to Churchill on 8 December, George VI enclosed a memorandum explaining why Wallis could not use the title 'Royal Highness'. 'I am quite ready to leave the question in abeyance for the time being, but I must tell you quite honestly that I do not trust the Duchess's loyalty.'[40]

The memo, marked 'Private and Confidential' read:

I have read the letter from my brother with great care, and after much thought I feel I cannot alter a decision which I made with considerable reluctance at the time of his marriage . . . When he abdicated, he renounced all the rights and privileges of succession for himself and his children – including the title 'Royal Highness' in respect of himself and his wife. There is therefore no question of the title being 'restored' to the Duchess – because she never had it . . . I know you will understand how disagreeable this is to

[38] Pye, p. 56.

[39] The Duke to Churchill, 10 November 1942, CHAR 20/63/84–93, Churchill College Archives.

[40] George VI to Churchill, 8 December 1942, CHAR 20/52/96–100, Churchill College Archives.

me personally, but the good of my country and my family come first . . . I have consulted my family, who share these views.[41]

The news was transmitted to the Duke by Churchill three days before Christmas.[42]

* * *

In May 1943, the Duke paid his third visit to America, visiting Bahamian labourers in northern Florida, seeing executives of General Foods in New York about the possibility of setting up fishing and canning operations in Bahamas, and socialising in Palm Beach. He had two meetings with Roosevelt, was invited by Churchill to hear him address Congress – where both men were given standing ovations – and lobbied for a new appointment.

The best that Churchill could come up with was Governor of Bermuda, marginally up the pecking order and a better climate, but further from the United States and, after three days consideration, the Duke refused.[43] As Wallis wrote to her aunt, 'I can't see much point in island jumping. I'm for the big hop to a mainland.'[44]

Through Halifax, the Duke now asked for Wallis's letters to be exempt from postal censorship because of his diplomatic status, a request that was refused by the State Department. Adolf Berle wrote to Cordell Hull:

[41] CHAR 20/52/96–100, Churchill College Archives.
[42] Churchill to the Duke, 22 December 1942, CHAR 20/63/107, Churchill College Archives.
[43] The offer was made on 10 June 1943, CHAR 20/100/10, Churchill College Archives, and FO954/33A/213, TNA, and refused 13 June 1943, CHAR 20/100/15, Churchill College Archives.
[44] Michael Bloch, *Secret File*, p. 200.

Quite aside from the shadowy reports about the activities of this family, it is to be recalled that both the Duke and Duchess of Windsor were in contact with Mr James Mooney of General Motors, who attempted to act as mediator of a negotiated peace in the early winter of 1940; that they have maintainèd correspondence with Bedaux, now in prison under charges of trading with the enemy and possibly of treasonous correspondence with the enemy; that they have been in constant contact with Axel Wenner-Gren, presently on our blacklist for suspicious activity etc. The Duke of Windsor has been finding many excuses to attend to 'private business' in the United States, which he is doing at present.[45]

Reports about the couple's controversial views and associations had continued to be passed to the authorities. In October 1942, a letter from Gerald Selous, the trade commissioner in Vancouver, was forwarded to Sir John Stephenson at the Dominions Office, reporting that Baron Maurice de Rothschild, had 'set various drawing-rooms of Vancouver "goggling" with his tales, amongst which that he saw much of the Windsors . . . that the Duke had told him they loathed Nassau, that they daily regretted having left the South of France, that he (the Duke) was on very friendly terms with Ribbentrop and Goering, and that he was sure the Germans would not have bothered them (the Windsors) at all.'[46]

The following April, the First Secretary at the British embassy in Washington, Sir John Balfour, wrote to Oliver Harvey at the

---

[45] Adolf Berle to Cordell Hull, 18 June 1943, 811.711/4039, NARA.

[46] Gerald Selous to Ian Maclennan, 16 October 1942, CO 967/125, TNA. Maurice was a cousin of Eugene de Rothschild. He also claimed that the Duke had lobbied Roosevelt to request he be made Ambassador to Washington. See DO 127/42, TNA.

Foreign Office after Marcus Cheke, the First Secretary in Lisbon, minuted a meeting with a young Spaniard called Nava de Tajo.

De Tajo had known the Duke pre-war and then met him again in the summer of 1940, and he had relayed the Duke's views, which Balfour thought were 'of interest as corroborating what one has heard on the subject from other sources':[47]

> It was clear from the conversation of HRH that he expected the British Cabinet to resign in the near future, and to see the creation of a Labour Government which would enter into negotiation with Germany. He expected also that King George VI would abdicate, following a virtual revolution brought about by the fact that the ruling classes had utterly disgraced themselves and that he (the Duke of Windsor) would be summoned to return to England to occupy the throne. HRH also spoke of how England would become the leader of a coalition consisting of France, Spain and Portugal, while Germany would be free to march against Russia! . . . HRH said he thought the age of constitutional monarchy had passed, evidently believing that an age of fuehrers such as Petain, Franco and Salazar, had opened . . . He also expressed himself with some force about the present Queen of England, whom he termed 'an ambitious woman'.[48]

What of Charles Bedaux, last viewed abandoning the American tour for the Duke in November 1937? He had continued his activities, happy to do business with anyone who served his interests, but also suspected by all. In October 1940, he had gone to North Africa to work with the Vichy governor general, Maxime Weygand, on

[47] John Balfour to Oliver Harvey, 3 April 1943, FO 954/33A/212, TNA.
[48] John Balfour to Oliver Harvey, 3 April 1943, FO 954/33A/212, TNA.

developing railways, power plants, and water and coal production. In return for his services, his confiscated Dutch companies had been returned.[49]

A State Department official, who had met Katherine Rogers in Portugal in August 1941, reported that she had denounced Bedaux as a collaborator. An FBI memo noted:

> Mrs Rogers stated that she had definite information that Mr Bedaux was using his talents on behalf of the Germans in acquiring for the account of certain German individuals and for himself large properties in and about Paris, and that he travelled about without apparent restrictions, and with all indications that he was persona grata to the German occupying forces.[50]

She had also reported that the Château de Candé had been the only building in the surrounding area not bombed by the Germans.

Herman Rogers had also given a statement to the FBI, after a routine interview by the Bermuda censorship authorities, telling the British that Bedaux:

> had always held pro-Fascist views. At the time of the battle of France, he had personally welcomed the German General Staff to his house near Tours. He was now installed in an office in Paris in the Rue des Petits Champs, where he controlled a large German staff. The work of the office was to organise Jewish industries taken over by the Germans in France, and to see that the maximum production . . . was achieved.[51]

---

[49] More details, Higham, *Trading with the Enemy*, p. 184.

[50] Memo, 24 November 1941, FBI file 100-49901.

[51] FO 1093/23, TNA.

Bedaux had been automatically arrested by the Germans after Pearl Harbor, but released after the intervention of Otto Abetz. Returning to North Africa, he began plans to build a pipeline across the Sahara carrying water and peanut oil. Later he had worked with the Germans to camouflage refineries at Abadan against Allied bombing.[52]

According to the December 1941 war diary of General von Lahousen, head of the Abwehr Division II, Bedaux demanded various conditions for his involvement in the Abadan refinery, including being given the rank of major-general in the Wehrmacht, and was described as an agent of the 'First Magnitude'.[53]

In September 1942, he had again been picked up – and imprisoned with his wife in Paris Zoo in a cage usually used by monkeys – but was released, after persuading General Otto von Stülpnagel, commander of German forces in Occupied France, that he could best serve the interests of the regime in French North Africa.

In October 1942, Bedaux had arrived at the American consulate in Algiers and brazenly told the minister, Robert Murphy, he was on a mission on behalf of the German government. Shortly afterwards, he and his 33-year-old son were arrested by the French, on American orders. Two FBI agents were sent to interrogate him, but were killed when their plane crashed. Subsequently two more FBI agents were sent, though Algiers was outside their jurisdiction.[54]

Hoover immediately wrote a confidential memo for his senior FBI staff, outlining the incriminating evidence that Bedaux carried linking him to the Germans, which included two German

---

[52] Full details of Bedaux's wartime activities can be found in Charles Higham, *Trading with the Enemy* (Delacorte, 1983), pp. 183–8.

[53] December 1941, war diary of General von Lahousen, Hoover Institute.

[54] One of those killed was Percy Foxworth, who had previously reported on the Duke.

passports, a pad for sending coded messages, and instructions to spy on 'military formation', 'armaments', 'troop movements', and 'the acquisition of military codes'.[55]

'Bedaux has not only been pro-Nazi and pro-Fascist since the collapse of France, but was very much so in his sentiments for a number of years before Munich,' an OSS Report stated. 'His pro-Nazi sentiments can perhaps be described as those of a conscientious believer in Hitler's "New Order" in Europe.'[56]

The Duke's old friend was in deep trouble, but it was a more recent friend, the richest man in the Bahamas, who was to bring his next problem.

---

[55] Hoover to Tolson, Tamm and Ladd, 4 January 1943, FBI file 100-49901.

[56] 15 January 1943, RG 226, OSS report, NARA. Bedaux died from an overdose on 18 February 1944 in Miami shortly before he was due to be indicted for Trading with the Enemy. Suspicions persist it was not self-administered. After the war the French Government awarded him a posthumous knighthood of the *Légion d'honneur* on the grounds he had worked against the Germans, but his MI5 file confounds this with extensive references to his espionage activities on behalf of the Germans, KV2/4412, TNA.

CHAPTER 14

Murder in Paradise

On the morning of Thursday 8 July 1943, the bloodied corpse of Sir Harry Oakes was found in his bed at Westbourne, one of his homes on New Providence. He had four distinct triangular-shaped wounds by his left ear, he had been set alight, feathers from a pillow were scattered over the body and his genitals had been almost burnt off. Although he lay on his back, there was blood running across his face, suggesting he had been moved after the fatal blows. A set of false teeth still sat in a glass of water on the table next to the bed.

He had been discovered at 7 a.m. by Harold Christie, who had dined with Oakes the previous night and unexpectedly stayed over because of a thunderstorm outside. Christie claimed at the subsequent trial that he had assumed Oakes was still alive, wiped his bloody face and given him a glass of water. Then realising his business partner was dead, he had made a series of phone calls: to Madeline Kelly, the wife of Oakes's business manager, who lived in a cottage nearby; to his brother Frank; to Reggie Erskine-Lindop, the commissioner of the Bahamas Police, and finally to Government House.

The Duke, who was woken by Gray Phillips and told the news just before 8 a.m., was shocked. Unsure what to do, the Duke immediately imposed a news blackout, but he was too late. Etienne Dupuch, the editor of the *Nassau Gazette,* had already been told and had begun filing the story. The question soon began to be asked: 'What was there to hide?'

The Duke then made a decision for which he was to be heavily criticised. Serious crime was rare on the islands and he later argued that he did not feel that the local police were sufficiently experienced to investigate.[1] The obvious decision would have been to call on Scotland Yard or, if he felt that they were too far away, the FBI or even the local RAF base.

Instead, after several hours of discussion with Wallis and Christie, at 10.30 a.m. he rang the head of the Miami City Police Homicide Department, Captain Edward Melchen, with whom he had had dealings on his American trips, saying he needed help 'to tidy things up a bit'. Melchen, a veteran of over 500 murders in his almost twenty years with the force, immediately jumped on a plane, bringing with him Captain James Barker, the head of the fingerprint squad. By early afternoon, they were at Westbourne.

The police investigation was flawed from the beginning. The house was not sealed and much of the evidence was disturbed by the numbers of people who had arrived when they heard news of the death. Amongst the first to arrive was a local doctor, Dr Hugh Quackenbush, who estimated death between 2.45 a.m. and 5.15 a.m., and he was soon joined by Major Herbert Pemberton, the deputy commissioner, and several detectives.

The police quickly identified a suspect, Harry Oakes's son-in-law, Count Alfred de Marigny. De Marigny, whose French title came from his mother, was a Mauritian playboy then in his early thirties. Twice-divorced, he had married the eldest of Oakes's five children, Nancy, just over a year before and two days after her eighteenth birthday.

---

[1] Wallis later claimed in her memoirs that 'the Bahamas police had no up-to-date detection equipment', but there was such equipment at the RAF base. *Heart*, p. 354.

Relations with Sir Harry were strained and de Marigny was felt to have a motive for killing Oakes. He had been near Westbourne at the time of the murder, the hairs on his arms were scorched by fire, and he was unable to produce the shirt and tie he had been wearing on the night of the murder.

De Marigny owned a yacht, the *Concubine*, on which he won many races – and also smuggled goods. An FBI background check on de Marigny revealed 'that the Bureau had conducted some investigation in the past of de Marigny during which some evidence was developed indicating that de Marigny had been engaged in the illicit traffic of drugs.'[2]

There was no need for the Duke to become involved in the investigation, but on Friday 9 July he appeared at Westbourne and had a private twenty-minute conversation with Barker. No record of what was said was kept. Two hours later, de Marigny was arrested and charged with the murder of Sir Harry Oakes. If found guilty, he would hang.

Murders were bad for tourism and a quick resolution to the crime was needed. De Marigny had few friends amongst the officials in the Bahamas and he was a convenient scapegoat. The Duke reported immediately to the Colonial Office that the two Miami detectives had rendered 'most valuable service by their relentless investigations, which have in a large measure resulted in the arrest of the accused.'[3] What he had not said was that there was history between the Governor and de Marigny.

De Marigny had no respect for the Governor and enjoyed taunting him – on one occasion inviting the English actress Madeleine Carroll, who was on the island filming *Bahamas Passage*, to dinner

[2] 15 October 1943, FBI report 6273197.

[3] Charlotte Gray, *Murdered Midas: A Millionaire, His Gold Mine, and a Strange Death on an Island Paradise* (Collins, 2019), p. 176.

when the Duke hoped to entertain her, and on another offering to sell at an outrageous price some cognac that the Governor expected to be given free.

In the past, the two men had also argued about the treatment of some prisoners who had escaped from Devil's Island and a visa for de Marigny's yachting coach. The final straw had been when the Duke refused be the guest of honour at a fundraising dinner for the dependants of Bahamian servicemen overseas with which de Marigny was involved.

'We are endeavouring to keep as clear from this awful case as is possible,' wrote the Duchess to her Aunt Bessie on 24 August:

> I am afraid there is a lot of dirt underneath and I think the natives are all protecting themselves from the exposure of business deals – strange drums of petrol, etc. – so one wonders how far it will all go. Most unpleasant as I do not think there is a big enough laundry anywhere to take Nassau's dirty linen.[4]

In mid-September 1943, the Windsors made their fourth visit to the United States, in spite of objections from the British ambassador Lord Halifax.[5] They would be away until the end of November. Starting in Miami, they moved north, staying for three nights at the British embassy in Washington and then at a hotel in Hot Springs, Virginia, where a fellow guest was their old friend from Paris, the US ambassador William Bullitt.

'The Duke and Duchess of Windsor were there the entire time, occupying rooms on the same floor, only three or four rooms from ours,' he wrote in his diary. 'He is quite small and dissipated looking.

---

4 Duchess of Windsor to Aunt Bessie, 24 August 1943, quoted Michael Bloch, *The Duke of Windsor's War* (Weidenfeld & Nicolson, 1982), p. 308.

5 Lord Halifax to Colonial Office, 6 September 1943, FO954/ 33A/219, TNA.

She looks like her pictures. I think she is a disgusting kind of person, and didn't want to have anything to do with her or him either.'[6]

And then it was on to New York, where the Duke signed an agreement to drill for oil on his Canadian ranch. One of the highlights of the trip was a visit to the FBI to see the exhibit rooms, communication section, laboratory, firearms range and Identification Division, where they were shown round by J. Edgar Hoover himself. The couple visited art galleries, service canteens and navy yards, inspected training units at Harvard, and reviewed naval troops at Newport, Rhode Island, where they dined with Mrs Cornelius Vanderbilt. Finally they saw Aunt Bessie in Boston.

Their timing was deliberate, because shortly after they left, the trial of Alfred de Marigny opened.[7] The evidence against him looked strong, not least the discovery of his fingerprints on the bloodied Chinese screen in Oakes's bedroom, a room that de Marigny was supposed not to have visited, but the prosecution's key evidence soon began to unravel. Even though the two detectives had been working closely together, Captain Barker had only announced the discovery of the fingerprint to his colleague when he and Captain Melchen saw Lady Oakes at Oakes's funeral several days after the print had been discovered, and long after de Marigny had been arrested.

The fingerprint produced in court had supposedly been lifted from the screen but, on cross examination, it became clear that the detectives were not sure from where it had been taken on the screen. It then became apparent from the patterns behind the fingerprint

[6] William Bullitt diary, Mss A B937c1724, Filson Historical Society.

[7] One of the reporters was Erle Stanley Gardner, creator of Perry Mason, on his first newspaper assignment. The Duke wrote to Oliver Stanley on 8 March 1944: 'It was the lack of training of the local CID that caused me to call in the American Detectives . . . I purposefully absented myself and the Duchess from the Colony during the de Marigny trial to avoid adverse publicity.' CO23/967/126, TNA.

that it had actually been lifted from a water glass – a glass given to de Marigny by the detectives when interviewing him.

It now emerged that the detectives, in particular Barker, were not quite as reputable and experienced as had been assumed. According to his FBI file, Barker, who had started his police career as a traffic cop and clerk, had been suspended for drunkenness and demoted for insubordination, and had close connections with organised crime, especially Meyer Lansky, also known as the mob's accountant and instrumental in the establishment of illegal gambling in the US.[8]

De Marigny's defence lawyers were able to explain away the burns on his hands from lighting candles in hurricane shades and his friend, the Marquis Georges de Visdelou, provided an alibi for the night of the murder, saying he had spoken to de Marigny at 3 a.m. in the flat they shared. It was, however, the planted fingerprint evidence that was to be decisive.

On 14 November, after just over an hour's deliberation, the jury by a majority of 9 to 3 returned a verdict of not guilty. It was clear the authorities, especially the Governor, did not want de Marigny around. The next day he and de Visdelou were ordered to be deported. Writing to the Colonial Office that day with copies of the newspaper editorials, Heape noted of one of the Bay Street Boys factions: 'The Solomon gang are out for blood and we may expect another Committee of Enquiry by the House. The general opinion is [that] Marigny is guilty of the murder, but the Chief Justice could only sum up in his favour on the evidence produced in Court.'[9]

Ten days later, the Duke in a telegram to the Secretary of State for the Colonies added of de Marigny that he was 'an unscrupulous

---

[8] Barker was discharged early on medical grounds and at Christmas 1952, high on drugs, was shot dead by his son, who it was said suspected his father of sleeping with his son's wife, in what was described as a justifiable homicide.

[9] W.L. Heape to Mr Beckett, 14 November 1943, CO 23/714, Bahamas Archives.

adventurer . . . gambler and spendthrift. Suspected drug addict. Suspected of being concerned in the unnatural death of his godfather Ernest Bronard.'[10]

Ridding the colony of the two men proved more difficult than anticipated. The War Office refused to provide transport and the American authorities denied visas for travel via Miami. In the event, it was not until early December that de Marigny and Nancy sailed to Havana and the finca of their friend Ernest Hemingway – where Nancy proceeded to have an affair with Hemingway's son Jack.[11]

The trial and verdict had been a disaster for the Duke, showing his lack of authority and judgement and revealing how he had tried to frame an innocent man. He and Wallis always stressed in subsequent interviews that they had deliberately not involved themselves in the case, but in the Royal Archives is a cryptic letter from Melchen to the Duke written shortly after the couple returned to the Bahamas:

> The enclosed is self-explanatory. There are many things I can enlighten you on and will be glad to do so at your request. Some of the things deal direct with the conduct of members of the Assembly, both in civil life and in their conduct in this case, and those things should also be investigated as well as the members who had knowledge of and were parties to some of those things. I told you of one matter.[12]

[10] Duke of Windsor to Secretary of State, 25 November 1943, CO 23/714, Bahamas Archives.

[11] Alfred de Marigny and Nancy divorced in 1949. She married several times, including the son of the German minister in Lisbon during the war, Oswald von Hoyningen-Huene.

[12] Melchen to Duke of Windsor, 26 November 1943, RA EDW/PRIV/ MAIN/5371.

The enclosure is missing, but it suggests Melchen privately knew more about the likely culprit than history has recorded.

To date, no one apart from de Marigny has been charged for the murder and speculation continues with a regular stream of books, each with their own theory of the killer. One candidate, however, remains particularly strong – Harold Christie.

Christie's family had been on the island since the mid-eighteenth century and he was now regarded as one of its most prominent citizens, being elected to the House of Assembly in 1928. He had made a fortune buying up beachfront properties from poor farmers and redeveloping them for British and American investors. But there was a darker side, with a police and FBI record as a bootlegger going back to 1923, when he had been charged with illegally transferring a schooner from the American to British registry of ships to make it easier to smuggle alcohol into the US.[13]

He was now a key witness and his testimony raised many questions. Though he had been sleeping a few doors away from Oakes, he claimed to have heard nothing. Why did he offer Oakes a glass of water on finding the body, when it must have been clear the magnate was dead? Was he actually at Westbourne that night? How did he explain the sighting by an old school friend, Captain Edward Sears, the head of the Bahamas police traffic division, of him in a car in central Nassau at midnight on 7 July, supposedly with his brother Frank? Why did he park his car at the country club, rather than outside Westbourne, if he was not to use it until the morning? Why were the bloodstains found in the bedroom that Christie slept in not investigated?

Christie certainly had a motive. There were rumours he had double-crossed Oakes in a property deal. In revenge, Oakes had called in Christie's IOU notes, sought repossession of Christie's

[13] His FBI file is 62-4138.

only fully-owned asset, the island of Lyford Cay, and talked of planning to move to Mexico, taking much of his business with him and thereby ruining Christie. What no one doubted was that, as a key figure amongst the Bay Street Boys and a member of the Executive Council, Christie was not someone who was ever going to be fully investigated.

Other mysteries remain. De Marigny's friend, Basil McKinney, himself to be charged the following year with smuggling drugs onto the islands, claimed that two watchmen at Lyford Cay told him they had seen a cabin cruiser arrive at 1 a.m. on the night of the murder, two men being collected by car and returning an hour later. According to de Marigny, shortly afterwards one drowned and the other was found hanging from a tree. Were these hit men brought in from the outside?

Why was the commissioner of police since 1936, Reggie Erskine-Lindop, a policeman of great experience and integrity, taken off the case and transferred sideways as the commissioner in Trinidad, especially when he was narrowing in on a suspect? Lindop later revealed that 'de Marigny was an unprincipled rascal, but he did not kill Oakes. My investigations had just reached the point where, during the interrogation of a possible subject, I extracted information that I am sure was a clue to the murderer or his accomplice, when the case was taken out of my hands. I was transferred to Trinidad and not asked to give evidence at the trial.'[14]

And who ensured the transfer? The Governor. 'It was largely at the insistence of HRH that we moved Lindop and landed Trinidad with a problem,' states a Colonial Office report re-examining the

---

[14] Dupuch article, *Nassau Daily Tribune*, 26 August 1974, reprinted 1983. Erskine-Lindop took his secrets to the grave, refusing to ever discuss it or leave an account in a bank vault after his death. Jennifer Kawar, his granddaughter, to the author, 8 March 2021.

case.[15] Why was the Duke so keen to shut down the story? In July 1942, a secret State Department memo had noted that Axel Wenner-Gren had $2,500,000 frozen on deposit in the Bahamas, 'made at the express request and in part for the benefit of the Duke of Windsor'.[16]

This was money that the Duke hoped could circumvent currency regulations and either use in America or invest in Mexico – he had plans to buy a villa there – safe from the ravages of war. Oakes and Christie had also invested heavily in Mexico through the Banco Continental, set up by Wenner-Gren in June 1941, in the hope of protecting their money from the war and consolidating their fortunes.

According to Pat Wertheim, who has studied the case:

a careful accounting of Oakes' estate at the time of his death came up $15,000,000 short . . . Oakes had put that money into Banco Continental (supposedly created as a stash house for Nazi war loot being moved out of Germany prior to the end of the war), along with money put there by Christie and the Duke. My interpretation, if not the overt suggestion, was that when Oakes was killed, only Christie, the Duke, and Maximino Comacho (the banker and brother of the President of Mexico) knew of Oakes's money stashed there. The conclusion, then, was that after things had cooled down, they realised that money was free for the taking and split it. That would

---

[15] 30 May 1945, CO 23/785/7, Bahamian National Archives. The minute has been weeded from the UK version of the file in the TNA. According to an expert on the Oakes murder, Pat Wertheim, Erskine-Lindop ' had some scruples against cooperating with the Duke's scheme to frame DeMarigny for Oakes's murder and he made no secret, at least among the whites on the Trinidad & Tobago Police, that he had been transferred for his refusal to participate in the scheme.' Pat Wertheim to the author 16 Feb 2022.

[16] 21 July 1942, RG 59/2682K/1940–1944, NARA.

have put an extra $5 million into Christie's pocket for his real estate developments and another $5 million into the royal coffers when the Duke returned to England.[17]

Finances certainly seem to have connected many of those associated to the murder. When investigators called at de Marigny's apartment on 8 July, they found him with John Anderson, an accountant who was responsible for Wenner-Gren's businesses after the Swedish tycoon's blacklisting. It was Anderson who had driven de Marigny to the scene of the crime on the 8th, who had spent most of the day with him, and whom it was discovered owed de Marigny $1,000 – Anderson was a compulsive gambler:

> The Miami police investigator stated that Anderson had been questioned regarding de Marigny's possible connection with Axel Wenner-Gren and when this subject was brought up, Anderson became extremely nervous and did not volunteer any information. The investigators felt that Anderson had some possible tie-in with de Marigny and Wenner-Gren, and they viewed his operations with suspicion.[18]

Anderson, then in his late thirties, had originally worked as an accountant in Montreal before taking over the Bahamas General Trust Company in 1936 and heading the Bank of the Bahamas owned by Wenner-Gren. The Bahamas General Trust had been set up by Lord Beaverbrook and he held 10 per cent of the 5,000 shares with Arthur Vining Davis, president of the aluminium producer Alcoa, holding the controlling interest.

[17] Pat Wertheim to the author, 11 December 2020.
[18] Memo, district cable censor, 10 December 1943, FO 115/4140, TNA.

Sir Harry Oakes, Harold Christie and Sir Frederick Williams-Taylor were also shareholders and, according to one report, 'prior to the death of Sir Harry Oakes, a scheme was afloat for this controlling interest to be distributed between Mr A.V. Davis, Sir Harry Oakes and Hon. H.G. Christie. The proportions and considerations are not known.'[19]

In October 1942, de Marigny had told his friend, Georges de Visdolou, that Oakes planned to replace Anderson as managing director with de Marigny and that the Oakes family was 'surrounded by sharks whom they distrust and for this reason they make hardly any use of their capital in Nassau.'[20]

Anderson had been the subject of numerous censorship and security reports and had come to the authorities' attention 'when a Miami police officer called at this office to attempt to locate a message in our files which he believed would establish the motive for the murder of Sir Harry Oakes'.[21]

Censorship interest had been aroused because it was thought Sir Harry Oakes and de Marigny 'might be intermediaries between J.H. Anderson and H.B. Griffiths in Nassau and Axel Wenner-Gren in Mexico.'[22]

Anderson, interviewed about the murder, told the FBI:

> that Christie and Wenner-Gren brought in Duke of Windsor into a plot to divert millions of dollars to Mexico, to be exploited there after the war . . . I was told that Anderson does not know where the records were kept or how, but Wenner-Gren let it be known that he was holding $2,500,000 (US

[19] A. Whitmore report, 23 December 1943, FO 115/4140, TNA. The file is marked: 'Secret to be kept by secret registry.'

[20] A. Whitmore report, 23 December 1943, FO 115/4140, TNA.

[21] Memo, district cable censor, 10 December 1943, FO 115/4140, TNA.

[22] A. Whitmore report, 23 December 1943, FO 115/4140, TNA. H.B. Griffiths was a banker.

currency) for Windsor – some of it the Duke's money, all of it available to him . . . unthinkable that former King of England might have a hand in it.'[23]

It seemed the murder might not be as simple as it seemed.

* * *

Nancy Oakes had stood by her husband throughout the trial. She had also brought in a private detective, at $300 a day plus expenses, to conduct his own investigation. A master of self-promotion, the Alfred Hitchcock lookalike, Raymond Schindler, was the most famous and highest paid American detective of the day.

'It is my considered opinion that the murderer of Sir Harry (Oakes) can be found, identified, convicted and brought to justice,' wrote Schindler, who remained obsessed with the case, to the Duke in July 1944, offering to work on it for free with his colleague Leonard Keeler, the developer of the lie detector.[24] The Duke politely declined. The detective was not put off, speculating in the magazine *Inside Detective* shortly afterwards that the body had been moved to the bedroom and that there was a voodoo element.[25]

The following month, Christie met with an FBI officer to find a New York private investigator to re-examine the murder paid for 'by contributions of a few influential people in Nassau'.[26] An FBI report of August 1944 thought that 'in view of Oakes' background, it might have been committed by some of the big time mobsters

---

[23] D.H. Ladd, FBI memo on Harold Christie, 23 October 1943, Bob Cowan, *Sir Harry Oakes, 1874–1943: An Accumulation of Notes* (Highway Bookshop, 2000), pp. 230–1.

[24] Parker, p. 231, and Marshall Houts, *Who Murdered Sir Harry Oakes?* (Robert Hale, 1976), p. 306.

[25] 'I Could Crack the Oakes Case Wide Open', *Inside Detective,* October 1944.

[26] 31 May 1944, FBI file 62-73197.

with whom Oakes had previously been associated.'[27] In the spring of 1945, the FBI were tipped off by Scotland Yard of 'possible additional evidence' of 'a native of the Bahamas but who is presently in the United States', but they were not interviewed.[28] The inference was that this was Harold Christie.

In August 1946 a new Governor, Sir William Murphy, asked the Colonial Office to reconsider the evidence against de Marigny and Scotland Yard conducted a review of the case, but only on the basis of the trial transcript. They concluded that 'in our opinion, de Marigny was the murderer and, with great respect, we think the case was mishandled . . . There should have been a conviction if the facts had been investigated and put before the Court in a proper manner.'[29] They saw no purpose in reopening the case, especially after de Marigny could not be retried. It suited everyone's purposes to let sleeping dogs lie.

In September 1950, Edward Majava, a seaman on holiday in California, was arrested for drunkenness and claimed that he had been told the name of the killer by a society portrait painter, Mrs Hildegarde Hamilton. He was sufficiently convincing for August Robinson, an assistant superintendent in the Bahamas police, to fly to Oakland. Majava told him that Christie had paid a Bahamas hit man.

The next month the *Washington Star* quoted a woman who claimed, 'Everybody in Nassau knows who did it and why. But he is so powerful nobody dares touch him.' According to the unnamed woman, the actual slayer was the son of a white father and Negro mother, and 'he acted only as the hireling of a "powerful" plotter'.[30]

---

[27] 6 August 1944, FBI file 62-73197.

[28] FBI file 62-73197.

[29] Owen, p. 257.

[30] *Washington Star*, 3 October 1950

The lawyer Felix Cohen wrote to the British embassy in Washington in November 1950 after a colleague, Bettie Renner, who was supposedly looking into the case, was murdered, complaining that the authorities were turning a blind eye to various murders and witnesses felt intimidated about coming forward. He singled out Newell Kelley, Harold and Frank Christie.[31]

Three years later a local American hotelier, Daniel Cusick, told the FBI that 'the Bahama Islands are controlled by Harold and Frank Christie' and that 'on one occasion someone shot him, and he feels confident it was a Christie hired gunman.' The FBI said they could not help as they had no investigative jurisdiction.[32]

The first full-length study of the murder, *The Life and Death of Harry Oakes*, was written by the *Daily Express* journalist Geoffrey Bocca in 1959. He was helped in his research by Christie and initially by his former employer, Lord Beaverbrook, who had a house in Nassau; but during the course of the research, Beaverbrook suddenly withdrew his support. 'I am opposed to the book about Oakes,' he wrote to his former protégé. 'I dissociate myself from it altogether because of the implications in relation to other people.'[33] Bocca, who had planned to name Christie, subsequently suggested the killers were a 'syndicate of financial adventurers involved in an intricate plot to get their hands on Oakes's fortune.'[34]

The Bocca book stimulated new interest in the case. In March 1959, Canadian television transmitted a programme on the murder. On 8 June, Raymond Schindler wrote to the Bahamian attorney

---

[31] Felix Cohen to J.K. Thompson, 17 November 1950, Harold Christie. FBI file 62-4138. Newell Kelly (1892–1976) was the manager of various properties owned by Oakes, and one of his trustees.

[32] Memo, 27 October 1953, FBI file 62-4438.

[33] Gray, p. 253.

[34] Bocca, p. 168.

general saying that the Duke had been responsible for a cover up.[35] Two days later Charles Bates, the legal attaché at the US embassy in London, sent an FBI report dated 28 May 1959 on the case to Hoover. That report remains closed.[36]

On 8 July, Nancy Oakes was interviewed at Scotland Yard, on the understanding that her information would not be made public without her permission. The following month, a Scotland Yard memo concluded that, 'One or more of the beneficiaries might have been responsible for the death of her father', naming as the hit man, a former narcotics officer in California called Stanley E. Halstead, who had known Oakes in his mining days.[37]

Later in 1959, Cyril Stevenson, leader of the Black Progressive Liberal party and editor of the *Bahamian Times*, began a campaign for a reopening of the investigation. 'I am prepared to say that, in my opinion, Oakes was killed by one of his close friends, whom he had no reason to suspect.'[38] Twenty-four hours later, four shots were fired into the office where he usually worked.

Christie's former secretary, sixty-year-old Dorothy Macksey, was raped and murdered in 1962. The authorities were quick to stress that there was no connection to the Oakes murder, but she was only one of many involved in the case who met sudden deaths. Sir Harry Oakes's heir, Sydney, died in a car accident in 1966. According to writer John Marquis, he 'had been working on documents relating to the Oakes's land holdings on New Providence. There is talk of a faulty drive-shaft and possible interference with the car.'[39]

[35] Schindler to Lionel Orr, 8 June 1959, MEPO 2/9533, TNA.

[36] Charles Bates to Scotland Yard, 10 June 1959, MEPO 2/9533, TNA.

[37] S. Shepherd, 11 August 1959, MEPO 2/9533, TNA.

[38] Parker, p. 274.

[39] John Marquis, *Blood and Fire: The Duke of Windsor and the Strange Murder of Sir Harry Oakes* (LMH Publishing, 2006), p. 183.

Another son, Pitt, suffered from years of mental illness and according to de Marigny, 'he would run through the house naked barking like a dog and raising his leg to relieve himself on the furniture.'[40] He had died shortly before Macksey of alcoholism but, according to the author John Marquis, his death was more sinister. 'He didn't die from drink, a source told me . . . Someone felt the need to silence him for ever.'[41]

As for Harold Christie, in 1959, aged sixty-two, he married a divorcee twenty years his junior. His business interests prospered. He eventually became chairman of the Bahamas Development Board and was knighted in 1964. But the increasing public suggestions of his involvement led Christie to issue a statement through his lawyers, threatening action against anyone who accused him.

His lawyers sent legal letters to Marshall Houts, an American academic who had served in the FBI and CIA, when his book *King's X* was published in 1972, seeking to have the book withdrawn. After discussions, Christie then asked that he be allowed in the second printing 'to make a statement that would detail Christie's side of the case.'[42] That statement never came.

The mystery remains unsolved, even if it seems that the real culprit's identity was an open secret. At a party in the south of France in the 1960s, Diana Mosley heard Lord Beaverbrook ask Christie, 'Come on, Harold, tell us how you murdered Harry Oakes.'

Christie smiled and said nothing.[43]

---

[40] Alfred de Marigny with Mickey Herskowitz, *A Conspiracy of Crowns: The True Story of the Duke of Windsor and the Murder of Sir Harry Oakes* (Bantam, 1990), p. 301.

[41] Marquis, p. 185.

[42] Houts, p. 332

[43] Mosley, *Duchess of Windsor*, p. 167. Christie died peacefully of a heart attack in 1973.

CHAPTER 15

Beyond the Bahamas

The Windsors were not happy. The Duchess was exhausted from her war work and increasingly suffering stomach pains, the Duke was caught between the strictures of the Colonial Office and the Bay Street Boys. His allies, Leslie Heape and Eric Hallinan, had now moved on to other postings and he felt exposed in his dealings with local politicians.

'I really feel that neither of us can stand this place either physically or mentally for another year,' wrote Wallis to her Aunt Bessie in January 1944. 'I do not think the Duke would hesitate to throw his hand in for this is no place for him and to think he is dumped here solely by family jealousy.'[1]

That month, Oliver Stanley, the Colonial Secretary, told Churchill that the Duke had asked to resign.[2] The Duke was now looking beyond the war and the Bahamas and lobbying hard for a job as a roving ambassador in the United States, or as Canadian governor general. At the Palace, there were serious discussions about the 'Windsor problem'.

'As you know, I was once closely associated with the Prince of Wales, and since that association began, nearly 25 years ago, I don't think any problems in my life have given me so much anxiety as

---

[1] Wallis to Bessie, 6 January 1944, Bloch, *Secret File*, p. 211.
[2] Oliver Stanley to Churchill, 6 January 1944, CHAR 20/148/1, Churchill College Archives.

those arising from his,' wrote Tommy Lascelles to Churchill's private secretary John Martin.[3]

Lascelles outlined four possibilities for the Duke:

1. Undertake Ambassadorial or Pro-Consular jobs abroad.
2. Live in this country as a quasi-younger brother of The King.
3. Live in this country as a private individual, and devote his great wealth to some useful object in which he is interested.
4. Do ditto in the USA.[4]

All of them had their problems. With regard to the first option, he felt 'that there is in the British cosmos no official place for an ex-King. How can a man who has renounced the British Crown personally represent the Sovereign, or even impersonally HM Government?' He argued the Duke could not distinguish between 'the wood of the public weal apart from the trees of private inclination' and that he had a 'Rehoboam-like tendency to take up with undesirables, and dangerous associates. The latter may have diminished; but, from the episodes of the scoundrel Bedaux and the egregious Gren, it doesn't look like it.'[5]

The second and third options were impractical – 'there is no room for two Kings in England' – and would cost him £20,000 in taxation, leaving just the fourth.

> The Prince, I understand, is one of the richest men in the world, without encumbrances of any kind. He could make himself a charming home – a thing he has never yet had; he

[3] Alan Lascelles to John Martin, 30 May 1944, CHAR 20/148/37–9, Churchill College Archives.

[4] *Ibid.*

[5] *Ibid.*

could make wonderful use of his money by furthering some of the many schemes that have successively caught his interest. Stettinius told me that he is at present absorbed in the de-hydration of vegetables. That sounds a somewhat dreary hobby for a man's middle-age but it is just as useful, and maybe as amusing, as agriculture, stock-raising and so on . . .

He concluded 'that the best chance for the Prince's own happiness and for the peace of the world at large, is that he should adopt course (4).'[6]

Churchill's response was 'that someone acceptable both to the King and the Duke should be sent out to talk all this over with the latter in order to ascertain what he wishes, and what he will or will not do.'[7] It was time to call in Walter Monckton.

Discussions carried on through the summer. The King suggested a South American ambassadorship, but Halifax was less keen, preferring the Duke settle as a private citizen in France or the United States. There was talk of the governorship of Madras and Churchill suggested Governor of Ceylon. Mackenzie King, the Canadian prime minister, was adamant there was no possibility of the Duke succeeding the Earl of Athlone as Governor General of Canada.[8]

Finally in a telegram to Churchill, marked 'Strictly Private and Personal', the King made the family views clear. 'In any discussion as to his future perhaps you would put forward my conviction, which you already know, namely that his happiness will be best promoted by making his home in the USA. Repeat USA.'[9]

[6] *Ibid.*

[7] Churchill to Lascelles, 27 June 1944, CHAR 20/148/44–5, Churchill College Archives.

[8] He was succeeded by Earl Alexander of Tunis in April 1946.

[9] King George VI to Churchill, 16 September 1944, Char 20/148/55, Churchill College Archives.

Meanwhile the Windsors were back in the United States, staying with their friend Robert Young in Palm Beach. There Wallis was admitted to the Roosevelt Hospital in New York for the removal of her appendix – when it was discovered she had stomach cancer.[10]

Another crisis presented itself. In New York the Duke called in the FBI to reveal that he was being blackmailed by a former girlfriend, Rhoda Tanner Doubleday, with whom 'he ran around with (her) quite a bit, over a period of five or six years'. Doubleday had been a nuisance for some time, writing to him after his marriage, 'claiming he should have married her', and then in 1941 threatening to write about their relationship in her memoirs – he had put the matter in the hands of his lawyers. In October 1943, on a visit to New York City, he had 'received some jewellery from her together with a note saying that the least he could do was to purchase her jewellery. This, too, he later turned over to his attorney.'[11]

Tanner was the same age as the Duke and had come out as a debutante in 1913. Two years later, she had married Felix Doubleday, part of the publishing family – they had divorced in 1924, she later suing him for $10,000 in back alimony. From 1924 to 1932 she had moved in the same circles as the Prince of Wales and they probably had an affair during this period.

Returning to the United States, she began a relationship with the businessman Harold McCormick, successfully suing him for $65,000 for breach of promise when he didn't marry her. The following year the FBI noted she had had an abortion and threatened to file rape charges against the thoroughbred racehorse owner Louis

---

[10] Without access to medical records, biographers have been unable to verify the type of cancer, or even if it was simply a major internal operation. Contemporary accounts refer only to her appendix being removed. In 1951 she was supposedly diagnosed with cancer of the ovaries or womb, but if so it is unlikely she would have lived to the age she did.

[11] FBI report to Hoover, 4 September 1944, FBI File 62-76544-3.

Rowan, 21-year-old son of the Italian Princess Orsini. A heavy drinker and mentally unbalanced, by August 1944 she was working as a sales lady at the Gunther Fur Shop on Fifth Avenue.

An FBI agent, Jerome Doyle, saw the Duke at the Waldorf Towers on 29 August. 'The Duke was very, very impressed with the information obtained,' FBI deputy director Edward Tamm told Hoover. 'As a matter of fact, Mr Doyle stated he [the Duke] almost fell off his chair three times when he realised what he had almost become mixed up with. He wanted to be sure you understood how much he appreciated this information.'[12] The Duke heard no more from Mrs Doubleday and the matter was hushed up, but it was yet more evidence to the authorities of the embarrassments in his private life.[13]

This was not his only involvement with the FBI. In June, the journalist Helen Worden had published a long and critical profile of the Duchess in the magazine *American Mercury,* based on interviews with a number of acquaintances and various retailers Wallis frequented, suggesting that the Duchess was profligate, ambitious – 'it was her dream that the Duke would be appointed Viceroy of India . . . She hoped the Duke could be Great Britain's ambassador to the United States' – and mean:

At the end of her first New York visit as the Duchess of Windsor, she called in the detectives who had been assigned to guard the royal suite which she and the Duke occupied at the Waldorf. 'I have a little memento for you,' she told them. Very seriously, she distributed eleven hotel postcards, each autographed by the Duke and herself.[14]

---

[12] Tamm to Hoover, 14 September, FBI file HQ 94-4-6650.

[13] She did, however, make approaches to his cousin Louis Mountbatten in 1961 after the death of his wife Edwina. Doubleday died aged ninety-one in 1986.

[14] *American Mercury,* June 1944.

In the article, Worden had said of Wallis that 'An autographed photograph of von Ribbentrop once hung over her toilet table in Nassau, according to a friend who visited her last winter. When this friend commented on the picture, the Duchess said she had known and liked von Ribbentrop before the war.'[15]

The Duke's reaction was to 'demand a correction of criminally libellous statements'.[16] Worden fought back, replying in the October issue of the *American Mercury*:

> My information about the von Rippentrop photograph came from a friend of the Duke and Duchess, who had been their house guest in Nassau . . . The Duchess was reported as saying that von Ribbentrop was her friend before the war and she could see no reason why the fact of the war should make it necessary for her to remove the picture. My information came from a source in which I have complete confidence.[17]

The Duke asked the FBI to investigate and find out if there was a vendetta against the Windsors in publishing circles, hinting that, as Worden was Jewish, that may have been the motivation. The FBI director J. Edgar Hoover approached Jerome Doyle, chief of the US Special Intelligence Service, who undertook 'a discreet survey of SIS contacts in New York city to ascertain if there were any concerted efforts being made in literary circles in New York to injure the character of the Duchess of Windsor.'[18] He found nothing to support the Duke's suspicions, including on Worden's background, raising questions not only about the couple's loyalties,

---

[15] *American Mercury,* June 1944.

[16] *Guardian,* 25 September 1944. He was successful.

[17] Helen Worden papers, Box 79, Folder 3, Columbia University.

[18] Edward Conroy to Hoover, 1 August 1944, FBI file HQ 65-311113.

but judgement. 'Miss Helen Worden makes her case well and it is a damaging one,' stated one Foreign Office memo that was following the spat.[19]

The article also drew attention to the Duchess's extravagance, describing her expenditure on recent shopping trips:

> She also ordered six costumes from Valentina, five suits from Saks-Fifth Ave and a dozen or more sports things from Hattie Carnegie. She bought between twenty and thirty hats, chiefly from Miss Jessica of Bergdorf-Goodman, Walter Florell, and Braagaard, the latest rave in men milliners. Her purchases, since she moved to Nassau, have averaged a hundred dresses a year. Most of them cost about $250 apiece, though many ran much higher. Mainbocher's black afternoon dresses are now $500.[20]

Worden continued:

> All of her lingerie is hand-made. She hunts the kind of little out-of-the-way shops which delight most women. She discovered such a one on West 57th Street run by a French refugee, and asked the woman, over the phone, to bring her collection to the Waldorf. The woman refused. A customer, hearing the conversation remarked, 'I should think you'd find it a great honor to serve the Duchess.' 'Madame,' was the reply, 'it is an honor I cannot afford.'
>
> I've run across a lot of modists and jewelers who say they wouldn't take the Duchess' accounts on a bet that she never

[19] 23 November 1944, J. Donnelly, FO 371/38705, TNA.
[20] Helen Worden papers, Box 79, Folder 3, Columbia University.

pays her bills. Some say that is one reason she bought at so many shops on her last visit – that she was staggering her orders because of the OPA freezing of accounts.[21]

In mid-September the Duke, partly influenced by Wallis's health, met Churchill at Roosevelt's estate at Hyde Park and obtained permission to resign from the Bahamas, on condition that he did not return to Britain. The next day Churchill reported to the King how the Duke 'hoped that he might perhaps be found some work in France at the head of some Anglo-French organisation or other.'[22]

But there were problems there. After a conversation about such a return with the French foreign affairs minister, Rene Massigli, Oliver Harvey wrote to Churchill that:

> in view of some of the acquaintances that the Duke and Duchess had previously had in France, it would really be preferable that they should stay away until the situation had been cleared up. What Monsieur Massigli evidently had in mind, although he did not say so, was that he feared that the Duke and Duchess might seek to renew acquaintance with many who had turned out to be collaborators, and this would cause a most embarrassing situation.[23]

In October, whilst the Duchess was recuperating from her operation at Hot Springs, Virginia, the Duke had written to Churchill asking again for a job 'if there was any sphere in which it were

---

[21] Helen Worden papers, Box 79, Folder 3, Columbia University.

[22] Churchill to King George VI, 19 September 1944, CHAR 20/148/58, Churchill College Archives.

[23] Oliver Harvey to Churchill, 8 November 1944, CHAR 20/148/64, Churchill College Archives, and FO 371/42121, TNA.

considered my experience could still be appropriately utilised.'[24] He continued, touching on the subject of his return to Britain, that 'I would not have thought that my presence in their midst could any longer be considered so formidable a menace to the solidarity of the monarchy.'[25] He also pressed for a meeting with his brother, stressing he was entitled to do so solely on grounds of protocol as a former Colonial governor:

> It could never be a very happy meeting, but on the other hand it would be quite painless, and would at least have the merit of silencing, once and for all, those malicious circles who delight in keeping open an eight year wound that should have been healed officially, if not privately, ages ago.[26]

With the end of the war looming, 'The Windsor Problem' had resurrected itself. Tommy Lascelles, writing in his diary, had noted that Churchill had urged:

> the Royal Family should bury the hatchet and 'receive' the Duchess, but the King thought 'such a gesture is wrong in principle, and would imply that the Abdication had been all a mistake'; and I have no doubt that a number of people all over the Empire might so interpret it, and ask themselves, 'If the Duchess of Windsor goes to luncheon at Buckingham Palace, what was all the row about in 1936?'[27]

---

[24] The Duke to Churchill, 3 October 1944, CHAR 20/148/5–7, Churchill College Archives.

[25] *Ibid.*

[26] *Ibid.*

[27] Lascelles diary, 9 November 1944, Duff Hart-Davis (ed.), *King's Counsellor: Abdication and War* (Weidenfeld & Nicolson, 2006), p. 269.

Traitor King

Lascelles conveyed the Palace's response at the end of December. 'I do not think there is any point of difference between the attitude of the King and that of the two Queens as to a meeting with the Duke of Windsor. All of them would be glad to see the Duke; none of them wishes to see the Duchess.'[28]

The following day, John Martin minuted to Churchill a conversation with Lascelles:

He explained orally that he did not feel he could say in writing that the King was unwilling to see the Duke; but in fact HM would not be sorry if his brother did not come to England for the next ten years. The chief objection, however, is of course to meeting the Duchess . . . There is no doubt that the King's preference would be that the Duke should settle in America, or failing that in France, but that at any rate he should not bring the Duchess to England.[29]

The position was clear: the Windsors were not welcome in Britain and henceforth they must make their home either in France or the United States. The Duke took six weeks to respond.

'We most certainly do not wish to expose ourselves unnecessarily to insults that can be so simply avoided, by travelling some other way to the continent of Europe, when the time is ripe for us to do so,' he wrote to Churchill on 12 February. 'We shall therefore make our plans accordingly.'[30]

[28] Tommy Lascelles to John Martin, 20 December 1944, CHAR 20/148 28–9, Churchill College Archives.

[29] John Martin to Churchill, 21 December 1944, CHAR 20/148 26, Churchill College Archives.

[30] The Duke to Churchill, 12 February 1945, CHAR 20/202/2, Churchill College Archives.

Members of his staff were also making plans for their future. George and Rosa Wood, who had accompanied the Windsors on their flight from the South of France in June 1940 to the Bahamas, now wished to leave the islands. Their request was seen as a personal betrayal.

'Our goodbye unfortunately was a very unpleasant one,' wrote Rosa to her friend Edith Lindsay:

> The moment the Windsors knew we were leaving they both suddenly became very nasty – made out that we were letting them down and only used them while it suited us. Almost funny when George worked for the Duke for four years without one penny pay, and I certainly did ALL to help Wallis. A very unpleasant ending and undeserved . . . it has somehow left us with a bitter and disillusioned feeling.[31]

On 15 March 1945, the Duke resigned as Governor of the Bahamas, several months before his term was officially up, but neither he nor Wallis could face another humid summer. It was dubbed the 'Second Abdication'.[32] Reviewing his tenure two days later, the *Nassau Tribune* wrote: 'We know of many views held by His Royal Highness in which we are in strong disagreement, but we have grown to respect him because he is no politician – he doesn't bluff and he is no hypocrite . . . We were sorry to see the Duke come to the Colony as its Governor. We are more sorry to see him leave.'[33]

The Duke's record was mixed. Much of his time in his final months had been spent dealing with a commission into the behaviour of the

---

[31] Rosa Woods to Edith Lindsay, December 1944, Amory notes, CAP, Box 845, quoted Andrew Morton, *Wallis in Love*, p. 282

[32] Lascelles noted that the Duke's resignation letter to the Colonial Office contained 'two bad grammatical errors'. Hart Davis, p. 299.

[33] *Nassau Tribune,* 17 March 1945.

unpopular police commissioner, Colonel Lancaster, and poor morale, pay and working conditions in the police.[34] He had introduced various programmes that had brought employment, but had failed to introduce income tax, though London had supported such a measure, and there had been little political, economic or social reform. His own views on self-government and race are clear in a report he sent to Churchill in November 1942:

> Those with experience of regions where the population is predominately coloured, realize that negroes in the mass are still children both mentally and morally and that while these liberal socialistic ideas of freedom and equality regardless of race or colour may sound fine theoretically, the forcing of these theories are to my way of thinking, both premature and dangerous so far as the Western Hemisphere is concerned . . .[35]

Wallis had done better, improving conditions whether the need for birth control, clinics for syphilitics, or canteens for soldiers, but there had been no official recognition in any Honours List.

'Should it ever be considered that there was any sphere in which my experience could still be appropriately utilised, my services will be available,' the Duke wrote to Churchill.[36] But the offers were not forthcoming and the couple faced an uncertain future.

Their past would now catch up with them with a discovery in the Harz mountains.

---

[34] See CO 23/785, TNA.

[35] The Duke to Churchill, 10 November 1942, CHAR 20/63 /84–93, Churchill College Archives. He had told Walter Monckton in July 1941 that improving the lot of the black population was a 'fence that must not be rushed'. RA EDW/PRIV/MAIN/A/4870.

[36] The Duke to Churchill, 22 March 1945, CHAR 20/202/30, Churchill College Archives.

CHAPTER 16

The German Documents

On 12 April 1945, Captain David Silverberg, part of the American First Army, was advancing through the Harz Mountains when he came across an abandoned German vehicle with papers strewn around it. Stopping to look at the papers, he noticed that one was signed by Joachim von Ribbentrop. His interest was aroused and he quickly found whole archives located in local castles, including a copy of the 1939 Ribbentrop-Molotov Pact at the nearby Schloss at Degenershausen. It was the almost complete archive of the German Foreign Ministry and a verifiable treasure trove.

As the material was in the Soviet zone of occupation, it was quickly moved to Marburg Castle in the American zone – some 400 tons of documents transported in a convoy of 237 trucks in shuttles over several days – where they were examined by a team under Dr Ralph Perkins of the State Department and Colonel Robert Thomson of the Foreign Office.

There were to be other discoveries. Karl Loesch, the assistant to Hitler's interpreter, Paul Schmidt, had been captured and was now bartering his freedom for some sensational information. Loesch, who had an English mother and had been at Oxford, approached Thomson and, in return for safe passage, led him to a large country house above the village of Schönberg, twenty-five miles from

Mühlhausen, telling him that a microfilm set of the ministry's most confidential papers had been made by Ribbentrop in 1943.[1]

'We had to descend, rather uncomfortably, a steep ravine banked with pine trees,' wrote Thomson in his report. 'Our guide halted at a certain spot where he and Captain Folkard with iron bars soon scraped the soil from a waterproof cape covering a large battered metal can. This Captain Folkard brought to the top of the declivity and placed under guard at the mansion.'[2]

There they found buried further microfilm files of the German Foreign Ministry in several metal suitcases. One series from State Secretary Ernst von Weizsäcker was entitled 'German-British Relations' and included a volume on the Duke of Windsor, which would come to be called the 'Marburg File'. The material was immediately removed for safekeeping to SHAEF (Supreme Headquarters Allied Expeditionary Force). There the British, realising the sensitivity of the material, immediately tried to prevent its sharing with the Americans, but two copies had already been made. One was now in the United States at the State Department.

The documents were flown to the SIS technical branch at Whaddon Hall in Buckinghamshire, where the Foreign Office's historical adviser, Ernest Llewellyn Woodward, declared the Loesch cache authentic. On 30 May, the MI5 officer Guy Liddell noted in his diary:

> Bill Cavendish-Bentinck rang me up about the case of Carl von Loesch, who was formerly attaché to Ribbentrop's *dienststelle* in this country. He has come into possession of

---

[1] Details of the collection at the National Archives can be found at http://discovery.nationalarchives.gov.uk/details/r/C8595, and the Loesch letter at FO 371/46712, TNA.

[2] The Thomson report, quoted Andrew Morton, *17 Carnations: The Windsors, the Nazis and the Cover-Up* (O'Mara, 2015), p. 245.

the secret archives of the German Foreign Office. They had been photographed and at the last moment it was decided to burn them. Von Loesch managed to bury them and the SD who were doing the job merely burned the empty boxes thinking they were burning the archives.[3]

By July 1945, the State Department had accumulated 750,000 documents and microfilm and by August, 1,200 tons of files were held under joint Anglo-American control inside the American zone. The Loesch material was especially important, showing the close collaboration between Hitler and Franco, the text of non-aggression agreements made between Germany and the Soviet Union immediately prior to the Second World War, and the revelation that Oswald Mosley had been funded by Mussolini's government.

On 19 June, there was a meeting at the Foreign Office to discuss the 'finds' of German and Italian documents. 'We are left with an embarrassingly large quantity of documents (far more than we expected), which throw light on every major aspect of German and Italian policy,' stated one memo.[4]

'The whole Windsor problem has recently been complicated by the discovery among the German Foreign Office archives at Marburg of a set of top-secret telegrams between Ribbentrop and Stohrer (German Ambassador in Madrid), regarding certain alleged overtures made to the Windsors by German agents when they were marooned in Portugal in May 1940,' wrote Tommy Lascelles in his diary on 12 August:

If the Windsors' reactions were as implied in this correspondence (which both Godfrey Thomas, to whom I showed them,

[3] Liddell diary, 30 May 1945, KV4/196, TNA.
[4] 'Notes for 19 June meeting', FO 371/46713, TNA.

and I agree cannot be wholly discounted; internal evidence indicates that there is at any rate, a substratum of truth in it), the result is, to say the least, highly damaging to themselves. Only one other copy of this set of telegrams is said to be in existence, and that is in American hands; the Foreign Office are taking steps to recover it. Meanwhile, I advised the King to discuss the whole thing with Bevin, and to urge him to let both Winston and Walter Monckton read the telegrams.[5]

The next day the Foreign Secretary, Ernest Bevin, advised the new Prime Minister, Clement Attlee – a Labour government had just been elected – that 'we should try to persuade the United States Government to co-operate with us in suppressing the documents concerned' and felt 'a disclosure would in my opinion do grave harm to the national interest.'[6]

On 15 August, VJ Day, Lascelles cornered Lord Halifax after the King and Queen appeared on the balcony at Buckingham Palace 'and made him read the Marburg telegrams. I had actually received them from the Foreign Office the day before, but had deliberately withheld them from the King, thinking that they would certainly upset him and that he should not be troubled with them on the eve of making two major speeches.'[7]

Two days later, the Chiefs of Staff Joint Intelligence Sub Committee met to discuss the 'Release of Captured German Documents' and decided that publication should be deferred and the circulation of the documents restricted.[8]

---

[5] Duff Hart-Davis (ed.), *King's Counsellor,* p. 351.

[6] Bevin to Atlee, 13 August 1945, FO 800/521.

[7] Duff Hart-Davis (ed.), *King's Counsellor,* p. 352.

[8] CAB 79/37/21, TNA.

The German Documents

Sir Godfrey Thomas, the Duke's former Private Secretary, was tasked with preparing lines of defence and sent various arguments to Tommy Lascelles:

1/ that the whole thing is a tissue of lies. Can one imagine, with his record of service to his country, ever having flirted with the enemy or been a defeatist.

2/ that of course he had no suspicion that the Germans, through their Spanish & Portuguese agents, were trying to detain him in Europe for their own ends.

3/ Anyhow he didn't fall for it. After accepting the appointment, it was always his intention to proceed as soon as possible to the Bahamas. Any delay was due to the shipping difficulties and – perhaps to the Duchess's natural alarm at the many threats & anon warnings received during their stay in Lisbon (infernal machines on board).

4/ He will scoff at the possibility of his host Espirito Santo having been a German agent. The Brit Embassy in Lisbon must have had more inkling of this, if true. Why didn't they put him wise?

5/ He is bound to deny the reference to the King & Queen or to say that any remarks made about TM have been distorted.

It is of course possible that the German representatives in Madrid & Lisbon, knowing how insistent were Ribbentrop's instructions, that the D of W should be detained at all cost & by any means in Europe, did to a certain extent 'colour' their reports to Berlin so as to give the impression that they were working on HRH on the desired lines and, up to the last moment, with good hopes of success . . .

It must be remembered too that remarks alleged to have been made by HRH would have been recorded by the agents in Spanish or Portuguese then translated into German for transmission to Berlin & now back again into English. There is ample room for misinterpretation of a word or the sense of a whole phrase after passing through this process.

So much for the defence.

On the other side one must with reluctance admit that a lot of it rings horribly true. 'If I'd been King of England this war never need have happened. I understand the German.' One can hear him saying this.

And there have been reports before (some of which I think 'C' had) of the Duchess of W at any rate having spoken in similar terms of the King & Queen.

There were a good many rumours after the fall of France of his defeatism but I can't remember their source. I think it's probably fair to say she was the defeatist of the party, with her grievances and little love of this country and her attitude, as always, was the dominating influence.

As regards flirting with the enemy, how could he think that the neutral agent, when suggesting, among other things, that circumstances might result in him being put back on the throne had been inspired by anyone but the Germans.

I can't remember to whom he is said to have expressed sympathy & admiration for the Fuhrer but that needs a lot of explaining away. Clearly he could deny it flat.

And what of the alleged arrangement whereby if after his departure he was required to return. His 'agent' could send him a code message. What would he be required for and by whom?

THE ROYAL DUKES walk in the procession as it leaves New Palace Yard: (L. to R.) the Duke of Edinburgh, the Duke of Gloucester, the Duke of Windsor and the Duke of Kent. BELOW, the Heads of State and foreign Royal representatives: (L. to R.) first rank, King Gustav of Sweden, King Paul of the Hellenes, King Frederik of Denmark, President Auriol of France; second rank, President Bayar of Turkey, King Feisal of Irak, President Ribar of Jugoslavia; third rank, the Crown Prince of Abyssinia; fourth rank, Prince Ali Reza (Persia), Prince Bernhard of the Netherlands, Prince Felix of Luxembourg, the Prince of Liège; fifth rank, Marshal Shah Wali Khan (Afghanistan), Prince Zeid of Irak, Prince Axel of Denmark.

Above: Mother and son reunited, September 1945. The Duke had hoped Queen Mary might accept Wallis as part of the family, but his hopes were in vain.

© Pictorial Press Ltd/Alamy Stock Photo

Left: A news clipping from the *Daily Telegraph* depicting the Duke walking with the Duke of Edinburgh, the Duke of Gloucester and the Duke of Kent at his brother's, King George VI, funeral on 15 February 1952.

© Kathy deWitt/Alamy Stock Photo

Above: Gare De Lyon, Paris, 17 August 1952. The Duke, suffering from lumbago, is supported by a plain clothes detective and Wallis, while his private secretary, Victor Waddilove, looks after their dogs. © *Jean Aubry/AP/Shutterstock*

Below: The Duke and Wallis with their friend, French actor and singer Maurice Chevalier, at the International Dance Festival at the Champs Élysées Theatre in Paris, 5 November 1963. © *Keystone/Getty Images*

The Duke sitting with his golf club in Cuba, 3 December 1954. © *Bettmann/Getty Images*

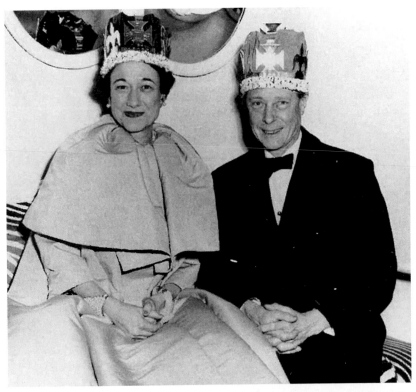

Above: The crowned Windsors seated on a zebra-striped 'throne', El Morocco nightclub, New Year's Eve, 1953.

Below left: Wallis with Jimmy. © *Topfoto*

Below right: Jimmy and the Duke in Venice, 1954.

OBJET : Séjour à Paris de la Duchesse de WINDSOR.

    Se disant souffrante, la Duchesse de WINDSOR a manifesté l'intention hier matin de garder la chambre toute la journée.

    Vers 15 heures, elle est cependant sortie pour assister à la présentation de la collection du couturier Christian Dior et elle a regagné sa résidence à 17h50.

    Vers 20 heures, M. James DONAHUE est venu la chercher. Ensemble ils ont dîné au restaurant "Paprika" 14, rue Chauchat et ils ont fini la soirée au cabaret de "Monseigneur", rue d'Amsterdam.

    M. DONAHUE a raccompagné la Duchesse à sa résidence vers 2h20 et n'a quitté lui-même l'hôtel de la rue la Faisanderie que ce matin à 5 heures.

Left: A surveillance report from the French Secret Service, noting that Jimmy appeared to leave the Duchess's home alone at 5 a.m.

© *Archives Nationales, France*

Right: The Duke reunited with Wallis in New York after he learns of the affair with Jimmy Donahue, December 1950. © *Bettmann/Getty Images*

Above left: 85 Rue de la Faisanderie, Paris, circa 1936, where the Windsors lived from 1949.

Below: The Windsors at home in Paris on 15 June 1951.

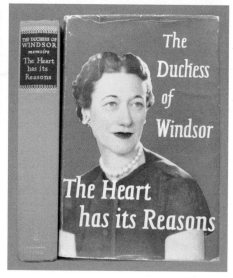

Above left: The Duke with his autobiography *A King's Story*, published 1951.
© *Erika Stone/Getty Images*

Above right: Charles Murphy (on left) who ghosted both of the Windsors'
autobiographies. © *Virginia Museum of History and Culture*

Below left: Cleveland Amory who started ghosting *The Heart has its Reasons* but
gave up because 'You can't make the Duchess of Windsor into Rebecca of
Sunnybrook Farm.' © *Hulton Archive/Getty Images*

Below right: Wallis's memoir *The Heart has its Reasons* published in 1956.

The Duke and Duchess of Windsor, 1956. In the 1950s, Philippe Halsman began asking his sitters to jump in front of the camera, because he noticed that doing so paradoxically seemed to relax people. © *Philippe Halsman/Magnum Photos*

And if all these mysterious negotiations with neutral agents were going on while he was in Lisbon, why didn't HRH say anything to the British Ambassador about them?

Either he knew perfectly well what they were driving at (in which his silence condemns him) or if he could probably claim he never grasped their real purpose, he should have gone to Walford, as a friend to whom he could talk freely, & say 'Several prominent Spaniards & Portuguese seem determined to persuade me to stay in Europe and are trying to make my flesh creep about the perils of going to the Bahamas. What do you think is behind it all?'

Perhaps I'm wronging him and something was reported about it at the time. Walford sent a spate of telegrams while HRH was in Portugal, some of which I remember seeing at the FO & all are presumably in the Private Secretary's files there. It might be interesting to re-read them in the light of the Marburg disclosures.

And I believe 'C' got a certain amount of Windsor gossip during this period from his chap in Lisbon.[9]

On 20 August, the British sent an *aide-mémoire* formally asking the State Department to destroy the Windsor file or hand it over to the British for 'safekeeping', arguing, 'It will be appreciated that the documents in question have no bearing on war crimes or on the general history of the war.'[10]

Guy Liddell of MI5 saw Lascelles at his club on 23 August, Liddell recording in his diary the next day, how he was then taken to:

[9] Godfrey Thomas to Tommy Lascelles, 17 August 1945, RA PS/PSO/GVI/ C/042A/397.

[10] Record Group 59, CDF, 1945–9, 862.4016-862.42, Box 6836, NARA.

look at certain papers on which he wanted advice. These papers were in fact German Foreign Office telegrams which had been found at Marburg ... The telegrams in question were dated about June – July 1940 and sent by Stohrer and Hoyneigen-Huehne (*sic*), the German ambassadors in Madrid and Lisbon respectively to Ribbentrop.[11]

He continued, 'There were also some from Ribbentrop to the ambassadors and one I think either to or from Abetz. The fact that Abetz had something to do with the scheme subsequently revealed in the telegrams might suggest that Charles Bedaux was behind the whole thing.'[12]

Liddell added that 'the Duke was staying in Lisbon as the guest of Esperito Santo Silva, the head of the bank of that name, which of course is known to us as an agency for the transmission of funds to German agents':[13]

He clearly rather felt himself in the role of mediator, if his country had finally collapsed, but he did not think the moment opportune for any sort of intervention ... Before the Duke left he fixed up, according to the telegrams, some kind of code with Espirito Santo Silva in order that he might fly back to Portugal from Florida if his intervention was required. It was further stated that about 15 August a telegram had been received from the Bahamas by Espirito Santo asking whether the moment had arrived.[14]

[11] Guy Liddell diary, 24 August 1945, KV 4/466, TNA.
[12] *Ibid.*
[13] *Ibid.*
[14] *Ibid.*

The German Documents

MI5 began to check telegrams sent during the period and decided to interrogate Walter Schellenberg, who was now in Allied custody. 'Ernest Bevin is *au fait* with all the information given above and is endeavouring to recover the copies and films of the telegrams in question since, if by any chance they leaked to the American press, a very serious situation would be created.[15]

He continued:

> I gather that Censorship obtained during the early days of the war a telegram from Madame Bedaux to the Duchess in the Bahamas which seemed to be of a singularly compromising nature. There were a lot of blanks in this telegram but the sense of it seemed to be that the question of either the Duke's mediation or of his restoration was discussed at some previous date and Madame Bedaux was anxious to know whether he was now prepared to say yes or no.[16]

Attlee decided to share details of the captured documents with Churchill, writing, 'Although clearly little or no credence can be placed in the statements made, nevertheless I feel sure that you will agree that publication of these documents might do the greatest possible harm.'[17] 'I am in entire agreement with the course proposed by the Foreign Secretary and approved by you,' Churchill replied the next day. 'I earnestly trust it may be possible to destroy all traces of these German intrigues.'[18]

---

[15] *Ibid.*

[16] *Ibid.*

[17] Attlee to Churchill, 25 August 1945, Annex D CAB 301/179, TNA.

[18] Churchill to Attlee, 26 August 1945, Annex D, CAB 301/179, TNA and BBK/G/6/20, Parliamentary Archives.

On 5 September, the 490-page dossier was signed out from Marburg on the orders of General Eisenhower, then the military governor of the American occupation zone, and sent to the Foreign Office. With the original at the Foreign Office and a microfilmed copy at the State Department, the only other existing copy of the Windsor file was the microfilm in British possession. It was promptly destroyed. The battle between British officialdom and American academia was about to begin.

On 27 August, David Harris, a Stanford University history professor seconded to the State Department as Assistant Chief of Central European Affairs, sent a memo to his boss John Hickerson, arguing that the Windsor file had historical value and the episode was a 'significant chapter in German and Spanish manoeuvres toward a negotiated peace with the United Kingdom in 1940', continuing that:

> in my judgement the documents are an essential part of the diplomatic record of 1940. There is I believe a moral responsibility resting on this government to preserve all the records in its possession, an obligation which takes precedence over a tender feeling for the ultimate reputation of the Duke of Windsor.[19]

The arguments raged over the autumn until in October, the new American Secretary of State, James F. Byrnes, informed Lord Halifax that for legal and historical reasons, the United States would not destroy the Marburg file, but provided a sop. The Windsor file would not be mentioned at the Nuremberg trials and 'The British Government is assured, however, that the

---

[19] Harris to Hickerson, 27 August 1945, Record Group 59, Lot File 78D441, Historical Office Records relating to the German Documents Project, 1944–83, Box 6, Historical Office, National Archives, quoted Morton, *17 Carnations*, p. 282.

Department of State will take all possible precautions to prevent any publicity with respect to the documents in its possession relative to the Duke of Windsor without prior consultation with the British Government.'[20]

Meanwhile MI5 were tasked to find out more about Operation Willi. On 1 September, Guy Liddell of MI5 passed Tommy Lascelles the interrogation of Schellenberg conducted two days earlier and marked 'Top Secret'. It revealed Hitler's offer to the Duke of 'the alternative right of residence in either Switzerland, Spain, France or Germany – a guarantee as to his own personal safety, together with an annuity of 100,000 US Dollar'.[21]

Liddell had sought to find a copy of Santo's message of 15 August 1940:

I find that our dealings with Espirito SANTO only began about December 1940, and unfortunately all records at Censorship headquarters and outstations before and after that date have now been destroyed. The only records therefore would be with interested departments if they saw fit to retain them. It is just possible that MEW might still have certain censorship submissions but I am clearing this point up.[22]

Three days later, Liddell again wrote to Lascelles after another interview with Schellenberg, who reported:

---

[20] Byrnes to Halifax, 11 October 1945, Record Group 59, Lot File 78D441, Box 13 Historical Office, National Archives, quoted Morton, *17 Carnations*, p. 284.

[21] The interrogation can be found at RA PS/PSO/GVI/C/042A/400.

[22] Guy Liddell to Tommy Lascelles, 1 September 1945, RA PS/PSO/GVI/ C/042A/399. MEW was the Ministry of Economic Warfare.

Von STOHRER took up a very optimistic attitude as to the prospect of carrying through RIBBENTROP's plan, remarking to SCHELLENBERG that he, SCHELLENBERG, had only to speak to W at the hunting expedition, and W would almost certainly accept. From this he supposes preliminary negotiations by von STOHRER and RIVERA to have made considerable progress, but he cannot enlarge upon the actual character and content of such negotiations . . . One basic fact he understood from both RIBBENTROP and von STOHRER's demeanour to be beyond all doubt, was W's serious intention to stay on in Europe.[23]

* * *

It was not only the Windsors whose private messages were being discussed. On 14 May, Tommy Lascelles recorded in his diary that Queen Mary, who had spent the weekend at Windsor, had sent for him 'ostensibly to discuss the possibility of guarding against the heirs of the Duke of Cambridge making undesirable use of two boxes of his letters deposited in their names in Coutts bank.' More importantly, he was alerted to the correspondence between the Duke of Connaught and his long-term mistress Leonie Leslie, Winston Churchill's aunt.[24]

The King was exercised about what might happen to them and Sir Owen Morshead, the Royal Librarian, was asked to rescue them.[25] This was to be just one of several missions by members of the Royal Household during 1945 to 'liberate' papers and artifacts in Germany for 'safe-keeping'.

[23] Guy Liddell to Tommy Lascelles, 4 September 1945, RA PS/PSO/GVI/ C/042A/402.

[24] The relationship lasted from the mid-1890s until the Duke's death in 1942.

[25] Duff Hart-Davis (ed.), *King's Counsellor*, pp. 324–5.

The German Documents

At the beginning of August, Morshead and Anthony Blunt, recently appointed Surveyor of the King's Pictures and still a member of MI5, left by military plane for Germany. *En route* they went to Schloss Wolfsgarten, where they interviewed Prince Louis of Hesse.[26] Officially, their mission was to recover correspondence at Schloss Kronberg between Queen Victoria and her eldest daughter, the Princess Royal, who had married Frederick III of Prussia in 1858.

The 4,000 letters known as the 'Vicky letters' were kept at the schloss just outside Frankfurt, which was the main residence of George VI's cousins, the von Hessen family. The letters contained details of Queen Victoria's relationship from the age of fifteen with the Captain of the Royal Horse Guards, the 13th Lord Elphinstone, twelve years her senior, who, when the affair was discovered in 1836, was exiled to India as Governor of Madras.[27]

Guy Liddell noted in his diary on 15 August, 'Anthony has returned from Germany and has brought with him Queen Victoria's letters to the Empress Frederick. They are only on loan.'[28] The 73-year-old Princess Margaret of Hesse had agreed to the transfer of the letters, but the problem was that the Americans were less keen to surrender any property. Kathleen Nash, the female American captain in charge of the castle, which had been commandeered as a social club, said she could not let any papers go as they were the property of the US

---

[26] OMGUS Records, p. 130, Ardelia Hall Collection, NARA.

[27] The story is told in Roland Perry's *The Queen, Her Lover And the Most Notorious Spy In History* (Allen & Unwin, 2014).

[28] Guy Liddell diary, 15 August 1945, KV4/ 466A, TNA. Cf. US Colonel John Allen memo, 'on 3 August 1945, however, the Victoria letters were officially received by Sir Owen Morshead and Major A.F. Blunt for transfer to Windsor Castle, England', RG 260, OMGUS Education and Cultural Relations, Box 226, Colonel John Allen to G-5 USFET, 6 August 1946, NARA, quoted Jonathan Petropoulos, *Royals and the Reich: The Princes von Hessen in Nazi Germany* (Oxford University Press, 2006), p. 338.

Army. Whilst Blunt distracted her, the packing cases of documents were loaded onto a waiting lorry.[29]

Yet Blunt's role in the collection of the letters seems to have been minor. In his report of the rescue, Morshead hardly mentioned Blunt and only justified his presence 'since he had in any case to go out to Germany on business I had brought him with me, for agreeable companionship and because his German is excellent.'[30] So why was Blunt there? What other business did he have? Morshead may have removed Vicky's letters, but no artwork was taken and Blunt simply made an inventory of thirty-one English works that belonged to the Empress.[31]

From Kronberg, Blunt travelled to Schloss Marienburg, in Lower Saxony, property of the Princes von Hanover. Prince Ernst August von Hanover was close to the Nazi hierarchy – he had joined the SS in 1933 – and there was concern that some correspondence there might reveal pro-German sentiment by British royals. There was also a worry that important cultural artifacts might fall into the hands of the advancing Soviets.[32]

---

[29] The Vicky letters were returned in December 1951 and can now be seen at Schloss Fasanerie. The Morshead/Blunt mission is documented in RG 260, OMGUS Education and Cultural Relations, Box 226, Colonel John Allen to G-5 USFET, 6 August 1946, NARA, quoted Petropoulos, p. 338. Also RA M SS A/1 report of Owen Morshead, 9 August 1945, and RA MSS Sir Owen Morshead's Mission to Germany 3–5 August 1945, quoted Petropoulos, p. 339. The visit alerted Nash that there might be other valuables in the castle. Together with her boyfriend, later her husband, Colonel Jack Durant, she stole the family's fabled collection of jewellery, worth up to $6 million. Quickly apprehended, Nash was sentenced to five years and Durant to fifteen years. Only a small percentage of what had been stolen was ever recovered.

[30] RA Add M SS A/1, report of Owen Morshead, 9 August 1945, quoted Petropoulos, p. 339.

[31] 'Hesse Crown Jewels Court-Martial', p. 95, NARA.

[32] Miranda Carter, *Anthony Blunt* (Macmillan, 2001), p. 316. Details of the mission to Duke of Brunswick can be found in FO 371/65327, TNA.

The German Documents

In 1979, Blunt was publicly revealed to have been a Russian spy since the 1930s, though he had privately confessed to the intelligence services in 1964. The MI5 officer Peter Wright, who interrogated him, was informed by the Queen's private secretary, Sir Michael Adeane, that Blunt had undertaken an 'assignment . . . on behalf of the Palace – a visit to Germany.' Wright was told not to 'pursue the matter . . . strictly speaking it is not relevant to considerations of national security.'[33]

It looks like the trip to Kronberg was a cover for a fishing expedition, which suggests there was something else the Royal Family was worried about. 'George VI had every reason to believe that the Hesse archives might contain a "Windsor file", because Prince Philipp of Hesse had been an intermediary, via the Duke of Kent, between Hitler and the Duke of Windsor,' claimed Prince Wolfgang of Hesse to the *Sunday Times*.

It was a belief supported by the wartime intelligence officer Hugh Trevor-Roper, later Regius Professor of Modern History at Oxford University.[34] It is confirmed by Andrew Sinclair, who spent eighteen months researching a biography of Vicky, *The Other Victoria*, who wrote that Blunt had retrieved 'the Duke of Windsor's correspondence with his German princely cousins, some of whom held high office in the Nazi party.'[35]

John Loftus, a lawyer with the US Justice Department, interviewed two former US military intelligence officers from the SHAEF T-groups attached to General Patton's forces, who confirmed they had seen references to communications between the Duke of Windsor and Hitler. The documents had been found in

[33] Peter Wright, *Spycatcher* (Viking, 1987), p. 223.

[34] C. Simpson, Leitch and Knightley, 'Blunt was Emissary', *Sunday Times*, 25 November 1979.

[35] Andrew Sinclair, *London Review of Books*, Vol. 37, No. 18, 24 September 2015.

a 'villa that was owned by a close relative of the Duke which was occupied as an American officer's club.'[36]

Douglas Price, an aide to General Dwight D. Eisenhower, was stationed at Friedrichshof in the summer of 1945. In the library he found an ornate cabinet containing letters between the Hesse family and the Duke of Windsor, dating back to when he had been Prince of Wales. It seems that these were the documents that Blunt had been sent to retrieve.[37]

According to the intelligence magazine *Lobster*, Blunt had also been sent to retrieve the minutes of the Duke of Windsor's 1937 meeting with Hitler, which were missing from the captured German documents.[38]

Donald Cameron Watt, the British historian who was part of the team dealing with the captured German documents at Whaddon Hall, later told the *Sunday Times*:

> Among the 400 tons of documents there was a section relating to the Duke of Windsor. Everything we thought should have been in this file was indeed there – with one exception. For example, we found all the Lisbon material and we found accounts of Windsor's conversations with Ribbentrop and various German officials. The exception was there was no account of the conversation with Hitler in October 1937. There was simply no trace of this in the archives.[39]

---

[36] John Loftus interview, John Costello, *Mask of Treachery* (Collins, 1988), p. 461.

[37] Interview Douglas Price, *Edward VIII: Traitor King* (Channel 4, 1996). See his diary entry for 29 July 1945, AD 37-1/47, Keble College Archives, Oxford.

[38] *Lobster*, summer 2015, referencing a *Daily Telegraph* report from 1978.

[39] *Sunday Times*, 25 November 1979.

The German Documents

The Windsors, unaware of what was happening with the captured documents, quietly left the Bahamas for Miami in early May 1945. They spent time with friends in Palm Beach, and then spent several months at a flat at the Waldorf Towers in New York, whilst they decided what to do. The Duke had lost $100,000 drilling for non-existent oil on his Canadian ranch and needed to make up his losses. He briefly toyed with the idea of a business career in America and visited Cleveland, Ohio, at the end of June to study industrial methods, courtesy of Robert Young, but decided it was not for him. In July, they were the guests of the Canadian philanthropist and banker Isaak Killan at his fishing lodge in New Brunswick, causing British officials to worry he might be lobbying to become Canadian governor general.[40]

In August, they stayed at the Washington embassy as the guest of Sir John Balfour, the First Secretary. Balfour had met the Duke pre-war and had always felt 'in spite of the hold on popular affection which he had acquired as Prince of Wales, he was unfitted to be King . . . My disquiet about the King was heightened by reports that innate pro-German sympathies were colouring his views on the subject of Nazi Germany.'[41]

Balfour found no reason on his visit to revise his opinion, regarding him as 'a mixed-up, unstable character':

> On the third evening of his stay, the Duke asked us to invite to dinner an elderly American friend of his – a railroad tycoon named Young. Both of them seemed oblivious to Nazi misdeeds and were at one in thinking that, had Hitler been

[40] See DO 127/54, TNA.

[41] 'Encounters with the Windsors', p. 5, Sir John Balfour papers, Columbia University.

differently handled, war with Germany might have been avoided in 1939.[42]

By September, the Windsors were back in Paris. Duff Cooper, recently appointed British ambassador in Paris, reported that the Duke 'seems to be making himself a bit of a nuisance, "talking big" to various French officials whom he meets at dinner, and telling them how to run their own country, which naturally they don't like. He was always given to holding forth, and indeed, as long ago as 1926, showed increasing signs of becoming a hearth-rug bore; with increasing years, he may be developing George IV's tendency to arrogate to himself capabilities, and performances which are actually beyond him . . .'[43]

His wife, Lady Diana Cooper, equally disparaging, thought 'both looking as thin as if just out of Belsen. She grown a little more common, and he more pointless, dull and insipid.'[44]

Shortly afterwards the Duke flew to London, staying at Marlborough House with Queen Mary. He had two objectives – to secure acceptance of Wallis from his family and a job from the new Labour Government. He failed on both counts. It was the first time he had seen his mother since 1936 and his brother since 1940 and the reunions, according to Tommy Lascelles, went 'far better than expected', but 'I gather that the King has at last convinced him that there is no possibility of his Duchess ever being "received" or getting the title HRH.'[45]

---

[42] *Ibid*, pp. 8–9. He writes in similar vein in his autobiography: John Balfour, *Not Too Correct an Aureole* (Michael Russell, 1983), p. 108.

[43] Lascelles Diary, 9 November 1945, Duff Hart-Davis (ed.), *King's Counsellor*, p. 367.

[44] Lascelles Diary, 11 October 1945, *Counsellor*, p. 361.

[45] Lascelles diary, 6 October 1945, *Counsellor*, pp. 356–7.

'Quite like old times; very well informed, knew everything that was going on,' Queen Mary told Owen Morshead about the visit. 'But still persisting about my receiving his wife, when he promised he'd never mention the subject to me again. His last words when he was going away – "Well goodbye – and don't forget: I'm a married man now." Don't forget, indeed: as if one ever could!'[46]

There was equally little comfort from Attlee. The Duke had hoped there might be a role for him as an Ambassador at Large in the United States. 'I would concentrate on the public relations aspect . . . Such a job would require my bringing Americans and visiting Britons together, providing a good table and a comfortable library for informal talks and helping along what Winston Churchill called "the mixing-up process".'[47]

But there was the continuing concern, as Halifax reported to the Foreign Office, that 'press reports of society engagements in Newport, New York and Long Island would, as they have done before, tell heavily the other way.'[48] And there were the questions about some of his associates. 'The Duke has certain disagreeable personal skeletons in his cupboard – e.g., Axel Gren, Bedaux and Ricardo Espírito Santo Silva, all proven German agents,' wrote Lascelles in his diary, after the Duke had asked to be made Ambassador at Buenos Aires. 'No professional diplomat with such associations would ever be given an important embassy – or indeed employed anywhere.'[49]

[46] Owen Morshead, 'Notes on conversation with Queen Mary', 18 February 1946, A AEC/GG/12/OS/2, quoted Shawcross, p. 600.

[47] *New York Daily News*, 11–16 December 1966.

[48] Halifax to FO, 4 March 1946, RA GV EE 13/48, quoted Ziegler, p. 506.

[49] Lascelles diary, 5 October 1945, *Counsellor,* pp. 355–6.

Sir Alexander Cadogan noted in his diary at the same time that 'the King fussed about the Duke of Windsor's file and the captured German documents.'[50]

But Churchill could see the merit of giving the Duke something to do. As he told the King, 'I would even go so far as to say that there might be serious disadvantages in utterly casting off the Duke of Windsor and his wife from all official contact with Great Britain, and leaving him in a disturbed and distressed state of mind to make his own life in the United States.'[51]

In mid-November, Churchill spent the day with the couple in Paris and drew up a memo, 'Concerning His Desire for Official Work in America after 1945'.[52] But nothing was forthcoming.

In March 1946, Tommy Lascelles suggested to Halifax that the Duke buy a house:

somewhere in the southern states, and make it a centre of private hospitality . . . where he could bring together worth-while Americans, English and foreigners . . . with this he could continue some line of his own (stock-raising, arboriculture, agricultural research, etc.) which would give him an interest, and which, with his considerable means, he could well afford to do on a useful and even profitable scale . . . The King feels strongly . . . that the USA is the only place in which he *can* live, and that he should be urged to make it his permanent home as soon as possible. He must not settle in the UK . . . The King hoped if Duke did settle in US it would be possible for British Embassy to establish a friendly and unofficial relationship with

[50] Cadogan diary, 25 October 1945, ACAD/1/15, Churchill College Archives.
[51] Churchill to George VI, 18 November 1945, RA GV EE 13/41, quoted Ziegler, p. 505.
[52] It is reproduced in Bloch, *Secret File*, pp. 315–18.

the Duke whereby HRH's wish to make himself useful in the sphere of Anglo-American understanding may be encouraged, and when necessary, controlled by private advice.[53]

The problem with the United States was taxation. The Duke had considerable wealth and, since diplomatic status was not being offered, he had no wish to pay tax, especially if it was backdated. Kenneth de Courcy, the editor of a series of international finance and intelligence magazines who had suggested the Duke adopt the role of roving foreign affairs expert lobbying those in power, continued to press the couple to stay close to the Royal Family and to:

set up a suitable home in England which should, at first, be visited for very short, sharp and brief periods for business and private purposes only . . . I think the public and the government should be allowed slowly to get used to the idea of Your Royal Highness and the Duchess coming over for private purposes from time to time. Slowly and wisely the thing could become habitual and presently the whole thing would be accepted by everyone as perfectly normal and harmless.[54]

Hearing that Fort Belvedere, which had been abandoned during the war, might be sold or leased, the Duke offered to buy it back. It was immediately taken off the market.[55]

It was clear that the couple's exile was to be permanent.

---

[53] Halifax papers, A4.410.4.10, quoted Sarah Bradford, *King George VI* (Weidenfeld & Nicolson, 1989), pp. 445–6.

[54] Kenneth de Courcy to the Duke of Windsor, 14 March 1946, de Courcy, Box 3, Folder 5, Hoover Institute.

[55] In 1955 it was sold to his nephew Hon. Gerald Lascelles on a 99-year lease, which was taken up in 1976 by the son of the Emir of Dubai. *Edward & Mrs Simpson* was filmed there in 1978.

CHAPTER 17

A Life Without Purpose

Susan Mary Patten, a US diplomat's wife and one of Duff Cooper's mistresses, sat next to the Duke at a dinner in Paris and wrote in her diary, 'He is pitiful, looks young and un-dissipated, and the famous charm is still there, but I never saw a man so bored . . . They are dining here on Saturday and I couldn't dread it more . . .'

He had recounted his day to her:

I got up late, and then I went with the Duchess and watched her buy a hat, and then on the way home I had the car drop me in the Bois to watch some of your soldiers playing football . . . When I got home the Duchess was having her French lesson, so I had no one to talk to, so I got a lot of tin boxes down which my mother had sent me last week and looked through them. They were essays and so on that I had written when I was in France studying French before the Great War . . . You know I'm not much of a reading man.[1]

---

[1] Susan Alsop, *To Marietta from Paris 1945–1960* (Weidenfeld & Nicolson, 1976), pp. 54–5. Patten continued to dine with the Windsors until April 1953, when her husband got into a row with the Duke after he called General Marshall a communist. Alsop, pp. 220–1.

Though there were too many sensitivities for the Duke to take on a business career or diplomatic appointment – the latter having a particular attraction because of the tax status – there was no reason he could not have devoted his time to a non-governmental job or charity, but he chose not to do so. Independently wealthy and with no dependants beyond his wife, he had greater freedom than most men of his generation – he was just fifty – to pursue his own interests.

The problem was that he had few interests. As he told Susan Patten, he was 'not much of a reading man'. When Churchill presented him with an inscribed copy of his memoirs, the Duke thanked him and said he would put it in the bookshelf next to the other volumes. He had no interest in the arts or helping others. Once, after sitting through a concert organised by Lady Cunard, he asked, 'Did that Mozart chap write anything else?'[2]

His life revolved around golf, gardening, being entertained, discussing his investments and musing about politics with the similarly minded – generally rich American businessmen who were antisemitic and anti-communist. The problem was that the Duke wanted status not a job, to be recognised rather than to contribute.

Patten was back dining with the Windsors in February. 'Awful evening at the Windsors,' she wrote in her diary, 'the Duchess determined to play word games, despite her complete lack of education and the competition of Lady Diana Cooper, who learned history with her mother's milk . . . the Duke couldn't remember Metternich and Castlereagh and the Duchess to help him screamed, 'Your turn, David, now take someone we all know.'[3]

---

[2] Cleveland Amory notes, CAP, Box 85, quoted Morton, *Wallis in Love*, p. 293.

[3] Alsop, p. 67.

'The Duke of Windsor came to see me this morning at his own request,' noted Duff Cooper in his diary:

> I thought he wanted to consult me about something – but not at all. He sat here for nearly an hour chattering about one thing and another. I expect the truth is that he is so *désoeuvré* that Wallis, to get him out of the house, said, 'Why don't you go round to see Duff one morning and have an interesting talk about politics.'[4]

After the Boulevard Suchet house was sold, the Windsors moved to an apartment at the Ritz and then moved back to La Croë. It had billeted Italians and German troops during the war and was in a sorry state, with curtains and oil paintings stolen, mines in the garden, rusting radar on the roof and huge pillboxes on the sea wall. Wallis, never happier than when making a new home, set about restoring it and their pre-war life. Within a month she had a staff of twenty-two and was entertaining furiously, helped by the fact that, as a major-general, the Duke was entitled to draw rations from the British Army depot at Marseille.

Here the couple lived the life denied to them in reality; here Wallis was given the status denied to her by the Royal Family. Georges Sanègre, who worked for the Windsors for almost forty years, was taken aside when he first joined the staff by Wilmott the butler. 'I have been instructed by the duke that all staff must bow or curtsy to the duchess and call her Your Royal Highness. You must never speak first, but wait until she has spoken to you; never

---

[4] 14 March 1946, John Julius Norwich (ed.), *The Duff Cooper Diaries: 1915–1951* (Weidenfeld & Nicolson, 2005), p. 403. *Désoeuvré* means 'with nothing to do' or 'at a loose end'.

turn your back to her, but take several paces backwards and then turn to leave her presence.'[5]

The Windsors always dressed for dinner – he in dinner jacket or kilt, she in long dress and jewels, and close attention was paid to the food, flowers and guests. They brought in well-known entertainers such as Maurice Chevalier, and guests might include Noël Coward. Once when a member of staff was surprised there were only six for dinner, Wallis quickly replied, indeed, 'but they are all kings.'[6]

Without any purpose in life, the Windsors' purpose became to entertain and be entertained. If they could not live in a royal palace or be posted to an embassy, they would create the ambience of one themselves. Their lives would become a spectacle. One guest remembered them taking a party to a gala in Monte Carlo. 'She had on every jewel. He wore a kilt. It was like watching a couple in pantomime – the studied gestures, the automatic smiles.'[7]

'In the evening the Windsors arrived,' wrote Noël Coward in his diary in spring 1946:

> The hotel got itself into a fine frizz . . . I gave them a delicious dinner: consommé, marrow on toast, grilled langoustine, tournedos with sauce béarnaise, and chocolate soufflé. Poor starving France. After that we went to the Casino and Wallis and I gambled until 5 a.m. She was very gay and it was most enjoyable. The Duke sat rather dolefully at one of the smaller tables.[8]

'You can't imagine the sense of luxury at La Croë in that first summer after the war,' said the French socialite and friend of the Windsors,

[5] Parker, p. 245.

[6] Parker, p. 246.

[7] Bryan and Murphy, p. 463.

[8] 6 April 1946, Graham Payn and Sheridan Morley (ed.), *The Noël Coward Diaries* (Weidenfeld & Nicolson, 1982), p. 55.

the Baronne de Cabrol. 'It was a really grand villa and to amuse us, the Duchess arranged to serve dinner in a different room each night over the ten days we stayed there.'[9]

'A dull reception at the Chamber of Commerce followed by a call on the Windsors – in a small apartment at the Ritz,' wrote Duff Cooper in his diary later:

> Wallis was looking strikingly plain. It is sad to think that he gave up the position of King-Emperor not to live in an island of the Hesperides with the Queen of Beauty, but to share an apartment on the third floor of the Ritz with this harsh-voiced, ageing woman who was never even very pretty.[10]

In plotting their return to mainstream British life, the royal couple continued to rely heavily on the advice of Kenneth de Courcy. Referring to 'the subject we discussed in Paris', the Duke wrote to de Courcy in March 1946:

> It certainly is a situation of great delicacy but, at the same time, one in which it would seem I hold fifty per cent of the bargaining power in order that the Duchess and I can plan for the future in the most constructive and convenient way. For obvious reasons, I prefer to say no more in this letter but look forward to another talk with you when there is an opportunity which I hope may be soon.[11]

[9] Suzy Menkes, *The Windsor Style* (Grafton, 1987), p. 76.

[10] 7 June 1946, John Julius Norwich, p. 412.

[11] Duke of Windsor to de Courcy, 19 March 1946, de Courcy Box 3, Folder 5, Hoover Institute.

In May, de Courcy stayed with them in the South of France to 'discuss world affairs and possible future activities.'[12] Those future activities soon became clear. De Courcy saw Lord Clarendon, the Lord Chamberlain of the Royal Household, asking if Fort Belvedere could be made available to the Duke as he 'was proposing to make some statement to the press in America retailing all his grievances against the King and the British government.' Clarendon reported the blackmail to Tommy Lascelles, who contacted Guy Liddell of MI5 and it was agreed 'to take the risk of the Duke giving a statement to the press which he does not think would cut much ice.'[13]

* * *

In October 1946, the couple paid a short visit to the United Kingdom, the Duke again lobbying George VI for a job. The trip was by way of an experiment to gauge the public reaction of their return to Britain – one that did not start well when it was revealed that three army lorries were required to transport their luggage. They were lent Ednam Lodge in Berkshire for a month by their friend William Ward, the 3rd Earl of Dudley, and it was there on 16 October that the Duchess was robbed of some of her jewellery, a *cause célèbre* that made news headlines around the world – much of it critical of the Windsors.

Whilst the couple were in London for the evening and staff were downstairs, a cat burglar climbed a drainpipe, crossed a flat roof and entered through the open window of the Duchess's secretary. Wallis had rejected an offer to put her jewellery in the house safe and instead it was simply kept under her bed. Accounts vary, but it is said that some £250,000 of jewels were stolen, though some items were later found abandoned on a local golf course, including

---

[12] Duke of Windsor to de Courcy, 15 April 1946, de Courcy Box 3, Folder 5, Hoover Institute.

[13] Guy Liddell diary, 16 May 1946, KV4/467, TNA.

a string of pearls valued then at £5,000 and gifted to the Duke by Queen Alexandra.[14]

The whole episode was distressing for everyone. The Countess of Dudley later wrote that Wallis showed:

> an unpleasant and to me unexpected side of her character . . .
> She wanted all the servants put through a kind of third degree.
> But I would have none of this, all of them except for one kitchen maid being old and devoted staff of long standing . . .
> the Duke was both demented with worry and near to tears.[15]

The robbery received wide publicity and did not endear the Windsors to a Britain living with rationing. When asked what jewellery she had been wearing that night, Wallis replied, as if perfectly obvious, 'A fool would know that with tweeds or other daytime clothes one wears gold, and that with evening clothes one wears platinum.'[16]

Mysteries remain about the burglary, raising suspicions of an inside job – possibly, according to rumours, even sponsored by the Royal Family keen to recover gifts made to the Duke. None of the Dudleys' guard dogs had barked and a detective at the front door had heard nothing. In 2003 the Scotland Yard case files were released, naming a well-known local burglar called Leslie Holmes.[17]

---

[14] Hugo Vickers, *Behind Closed Doors* (Hutchinson, 2011), p. 339, says only eleven pieces were stolen. Bryan and Murphy, p. 458, quoting a member of the Duke's staff, says the jewels were insured for £400,000, but in fact the insurers paid out £800,000. £250K and £5K is £10.7 million and £214K in today's money.

[15] Laura, Duchess of Marlborough, *Laughter from a Cloud* (Weidenfeld & Nicolson, 1980), pp. 104–5. To make up for the loss, he supposedly bought new jewels worth £75,000.

[16] *Evening Standard*, 17 October 1946.

[17] MEPO 2/9149, TNA, though parts still remain closed. Holmes's granddaughter Harry Leavey wrote a fictionalised account of the robbery, *The Duchess and the Soldier's Revenge*.

Holmes was imprisoned for five years in 1947 for other housebreaking offences and asked for twenty-six other cases to be taken into consideration, but he never confessed to the crime.

Other suspects included two criminals operating in the South of France, Rodney Mundy and Campbell Muir,[18] and both Suzy Menkes and Hugo Vickers have named a Norfolk burglar, Richard Dunphie, who confessed in 1960.

The official historian of the Queen's jewels, Leslie Field, later claimed:

> I believe the Duchess of Windsor defrauded the insurers by overstating the numbers and identifications of the jewels which had been disposed of. At least thirty items she named as being stolen turned up in the Sotheby's catalogue at Geneva in April 1987 and were sold for high prices. She clearly could never wear those jewels again after she and her husband had collected the insurance. They had from the beginning been in a strong-box in Paris and remained there.[19]

Meanwhile, the debate about the future of the captured German documents continued. 'I feel sure they would not hesitate to remove any which showed appeasement policies of high British personalities in an unfavourable light,' minuted Freeman Matthews, the Director of the State Department's Office of European Affairs, to the US Secretary of State, James F. Byrnes, in January 1946, concerned about the various British attempts to suppress the Windsor material. 'We have on occasion had difficulty obtaining microfilm copies of certain documents. The British, on one occasion, formally

---

[18] *Los Angeles Times*, 1 January 1950.

[19] Higham, *Mrs Simpson*, pp. 428–9. It is more likely that copies were made from the insurance money and were then sold as originals by Sothebys.

requested us to sanction the destruction of certain documents deal-ing with the Duke of Windsor's passage through Spain and Portugal in the summer of 1940.'[20]

In June 1946, an Anglo-American agreement was signed for publication of selections of the captured German diplomatic docu-ments, but the file on the Duke was not included in the archive given to the British and American historians.

In November 1946, *Newsweek* leaked the story of the Marburg file, to the irritation of Lord Inverchapel, the British ambassador in Washington, who wrote a 'Top Secret and Personal' letter to the Under Secretary of State, Dean Acheson: 'I am at a loss to know what explanation I can give to the Foreign Office with regard to this leakage in view of the special precautions which your Department agreed to undertake . . .'[21]

Rumours were already rife in British circles about the file. Bruce Lockhart noted in his diary the same month: 'Jack Wheeler-Bennett in his sifting of the German documents has found some damag-ing material on the Duke of Windsor. There are various protocols of Nazi conversations with him, including one at Lisbon during the war.'[22]

At the foreign minister's meeting in Moscow in March 1947, Bevin, an unlikely protector of the Royal Family, sent urgent requests to the new US secretary of state George Marshall, trying to suppress the Marburg file. In a 'Personal, For Your Eyes Only' telegram, Marshall asked Acheson about the microfilm copy of the Windsor file. 'Bevin says only other copy was destroyed by Foreign

[20] Freeman Matthews to James Byrnes, 31 January 1946, Record Group 59, CF 1945–49 (Conf), Box 5703, FW 840.414/1-2946, NARA, quoted Morton, *17 Carnations*, p. 288.

[21] Inverchapel to Acheson, 2 November 1946, FO 371/55526, TNA.

[22] 23 November 1946, Young, Vol 2, p. 572.

Office, and asks that we destroy ours to avoid possibility of a leak to great embarrassment of Windsor's brother. Please attend to this for me and reply for my eyes only.'[23]

In August 1947, Owen Morshead and Anthony Blunt flew to Huis Doorn, the home of Kaiser Wilhelm II, after Wheeler-Bennett had found a reference in the captured German documents to his son Frederich Wilhelm being used as a royal intermediary by Hitler. They returned with the Kaiser's Garter insignia and a portrait of the Duke of Clarence, but reported 'no documentary material was found'.

However, the story of the German documents was not over yet.[24]

---

[23] NA 841.001/3-157, NARA. Declassified in 1988 it carries a manuscript note 'no record in RM/R as of 2,28/58'. No copy of microfilm appears to exist in any archive. We don't know what it is, but its contents must have been highly sensitive.' Acheson's reply is also missing from the files.

[24] Owen Morshead to Tommy Lascelles, 28 September 1947, FO 370/1698, TNA.

CHAPTER 18

The Wandering Windsors

The Windsors spent the winter of 1947 with Arthur Vernay at his home in the Bahamas, the first time the couple had returned to the island since 1945. They had met Vernay, an English-born American art and antiques dealer, decorator, big-game hunter, and explorer, during the war and were to subsequently spend many winters with him in the Bahamas.[1]

From there they moved on to Robert Young in Palm Beach. Though never totally accepted in Newport or New York, the Windsors loved Palm Beach, where the Duke regularly played golf and they were treated as royalty, with bows, curtsies, positions at the head of table and being served first. Protocol required that no one could leave until they did, which often led to tensions, as the Duke enjoyed lingering. 'Sometimes at parties, for no apparent reason, the Duke would insist on speaking only in German,' one biographer remembered:

> Since German was a language with which most of the Palm Beach winter colony was not familiar, there were often evenings when, for long periods, no one had the slightest idea what the Duke was talking about. During the day, the male

---

[1] The Colonial Office were concerned about the protocol of such visits. CO 537/2250, TNA.

members of the Everglades Club would draw straws to see who would play golf with the Duke. The loser got him as a golfing partner; he was, it seemed, a painfully slow player, planning and discussing his shots for what felt like hours.[2]

King Leopold of Belgium, a regular golfing partner, remembered how the Duke was 'always eager to win and tended to forget his score. Once I saw David take three shots in a trap, then give himself a five.'[3]

* * *

In May 1947, the Windsors returned to London from the United States. Asked about a new job, the Duke replied, 'I might do something sometime, but I have nothing definite in mind. I never take life easy. I never have and I never shall.'[4] The Duke took the opportunity to lobby Clement Attlee for a job and see his mother on her eightieth birthday – though he was not invited to the birthday lunch. Cynthia Gladwyn, who saw the couple at a tea given by Sibyl Colefax, leaves a portrait of the former king:[5]

At first glance he appears extraordinarily youthful, a boyish figure and his small retroussé nose giving him a very juvenile look. But as one examines him more carefully, one is almost unpleasantly shocked to see how old, wrinkled, and worried his face is and how pathetic his expression. His hair is golden and I fancy must be dyed, for he must be over fifty . . . He was amiable and alert, but one was terribly aware of his instability. He talked a great deal, not interestingly, but keenly – in fact he

---

[2] Birmingham, p. 226.

[3] Cyrus Sulzberger, *A Long Row of Candles* (Macdonald, 1969), p. 392.

[4] Birmingham, p. 227.

[5] Other guests included Osbert Lancaster, Harold Nicolson and Ben Nicolson.

hardly drew breath. We discussed conferences, the Russians, servant difficulties, the French, places he'd been to, and so on. I envy his remarkable memory, he appeared to remember dates and names with ease and accuracy. He spoke with a profound American accent, and used American expressions which rather jarred on me. He kept looking at his watch and wondering why the Duchess didn't arrive, and finally dashed into the next room to telephone to find out what had detained her.[6]

When Princess Elizabeth shortly afterwards announced her engagement to Philip Mountbatten, there was no invitation to the November wedding – the Windsors were the only close relations not amongst the 2,200 guests.

'I am always hoping that one day you will tell me to bring Wallis to see you, as it makes me very sad to think that you and she have never really met,' wrote the Duke to Queen Mary. 'It would indeed be tragic if you, my mother, had never known the girl I married and who has made me so blissfully happy.'[7]

Instead they returned to the Waldorf Towers, where they had become friends with the composer Cole Porter, who also had an apartment there, and where on Christmas Eve they hosted a large dinner.

'We were a party of some twenty,' remembered the journalist Cecil Roberts:

I was astonished on entering their suite, which they kept permanently, by its almost regal magnificence. There were full-length paintings of George III and George IV in their

---

[6] 28 May 1947, Miles Jebb (ed.), *The Diaries of Cynthia Gladwyn* (Constable, 1995), p. 56.

[7] Duke of Windsor to Queen Mary, 15 August 1947, RA GV EE 3, quoted Ziegler, p. 529.

coronation robes. Others of the duke's ancestors were there, some in the Garter regalia, all illuminated, in the long salon. Two footmen wore liveries. It was a full-dress affair, the ladies décolleté, with jewels. The duchess wore a small tiara on her black, tightly drawn-back hair. A cerise silk gown moulded her svelte figure. The dining-room shone with silver, cut glass, flowers. The serviettes were embroidered with the royal arms. This did not look like exile.

In the salon after coffee we began to pull crackers and sing carols. After this there were general songs. The duke, in a plum-coloured velvet evening jacket, went to the grand piano and began to sing. He had a large repertoire, a good voice and was excellent in some German, Lancashire, Scottish and Irish songs. His à la Harry Lauder 'Oh it's nice to get up in the morning, but it's better to lie in bed' was the *chef d'oeuvre.* The party broke up at three a.m.[8]

* * *

In February 1948, the couple were in Florida and the following month they spent several weeks cruising the Caribbean – where they met Ernest Hemingway in Cuba – as the guests of Joseph Davies, the former American ambassador to Russia, and his wife Marjorie Merriweather Post.[9] In April and May the Windsors were on Long Island, staying at Severn, the Locust Valley estate of another friend, Polly Howe, where the local 'hostesses were somewhat put off when they were asked to submit their guest lists to the Duchess before

[8] Cecil Roberts, *The Pleasant Years* (Hodder & Stoughton, 1974), p. 36.

[9] Their yacht *Sea Cloud*, then the largest privately owned sea-going yacht in the world, was sold in 1955 to the President of the Dominican Republic, Rafael Trujillo. The Windsors often stayed at Post's home Mar-a-Largo, later owned by Donald Trump.

she would agree to attend any parties, and were even more put off when these lists were returned with certain names crossed out.'[10]

They were then the guests of honour at the reopening of Robert Young's Greenbrier Hotel in West Virginia, a four-day extravaganza paid for by Young for '300 leaders of business, government, society, the motion picture world and sports', including Fred and Adele Astaire, Sam Goldwyn, Herbert Hoover, Bob Hope, President Truman, Bing Crosby and William Randolph Hearst, where the Duke played the drums for 'How are things in Glocca Morra' during the intermission.

Concerned by radical leftist governments in France, the Windsors now thought of moving to Switzerland or Ireland – Kenneth de Courcy was brought in to take soundings with the Irish President, Éamon de Valera – and even bought a plot in southern Spain to build a house. The nine-month trip to America to June 1948 was part of a plan to settle in the United States, but eventually they were drawn back to France, partly because they could not find the right house, but largely because of the attractive tax break they were given by the French.[11]

The lease at La Croë had ended in spring 1949 – amongst their last guests were Churchill for his fortieth wedding anniversary and Beaverbrook. Now their only home was to be in Paris. They had

---

[10] Birmingham, p. 229. The son of their close friend Margaret Biddle relates the story of the Windsors being invited to dinner by the Biddles. Wallis first rang to ask the menu and then, clearly unsatisfied, asked if she could send her own chef to prepare the Biddle dinner party. Margaret Biddle replied that Wallis should indeed ask her own chef to cook for her that night – at her own home, as the invitation was withdrawn. Interview Tony Biddle, 16 April 2020.

[11] See for example, 'We had another blow about the Long Island house we wished to rent before buying.' Duchess to Marjorie Post, 25 August 1948, Box 26, Marjorie Post papers, Bentley Historical Library, University of Michigan. Amongst the houses they looked at on Long Island was one owned by Eugene de Rothschild. Bloch, *Duchess*, p. 186.

given up the Ritz apartment and taken a four-year lease on 85 Rue de la Faisanderie, near the Bois de Boulogne, which they rented from the industrialist and philanthropist Paul-Louis Weiller.[12]

Thick hedges and tall wrought-iron gates protected the *hotel particulier* from the street. The outer hall led to a large entrance hall, where portraits of the Duke, at various ages, lined walls and an elegant marble staircase led to a small landing, where a marble horse stood looking down the stairs – the Duchess did not like it and it was hidden behind a screen. The stairs continued to the drawing room, dining room, library, sitting room and the Duchess's study. Above were the bedrooms. One bathroom, decorated by Elsie de Wolfe, had leopard-skin walls and the house was furnished with Marcel Proust's desk and eight chairs, which had belonged to Marie Antoinette.

Neither Windsor ever liked the house. It was too cramped for entertaining – the dining room sat only twenty-four – the rooms were cold and dark and the Duke objected to a huge organ in the foyer, disguised as a bookcase. So sometimes they used the Ritz.

'My lost rank has its advantages – I don't have to sit next to the Duke,' remembered Lady Diana Cooper, now no longer ambassadress, of one such dinner in November 1948. 'The party was pretty, in the Ritz's best suite, candles and the choicest flowers, caviar, vodka. Wallis looking her very best in off-the-ground white and gold lamé, clipped with two new gigantic yellow diamonds, the whole *surmonté* and *panaché* by the faithful Bahamian Negro in fine gold livery.'[13]

Socialising was the only occupation the Windsors had, giving structure to a life without purpose and serving to keep them both

---

[12] He also owned the Villa Trianon.

[13] 12 November 1948, John Julius Norwich (ed.), *Darling Monster: The Letters of Lady Diana Cooper to Her Son John Julius Norwich 1939–1952* (Chatto & Windus, 2013), p. 333. *Surmonté* means 'topped off' and *panaché* means 'given panache'.

stimulated. It was something Wallis took extremely seriously with a close attention to detail. At the dinners she kept a golden notepad at her side – the servants called it her 'grumble book' – to note the successes and mistakes. She was a perfectionist – even the leaves of lamb's lettuce served at meals had to be the same size – and rather than serve one sort of bread, she would offer a choice of six. Each individual would have their own Sèvres butter pot with a porcelain-handled knife and one regular guest, the designer Jacqueline de Ribes, remembered there was 'so much cutlery you never knew what to pick up.'[14]

'The table had so much upon it that I got bewildered,' wrote Diana Cooper of a dinner for Henry Luce, the publisher of *Life* and *Time*:

> Saxe Negro slaves and monkeys and fruits falling from Nymphenburg cornucopias and flowers and candles and boxes for toothpicks and cruets of course, and matches individual and cigarettes in gold boxes and five equal-sized knives, ditto forks in white Dresden china (I had to ask which to take for what and further blotted my copybook by using my side plate as an ashtray instead of a gold dish) . . .[15]

There were certain rituals. Guests were asked for 8.45 with dinner punctually at 9.15. There was never soup, because Wallis claimed, 'After all those cocktails, it's just another drink.'[16] Rather than serve cheese, she preferred camembert ice cream – camembert mixed with cream, coated in breadcrumbs and then frozen – which was served with port.

[14] Menkes, p. 28.
[15] *Darling Monster*, pp. 379–80
[16] Menkes, p. 28.

The couple employed several well-known chefs, including Lucien Massey and René Legros, who was said to be one of the four greatest chefs in the world. Beneath the chef was an assistant, two kitchen boys and a pastry cook. There was then the butler, Ernest Willemotte, assisted by Sydney Johnson, the 'faithful Bahamian negro', and several footmen.

Under the housekeeper were four housemaids – two just to take care of Wallis's clothes, run her bath and iron her sheets twice daily. The Duke had a valet simply called Campbell. The two chauffeurs, Ronald Marchant and David Boyer, were in charge of the four cars – a Humber sedan, Buick sedan, a Buick estate car and a Royal blue Cadillac limousine with the Royal Crest on it, built to the Duke's specifications and a gift from James Mooney. Wallis's secretary, Denise Hivet, a former Air France stewardess, and the Duke's secretary, Victor Waddilove, a former stock jobber's clerk, brought the total to eighteen.

The annual wages came to over £125,000, but costs were controlled by several factors.[17] First the Duke, with his diplomatic status, bought his drink, tobacco, many of his household goods and petrol through the British embassy and military commissary duty free. Likewise their television set, many electrical goods, and cars were not taxed.

And the Windsors paid some 20 per cent below the going rate for wages, on the grounds it was an honour to work for them and the position invariably led to more lucrative job offers elsewhere. At Christmas, however, staff were given, as required by French law, an extra month's pay and either a wallet or cufflink with the royal cipher for men and a cashmere sweater or some nylon stockings for

[17] £4.6 million in today's money.

the women. An inducement to stay were the promises that servants would be taken care of in the couple's wills.

Even so, the writer Charles Murphy noted 'the turnover was high, though resignations – far less dismissal – received only the most meagre severance pay.'[18] Marchant was forced to resign after over twenty years' service because of ill health. He received no pension and was paid off with a few thousand francs. The other chauffeur, Boyer, stayed for twenty-seven years, only to be sacked with less than a week's notice.

'I knew many of her staff,' remembered Letitia Baldrige, who later worked as Jacqueline Kennedy's social secretary, 'and she did not treat them particularly well.'[19] The Hon. Sarah Morrison, the stepdaughter of the Earl of Dudley, then a teenager living in Paris, had dinner with the Windsors once a week for two years and related how rude Wallis was to staff, giving the impression that she 'thought someone was going to take advantage of her' and how she was 'pretty nasty to the Duke, domineering and bossy.'[20] Working conditions were not easy with long hours and very precise demands. Charles Murphy remembered, 'tongue-lashings, harsh and overt, were routine; holidays were ignored, as was overtime; nothing earned praise or seemed to give satisfaction.'[21]

A woman who worked for the Windsors for ten years recalled, 'It was impossible for either of them to express gratitude. Their servants were made to feel that they were anything but indispensable – the Duke and Duchess were doing them an honour by having them around.'[22]

[18] Bryan and Murphy, p. 493.
[19] King, pp. 426–7.
[20] Interview Hon. Sarah Morrison, 22 July 2020.
[21] Bryan and Murphy, p. 493.
[22] *Ibid*, p. 497.

One Christmas, the Duke's private secretary, John Utter, gave his employer 'a small bag for carrying his golf shoes out to the course'. The Duke shifted nervously from foot to foot. 'I'm sorry, John, but until the Mill has been sold, I'm afraid we can't afford a present for you.'[23]

Yet, according to one staff member, every Christmas a party was held for staff and the royal couple:

> took a great delight in the children, who although warned by their parents to be on their best behaviour, inevitably wound up racing through the rooms. Once, a boy playing with some tin soldiers accidentally knocked over the vase which was serving as his castle. It broke of course and he burst into tears. But the Duchess took his hand, helped him clean up the pieces, and spent the rest of the afternoon playing soldiers with him on the Grand staircase.'[24]

The Duchess kept up on all the arrivals of celebrities in Paris with a subscription to *Celebrity Service*. When a prominent American author was in Paris, the Duchess would not only send an invitation, but buy one of his or her books. She would then, Cleveland Amory remembered:

> pick out a particularly good line, and then during the dinner when there was a total silence, she would turn to the author and say, 'I really think your line' – and then she would slowly quote the exact line – 'is so wonderfully put.' After she had done this at least one guest would always say

[23] Bryan and Murphy, p. 543. The Mill was a property they later owned.
[24] King, p. 433.

to a companion, 'Isn't that just like the Duchess? She keeps up on everything.'[25]

Everything was focused on making themselves and their house look good. The Duchess had Édouard, from Alexandre's, come to the house daily and comb her hair. There were then her regular hair and makeup treatments at Elizabeth Arden's salon in the Place Vendôme, where she was treated like royalty. A bouquet of her favourite flowers was placed in a special cut-glass vase in her private treatment room. On call were her favourite *coiffeurs*, Claude, Roger and Manuel, who would apply the specially formulated secret dye, which she always carried with her whenever she travelled, and Madeleine the makeup expert, with a specially created foundation designed to extenuate her eyes and draw attention away from her prominent jawline.

She could be a demanding customer, complaining once when she felt she had not been 'properly received and escorted'. The salesgirl was immediately sacked. 'For all the special treatment she received at Arden's, Wallis was not known as a good tipper,' wrote one of her biographers. 'Indeed, she was a non-tipper.'[26] Instead if they were lucky, the women would receive gold and diamond pins in the shape of the Prince of Wales's feathers and the motto *Honi soit qui mal y pense*, and for the men, gold cufflinks stamped with the royal crest. 'The historical significance of these gifts was often lost on their recipients, who would have much preferred a cheque or cash.'[27]

* * *

[25] Cleveland Amory, *The Best Cat Ever* (Little, Brown, 1993), p. 127.

[26] Birmingham, p. 238.

[27] Birmingham, p. 238.

In February 1947, the Duke had accepted an offer from Henry Luce, the proprietor of Time Life, to write four articles under the title 'The Education of a Prince', covering his career up to the First World War and ghosted by a Time Life journalist, Charles Murphy. They appeared in *Life* in December and were syndicated around the world with a further four running in May 1950.

Tommy Lascelles was incensed by them, but realised little could be done, writing in a memo: 'I am sorry to say that long experience has convinced me that he has no such feelings when the interests of the Monarchy or the Royal Family conflict with what he imagines to be the interests of himself and the Duchess.'[28]

Encouraged by the public reception and earnings from the articles and keen to set down his own version of events, fill his time, and make some more money, in July 1948 the Duke agreed to work with Murphy on an autobiography – codenamed Operation Belvedere. The target delivery date was September 1949, but the book was to be bedevilled by delays – never particularly self-disciplined, the Duke preferred to spend his time socialising – and new sensitivities.[29] For example, Churchill was nervous that his support of the Duke during the Abdication would affect his relationship with the Royal Family and asked that his private correspondence not be used and publication be delayed until after the General Election.

Murphy was later to write of the Duke that 'his span of attention, by Murphy's measurement, was two and a half minutes maximum; and when the story of the preceding night was plainly written in his trembling hands and bloodshot eyes . . . knew that another work-day would have to be scrubbed.'[30] It was not helped by Wallis's

[28] Lascelles memo, 19 September 1947, RA KEVIII Ab. Box 3, quoted Ziegler, p. 523.

[29] Duke of Windsor to Monckton, 8 December 1948, Monckton Trustees, Box 20, Folio 24, Balliol College.

[30] Bryan and Murphy, p. 465.

lack of support for the enterprise, giving precedence to the couple's social life over the looming delivery deadline. It was almost as if she resented the Duke doing something for himself and did not want him to revisit the past.

* * *

In the spring of 1949, George VI lay in bed in Buckingham Palace, following an operation to cut a nerve at the base of his spine. It was designed to counteract the arteriosclerosis from which the King now suffered, as a result of too much stress – and too many cigarettes – and there was a danger that both his legs might have to be amputated. The King's incapacity provided an opportunity for his older brother.

'The King is gravely ill and out of circulation and he will not be in circulation again,' wrote Kenneth de Courcy to the Duke:

> I may tell you most confidentially that a Regency has already been discussed and it seems likely enough that presently [a Regent] will be appointed. I do not think it too much to say that if the Regency should be one primarily influenced by the Mountbattens [i.e., Lord Mountbatten and Prince Philip], the consequences for the [Windsor] Dynasty might be fatal and I have no doubt from my information that the Mountbattens, thoroughly well-informed of the situation, will do everything in their power to increase their influence with the public regency, secondly with the future monarch . . . All these dangers could be averted, the whole position balanced and I believe the Dynasty heavily protected if the Duke were to return to live in England.[31]

---

[31] Kenneth de Courcy to Duchess of Windsor, 13 May 1949, De Courcy, Box 3, folder 5, Hoover Institute.

The Windsors' ambitions to settle, even temporarily, in Britain since the war had all been predicated on knowledge of George VI's poor health and the wish to be available should the call come for the Duke to act as a caretaker regent. Such were their suspicions that Prince Philip's uncle, Lord Mountbatten, would seek to influence the young Queen Elizabeth II, that the Windsors and de Courcy took the idea of a soft *coup d'état* seriously. In the event, there was no regency and any opportunity for the Duke to help shape events passed.

*   *   *

In August 1950, the Windsors were invited to the second wedding of Herman Rogers – Katherine had died in May 1949.[32] His new bride was a widow, Lucy Wann, who had been part of his social circle. What he had not realised was that Wallis, long in love with Herman herself, still had designs on him. 'There is no question that these women were rivals in love,' remembered Lucy's daughter-in-law, Kitty Blair. 'Both wanted Herman. Wallis would have grabbed him and told the duke to go.'[33] Wallis made her feelings clear, telling Lucy Wann, 'I'll hold you responsible if anything happens to Herman. He's the only man I've ever loved.'

'How nice for the duke,' Lucy icily replied.[34]

'Her boredom in her own marriage had become acute, and she was no longer as discreet as before when it came to hiding her feelings,' according to one friend of the Windsors.[35] Having failed to dissuade Herman from marrying Lucy, Wallis sought her revenge in other ways. The wedding present – an antique silver salver – bore

[32] Herman had been shocked that, when asked to choose a keepsake of Katherine's, Wallis had picked not a modest personal item but two gold bracelets valued at 10,000 francs.

[33] Interview February 2016, quoted Morton, *Wallis in Love*, p. 295.

[34] Morton, *Wallis in Love*, p. 299. According to Michael Bloch, Herman was bisexual.

[35] Bryan and Murphy, p. 523.

the inscription: 'To Herman Livingstone Rogers on the occasion of his marriage August 9th 1950 from Edward and Wallis.' No mention of Lucy and the wrong date.[36]

On the morning of the wedding, the date of which had been brought forward to suit the Windsors, just as Lucy was setting off to the *marie* for the civil ceremony, Wallis had begun to tug at the collar of Lucy's wedding dress. 'We can't have you looking like this *today*!' She pulled and twisted the satin until it was completely shapeless. 'There!', she said, 'That's better!'[37]

The reception was to be held between 6 and 8 p.m., with the Windsors regarded as an equal attraction to the newly married couple. When they had not arrived by 8.15 p.m., the guests began to leave. At 8.45 p.m. the Windsors appeared, claiming they had been with their architect. 'But Wallis, he was at our reception,' said Lucy sweetly.[38]

Afterwards at dinner, Wallis monopolised Herman, suggesting they talk Chinese together. Herman, still fluent himself but knowing she spoke only three words, and not wishing to be drawn into her games, pretended he had forgotten the language. Her parting shot was to bustle the Duke into their car and drive off leaving the bride and groom to find their own way home.[39]

The Duke and Duchess and their relationship continued to intrigue those that met them. Diana Cooper, dining with them in October 1950, later wrote:

Wallis dreadfully over-animated and I don't somehow think it's drink – benzedrine rather. She repeats herself embarrassingly . . .

I talked to the Duke after dinner (a particular agony) about the

---

[36] Bryan and Murphy, p. 523.

[37] *Ibid*, p. 523.

[38] Morton, *Wallis in Love*, p. 299.

[39] Bryan and Murphy, p. 524.

Bahamas. 'It was a bit difficult for me, you see. I'd been King Emperor and there was I, a third-rate Governor.' He says things like that so simply – no boggle, no laugh, no inverted commas.[40]

'When they are together they are like two automata. They have no intimacy – they seldom talk of anything at all serious. They drift,' noted Cecil Beaton in his diary:

Meanwhile the Prince is happy in his relationship with her. He depends on her utterly. It is a mother-mistress relationship. She looks after him like a child, & yet makes entertainment for him as she did in the days when he was the Prince coming to her home for relaxation at the end of a long day. She now gives him the antidote to hard work, but he has none of the hard work. He has nothing to do. She is nearly driven mad trying to find ways of amusing him. He has no interests. He thought he was bored at being a Royalty and he has no reason since to consider he has stopped being bored. He has no intellect. He never opens a book, & in many ways his memory has gone. Steam baths & brandy have made him very weak. The years as Prince have gone by in a flash. He has a 'train driver's' memory of places he has visited, but remembers nothing of what happened in any of them.[41]

The years of the Wandering Windsors had begun.

---

[40] 1 October 1950, *Darling Monster*, p. 430.

[41] Cecil Beaton papers, quoted Vickers, p. 343.

CHAPTER 19

Secret Affairs

In May 1950, the couple sailed from New York to France on the *Queen Mary*. With them was Jimmy Donahue, the 35-year-old heir to the Woolworth fortune and a cousin of the American socialite, Barbara Hutton. The Windsors had got to know Jimmy and his mother Jessie in Palm Beach early during the war, through a mutual friend Hugh Sefton – Wallis had been placed next to Jimmy at a lunch on 18 April 1941 – and the friendship had developed over the next decade, helped by the fact that the Donahues always picked up the bill.

Jimmy had had an unhappy childhood – his father had committed suicide in 1931, probably over a homosexual affair – which he covered up with outrageous behaviour and attention seeking; a favourite party trick was to put his penis on a dinner plate and ask a waiter to carve it thinly. Reputedly his family kept a lawyer on 24-hour call to buy him out of the most dangerous scrapes, as stories circulated of orgies at his mother's Palm Beach estate, the castration of a lover, and police investigations into callboys and drug use.

Apart from dancing in the chorus of a musical comedy, *Hot and Bothered*, Jimmy had never had a job, except perhaps as a court jester. Now he had his court with both the Duke and Duchess captivated by his exuberance and skills as a *raconteur*. Jimmy intrigued

Wallis with his unpredictable and flamboyant behaviour and the fact that he was the opposite of her husband.

Where Jimmy was carefree and impulsive, the Duke was organised and precise. Where Jimmy was generous, the Duke was penny-pinching. Where Jimmy was exciting and cheerful, the Duke was dull and depressed. Where the Duke reminded her of her age, Donahue made her feel young again. She had had to entertain the Duke for the last thirteen years, now Jimmy entertained her. Tired of emotionally supporting her husband, she relished being swept up in Donahue's dynamic and spontaneous world. 'She gave herself willingly to the charms of Jimmy Donahue,' says Grace, Countess of Dudley. 'It is easy to see why. He was very amusing.'[1]

Wallis was now in her mid-fifties and taking stock of her life. Her first husband had died in May and the remarriage of Herman Rogers had affected her deeply. She was bored, vulnerable, flattered by Jimmy's attentions, intrigued by him, his youthful energy and talents – a qualified pilot, he not only could play *Tosca* on the piano but supposedly could sing it in half-a-dozen languages – and drawn to him by the same sense of humour and fun.

He also had the attraction of being rich and generous. Encouraged by him, she began to amass a substantial collection of furs; one afternoon she picked out thirteen dresses and Jimmy paid the $3,105 bill.[2] As a publicly gay man, Donahue was also regarded as safe. The friendship now turned into an affair. She was giving up a king for a queen.

For him, she was a game and, given his detached cold mother Jessie, a maternal figure. There was also a darker side for her. 'Jimmy also said that she resented the fact that the Duke had lost

---

[1] Menkes, p. 163.
[2] Wilson, p. 165. Just under £35K.

his throne,' wrote Mona Eldridge, who knew the couple. 'Naively she had believed his promise of making her Queen. She despised his weakness and boring ways.' With Jimmy, she found revenge and enjoyed humiliating her husband – in public if necessary.'[3]

It was a view shared by Kenneth de Courcy. 'I think she enjoyed annoying the Duke of Windsor over that. I think it gave her a kick to see him enraged by it, which he was. I think it gave her a feeling of power, that after all those years she could still make him extremely jealous and angry over another man.'[4] But there are suggestions that it was not only Wallis who was attracted to Donahue. 'I think the Duke was in love with Jimmy,' claims the interior decorator Nicky Haslam, who knew the couple during this period.[5]

There have long been rumours of the Duke's bisexuality, which have never been denied. The Duke's biographer Michael Bloch, him-self gay, 'insisted that Maître Blum never objected to any hints that the Duke of Windsor was a homosexual. She never sued if any such insin-uation appeared in print.'[6] Anne Seagrim, who worked for the Wind-sors in the 1950s, in her draft notes for her memoir, wrote that Frances Donaldson in her biography missed 'the essential point about his char-acter – his fundamental uncertainty about his sexuality – his ability to be a heterosexual man. He was fundamentally afraid of women.'[7]

A similar view was advanced by a psychiatrist interviewed for a Windsor biography, *Lese Majesty,* published in 1952. Dr Werther believed the Duke was not a repressed homosexual but an overt one. 'There is no doubt that Wales has a strong feminine identification,

---

[3] Mona Eldridge, *In Search of a Prince* (Sidgwick, 1988), p. 93.

[4] Kenneth de Courcy, BEN 2/2/5, p. 45, Churchill College Archives.

[5] Interview Nicky Haslam, 5 April 2021.

[6] Blackwood, p. 130. Maître Suzanne Blum became the custodian of the Windsors' reputation after the Duke's death.

[7] Notes for memoir, Seagrim, Acc. 1053, 1/7, Churchill College Archives.

and that it is only with great effort that he can think of himself as a man, or feel like one.'[8]

Many of the Windsors' friends were gay, from Somerset Maugham and Noël Coward to the Mendls, from their decorator John McMullin to the equestrian Harvey Ladew, who often acted as the Duchess's escort. 'I just love your pansies,' said one guest at the Moulins de la Tuilerie, looking at the herbaceous borders. 'In the garden or at my table?' replied the Duchess.[9]

The Duke, however, never appeared comfortable in the company of gay men. 'I have always thought that Edward VIII suffers from sexual repression of another nature,' wrote Chips Channon in his diary in December 1936:

> His horror of anything even savouring of homosexuality was exaggerated, especially in a world where it is *far* from unknown; and at the same time there are tales (I have heard them all my life and some I believe to be half true) which reveal him in *quite* another light. Certainly, too, he has *always* surrounded himself with extremely attractive men. One knows almost in advance the type of man he would like – Fruity Metcalfe, Dicky (Lord Louis) Mountbatten, Sefton, Mike Wardell, Bruce Ogilvy, and even these he dropped as they aged.[10]

In the 2004 updated edition of his biography of Wallis, Charles Higham reveals that Dudley Forwood had told him that Fruity Metcalfe 'was an active homosexual and that he had a physical affair

[8] Norman Lockridge, *Lese Majesty: The Private Lives of the Duke and Duchess of Windsor* (Boar's Head Books, 1952), p. 115.

[9] Menkes, p. 31.

[10] December 1936, Heffer, p. 626.

with the Prince of Wales', a revelation he only wanted made public after Forwood's own death.[11]

'I like Jimmy,' Noël Coward told Truman Capote of Jimmy Donahue. 'He's an insane camp, but fun. And I like the Duchess; she's the fag-hag to end all – but that's what makes her likeable. The Duke, however well he pretends not to hate me, he does, though. Because I'm queer and he's queer but, unlike him, I don't pretend not to be. Anyway, the fag-hag must be enjoying it. Here she's got a royal queen to sleep with and a rich one to hump.'[12]

Nicky Haslam recounts how a colleague, the curtain-maker Eddie Page, told him that as a young man he used 'to go with boys to Hyde Park, that bit by the barracks, which was a great picking-up place for toffs. One day Prince David came with a friend, who approached me on his behalf. They took me to a queer nightclub in Seven Dials, run by Elsa Lanchester's sister.[13]

The Duke was the honorary president of the Austrian Sports and Shooting Club, which German police files suggest was a cover for homosexual activities. 'One royal member has recently fled Vienna because he was under threat of arrest on charges of homosexuality,' the report ran. 'In connection with this the (police) report also charges the Duke of Windsor with bisexuality.'[14]

On the gay forum, Datalounge, a couple of elderly posters shared anecdotes:

We had a good family friend here, who owned a flower shop in our city. In his young adulthood (1940s) he was part owner

---

[11] Higham, *Mrs Simpson*, p. 95. Forwood died in 2001.

[12] Truman Capote, 'Indelible Exits and Entrances', *Esquire*, Vol. 99, No. 3, March 1983.

[13] Nicholas Haslam, *Redeeming Features: A Memoir* (Jonathan Cape, 2009), p. 195.

[14] Report of Professor Lehofrich of Vienna, quoted Higham, *Mrs Simpson*, p. 198.

of a shop in NYC. His business catered to the society crowd. He told us many great stories over the years. One story he told was how he took care of the fresh flowers for the Duke and Duchess when they were in NYC. Our friend told us that sometimes he would literally be chased by the Duke while taking care of the flowers in their apartment.[15]

One of the Duke's lovers was supposedly Walter Chrysler Jr (1909–88), son of the founder of the Chrysler Corporation. Walter Jr was an art collector, museum benefactor, theatre and film producer, and had probably met the Duke at the Palm Beach Golf Club. Though Chrysler was twice briefly married, his homosexuality was well known. In 1944 he had been forced to resign from the Navy due to wild homosexual parties – sixteen enlisted men had signed affidavits that Chrysler, known as 'Mary', had committed unnatural acts with them – and *Confidential Magazine* had outed him in the 1950s.[16]

One regular poster to Datalounge, 'Charlie', wrote that Chrysler Jr had told him:

> a story about him and the Duke of Windsor (the former king of England) throwing a party on a Navy ship docked at Jacksonville, Florida, during World War II, I think. He said there were more than 1,000 sailors, and Walter and 'David' hired 200 hookers, but Walter and David sucked so much cock our lips were chapped for a week.[17]

---

[15] http://grumpyoldbookman.blogspot.com/2006/04/man-who-cut-off-cocks.html.

[16] 'The Strange Case of Walter Chrysler Jr', *Confidential Magazine*, July 1955 and 'How the Navy Ousted Its No. 1 Gay Gob', *Confidential Magazine*, January 1958.

[17] https://www.datalounge.com/thread/8581470-walter-chrysler-jr.

Chrysler had been based at the Key West Naval Base in Florida between April 1942 and December 1944 and was the subject of an investigation by the Office of Naval Intelligence. Subsequent enquiries revealed that all of the investigation files had disappeared.[18]

* * *

A few days after arriving in Paris, the *ménage à trois* of the Windsors and Donahue went to a charity ball in a seventeenth-century mansion, the Hôtel Lambert on the Île Saint-Louis, with 700 members of Parisian society. Amongst the guests were Barbara Hutton, Henry Ford, Cecil Beaton, Lady Diana Cooper and Elizabeth Taylor. The Duke left at midnight. Two of the last guests to leave close to dawn were Jimmy and Wallis.

On 11 June, Jimmy celebrated his thirty-fifth birthday at Maxim's with the Windsors as the guests of honour. At the end of the month, the Duke and Duchess joined Jimmy and his mother in Biarritz, where the affair continued. The Duke played golf during the day and then retired early, leaving Wallis and Jimmy to spend both the days and evenings together.

In November, Wallis returned alone to the United States, the Duke staying behind to finish his book. The affair continued. The designer Billy Baldwin noticed that the two lovers began to frequent a restaurant he often used, off Park Avenue at 59th Street, and then:

> after lunch they would just quietly go to Jimmy's apartment. The duchess was always well-behaved, but a couple

---

[18] An FBI file (62-63369) was opened on him in 1941 and has full details of his drinking, homosexual activities, failed business ventures, his pornography collection, and how he killed two children in separate car accidents.

of times I saw that she was rather tight, because she liked to drink. They were inseparable in New York, and I know that during that time in her life she had more fun than she ever had before.[19]

Alone back in Paris, the Duke could not concentrate. For two weeks he would ring Wallis both at bedtime and first thing in the morning, but whenever he called, the Duchess's maid was unable to say where she was. When he did reach her, his wife simply replied she 'had been with friends and cut the conversation short. Three weeks of her evasiveness brought him to the edge of a breakdown.'[20]

After he had opened some press clipping from a news agency addressed to the Duchess, it became clear what was happening. The Duke abandoned the book and decided to go to New York; Murphy, keen to keep him working on the book, went with him. So concerned was the ghost writer about the Duke's mental health that he would not allow him on deck alone at night, for fear of him committing suicide. It was the greatest test of the Windsors' thirteen-year-old marriage.

The Duchess met the Duke, accompanied by their cairn terriers Thomas and Pookie, on arrival and they laughed heartily at published reports they were estranged. But despite their public displays of affection, she continued to see Jimmy during the day – lunching and shopping at Cartier and Mainbocher – and the Duke in the evenings.

That Christmas the three of them attended Mass at St Patrick's Cathedral, the first time since the reign of Charles I that a British monarch or ex-monarch had taken the sacrament from a disciple of

---

[19] Billy Baldwin with Michael Gardine, *Billy Baldwin, An Autobiography* (Little, Brown, 1985), p. 295.

[20] Bryan and Murphy, p. 472.

Rome. Ten days later, the Windsors gave a luncheon for Cardinal Spellman – a homosexual friend of Jimmy's with a penchant for cross-dressing – all part of Jimmy's mischievous attempt to persuade Wallis to convert to Roman Catholicism.

Almost nightly, the Windsors and Jimmy would find themselves at the El Morocco nightclub, but the Duke would leave alone at midnight and then:

> Jimmy came into his own, wisecracking, cavorting, camping, telling naughty stories and gossiping about the other patrons . . .
> Next morning, the haggard Duke would make his way to the Duchess's room to assure himself of her safe return, only to be brought up short by a scrawled warning taped to her door: KEEP OUT, STAY OUT or DON'T COME IN HERE.[21]

At the end of January, the three decamped to Horse Shoe Plantation at Tallahassee, Florida, the home of the Windsors' close friend Edith Baker and a regular haunt. 'What do you and the Windsors talk about?' Baker was once asked. 'She seemed startled by the question. "Well, where they've just been and who they've just seen," she said at last.'[22]

On Valentine's Day, the Windsors were guests of Jessie Donahue at the Venetian Ball. The gossip was that she had 'bought' the Windsors in the way she had seduced the writer and socialite Elsa Maxwell and columnist Maury Paul with substantial cash presents at Christmas and birthdays.

Wallis had also taken a fancy to another young man, Russell Nype, a thirty-year-old actor and singer, starring with Ethel Merman

---

[21] *Ibid*, p. 476.

[22] Birmingham, p. 231. Home movies of these visits can be seen in the Baker family papers at Harvard University.

in Irving Berlin's *Call Me Madam*.[23] Often he and Merman would join the Windsors for dinner after the show and the inference in the press was that the relationship with Wallis was more than just friendship. 'She had been phoning the young man nightly, and sometimes called for him in her car,' reported Walter Winchell in his 'Man About Town' column.[24]

It was said that the Duchess, whose pet name for Nype was 'Harvey', gave the actor expert advice on interior decoration when he moved to a new apartment.[25] 'What could there be romantic between a middle-aged Duchess and a young man who reminds her of an invisible rabbit?' asked *New York Journal-American* in October 1951.[26]

The journalist Alice Moats, researching the story for the columnist Westbrook Pegler, was able to tell him:

It seems to be common gossip that she has a crush on a fellow called Nype who plays in 'Call Me Madam'. The Duke goes home at night because he theoretically has to write his book – inasmuch as he hasn't written a line of it or the *Life* pieces that seems odd, but there it is – and she plays about in night clubs with Mr Nype. However, things don't seem to be quite as simple as all that; Jimmy Donahue has just written to his boyfriend to tell him that their liaison is over – he has at last fallen in love with a woman (the Duchess) and he is going to

[23] 'The rumour was that Wallis's real and only attachment was Russell Nype', Haslam, p. 194. 'She had a whirl with the leading man in the Broadway show *Call Me Madam*, and it was the talk of the town.' Eleanor Davies Tydings Ditzen, *My Golden Spoon* (Madison Books, 1997), p. 177.

[24] 'Man About Town', 29 January 1951, quoted Iles Brody, *Gone with the Windsors* (John Winston Company, 1954), pp. 31–2.

[25] *Ibid*, pp. 31–2.

[26] *New York Journal-American*, 19 October 1951.

marry her! That I got almost straight from the horse's mouth or whatever – the person who told me had it from Jimmy's boyfriend who confided the story to her in his anguish.[27]

According to Nype's son, also Russell, there was nothing more to the relationship than friendship. 'Lots of people have tried to suggest things happened between them, but I don't believe it for one moment. Humour and fun was the bond between them. They just genuinely liked being together.'[28]

Nype, young, talented, straightforward, a little unsophisticated and good company, provided a distraction from the Duke, and Wallis enjoyed the fact that her visits to nightclubs with the young singer made her husband jealous. Even after Nype married in 1953 and had a young family, he and his wife continued to socialise with the Windsors in New York and Palm Beach and remained in touch for the next twenty years.

Rumours began to circulate that the Duke and Duchess's marriage was on the rocks. The novelist Rebecca West, who had been mooted as a possible ghostwriter for the Duchess's memoirs, wrote to Ewart Robertson, the right-hand man to Lord Beaverbrook at the *Daily Express*, 'I have been thinking very seriously over your letter, and I have come to the conclusion that if what you predict comes to pass and the Duke and Duchess of Windsor part, I would not care to have anything to do with her Memoirs.'[29]

---

[27] Alice Moats to Westbrook Pegler, 23 January 1951, 'Duke and Duchess of Windsor'; Subject Files; James Westbrook Pegler Papers; Herbert Hoover Presidential Library.

[28] Interview Russell Nype, 6 June 2021.

[29] RA PS/PSO/GVI/C/042A/389 and Robertson, EJ, 1951, 1986.002.1.1-70, Box:44, Folder:7, The University of Tulsa, McFarlin Library, Department of Special Collections & University Archives.

In February 1951, Wallis entered the Harkness Pavilion in New York, registering as Mary Walters, where she was successfully treated for cancer of the womb, which required a hysterectomy. She was in hospital for three weeks, during which the Duke pottered aimlessly around the Waldorf Towers, refusing to see people, and showering her with red roses and beluga caviar – which she complained was too salty.

At the end of May, the Windsors returned to France on the *Queen Mary*, accompanied by Jimmy, who had taken a suite at the Ritz. The relationship continued, especially when the Duke paid a week's visit to London, where he desperately went round the Grosvenor Antiques Fair trying to find gold snuffboxes to go with the collection that Jimmy had given to Wallis.

Diana Cooper continued to provide a useful commentary on the Windsors' behaviour from a succession of dinner parties. In May, she joined Wallis at the Monseigneur nightclub, a regular haunt. 'We must go on to Monseigneur – the Duke would like it, so don't argue. She seldom calls him the Duke now, but rather "My Romance" with a funny tone – not sneery but not straight.'[30]

They were joined by Jimmy 'shouting, singing and yelling "hit it up, hit it up". Then he was up to the piano playing Rachmaninoff's Prelude.' In the car on the way back, Jimmy confessed to Diana, 'I adore Wallis – she knows she's only got to call on Jimmy and I'll do anything for her. I *love* her – like my mother, you know – not any other way because I'm not that sort, etc, etc.' Diana for once took pity on the Duke and the situation. 'Isn't it all desperately sad? He showed nothing, I have to admit, on his royal wizened face, but if it's true and he learns it, the wife is gone, the legend dead, he'll have to throw himself off the Empire State Building.'[31]

---

[30] *Darling Monster*, p. 442.
[31] *Darling Monster*, p. 443.

In July, Jessie chartered a boat, with the Windsors as her guests, visiting Antibes, Monte Carlo, Genoa, Viareggio and Elba. The yacht was not sufficiently large to carry all of Wallis's wardrobe, so her maid Ophelia and the Duke's valet followed the yacht along the coast in the Windsors' black Cadillac with a van carrying the luggage. Each evening Ophelia would bring on board the outfit for the evening and next day.

The affair was now blatantly obvious, a humiliation that seemed to excite both Jimmy and Wallis. Lunching with Lady Kenmare in her villa at Saint-Jean-Cap-Ferrat, Wallis made an excuse that she wanted to show Donahue the view from the first-floor guestroom. They disappeared upstairs. Meanwhile the Duke remained at the lunch table reminiscing about his time as monarch, the embarrassed guests knowing 'the duchess was having it off with Jimmy in one of the upstairs guest rooms.'[32]

In Portofino, which they used to visit each year, the royal couple were guests of the actors Rex Harrison and Lilli Palmer, who had a house there. The Windsors had first met the couple in New York and, according to Palmer, the acquaintanceship had developed after the Duke 'in the middle of boisterous parties . . . would seek out a quiet corner to recite German poetry' with her.[33]

Palmer remembered that:

> although it was twenty years since he had abdicated, he liked to see protocol observed, only you had to guess when to observe it and when to ignore it. Naturally you had to be punctual to the minute and stand up whenever he stood up;

[32] Patricia Cavendish O'Neil, *A Lion in the Bedroom* (Park St Press, Sydney, 2005), p. 298. Lady Kenmare told her daughter, 'The duchess was famous for her expertise in fellatio', p. 299.

[33] Lilli Palmer, *Change Lobsters and Dance: An Autobiography* (Macmillan, 1975), p. 209.

even if he was only going to the toilet, respectful attention was drawn to a function that common people prefer to attend to as inconspicuously as possible. When you greeted him, a little bob or rudimentary curtsey was appreciated. I only bobbed to him. His duchess got a firm handshake.[34]

Entertaining the Duke generally proved a challenge:

His sense of humour on the subject was disturbing. 'You know,' he once said to me with a smile, 'I've got a low IQ.' 'But, sir,' I protested loyally, 'just think of your book, *A King's Story*. That's a fascinating tale and very well written.' 'Didn't write it myself,' he said. 'Anyway, that's all I know.'[35]

The Duke and Palmer always talked in German and he confessed to her he never felt at home in England:

When I first set foot on American soil as a very young man, it came to me like a flash: this is what I like. Here I'd like to stay. And when I married an American, I hoped we would live in America. But as fate would have it, my wife hates America and only wants to live in France. That's the way it goes.[36]

One night during the Windsors' visit, Greta Garbo and her long-time companion George Schlee were in Portofino and the Harrisons invited them to meet the Windsors. Amongst the subjects of conversation was who might play the Windsors on film.

'Katharine Hepburn,' said the Duchess without hesitation.

[34] Palmer, *Change Lobsters and Dance*, p. 210.

[35] Palmer, *Lobsters*, p. 211.

[36] Palmer, *Lobsters*, p. 211.

'And to play the Duke?'

Wallis didn't answer. But Windsor nodded politely in Rex's direction and said: 'I think perhaps you would be the best choice.'[37]

Then Rex, in their open US-Army jeep, drove the Windsors from their villa, perched high above the town, down the perilously steep goat track to the harbour, the Duke clutching the windshield. '"Don't you ever have the seats recovered?" said Wallis reproachfully . . . settling gingerly in her white dress on the lumpy back seat, as if she were about to sit on a raw egg.'[38] Returning, Rex, who didn't like the Duke, muttered gleefully, 'Nearly lost the little bugger on the curve.'[39]

The next day the Harrisons, with Greta and Schlee, joined the Windsors on their yacht moored in the harbour, to find Wallis furious because Jimmy had not yet returned from the port.

At that moment, Jimmy appeared in the doorway, helloing exuberantly in all directions, his arms full of gardenias, which he deposited grandly on the Duchess's lap by way of a peace offering. She swept them to the floor, stood up, and said, 'Do you know what time it is?'[40]

From there the evening got progressively worse. The only other guest was a former American senator and his wife, the Isolationist senator drunkenly 'carrying on about his pet aversion, the British who over and over again had sacrificed innocent American boys to save their empire.'[41]

Jimmy tried to change the subject without success. Now, in order to divert attention, he rose from the table and, still dressed in his

---

[37] Palmer, *Lobsters,* p. 214.

[38] Palmer, *Lobsters,* p. 215.

[39] Carey Harrison to author, 5 April 2021.

[40] Palmer, *Lobsters,* p. 218.

[41] *Ibid,* p. 219.

midnight-blue velvet dinner jacket, leather pumps and diamond cufflinks, casually jumped into the sea. The Duke was stunned. 'But there must be some protocol . . . !'[42]

The crowd in the harbour howled with delight at the sight of Jimmy swimming in the harbour, which was 'full of refuse, dead rats and condoms'.[43] Wallis's 'jaws were clenched and her nose white with shock and anger. "That boy has no manners," she finally managed to say. "I'd like to ask you all not to speak to him when he comes back. We'll act as if nothing's happened."'[44]

Jimmy now returned in a green velvet dinner jacket, to discover the senator still droning on. 'We'll just have to try again.'[45] Once more he leapt into the water. It was the end of the dinner party. The guests left silently whilst the hosts engaged in a 'passionate "conversation" in the library'.[46]

The Windsors now moved to Biarritz. Doreen Spooner, sent to photograph the Duke, was not impressed by the couple:

> It was so hard to see why a king had abdicated his throne for that woman . . . I didn't take to her at all. The shots were taken out in the garden of the villa. As with so many photographs taken of them, the couple seemed to have an agenda of showing how blissfully happy they were and that the crisis that rocked the monarchy had all been 'worth it'. The ex-King Edward VIII, though quite formal in manner, was pleasant and willing to please, but the ex-Mrs Simpson wasn't. She was

[42] *Ibid*, p. 220.
[43] *Ibid*, p. 221.
[44] *Ibid*, pp. 220–1.
[45] *Ibid*, p. 222.
[46] *Ibid*, p. 222.

brittle, angular, devoid of all warmth. She smiled for the camera, but like a robot. There was no feeling behind it.[47]

By September, the Windsors were back in Paris and under surveillance by the French Secret Service. When the Duke left for London at the end of the month to see George VI, who had been operated on to have his left lung removed, the relationship with Donahue continued. As one surveillance report noted:

> JAMES DONAHUE (said to have had an affair with her for four years) rolls up in the evening, and takes her to the Paprika restaurant and then to the Monseigneur nightclub, where there's a cabaret. DONAHUE returns to the Duchess's home at 85, Rue de la Faisanderie in the 16th with her at 2.20 a.m., and then he's seen leaving alone at 5 a.m.[48]

The nature of the physical relationship between Wallis and Jimmy intrigued people. According to Billy Baldwin, Jimmy once when drunk had tried to circumcise himself with a pen knife, which made intercourse painful, and therefore they relied on oral sex.[49] According to one biographer, Donahue had claimed Wallis as 'the best cocksucker I've ever known'.[50]

'Some said they had oral sex, but I can't believe Jimmy was into that,' thought Nicky Haslam. 'He enjoyed her company. There was no way Jimmy could have done it with a woman. He was *so* gay . . .' 'Oh, they did have sex,' says the art historian John Richardson . . .

---

[47] Doreen Spooner, *Camera Girl* (Mirror Books, 2016), pp. 55–6.

[48] 20 September 1951, declassified French Government file 4AG73. It focused on individuals placed under surveillance by the RG between 1947–53. I'm grateful to Peter Allen for discovering the file and translating it.

[49] Baldwin, p. 289.

[50] Birmingham, p. 239.

'I asked Jimmy Donahue when he was drunk and ready to say anything, "What was it like going to bed with the Duchess of Windsor?"' says Richardson. 'And he said, "It was like going to bed with a very old sailor."'[51]

The American journalist Cy Sulzberger often met the Windsors during the 1950s. 'He is a curious, somewhat pathetic fellow,' he wrote in his diary after one dinner in October 1951. 'Although he has, of course, given up any rights to the throne, he still maintains a strict atmosphere of court etiquette; there is much curtseying and bowing, despite the fact that he is extremely informal and friendly.'[52]

The Duke had just returned from a trip to London and Sulzberger was touched by his obvious affection for Wallis. 'After dinner we were sitting together talking and every now and then he would look across the room at the Duchess and say: "It's so wonderful to see her. You know I have not seen her for a week. Isn't she charming?"'[53]

Sulzberger found him a little eccentric:

After dinner there was a pianist. The Duke was transported with joy. He sang a few songs rather badly and joyfully imitated the playing of various instruments such as the cello and the violin, waving his arms around like a happy schoolboy . . . The Duke drank a bit and seemed just slightly tight at the end of the evening. He talked steadily during dinner. At one point the Duchess leaned over the table and said: 'You promised you were going to listen tonight because there are a lot

[51] 'The Oddest Couple', James Fox, *Vanity Fair*, September 2003.

[52] 2 October 1951, Sulzberger, *Long Row*, p. 587–9.

[53] 2 October 1951, *Long Row*, p. 587–9.

of brains around, but you are talking all the time.' He replied: 'I have to talk or otherwise I would fall asleep.'[54]

A few weeks later Sulzberger attended a ten-course dinner, given for a UN delegation and including the French prime minister René Pleven, for what he described as 'a weird collection of social derelicts':

> The dinner itself was lavish in the extreme. Cocktails were accompanied by plates spread with caviar or covered with slices of lobster. The dinner comprised about ten courses and was heavily sliced with sherry, white wine, red wine, pink champagne and huge slugs of brandy. During course Number Seven, a complete string orchestra popped in and started playing away in a fashion reminiscent of pre-war Vienna . . . From then on, the Duke couldn't eat because he was too busy waving his arms around in time to the music – his favourite habit. Whenever I have seen him anywhere near music, out comes his conductor's complex.[55]

* * *

Progress on the Duke's memoirs had been slow. 'I have read Chapters 19, 20, 21 and 22, which Miss Swann sent me yesterday, and I return them,' wrote George Allen to Walter Monckton in October 1949. 'I do not think that HRH himself can possibly be the author of these Chapters. I feel that they are so bad that I am impelled to suggest to you that it may be our duty to advise him against publication, because if they appear in their present form,

[54] *Ibid*, p. 587–9.
[55] 12 November 1951, *Long Row*, p. 599.

they will be condemned and must do him untold injury in every quarter.'[56]

The press magnate Lord Beaverbrook, who had been actively involved in the drama, was brought in to write the chapter on the Abdication, telling Henry Luce, the publisher at Time Life:

> I took the 'Murphy' chapters and from his material I prepared the account marked 'Beaverbrook'. If we decide on the 'Beaverbrook' narrative, then we must all join together in pressing it upon the Duke. Your own authority will be required as well as my influence. And we must be tactful. Murphy, of course, could not have secured from the Duke the story I have told. The Duke did not know it. He never grasped the meaning of his own crisis . . . It is imperative that the Duke should not have knowledge of this letter to you. He must be persuaded to recognise that these writings represent his talks with Murphy and me.[57]

Eventually in January 1950 it was decided that the book was ready for submission and a contract was signed with Putnam, but it was to be another year before it was delivered. 'In many ways I am disappointed with the state of the work,' wrote Charles Murphy to George Allen in January 1950:

> Certain chapters – notably Four, Five, Six, Seven and Eight – have never been gone over by me. They consist primarily of the original LIFE material of the first series (partly finished

[56] George Allen to Walter Monckton, 13 October 1949, Monckton Trustees, Box 20, Folio 25, Balliol College.

[57] Lord Beaverbrook to Henry Luce, 13 September 1949, BBK/G/6/23, Parliamentary Archives. BBK/G/6/24 has 'The Duke of Windsor's Story text, 8 September 1949, as rewritten by Lord Beaverbrook'.

notes and experimental undertakings which the Duke himself grouped together, adding various bits and pieces of his own). Stylistically they are certainly not up to the standard of the rest . . . it has been like trying to make a rope of sand.'[58]

The reasons were clear. The Duke had lost interest in the book, focused on saving his marriage.

In April 1951, *A King's Story*, which recounts his life up to the Abdication, was published. The Windsors launched it from the Waldorf Towers and then travelled around the States, promoting it. 'I had editorial advice and assistance in compiling the book, of course, but I wrote every word of it myself,' the Duke told Nancy Spain for *Good Housekeeping*, adding, 'I worked an average of eight hours a day; nine until one o'clock, and then four hours more between lunch and dinner.'[59]

Reviews were mixed. *The New York Times* described the book as 'a character study of a well-meaning, undistinguished individual, destined from birth to a life of monumental artificiality', whilst Noel Annan, reviewing the British edition in the *New Statesman*, thought 'reflections of inconceivable banality succeed descriptions of Court life so bizarre that the characters seem permanently to be playing charades.'[60]

The *Scotsman*, however, thought it 'well written and lively',[61] *The Economist* 'a most dignified, objective and historically valuable work whose readers will, it is safe to say, look on the Throne with

---

[58] Charles Murphy to George Allen, 22 January 1950, Monckton Trustees, Box 20, Folios 40–2, Balliol College.

[59] *Good Housekeeping,* June 1951.

[60] *New York Times,* 16 April 1951; *New Statesman,* 29 September 1951.

[61] 27 September 1951.

an enhanced and deepened respect',[62] whilst the *Observer* found it 'frank and absorbing', but 'The wisdom of publication is arguable ... the hero emerges as rather a pathetic figure.'

Tommy Lascelles had no illusions about the book. 'I daresay the Duke of Windsor has written a good book; but it is wrong (and disloyal) for a former King of England to write such a book for profit and to sell things that are not his to sell.'[63]

The reviews did not prevent *A King's Story* from sitting on the bestseller lists for seven months, being translated into over twenty languages, and earning the Duke more than £300,000.[64]

[62] 29 September 1951.

[63] Tommy Lascelles to Roger Fulford, 6 October 1951, PS/PSO/GVI/C/042/368.

[64] £9.6 million today.

CHAPTER 20

Settling Down

On 31 January 1952, looking frail, George VI saw his daughter Elizabeth and husband Philip off at Heathrow for a tour of Africa. He would never see her again. On the morning of 6 February, he was found dead at Sandringham by his valet. The Duke, who was told the news by a reporter, immediately made plans to attend the funeral, but his wife was told she would not be welcome.

Back in Britain, he had tea with Queen Elizabeth; the new Queen, his niece Elizabeth; Prince Philip and Princess Margaret. He then viewed the coffin at Westminster Hall. Dressed in the uniform of Admiral of the Fleet, which drew some criticism, he was one of the chief mourners at the funeral, but played little part in it.

Never one to miss an opportunity, he used the visit to lobby for a job and to make his case for recognition of Wallis but, as usual, to no avail. He brought with him his lawyer Henry 'Hank' Williams, having learnt that the £10,000 annual allowance had lapsed with the death of the King. After negotiations, it was continued on the understanding that he kept out of Britain or he would be taxed. Meanwhile, in his absence, Wallis continued her affair with Jimmy.

In the knowledge that it was very unlikely they would ever be allowed to settle in Britain and with the monies made on *A King's Story*, the Duke and Duchess decided to lease a country home from the stage designer Etienne Drian. They chose a seventeenth-century mill, Le Moulin de la Tuilerie, about twenty miles outside Paris, consisting of four stone buildings with a cobbled courtyard and set in twenty acres of land.

The following year they decided to buy it, the first and only home they ever owned. Bathrooms were added to each bedroom, a modern kitchen created and a swimming pool built. This was to be the Duke's new Fort Belvedere and over the next twenty years it was to be the house where the couple felt most relaxed.

John Fowler and Nancy Lancaster, from the celebrated firm Colefax & Fowler, were brought in to decorate the house, choosing to create in the main house a pink and apricot drawing room with French windows leading onto the garden. Jessie Donahue paid for the redecoration of Wallis's bedroom, which was all white with beams waxed to dull gold and filled with a huge four-poster bed covered with pillows. The Duke's bedroom with its barracks cot 'had the feeling of a loft, littered with golf books, an autographed picture of Arnold Palmer, old 78 rpm records of *Carousel*, sheet music from *Gypsy*, stacks of old magazine articles and newspaper clippings.'[1]

There was colourful Italian pottery, comfortable divans, stone fireplaces, vivid yellow and flame curtains and scores of pillows with embroidered messages such as 'Never Explain – Never Complain'. 'It was very bright with patterned carpets, lots of apricot and really more Palm Beach than English or French,' remembered Diana Mosley.[2] 'Overdone and chichi . . . Medallions on the walls, gimmicky pouffs, bamboo chairs. Simply not good enough,' was Cecil Beaton's verdict.[3] The designer Billy Baldwin was even more blunt. '. . . most of the Mill was awfully tacky, but that's what

[1] Ralph Martin, *The Woman He Loved* (WH Allen, 1974), p. 453.

[2] Menkes, p. 62.

[3] *Ibid*, p. 62.

Wallis had: tacky Southern taste; much too overdone, much too elaborate, and no real charm.'[4]

The main guest cottage had two bedrooms and baths and was lined with framed prints of George IV's coronation and a display of the Duke's collection of seventy walking sticks. Everything was geared for the comfort of their guests. With 'a small bar supplied with whisky, gin, vodka, bitters, glasses, ice, and all conceivable cocktail garnishes . . . Each bedroom was also supplied with a thermos of iced water, with the newest books on the bedside table, with writing paper and postcards (even stamps), pen, ink, cigarettes – filtered and unfiltered, plain and mentholated – matches (green folders with "Moulin de la Tuilerie" stamped in white, cigarette lighter, and a radio.'[5]

The forty-foot barn was converted into a shrine to the life that the Duke had rejected, the walls hung with the pipe banners of the Seaforth Highlanders, pig-sticking and steeplechasing trophies, drums of the Grenadier and Welsh Guards used as occasional tables, 1937 coronation mugs, a frame with a sample of every button used by the British Army during the First World War, commemorative medals, and the Chippendale table on which he had signed the Instrument of Abdication.

The garden designer, Russell Page, was commissioned to design a traditional English country garden with herbaceous borders, a rock garden and various water features, and the Duke was to spend most of his weekends creating in this 'corner of a foreign field' the England he had left behind, with its walled garden, 'phlox and lupines, chrysanthemums and asters and roses of a dozen colours.

[4] Baldwin, p. 292.
[5] Birmingham, p. 246.

His prize was the Duke of Windsor rose, which an English gardener had created and named for him.'[6]

Here the couple would entertain most weekends following a strict ritual. First the invitation by phone, followed by an engraved card emblazoned with the ducal crown in green and crimson, which read: 'This is to remind you that the Duke and Duchess of Windsor expect you on Saturday . . . for the weekend at teatime.' Enclosed would be a note with directions. The Duke would be driven down in his Daimler, the Duchess following in a Cadillac with her maids.

After tea, the guests would retire to bathe and dress for dinner, which was always black tie, though the Duke often wore one of his kilts. Guests would find their cases unpacked, clothes pressed and shoes polished. After drinks in the hall with hot savouries served in silver dishes, at 9 p.m. the Duchess led the ladies into dinner. The finest food and wine would be served by the Windsors' liveried staff. The meal would finish with a savoury, a practice they introduced to the French, who claimed it 'impossible to eat scrambled eggs after chocolate ice'. The Duke and the men might remain drinking port.

The next morning, breakfast, which had to be ordered the night before on a menu card by their bed, was served in each room. There would then be pre-luncheon drinks on the terrace and lunch in the barn at two tables, which each Windsor hosted. The guests were then encouraged to leave.

It was at the Mill that they entertained Maria Callas, Marlene Dietrich, Elizabeth Taylor and Cecil Beaton, as well as old friends such as Eric Dudley, Gray Phillips, Alastair Mackintosh, the Marquesa de Portago, Princess Ghislaine de Polignac, and a series of friends from deposed royal lines and obscure European dynasties.

* * *

[6] Martin, p. 455.

Settling Down

In the spring of 1953, the Duke was back in London after his mother Queen Mary became ill and then died. Here was another reminder of the past that he had left behind. Theirs had been an intense relationship. Though he could never forgive her for the way she had treated Wallis, he had sought his mother's love and approval all his life, which is why her rejection of his wife had been so painful.

The Duke had mixed feelings about her death, telling his wife, 'My sadness was mixed with incredulity that any mother could have been so hard and cruel towards her eldest son for so many years, and yet so demanding at the end without relenting a scrap. I'm afraid the fluids in her veins have always been as icy-cold as they now are in death.'[7]

The funeral took place on 30 March, but again the Duke played little part in the organisation, or even the service. The next day Queen Mary was buried at Windsor. 'What a smug, stinking lot my relations are and you've never seen such a seedy, worn-out bunch of old hags most of them have become,' wrote the Duke to Wallis. 'I've been boiling mad the whole time that you haven't been here in your rightful place as a daughter-in-law at my side.'[8]

His mother's death did not bring the family together. There was to be no invitation to the Coronation in May, on the grounds that there was no protocol for a former sovereign to attend a coronation. Instead, the Duke watched it in Paris at the home of a friend, Margaret Biddle, providing a commentary to the other guests, and in return for a large fee from United Press for the exclusive right to photograph him.

Meanwhile, in his absence at the funeral, Jimmy and Wallis continued their affair with dinners at the Colony and dancing at the El Morocco.

[7] Michael Bloch, *Secret File*, p. 277.
[8] *Ibid*, p. 279.

In June, the Windsors signed the lease on 4 Route du Champ d'Entraînement, a house on the edge of the Bois du Boulogne, which was to be their main residence for the rest of their lives. Built in the style of Louis XVI, it was owned by the City of Paris and had previously been occupied by Georges-Eugène Haussmann, the planner of modern Paris, and Charles de Gaulle.

The Windsors paid a nominal rent and free security was added to the diplomatic status negotiated by Walter Monckton. It meant that they paid no income tax, their foreign purchases were duty free, and the profits from their investments were free of tax. The Duke's personal fortune at the time was at least £3 million.[9]

The mansion stood in two acres, guarded by a lodge and enormous iron gates, crowned with gilded spikes, and approached by a long sweeping gravel drive, flanked by lawns, oak and chestnut trees, and with a tall black lamppost topped by a gilded crown. A colonnaded portico led into a dimly lit grand marble hall, dominated by a silken banner emblazoned with the Prince of Wales's coat of arms, which had originally hung above his stall in St George's Chapel at Windsor. Above was a sky-blue vault with fluffy clouds, flying geese, and framed by a *trompe-l'oeil* balustrade. The room, which was adapted at night for dances, was furnished with a sedan chair, an outsize globe of the earth, five-foot-high octagonal mirrors, and one of the red boxes he had used as King. A marble stairway climbed along the left wall to an open gallery.

Straight through from the hall was the high-ceilinged drawing room, with French windows leading on to a terrace and lawn. Pictures included a landscape by Degas, some flower paintings by Fantin-Latour, a Utrillo, a picture of Queen Mary, and one of the Duke as Prince of Wales in his Garter robes:

[9] Parker, p. 265. Today £86.6 million.

Small, low tables were everywhere: marble tables, lacquer tables, marquetry tables. Some were for cigarettes, ashtrays, flowers. Others, larger, held the gold and silver caskets, the swords of honour, the Maori greenstone war clubs, and the silver-lidded, rock-crystal inkwells that had been bestowed on the Prince of Wales during his Empire tours.[10]

Other tables held Wallis's collections of china and porcelain, with one reserved for thirty-one Meissen pugs. A cushion in needlepoint displayed the Prince of Wales's three feathers and his motto 'Ich Dien', and in the corner was a blue and silver grand piano.

The east end of the drawing room opened into the dining room, which had a 'musicians gallery' high on one wall and could seat twenty-six, whilst leading off from the west was the library, which they used as a sitting room. This was dominated by Gerald Brockhurst's portrait of the Duchess painted in 1939, whilst on an adjacent wall hung Alfred Munning's equestrian portrait of the then Prince of Wales.

Upstairs there was an informal sitting room overlooking the garden, where they met each morning, took tea, and ate dinner on trays watching TV if they were not entertaining, and their bedrooms. At the foot of the Duchess's bed was a chaise longue, where she had her daily massage and her assorted stuffed toy pugs were displayed. The room was scattered with pictures of the couple and their dogs, and cushions embroidered with mottoes such as 'Take It Easy', 'Don't Worry – It May Never Happen' and 'You Can Never Be Too Rich or Too Thin'.

The Duchess's bathroom was like a circus tent, with the ceiling painted *trompe-l'oeil* with marquee stripes and hanging tassels, and on the walls a fantastical mural of ballet dancers, ribbons and flowers, and Cecil Beaton's picture of Wallis. His suite was much

[10] Bryan and Murphy, p. 486.

more spartan and dominated with pictures of the Duchess and their pugs or cairns. As he preferred to shower, his bath was used to store his papers and photos. Two guest rooms and a bath on the top floor completed the set-up.

* * *

In 1953, Volume 10 of the captured German documents, which related to the Duke's entrapment in Spain and Portugal, was close to publication, and the problem of how to deal with it returned to exercise the minds of leaders on both sides of the Atlantic.

On 27 June, Churchill wrote to President Eisenhower, 'My purpose in writing this letter is to ask you to exert your power to prevent publication,' concluding, 'I hope you will join with me and the French Government who I am also approaching, in refusing to allow the official publication of the telegram or their revelation to anybody outside the secret circles.'[11] He followed up a few days later with a telegram marked 'Most Secret and Personal': 'I am venturing to send you some papers about the Duke of Windsor which I hope you will find time to consider.'[12]

On 3 July, General Walter Bedell Smith, Under Secretary of State and formerly Chief of Staff to Eisenhower at SHAEF, arranged to see Bernard Noble, head of the Historical Division at the State Department. Noble later recounted the conversation to the US editor in chief, Paul Sweet:

I have instructions to tell you that the British government is going to communicate a list of the documents on the Duke of

---

[11] Churchill to Eisenhower, 27 June 1953, Annex B, CAB 301/179, TNA. Copies can also be found at BBK/G/6/20, Parliamentary Archives and RA PS/PSO/GVI/C/042/368.

[12] Churchill to Eisenhower, 1 July 1953, PREM 11/1074, TNA.

Windsor which it wishes to have left out of Volume X [10]. You are to inform the editor of the German documents that when he receives the list, he will agree to the elimination of these documents.[13]

On 12 August, Churchill circulated a paper to the Cabinet, 'Publication of Captured German Documents', writing:

Subject to the views of my colleagues, I propose to interview the British Editor-in-Chief and to propose that publication be postponed for at least ten or twenty years on the grounds that these papers, tendentious and unreliable as they should undoubtedly be regarded, would give pain to the Duke of Windsor and leave an impression on the minds of those who read them entirely disproportionate to the historical value.[14]

Two weeks later, the Cabinet met to discuss the publication of Volume 10, Churchill explaining that he 'was not persuaded that there was any historical need to publish this correspondence, at any rate during the lifetime of the Duke of Windsor. Its publication would certainly be damaging to the Duke and would cause him unnecessary distress.'[15] Churchill had written to Eisenhower, who 'had promised full co-operation and the chief American historian had been instructed that, if his British colleague asked that these documents should, after all, be omitted from the forthcoming volume, he should acquiesce.'[16]

---

[13] Morton, *17 Carnations*, p. 300.

[14] 12 August 1953, CAB 301/179, TNA.

[15] 'Confidential Record of Cabinet discussion on 25 August 1953', CAB 128/40/10, TNA.

[16] CAB 128/40/10, TNA.

The problem was that the British editor Margaret Lambert did not agree and had threatened to resign if documents were omitted. The British Government were aware that the existence of the documents was widely known both in the United States and in this country; that copies of the actual documents might even be in private hands; and that intervention to prevent the inclusion of these documents in the official publication might provoke unofficial publication, at least of the substance of the documents and possibly of the actual texts.[17]

Supressing the documents might, it was realised, be more damaging than allowing them to appear. Eventually after pressure, Lambert agreed to delay publication of Volume 10 and instead bring out a volume on the Weimar Republic.[18] Walter Monckton was sent to Paris to update the Duke.[19]

But the problem continued to worry the Government. At the beginning of March 1954, the minister of state at the Foreign Office, Anthony Nutting, raised concerns about the former German ambassador von Hoesch's reports that the King had actively interfered politically in the Rhineland Crisis and told the Germans that Britain would not intervene in the reoccupation.[20]

At the end of March 1954, the Cabinet again discussed publication of the German documents and their return to Germany, with Churchill taking the view that publication should be deferred until

[17] CAB 128/40/10, TNA.

[18] CAB 128/40/10. Cf. FO 370/2343, TNA.

[19] Beaverbrook had advised 'that publication of the documents will make a newspaper story; but suppression of them, their probably subsequent publication by some private individual and the resignation of Miss Lambert would make a really big newspaper splash.' John Colville to Tommy Lascelles, 20 July 1953, RA PS/PSO/GVl/C/042A/392-435. Consideration was also given to 'deliberately to leak to the Press, at a time chosen by ourselves . . . The idea would be to take the sting out of publication in advance.' *Ibid.*

[20] 4 March 1954, FO 370/2371, TNA.

after the death of the Duke of Windsor and that the file relating to the Duke 'should not be returned to the custody of the German Federal Government . . . but should be retained in British custody, at any rate during the Duke's lifetime.'[21]

In November 1954, the Stationery Office published Volume 8, aware that Walter Schellenberg's memoirs covering the subject were about to be published, but it was carefully controlled, with review copies only sent out to a limited number of dailies. The permanent under-secretary at the Foreign Office, Sir Ivone Kirkpatrick, reassured the Foreign Secretary, Sir Anthony Eden, that, 'Publication was accompanied by a press release drawing attention to its salient features, but not to the documents referring to the Duke of Windsor.'[22]

The Duke had come to London, having prepared a denial. The next challenge would be Volume 10.

* * *

Wallis's affair with Jimmy Donahue continued throughout 1953, with the Duke trailing in their wake. In July they were all in Biarritz, paid for by Jessie Donahue, and in August Jimmy chartered a yacht for a month around the Gulf of Genoa to Monte Carlo, Rapallo, San Remo and Portofino. It reached a notable humiliation on New Year's Eve, when the couple were photographed sitting awkwardly in the El Morocco nightclub on a zebra-striped 'throne' and, to widespread laughter, being crowned with paper crowns by Jimmy.

In the summer of 1954, Jimmy chartered the yacht *The Narcissus*, with a crew of fifteen, to again cruise around the Mediterranean,

[21] 'Cabinet minutes, Top Secret', 1 April 1954, CAB 128/40/13, TNA.
[22] Ivone Kirkpatrick to Anthony Eden, 11 November 1954, FO 800/847, TNA.

visiting Rapallo, Capri (where Jimmy was robbed of $2,000 cash and his passport – probably by a casual gay pickup), Naples, Ischia, Ponsa, Livorno, and Venice, where they stayed at the Gritti Palace. They ended with a few days in Austria, driving to the magnificent Schloss Velden on Lake Wörthersee in a motorcade of five cars – the Windsors' Rolls-Royce, Jimmy's Cadillac, a staff car, and two others containing luggage.

But tensions were mounting. Jimmy was bored by then – not least stuck playing gin rummy with the Duke every afternoon – and annoyed at their sponging. This came to a head during a five-night stay at the Brenner's Park hotel at Baden Baden, when Jimmy took exception to a disparaging reference by Wallis about his breath. He kicked her under the table leaving her bleeding and her stocking torn. It was the final straw for the cuckolded Duke, who told Jimmy to leave. 'We've had enough of you, Jimmy. Get out!'[23]

There was to be no further contact between the Windsors and the Donahues and Wallis made no reference to her lover and benefactor in her memoir. Like Fruity and the Drurys before, the Donahues were airbrushed out of the Windsors' lives.

Twelve years later, in December 1966, Jimmy was found dead by his mother in their apartment at 834 Fifth Avenue. The official explanation was 'acute alcoholic and barbiturate intoxication', but the suspicion was that it was suicide. In his bedroom were found thirteen framed photographs of Wallis.[24]

[23] Bryan and Murphy, p. 483.
[24] *Ibid*, p. 483.

CHAPTER 21

The Heart Has Its Reasons

The financial, if not critical, success of *A King's Story* had persuaded Wallis that she, too, should write her memoirs. The deciding factor was the cost of doing up the Paris house. Contracts were signed in November 1954 for $500,000, with *McCall's* magazine paying $250,000 for serial rights alone and delivery promised for the following October.[1]

The ghost writer was to be Charles Murphy, who had ghosted *A King's Story*.[2] He stipulated three conditions – 'that her account of her divorce from Ernest Simpson would be straightforward; second, that the Duke's dealings with the Nazis would not be glossed over; and third, that she would not use the book as a rostrum from which to beat or ridicule the Royal Family.'[3]

By May 1955, two-thirds of the book was written, but relations with Murphy had broken down and he was fired. Murphy was later to write that: 'She saw herself as the *ingenue* star of a perpetual light opera.'[4] He was replaced by Cleveland Amory, who specialised in writing about the jet set, at a fee of £8,000 and Amory spent

---

[1] Almost $5 million and $2.5 million.
[2] Others in the frame had included Rebecca West and Ernest Hemingway, Morton, *Wallis in Love*, p. 316.
[3] Bryan and Murphy, p. 516.
[4] *Ibid*, p. 517.

several months interviewing Ernest Simpson, Fruity Metcalfe, Perry Brownlow, Herman Rogers, and even the Queen. 'We loved them and learned so much from them,' wrote Cleveland's wife, Martha, to her in-laws, adding, 'So much that we can't use, but it was exhausting and fascinating.'[5]

Many of the interviews were arranged by the Windsors' lawyer, now Sir George Allen. 'He was wonderful to us in London, but we felt he didn't think much of either of them and had done his best to give us the TRUE story through others,' wrote Martha to her parents.[6]

The relationship with Amory also soured and he withdrew in September 1955, saying he could not be associated with such a 'dishonest' book in which she portrayed herself as 'Rebecca of Sunnybrook Farm.'[7] He later claimed that everything she told him about Ernest, his first wife, and the divorce was untrue.

'It is all coolly amicable,' wrote Martha Amory to her in-laws. 'The casual way they can be dishonest makes you know that ice runs through their veins. Sir George Allen looked at Clip [Cleveland] this morning as though he'd wished he had the guts to do what Clip was doing twenty years ago.'[8] Murphy was then re-hired at the insistence of the publishers.

The book, titled *The Heart Has Its Reasons* – the phrase comes from the French philosopher Blaise Pascal – eventually came out in February 1956.[9] It differed in many respects from the Duke's version of events and sold less well – 26,000 copies compared to his

---

[5] Morton, *Wallis in Love*, p. 322.

[6] Martha Amory, CAP Box 138, quoted Morton, *Wallis in Love*, p. 322.

[7] *Associated Press*, 5 October 1955.

[8] Martha Amory, September 1955, CAP, Box 138, quoted Morton, *Wallis in Love*, p. 323.

[9] Amory had first suggested *Untitled*, which had been received in stony silence by the royal couple.

120,000 in America.[10] The reviews ranged from the gently mocking to bad. *The Times* felt it could only say: '*The Heart Has Its Reasons* carries the memoirs of the Duchess of Windsor from her childhood in Baltimore to the present day.' It was overshadowed by a review of a book on alpine flowers.

In September, the couple agreed to an interview on CBS with Ed Murrow to help promote the book. 'Do you two ever have occasion to discuss what might have been?' he asked them. They shifted awkwardly, looked at each other, and the Duke replied, 'No. We both feel that there is no more wasteful or foolish or frustrating exercise than trying to penetrate the fiction of what might have been.'[11]

On the advice of PR experts and as part of the book promotion, they tried to improve their public image. In April 1956, Wallis had set up a clinic for the rehabilitation of the handicapped in New York and the following September they announced the Windsor Awards, an attempt to present themselves as patrons of the arts. The plan was each year to finance a French or American artist selected by jury. One award was given – $1,500 for a year's study in Paris – but the scheme was quickly abandoned through their lack of interest.

Cynthia Gladwyn, at her annual dinner with the Windsors in July 1956, reflected back on the Donahue affair, which had done so much to damage Wallis's reputation, and remembered how she had become 'rude, odious and strange. One had the impression that she was either drugged or drunk. She spent all her time with the effeminate young man, staying in nightclubs till dawn and sending the Duke home early: "Buzz off, mosquito" – what a way to address the once King of England!'[12]

---

[10] Birmingham, p. 251.

[11] 'Person to Person', 28 September 1956, quoted King, p. 447.

[12] Jebb, *Diaries of Cynthia Gladwyn*, p. 179.

Her version of the end of the affair differs from other accounts. 'Finally Donahue's boyfriend is alleged to have told him, "It's either her or me", and so he chucked the Duchess. Since this extraordinary and unnatural affair, she has become quite normal, but always hard.'[13] Frank Giles, who had not seen the couple since 1940 and was now *The Times* correspondent in Paris, dining with them:

> found very little change in him, he was extremely youthful looking, he always was I think to the day of his death, almost like a boy more than a man, and when he was not making remarks about the Jews could exert considerable charm in the way, I believe, he always could . . . She, on the other hand, whom I had admired so much twenty years earlier had become, to my way of thinking, rather coarse and raucous – her voice, instead of being a nice, soft Baltimore voice, had become a sort of twangy Yankee voice. Her opinions and her sort of cackling laughter were very unattractive . . .[14]

After dinner the Duke chatted to Giles, who was not drawn to his opinions either. 'There'd have been no war if Eden hadn't mishandled Mussolini,' he said. 'It was all his fault.' He added, as an afterthought, 'Together of course with Roosevelt and the Jews.'[15] Giles found him 'an object of pity as of despisement'[16] and 'his views would generally lie somewhere between the naïve and the silly.'[17]

[13] Jebb, p. 179.
[14] Frank Giles, p. 25, Bren 2/2/7, Churchill College Archives.
[15] Frank Giles, *Sundry Times* (John Murray, 1986), p. 131.
[16] *Ibid*, p. 131.
[17] *Ibid*, p. 132.

'He chatters and chatters. He pretends to be very busy and happy, but I feel this is false and that he is unoccupied and miserable,' wrote Harold Nicolson in his diary after dining with the Duke in November 1956. 'He is as nervous as ever. He has a vast cigar, which he chews and wets but does not even light and then lays aside. Although he must have talked to me for three-quarters of an hour without stopping, there was nothing of any interest at all that he had to say but his memory is acute.'[18]

* * *

The following year, at the end of July 1957, Volume 10 of the German Documents, covering the Duke's stay in Spain and Portugal in July and August 1940 was published. A few weeks earlier, the Cabinet had agreed the wording of a statement at the time of publication and 'steps had already been taken to inform the Queen, the Queen Mother, the Duke of Windsor and Sir Winston Churchill of the impending publication of this volume'.[19] Samuel Hoare, now Lord Templewood, was brought in to write a supportive article in the *Daily Express*.

With regard to the suggestion that the Duke did not plan to take up his appointment in the Bahamas, the Duke was adamant in a statement, carefully drawn up by Sir George Allen, that 'At no time did I ever entertain any thought of complying with such a suggestion, which I treated with the contempt which it deserved.'[20] This was reinforced by a press briefing note, carefully coordinated

---

[18] 9 November 1956, Harold Nicolson diary, Balliol College.

[19] 11 July 1957, CAB 128/40/31. The Royal Family had already been briefed. Norman Brook, Cabinet Secretary, to Sir Michael Adeane and Adeane's reply, 20 July. CAB 21/3776, TNA.

[20] Donaldson, *King Edward VIII*, p. 402.

between the State Department and the Foreign Office, which called the documents 'a tainted source'.

This surprised the historians who had fought so hard to ensure the historical documents had seen the light of day, given that the Germans could have had no expectations that the documents would be discovered, that they had been assembled by world-class historians, some had been used as evidence in the various Nazi war trials, and there was no logic in several, respected and experienced German ambassadors having separately misled their own Foreign Ministry. The press release continued, 'His Royal Highness (the Duke) never wavered in his loyalty to the British cause or in his determination to take up his official post as Governor of the Bahamas on the date agreed.'[21]

The truth, as Whitehall and Buckingham Palace knew, was very different. Tommy Lascelles confirmed a few days before the publication that the Duke had in August 1940 applied for a code to keep in touch with the Germans. 'He will deny it all, of course, but I am afraid it is all true.[22]

* * *

In December 1958, James Pope-Hennessy stayed at the Mill to interview the Duke for his life of Queen Mary.[23] He found him:

exceedingly intelligent, original, liberal-minded and quite capable of either leading a conversation or taking a constructive part in one. He is also one of the most considerate men

---

[21] *The Times,* 1 August 1957.

[22] 25 July 1957. 'Notes of a conversation with Sir Alan Lascelles by James Pope-Hennessy', Pope-Hennessy papers, Getty Library, quoted Vickers, p. 352.

[23] Pope-Hennessy had also 'intended to write a biography of the Duke which would be authorised by them', but negotiations broke down. Frances Donaldson, *A Twentieth Century Life* (Weidenfeld, 1992) p. 194.

I have ever met of his generation. Like the Duchess, he is perhaps too open and trusting towards others; or else he was determined to be especially helpful to me.[24]

Pope-Hennessy was less impressed with Wallis:

this is one of the very oddest women I have ever seen. It is impossible to assess what makes her function or why. I should say she was on the whole a stupid woman, with a small petty brain, immense goodwill and a stern power of concentration . . . suspicion that she is not a woman at all. She is, to look at, phenomenal. She is flat and angular, and could have been designed for a medieval playing card . . . Her jawbone is alarming, and from the back you can plainly see it jutting beyond the neck on each side.[25]

Their lifestyle at the Mill staggered him. 'Every conceivable luxury and creature comfort is brought, called on, conscripted, to produce a perfection of sybaritic living. It is, of course, intensely American, but I would think consciously aimed. The Queen Mother at Clarence House is leading a lodging-house existence compared to this.'[26]

Shown to his room, Pope-Hennessy discovered 'there was nothing on earth that you might conceivably want that wasn't there – every kind of writing paper, nail-file, brush, fruit, ice-water; the bathroom loaded with scent-bottles like a counter at a bazaar – a delicious sense of self-indulgence.'[27]

[24] Peter Quennell, *A Lonely Business* (Weidenfeld & Nicolson, 1981), p. 210.
[25] *Ibid*, p. 211.
[26] *Ibid*, pp. 210–11.
[27] *Ibid*, p. 212.

His observations of the couple and their home during his week-end stay are acute and amusing – he was surprised to see the Duke at dinner 'wearing red trousers, a fur coat, and a peaked flying cap with fur ear-flaps'[28] – but he persuaded his host to open up to him about his upbringing. 'My father had a most horrible temper. He was foully rude to my mother. Why, I've often seen her leave the table because he was so rude to her, and we children would all follow her out.'[29]

The Duke continued arguing that because his mother had never been in love herself, she could not understand his own strong feelings towards Wallis. 'My mother was a cold woman, a cold woman.'[30] The result was that Queen Mary would never discuss the Abdication:

> I'm afraid my mother was a *moral coward*. She would never, NEVER, talk to me about it. Right up to the end, if I said anything to her, she'd just cough slightly, hm, hm, like that and that was all. She evaded all discussion.[31]

At the end of 1958, the Duke discovered that his secretary, Victor Waddilove, had been defrauding him on the French currency transactions that the Duke had been conducting on the black market. Waddilove blamed an innocent secretary, Anne Seagrim, who was sacked, but further investigations revealed the extent of the fraud. The Duke contacted his new lawyer Alan Philpotts, who advised a full audit and then either to sack Waddilove or ask him to resign with a year's salary.

[28] *Ibid*, p. 218.
[29] Quennell, p. 214.
[30] Quennell, p. 219.
[31] Quennell, p. 221.

Waddilove wrote to Walter Monckton, who was dealing with the matter, seeking his advice:

> I have operated on the black market on their behalf for the past ten years, against my own conscience and the advice of the late Sir George Allen. Unfortunately, I did not take that advice and in devotion to my employers continued these illegal operations to please them, and to benefit them to the extent of well over £200,000 . . . I am now very worried that with the extension to others of the knowledge of these transactions there may be a leak of information. They have totalled over one and half billion Francs and have only been known to my principals and myself.[32]

The two men met several times throughout January. Monckton was keen to sack him, but realised the story might then go public – Waddilove was hinting he had been offered a six-figure sum by the press. Sir Edward Peacock, former Receiver-General to the Duchy of Cornwall, and another director of Barings Bank, Lord Ashburton, were brought in and advised that a deal should be done.

Negotiations continued until May, during which the Windsors' finances were checked by John Masters, a former Barings employee who had worked for the Duke as Prince of Wales. He reported that 'the deals in which the Duke has been engaged in French Francs on the black market' had been part of a wider crime ring. 'It would appear that the sum involved is something like FF 1.5 billion, and that in the last year or two a profit of something like FF 600 million has been shown.' One of the intermediaries had been a banker

---

[32] Waddilove to Monckton, 15 December 1958, quoted Andrew Roberts, *Eminent Churchillians* (Weidenfeld & Nicolson, 1994), p. 280. Allen had died in 1956. £4.7 million in today's money.

called Lacazes, who was now in prison. Masters also reported that 'on occasions he believes the Duke has done the actual work on the market himself personally.'[33]

There were concerns that the Windsors' private banker, Maurice Amiguet of Swiss Bank, might go public on the transactions, that 'the fact of the Duke's business in the black market is known to Montreal bankers', and that General de Gaulle was 'probing into all these black market deals'. Ashburton had also had 'some more or less informal talks with the Queen's private secretary, Sir Michael Adeane, because he feels that the position and reputation of the Crown may be affected.'[34]

In the end, Victor Waddilove was paid off and the scandal was hushed up.

---

[33] 12 May 1959, Monckton papers (then with Monckton family and now supposedly in the Royal Archives), quoted *Eminent Churchillians*, p. 281.

[34] *Eminent Churchillians*, p. 282.

CHAPTER 22

Coming In From the Cold

The success of their two volumes of memoir, especially in the United States, had led to invitations to write further books. A series in *McCall's* magazine in the summer of 1960 became *A Family Album*, ghosted by Patrick Kinross, where the Duke ruminated on clothes and the Royal Family. Clothes had always been of great interest to the Duke – a wardrobe inventory that year included fifty-five lounge suits, fifteen evening suits and hundred pairs of shoes – and, like his wife, he was regularly voted one of the best-dressed people in the world.

Clothes expressed his individuality and vanity and he became a style icon on both sides of the Atlantic, known for his Prince of Wales checks, wide Windsor tie knot, Oxford bags, plus-fours, Stuart plaid trousers, cummerbund with a dinner jacket, magenta linen dinner jacket, and bright socks. The Duke, often known as the 'Little Man', stood five foot, five inches and he maintained the slimness of his youth through careful dieting.

He favoured comfort and free movement, a style referred to as 'Dress Soft' and preferred American-style trousers, always with a zip, and English-style jackets, so the former were made in New York and the latter in London, in what Wallis called 'Pants across the Sea'. His jacket waists were uniformly set high to elongate his silhouette, his pockets cut wider on the left side of the trousers to take his cigarette case, and he wore elasticised girdles in his waistbands to preserve the flat appearance of his stomach.[1]

There were also contracts for a book, *My Hanoverian Ancestors*, to be written by Kenneth Young, and a childhood memoir ghosted by Charles Murphy. The latter was to be based on the diaries that he had kept until after the First World War and the 2,000 letters, strung in chronological order on scarlet strings fastened with small brass toggles, that he had written to his parents, but he became discouraged after Wallis told him, 'Who'll want to read about a boyhood as dull as yours? It's a waste of time!'[2] This was a part of his life she could not control. Neither book was ever written.

But there were other ways to make money by exploiting their celebrity. The couple lent their brand name to everything from cutlery to dress collections. Wallis launched a syndicated pattern service that led the following February to a monthly column in *McCall's*, 'All Things Considered', ghost-written by the journalist Etta Wanger, which ran for a year and covered her own experiences in shopping, fashion and entertaining, and most controversially touched on the Royal Feud. 'My husband has been punished, like a small boy who gets a spanking every day of his life for a single transgression . . . His hurt has been deep.'[3]

Wallis worked well with Etta Wanger and they planned a further series of articles, but a 'Duchess of Windsor Etiquette Book' collapsed when no publisher would come up with the requested $50,000 advance.[4]

---

[1] For more on his clothes, see Elizabeth Dawson, 'Comfort and Freedom: The Duke of Windsor's Wardrobe', *Costume: The Journal of the Costume Society*, 1 June 2013, Vol. 47, No. 2, pp. 198–215.

[2] Bryan and Murphy, p. xvii.

[3] *McCall's* magazine, February 1961.

[4] $450K today.

Officialdom, however, remained concerned about their judgement and the commercialism of their royal status. In June 1960, Walter Monckton persuaded the Duke not to sign a contract for a TV series in which he would re-enact the Abdication speech.

But their lives were empty, an endless round of parties, travel, shopping and golf. At the beginning of January 1961, the Conservative MP Charles Curran asked what the Duke had made of his life:

> Instead of waiting for Britain to employ him, why does he not employ himself? . . . He is rich, healthy, childless . . . He has spent a quarter of a century treading the social treadmill and travelling to and fro, like an animated luggage label . . . a member of PG Wodehouse's Drone's Club, an ageing Bertie . . . His life is a vacuum – a vacuum, deluxe, mink-lined.[5]

In 1962, yet another volume of German documents was published – this time covering the period 1935–6 and suggesting that the Duke had favoured an alliance with Nazi Germany. The Duke's stock response was that the documents misrepresented his position and, 'It is obvious that these reports were slanted in order to curry favour with Hitler and thereby they give a generally false impression.'[6]

'The Duke of Windsor has been attacked in the Press for having hobnobbed with Hitler in the late thirties,' wrote Noël Coward in his diary on New Year's Eve. 'Secret papers have disclosed his pro-Nazi perfidy which, of course, I was perfectly aware of at the time. Poor dear, what a monumental ass he has always been!'[7]

---

[5] *Sunday Dispatch*, 22 January 1961.

[6] *Los Angeles Times*, 29 December 1962.

[7] 31 December 1962, Payn and Morley, p. 520.

The period also saw a thawing of relations with the Royal Family. When at the end of 1964, the Duke travelled to Texas to be operated on for an aneurysm on his aorta, the Queen sent flowers. Two months later, the Duke was operated on for a detached retina at the London Clinic and the Queen paid a brief half-hour visit – the first time she had met Wallis since before the Abdication. The Duke's sister, Mary, also visited, followed a few days later by Princess Marina. The Queen Mother went as far as to send flowers.

This was all part of a concerted public relations strategy, but it was done reluctantly. According to the writer Greg King, 'The Queen, however, originally had no intention of visiting her ailing uncle at all; only after her private secretary, Sir Michael Adeane, along with Walter Monckton's widow, Alexandra, and several others intervened, did Elizabeth II agree to the visits.'[8]

Ten days after her first visit, the Queen had tea with the Duke at his hotel suite in Claridge's and agreed to his request for the couple to be buried at Frogmore. It was during his London visit that Mary, the Duke's sister, suddenly died of a coronary thrombosis whilst walking with her family on her Yorkshire estate. Her memorial service at the beginning of April was the first public appearance of the Windsors together. They returned to Paris on the Royal Flight. The following month Princess Alexandra, on holiday with her husband in Paris, dropped in to see her uncle and his wife.

But every time the Royal Family tried to repair the relationship, the Windsors jeopardised the *rapprochement*. In May 1965, the New York premiere took place of a documentary based on *A King's Story*, a strange mixture of old newsreels and interviews, interspersed with footage of the Duke reciting passages and nervously sitting in the garden with the Duchess. It was made by Jack Le Vien, who

[8] King, p. 455.

had previously produced a telebiography of Churchill's *The Valiant Years*, and it was narrated by Orson Welles, and was calculated to have netted the Duke almost $400,000.[9] For the documentary, the Duke read out the Abdication speech.

The reception afterwards was held not at City Hall, but the department store Bergdorf Goodman. The Duke was increasingly being used to enhance his wife's social and financial ambitions. 'At a cocktail party among the main floor handbag, scarf and sunglass counters, the Duke stood stoically in a receiving line as hundreds of the well-to-do elbowed each other into racks of new umbrellas in an effort to greet him,' wrote the *New York Times*. 'In the end it was his lot to stand by, while the Duchess gave the newspaper interviews, described her clothes, and drew raffle numbers for men's shoes and sets of Wamsutta superscale sheets.'[10]

Then in 1966, for the thirtieth anniversary of the Abdication, the Duke wrote a series of newspaper articles that took his story on from 1936 and where he spoke frankly about the bitter relationship with his family. They were published in the *New York Daily News* and syndicated around the world. He also used the pieces to deny 'any dealing by me with German or Spanish agents in Lisbon.'[11] They did nothing to improve his relationship with the Royal Family.

In June 1967, the Queen invited the couple to attend the dedication of a plaque outside Marlborough House commemorating Queen Mary. The Queen Mother was 'adamant that if Wallis was invited, she would not attend.'[12] The Duke said he would not attend if Wallis was not invited. Eventually the Queen Mother relented and for the first time since 1936, the two women met.

[9] About $3.5 million today.
[10] *New York Times,* 29 May 1972.
[11] *Los Angeles Times,* 15 December 1966.
[12] King, p. 457.

The Windsors arrived at Southampton – now on the SS *United States* rather than Cunard's *Queen Mary*, as they were given a reduced price suite in return for attending some functions, posing for the ship's photographer, and holding a short press conference.[13] They stayed the night with Dickie Mountbatten at his Hampshire home and then took up residence at Claridge's – there had been no invitation to stay with a member of the family.

A crowd of 5,000 had gathered to witness the historic meeting. The Windsors' arrival was met with cheers and the Queen Mother kissed the Duke on the cheek. Though the Duchess refused to curtsy to her sister-in-law, they shook hands and talked briefly after the ceremony, which had lasted fifteen minutes. Afterwards a small lunch was hosted for them by Princess Marina at Kensington Palace, whilst the Queen, Prince Philip, the Queen Mother and the Duchess of Gloucester left to watch the Derby at Epsom. The Court Circular the next day mentioned every royal – except the Windsors.

Though the Duke was invited to the investiture of Prince Charles at Caernarfon Castle in July 1969, he chose not to go as Wallis was not asked. Nor, though invited, had the Duke attended the dedication of the King George VI Memorial Chapel at St George's Chapel a few months earlier.

In January 1970, the Windsors were interviewed for the BBC, an episode watched by 11 million people. The interview, conducted by Kenneth Harris, was in two parts. The first with the couple was dominated by Wallis, the Duke in an over-sized grey suit shifting nervously, his eyes averted from the camera and constantly looking to Wallis for assurance. Asked if she had any regrets, Wallis replied, 'Oh about certain things, yes, I wish it could have been different.

---

[13] They always occupied cabins U87, U89 and U91, known as the 'Duck Suite', which consisted of two bedrooms and a sitting room in-between, with a valet and maid in two nearby inside cabins.

I mean, I'm extremely happy . . . We've had some hard times, but who hasn't? Some of us just have to learn to live with that.'[14]

The second part was with only the Duke, where he was more confident, claiming to have had no regrets about the Abdication, except that he would have liked to have reigned longer, '. . . but I was going to do it under my own conditions, so I do not have any regrets, but I take a great interest in my country . . . which is Britain, your land and mine, and I wish it well.'

In October 1970, Prince Charles, shooting near Paris, made an unexpected visit at the suggestion of the British ambassador Christopher Soames, who accompanied him. It was not a success, as he wrote in his diary:

> The whole house reeked of some particularly strong joss sticks and from out of the walls came the muffled sound of scratchy piped music. The Duchess appeared from among a host of the most dreadful American guests I have ever seen. The look of incredulity on their faces was a study and most of them were thoroughly tight . . . To my relief I managed to escape into a small sitting room, where I was able to have a word with Uncle David by himself. He seemed in very good form, although rather bent and using a stick. One eye was closed most of the time, as a result of his cataract operation, but apart from that he was in very talkative form and used wide, expansive gestures the whole time, while clutching an enormous cigar . . .
>
> While we were talking the Duchess kept flitting to and fro like a strange bat. She looks incredible for her age and obviously has her face lifted every day. Consequently she can't really

---

[14] Wallis revealed she was an insomniac, who read detective novels to get to sleep and would like to have headed an advertising agency. The interview can be seen at www.youtube.com/watch?v=I02fZDd-BBc&t=4s

speak except by clenching her teeth all the time and not moving any facial muscle. She struck me as a hard woman – totally unsympathetic and somewhat superficial. Very little warmth of the true kind; only that brilliant hostess type of charm but without feeling. All that she talked about was whether she would wear a hat at the Arc de Triomphe the next day. The whole thing seemed so tragic – the existence, the people and the atmosphere – that I was relieved to escape it after 45 minutes and drive round Paris by night.[15]

The opportunity to resolve the 'Windsor problem' had been lost.

* * *

The health of the couple continued to deteriorate. Now in his seventies, the Duke was no longer able to work in his garden and his arteriosclerosis was affecting the blood supply to his brain, which resulted in memory lapses and a short temper. 'When asked questions, he would often fail to answer,' wrote one biographer. 'He would forget names and, for long periods, he would sit at parties silently staring into space, with an absent, melancholy look on his lined face. Once he was found wandering aimlessly in an upstairs hallway of Mrs Young's house, looking lost.'[16]

'We dined last night at the Windsors,' wrote Cyrus Sulzberger in his diary in October 1969. 'The poor old duke . . . is terribly frail. His bad left eye seems to half close and he has such arthritis in his left hip that he limps heavily and uses a cane . . . He is a tragic little man . . . The Duchess seems increasingly nervous and sad. She kept

---

[15] Jonathan Dimbleby, *The Prince of Wales* (Little, Brown, 1994), pp.178–9.
[16] Birmingham, p. 257.

telling me during the evening, as she looked across at him, 'He had everything – and he gave it all up for me.'[17]

Wallis, who had had several face-lifts and dyed her hair each week, did her best to appear younger than her age, but no one was fooled. 'The Duchess appeared at the end of a garden vista, in a crowd of yapping pug dogs. She seems to have suddenly aged, to have become a little old woman,' noticed Cecil Beaton, when he saw the couple in September 1970.

> Her figure and legs are as trim as ever, and she is energetic as she always was, putting servants and things to right. But Wallis had the sad, haunted eyes of the ill . . . Then an even greater shock. Amid the barking of the pugs, the Duke of Windsor, in a cedar-rose-coloured, velvet golf-suit, appeared. His walk with a stick makes him into an old man . . . But they are a happy couple. They are both apt to talk at once, but their attitudes do not clash and they didn't seem to have any regrets . . .[18]

Three months later, Richard Burton and Elizabeth Taylor were invited to dinner by the Duke and Duchess, Burton noting in his diary:

> with half a dozen of the most consummate bores in Paris. I don't know their names but I shall never need to remember them for I have an idea they are people who only go to the Windsors and one of them – probably the old Duke – must die very soon, though it is she who is now nearly completely ga-ga. It was a sad and painful evening and needs a long time to write about . . . They both refer continually to the

---

[17] Cyrus Sulzberger, *An Age of Mediocrity* (Macmillan, 1973), p. 581. The Duke was in fact seventy-five.

[18] Cecil Beaton, *The Parting Years* (Weidenfeld & Nicolson, 1978), pp. 110–11.

fact that he was once the King. 'And Emperor,' I said at one point. 'And Emperor,' she repeated after me. 'And Emperor, we always forget that. And Emperor.' He is physically falling apart, his left eye completely closed and a tremendous limp and walks with a stick. Her memory has gone completely and then comes back vividly in flashes.[19]

The Duchess was in the early stages of Alzheimer's. In November 1971, the Duke, who had smoked heavily throughout his life, was diagnosed with throat cancer and prescribed daily cobalt therapy. Though the couple were not told, the doctors knew it was only a matter of time.

Shortly afterwards, Cecil Beaton saw her. 'The Duchess of Windsor came in and behaved like a mad Goya. She is more than ever a personality and character, but God, what she looks like, her face so pulled up that the mouth stretches from ear to ear. She was galvanised, as if high, her body and arms and hands so thin that one feels she cannot last.'[20]

At the beginning of February 1972, Dickie Mountbatten, in Paris to dub the French version of a twelve-part television programme based on his career, took the opportunity to see the Duke whilst Wallis was having a minor operation in Switzerland. He thought the Duke had aged ten years.

The Duke was upset about a film based on his life that was being planned called *The Woman I Love*, starring Faye Dunaway and Richard Chamberlain, and sought Mountbatten's advice. Mountbatten suggested that the two Windsors be filmed side by side on

[19] Melvyn Bragg, *Richard Burton: A Life* (Little, Brown, 1988) , p. 393.

[20] Hugo Vickers (ed.), *The Unexpurgated Beaton* (Weidenfeld & Nicolson, 2002), p. 212.

Above: The Moulin de la Tuilerie, known as The Mill, twenty-two miles from Paris, and the Windsors' country home from 1951. © *Dave Pattison/Alamy Stock Photo*

Below left: The Duke with one of his pugs, who became substitute children.
© *Frank Scherschel/The LIFE Picture Collection/Shutterstock PREMIUM*

Below right: The Windsors in their walled garden, 15 June 1955.
© *Frank Scherschel/The LIFE Picture Collection/Shutterstock. PREMIUM*

Left: 4 Route de Champ d'Entrainement, the Windsors' main residence leased from the French government at a nominal rent from 1952 until Wallis's death.

© *United Archives GmbH/Alamy Stock Photo*

Right: The drawing room of the Duke and Duchess of Windsor's home in the Bois de Boulogne, Paris.

© *PA Images/Alamy Stock Photo*

Left: The Duchess's bedroom.

© *Manuel Litran/Getty Images*

Above: The library. The portrait of Wallis was painted by Gerald Brockhurst in 1939 and is now in the National Portrait Gallery. © *Wolfgang Kuhn/United Archives via Getty Images*

Below: Sydney, the butler who worked for the couple from their time in the Bahamas until after the Duke's death. © *Alan Davidson/Shutterstock*

Above: Scotty Bowers, the former marine who procured lovers for the Windsors in Los Angeles during the 1950s. © *Greenwich Entertainment/Kobal/Shutterstock*

Below left: Walter Chrysler Jnr, the Duke's golfing partner and alleged lover.
© *ANL/Shutterstock*

Below right: Tim Seely (born 1935) supposedly the illegitimate son of the Duke.
© *Popperfoto via Getty Images/Getty Images*

Above left: The Duke and Duchess of Windsor in Venice, 8 March 1961.

© *Keystone Press/Alamy Stock Photo*

Above right: The Windsors with John F. Kennedy, 14 June 1957. © *Bob Henriques/Magnum Photos*

Below left: Dancing at party hosted by Francoise de Lobkowicz (née De Bourbon-Parme), 11 December 1969. © *Sipa/Shutterstock*

Below right: The Windsors at a dinner given for them at the White House by Richard Nixon, 4 April 1970. © *Everett Collection/Bridgeman Images*

Attending the unveiling of the plaque to Queen Mary, 7 June 1967, the first time that the Royal Family had been seen with Wallis in public. © *Dennis Oulds/Central Press/Getty Images*

The Queen, the Duke of Edinburgh and Prince Charles visiting the Duke of Windsor, 18 May 1972, ten days before the Duke died. © *James Andanson/Sygma via Getty Images*

Above: The Duchess of Windsor watches the Trooping of the Colour, 3 June 1972.
© ANL/Shutterstock

Below left: The funeral of the Duke of Windsor at St George's Chapel, Windsor, 5 June 1972. © Bettmann/Getty Images

Below right: The Duchess visiting the Duke's grave at Frogmore with Lord Mountbatten and the Duke of Kent, July 1973. © Elizabeth Johnston/Camera Press, London

Left: The Duchess of Windsor, 23 September 1975. © *Central Press/Getty Images*

a sofa reading a statement repudiating the film. Wiser counsels prevailed and the advice was ignored.

It was an opportunity to review the past and patch up a friendship that had never fully recovered from the misunderstandings over the wedding and Mountbatten's acting as best man. As they parted at midnight, the Duke paused for a final reflection. 'There's something I'll bet you don't realise. If I hadn't abdicated, I'd have completed thirty-six years of my reign by now – longer than either my father or my grandfather.'[21] It was a rare admittance of what might have been.

A few weeks later, the Duke was admitted to the American hospital in Paris under the name Mr Smith. 'How pitiable it all is. Now at the end, except for the black Sidney (*sic*), a late imperial acquisition from the Bahamas, they are quite alone among comparative strangers,' Charles Murphy wrote to his co-writer Joseph Bryan. 'The lady made it so. Whatever Court there was, she was determined to rule. And now it is made up mostly of shadows – and the worst of the collaborationists and the robber barons.'[22]

On 18 May 1972, the Queen, on a state visit to Paris with Charles and the Duke of Edinburgh, visited the couple for tea. The Duke, who now weighed less than six stone, insisted on getting dressed and seeing her, a herculean task that took four hours. He was so weak that he had to be given a blood transfusion and was on a concealed intravenous drip, which he called 'damned rigging'. The visit lasted only thirty minutes.

The end was now in sight, with nurses caring for him on a 24-hour basis, and an opportunity to reflect on his life. 'I've spent the best part of my life with her, and I can tell you that nothing I gave up

[21] Bryan and Murphy, p. 545.

[22] Charles Murphy to Joe Bryan, 3 April 1972, Murphy papers, Mss 5.9 B 8405:97–119, Virginia Museum of History and Culture.

for her equals what she has given me: happiness, of course, but also *meaning*,' he told his friend David Bruce. 'I have found her to be utterly without faults, the perfect woman.'[23] To C.Z. Guest, he was more succinct: 'The Duchess gave me everything that I lacked from my family. She gave me comfort and love and kindness.'[24]

The night nurse, Julie Chatard Alexander, was shocked that Wallis, whose bedroom was on the same floor, 'never came to see him or kiss him good night or see how he was. Not once. Poor fellow. He would call her name over and over: "Wallis, Wallis, Wallis, Wallis." Or "Darling, darling, darling, darling." It was pitiful and pathetic. Just so sad, like a lamb calling for its mother.'[25]

At 2.30 a.m. on 28 May, the former King Edward VIII died, though versions of the death vary. The myths, which had surrounded the couple throughout their lives, continued even in death. According to Wallis's close friend, the Countess of Romanones, Wallis was called in the middle of the night and rushed to his bedside. 'I took him in my arms. His blue eyes looked up at me, and he started to talk. He could only say, "Darling . . ." Then his eyes closed, and he died in my arms.'[26]

It's an account confirmed by one nurse, Oonagh Shanley, interviewed by biographer Greg King, who says Wallis was woken and kissed her husband's forehead, 'My David.' Cupping her hands gently round his face, she said, 'My David – you look so lovely.'[27] But John Utter, the couple's secretary, told author Hugo Vickers that the Duchess was asleep when the Duke died and he had to wake her.

---

[23] Bryan and Murphy, p. 546.

[24] Bryan and Murphy, p. 546.

[25] Interview quoted Morton, *Wallis in Love*, p. 334.

[26] 'The Dear Romance', *Vanity Fair*, June 1986. Murphy, p. 548 says the same.

[27] Shanley interview, quoted King, p. 473.

'Well, it is good that she did not die before him,' wrote Cecil Beaton in his diary later that day, 'What will happen to her is not of interest. She made no friends. She will have less now. She should live at the Ritz, deaf and a bit gaga. It is sad because age is sad, but her life has not been a commendable one, and she is not worthy of much pity.'[28]

Buckingham Palace was immediately informed and an official statement issued just after 6 a.m. The Queen and Queen Mother sent telegrams of condolence to the widow and nine days of court mourning was declared. The former King Umberto of Italy was one of the first to visit and give his condolences, followed by the French foreign minister, Maurice Schumann, who, as a journalist, had attended the Windsor wedding.

Dickie Mountbatten was asked by the BBC to pay tribute to his former best man. Initially he refused, but he felt there should be some response from the Royal Family and he was happy to provide it. He rang the Queen, who 'after considerable thought, had approved, provided I spoke about him in a balanced way.'[29] Mountbatten, who had seen little of the Duke over the last thirty-five years, spoke of how, 'He was more than my best man, he was my best friend all my life.'[30]

Other tributes were more measured. The *Times* obituary confined itself to the facts with few references to Wallis, whom it called 'Mrs Simpson' throughout. To Richard Nixon, who had hosted a white tie dinner for the couple at the White House a few years earlier, 'He was a man of noble spirit and high ideals, for whom millions of Americans felt deep respect and affection.'[31]

[28] Vickers, *Unexpurgated Beaton*, p. 252.
[29] Philip Ziegler (ed.), *From Shore to Shore: The Final Years* (Collins, 1989), p. 251.
[30] MB1/K45, Mountbatten papers, Hartley Archives, Southampton University.
[31] *New York Times*, 29 May 1972.

* * *

On 31 May the Duke's body was flown to RAF Benson, where it was met by a Royal Guard of Honour, by the Duke and Duchess of Kent, members of the government and the French Ambassador. A band played the first six bars of the National Anthem. The coffin, its whole length covered by flowers from the Duchess, lay overnight in the RAF chapel with RAF officers keeping a vigil. It bore a simple inscription:

HRH The Prince Edward Albert Christian George
Andrew Patrick David, Duke of Windsor
Born 1894 Died 1972
King Edward VIII
20 January–11 December 1936

The next day, the body was taken to St George's Chapel at Windsor, where it lay in state for two days whilst 60,000 mourners filed past.

On 2 June, the Duchess, who had been too distressed to accompany her husband's body, flew to London in an aeroplane of the Queen's Flight accompanied by Grace Dudley, Mary Soames, John Utter, whom she had tried to dismiss only ten days before, the Duke's American doctor and a former equerry, Douglas Greenacre. She was met at Heathrow by Mountbatten and driven to stay at Buckingham Palace – the first time she had been there since a State Ball in May 1935, celebrating George V's Silver Jubilee, and the first time she had appeared in the Court Circular.

'She said how extremely nervous she was of having to confront the whole Royal Family without David to support her,' wrote Mountbatten in his diary. 'She had only seen them once before briefly at the unveiling of Queen Mary's Memorial at Marlborough

House, and then he had been with her. This was going to be very different and she was really apprehensive. Wallis was particularly worried about Elizabeth the Queen Mother who, she said, had never approved of her,' but Mountbatten reassured her that, 'She is so deeply sorry for you in your present grief and remembers what she felt like when her own husband died.'[32]

But her apprehensions were confirmed. 'They were polite to me, polite and kind, especially the Queen. Royalty is always polite and kind. But they were cold.'[32] A former courtier confirms the reaction. 'The Queen didn't want to have much to do with Wallis. Dinner was given in the Chinese Room – with anybody else, it would have been in the Queen's own dining room. She preferred to go down to where Wallis was set up. It was okay – everybody behaved decently. Charles was there, and helpful. But there was certainly no outpouring of love between the Queen and the Duchess of Windsor or vice versa.'[33]

The next day Wallis was invited to Trooping the Colour with the Queen wearing a black armband and a minute's silence in the Duke's honour. Heavily sedated, Wallis chose to watch it on television from a neighbouring building, though a few press pictures captured her at a window, her face gaunt, her eyes sad.

That evening Mountbatten and Prince Charles took her to St George's Chapel to see her husband lying in state after the crowds had gone. Mountbatten later wrote how she stood 'for a few moments alone, her head bowed in grief . . . At the end she stood again looking at the coffin and said in the saddest imaginable voice, "He was my entire life. I can't begin to think what I am going to

---

[32] Bryan and Murphy, p. 551.

[33] Ben Pimlott, *The Queen: A Biography of Queen Elizabeth II* (Collins, 1996), pp. 408–9.

do without him, he gave up so much for me and now he has gone. I always hoped that I would die before him."'[34]

Prince Charles remembered how she 'stood alone, a frail, tiny, black figure, gazing at the coffin and finally bowing briefly . . . As we stood, she kept saying, "He gave up so much for so little" – pointing at herself with a strange grin.'[35] It was her thirty-fifth wedding anniversary.

The hour-long funeral took place on the Monday in St George's Chapel, attended by the Queen and Duke of Edinburgh, with Wallis dressed in a simple black dress and coat quickly run up by Givenchy. Several times during the service, Wallis appeared confused and the Queen had to help her find her place in the order of service. Clarissa Avon told Cecil Beaton, one of the guests, how the 'Queen showed a motherly and nanny-like tenderness and kept putting her hand on the Duchess's arm and glove.'[36]

'Wonderful as the service was, I was not moved by the death of this man who for less than a year had been our King,' wrote Beaton in his diary:

> History will make his love story into a romance. In fact, for us so close, it is hard to see that. Wallis has been a good friend to me, I like her. She is a good friend to all her friends. There is no malice in her. There is nothing dislikeable. She is just not of the degree that has reason to be around the Throne . . .[37]

After the service, there was a lunch for forty in the state dining room. 'I was seated with the sun shining in my eyes,' Wallis told her friend

[34] Ziegler, *From Shore to Shore*, pp. 253–4.

[35] Dimbleby, p. 180.

[36] *Unexpurgated Beaton*, p. 256.

[37] *Ibid*, p. 256.

the Countess of Romanones – not always a reliable source. 'I was in pain from it. I sat next to the Duke of Edinburgh, who I had always imagined would be better, kinder, perhaps more human than the others, but you know, Aline, he is just a four-flusher. Not he, or anyone else, offered me any solicitude or sympathy whatsoever.'[38]

After the lunch, the party moved to the committal at Frogmore and burial at a site the Duke had chosen, near where he had played as a boy, and where it had been agreed Wallis would also be buried. The Duchess was shocked by how little space was left for her 'just a sliver, up against a hedge. I looked at the archbishop and said, "I realize that I am a very thin, small woman, but I do not think that even I could fit into that miserable little narrow piece of ground next to His Royal Highness's burial plot."'

'I don't see that there's much that can be done about it. You'll fit, all right,' he replied.[39]

The Lord Chamberlain then escorted her party back to the airport. As she left the plane, she thanked the pilot. 'You must come out and see us, next time you're here. The Duke would so enjoy meeting you!'[40]

---

[38] 'The Dear Romance', *Vanity Fair*, June 1986.

[39] *Ibid.* The hedge was later moved to accommodate her.

[40] Bryan and Murphy, p. 556.

CHAPTER 23

The Duchess Alone

Wallis returned to a home filled with reminders of their life together. She may have strained at his devotion and her lack of freedom, but he had given purpose and structure to her life. Now at seventy-six, she was a widow with no immediate family and a dwindling circle of friends. 'I think that the Duke was more in love with the Duchess than the Duchess with him,' the Countess of Romanones later claimed, 'but by the time he was dying, she had begun to realise how much in love with him she was. He meant more to her than anyone.'[1]

The house became a shrine with everything left as it had been. 'His suits still hang in his dressing-room cupboards. His shirts are stacked in their drawers, his toilet articles spread in his bathroom, his desk ready for instant use, with supplies of pipe cleaners and assorted stationery, all as during his lifetime.'[2]

She was terrified that she would not have enough money and that the French Government would end the agreement over the house. The Mill, which had been on the market for two years, was sold to a Swiss millionaire for £350,000, together with the 3.5 acres in Marbella for £82,000.[3]

---

[1] Romanones interview, quoted King, p. 486.
[2] Bryan and Murphy, p. 563.
[3] £4.7 million and £1.1 million today.

In fact, Wallis inherited everything – little was left to charity, friends, godchildren or staff.[4] She received $19,500 from the United Kingdom and $2.5 million of French assets, the Queen continued the annual allowance, now reduced to £5,000, the French did not impose death duties, and she remained immune from tax during her lifetime, but the Paris staff was still reduced from twenty-five to fourteen.[5]

One of those to go was Sydney, the butler, who had been with the Windsors since the Bahamas. His wife had just died, requiring him to put his three small children to bed. Having failed to engage a nurse or housekeeper, he asked if he might begin going home at five. Wallis's response had been, 'If you go at five, don't come back.' He left and did not come back.[6]

Later in June, the art historian Roy Strong dined with the Windsors' friends Charles and Jayne Wrightsman, with Cecil Beaton amongst the guests. Strong recollected Charles Wrightsman telling him that:

> The Duchess was, however, the 'bad lot', a chronic insomniac who needed only three hours' sleep and demanded that people talk to her till four in the morning. She sponged off everyone and had boyfriends, in particular Jimmy Donohoe (*sic*), whom she had times with on her own at Palm Beach, the Duke arriving later. Charlie Wrightsman categorised her as the 'nurse'. He was like a child of ten. The Duchess ran the whole show, embarking on memoirs and television for the money. She had invested in jewellery, which was a mistake, because on his death her income collapsed as certain revenues

4 His godchildren included: Edward Brownlow, son of Perry; Alexander Guest, son of Winston; David Metcalfe, son of Fruity; David, Marquess of Milford-Haven; David Seely, 4th Baron Mottistone; David, Earl of Westmoreland, and North Dalrymple-Hamilton.

5 The annual allowance was worth £67,000 today.

6 Bryan and Murphy, p. 549.

from Wales ceased to come any more. She had been virtually doped for his funeral and it was thought safer to take her into the Palace rather than having her freak out at Claridge's.[7]

At the lunch at the funeral, Wallis had deliberately been placed between Mountbatten and Prince Philip, whose task was to persuade her to part with sensitive papers and royal heirlooms. 'Within a day or two of her return to Paris, a truck drew up and whisked them away,' wrote Kenneth Rose in his diary. 'They are now in the Royal Archives at Windsor.'[8]

Exactly what was removed to the Royal Archives, when and whether it was all above board, has never been clear. The Duchess's lawyer, Maître Blum, later claimed 'that two individuals, authorised either by Lord Mountbatten, or "some other person" acting upon what she alleged to be Royal authority, had somehow obtained the keys to the Duke's boxes and confidential filing cabinet and burgled the contents . . . The contents included the Duke's private correspondence, the documents of divorce from Win Spencer and Ernest Simpson . . . and a certain amount of the Duchess's personal correspondence.'[9]

But, according to Kenneth de Courcy, the first consignment of papers was handed to the Queen's Librarian Sir Robin Mackworth-Young with the Duchess present on 15 June 1972. A second tranche, again collected with the Duchess's knowledge, was picked up on 13 December.[10] A third was picked up by Mackworth-Young on 22 July 1977.[11]

---

[7] 20 June 1972, Roy Strong, *Splendours and Miseries: The Roy Strong Diaries 1967–87* (Weidenfeld & Nicolson, 1997), p. 105.

[8] 21 January 1983, Kenneth Rose, Vol. 2, pp. 68–9.

[9] Higham, *Wallis*, pp. 484–5. Also Parker, pp. 297–8.

[10] Kenneth de Courcy, Box 3, Folder 5, Hoover. This is supported by Ziegler, pp. 680–1 and Vickers, p. 10.

[11] *Daily Express*, 23 July 1977.

Mountbatten now found the opportunity to drop in more often, anxious to know what would happen to her wealth and possessions after her death. He suggested that some of the jewellery might be given to some of the younger female royals; that he might serve as an executor of her will; the setting up of a Duke of Windsor Foundation chaired by Prince Charles and with Rear Admiral Philip de Gaulle, son of the President, as the French trustee; and that she might support the United World Colleges, of which Mountbatten was International President. Eventually Mountbatten was told not to visit her by her doctor, Jean Thin, because it raised her blood pressure.

Initially enthusiastic, at the beginning of 1973 she decided against the foundation, dismissed her London solicitor, Sir Godfrey Morley of Allen and Overy, and appointed Suzanne Blum to act for her exclusively in future. It was to mark an important new chapter in the Duchess's life.

Blum had been born in north-west France in 1898 and had graduated from the University of Poitiers in 1921. In the same year she had married Paul Weill, later the Paris representative of Allen and Overy. She had built a successful and high-profile practice, representing Rita Hayworth in her divorce from the Aly Khan in 1958, and her Hollywood clients included Charlie Chaplin, Jack Warner, Darryl F. Zanuck, Walt Disney, Douglas Fairbanks and Merle Oberon. One of her first briefs had been successfully defending Warner Brothers against an action brought by the composer Igor Stravinsky for misuse of his music.

She had first been introduced to the Windsors in 1937, through the US ambassador William Bullitt, but had only started acting for the Windsors shortly after the Second World War. From 1973 her influence over the Duchess would be absolute. In March 1973, partly as a thank you for their generosity, Wallis signed an agreement to give the French government almost 140 pieces of furniture worth £750,000 and works of art.[12] Her gold boxes, some costing £25,000 each, were donated to the Louvre, a Stubbs picture went to Versailles, and some porcelain to the National Ceramics Museum at Sèvres.[13]

Writing to Joe Bryan that month, Charles Murphy related how:

> Biddy Mokcton (*sic*), now back in London, has called me here in great distress. A classical situation seems to have taken shape. Morley has been fired. Utter has taken over the management of the household. An English nurse from the staff of the American Hospital, who brought the Duchess home and has been with her four weeks or so, says that his (Utter's) office is maneuvering (*sic*) to take over the possessions. Most correspondence he throws into the waste basket. She has seen him do it. He allows few calls to go through to the Duchess. The effect is to persuade her that she is quite alone except for him. Even Biddy Monckton, who gave up her own comfort to be with the Duchess, was required by Utter, until the last visit, to stay in a hotel.
>
> It seems that Utter has made an art of cultivating the affection of rich elderly ladies who leave their possessions to him. I shall tell you this: the other day as I left the gate, Boyer, the English chauffeur, was standing outside. 'I must see you, Mr Murphy. You can't believe what is going on in that house. It will shock you.' Later, I told him. Think of the value of the jewels, the jewelry, the little bibelots and Meissen, that today are no longer under surveillance . . .[14]

---

[12] Now £9.2 million.

[13] Just over £300K.

[14] Charles Murphy to Joe Bryan, 10 March 1973, Mss 5.9 B 8405:97–119, Virginia Museum of History and Culture.

Wallis became increasingly obsessed with security. Beside the spiked fence and guarded gate and alarm system, she kept a pistol on her night table – unknown to her it was a fake – and hired a former French paratrooper to patrol the grounds. She began to drink more heavily – preferably vodka in a silver cup – and to become more reclusive.

She still sat on the boards of the American Hospital and the Animal Society, but contributed little in time or money. When her secretary John Utter tried to persuade her to visit hospital patients 'to redeem her image', she refused.[15] She turned down a suggestion from Jackie Onassis, now a publisher, to write another volume of memoirs, but in March 1975 she put many of her documents in the care of Maître Blum, with instructions that they be turned into a book. She had always been interested in cancer research, and as a means of thanking the French for years of low rent, she now wrote a new will making the Pasteur Medical Institute her main beneficiary.

She still saw some friends and travelled. In May 1973, the businesswoman Francine Farkas lent Wallis her villa at Cap Ferrat – as a thank you, Wallis gave her a silver urn with the royal crest. Farkas had met the Windsors through her husband, Alexander Farkas, who ran the department store Alexanders. The couples had met whenever the Windsors were in New York or the Farkas's in France.

'Her life was devoted to him and his needs,' recollected Ms Farkas:

> She would even check if there were bones in his sole filet at a restaurant. Her conversation was animated and she could talk engagingly about business, politics and especially food about which she knew more about than anyone I knew. Everything was done to perfection and when entertaining she'd have a

[15] Bryan and Murphy, p. 561.

small string quartet playing in the dining room gallery. He was the most charming person with real presence. Though a small man physically, people parted in front of him. He loved gardening and I remember how he showed me how to cut roses correctly, always the fifth rose down. People liked being with them. She always held court. She was like an older sister to me, someone who one valued being around.[16]

The following year, Wallis stayed at the Hotel du Palais in Biarritz with another old friend, 'Foxy' Sefton. She visited New York, where she had another face-lift, and stayed at the Waldorf Towers where a friend, Nathan Cummings, the founder of Consolidated Foods, had lent her some Renoirs and a Sisley to furnish the suite, and according to one biographer, 'the hotel staff talked for weeks about her abusive treatment of servants, waiters, bell-boys, and the drivers of her cars.'[17]

She continued to socialise, attending occasional dinner parties with a 26-year-old companion, Claude Roland. In 1974, it was rumoured she would marry Prince Borromeo, the ageing owner of the Borromean Islands and an old friend, but she was becoming increasingly aggressive and forgetful. At one dinner party that year, gesturing towards John Utter, she asked, 'Who's he? . . . I never saw him before in my life.'[18]

The *Vogue* editor-in-chief, Diana Vreeland, found her confused when she visited:

She was so affectionate, a loving sort of friend – very rare, you know . . . So we were talking after dinner, the two of us. And then suddenly she took hold of my wrist, gazed off

[16] Interview Francine Sears, 8 May 2020.

[17] Birmingham, p. 267.

[18] Bryan and Murphy, p. 566.

into the distance, and said, 'Diana, I keep telling him he must not abdicate. *He must not abdicate . . .*' Then, suddenly, after this little mental journey back more than thirty-five years, her mind snapped back to the present; she looked back at me, and we went on talking as we had been before.[19]

The friends began to stop coming or being invited.

She increasingly suffered ill health with broken legs and cracked ribs. In February 1976, she was admitted to the American Hospital with an intestinal haemorrhage – arriving with her own maid and linen, the latter changed daily. To fund medical treatment, Blum had quietly begun to sell possessions, some on the open market, others to friends – Nathan Cummings bought a dining-room table, some silver, and a Meissen Tiger dinner service.

In May 1976, *France Soir* published pictures of her in a chaise longue on the terrace at Route du Champ d'Entraînement. 'The Duchess looked pitiful. Her tiny shrunken body was being lifted by a nurse. Her legs were cigarette-thin and they dangled uselessly. Her hair was tied tightly back in a knot. Her head lolled helplessly on her chest. There was a close-up of her face and she looked a little like a Chinese mandarin, but more like a dead monkey.'[20] Blum sued for 'wrongful intrusion on her privacy' and was awarded 80,000 francs damages from each photographer.

Later that month, Wallis was admitted to the American Hospital with a bacterial infection, remaining until September. The photograph of her leaving would be the last glimpse the public would have of her. The following month, the Queen Mother arranged to see the Duchess on a visit to Paris, but Wallis was too ill to receive her.

[19] Diana Vreeland, *DV* (Knopf, 1984), p. 68.
[20] Blackwood, p. 110.

Instead she sent roses with the message 'In Friendship, Elizabeth'. The feud was over.

The Duchess was lonely, depressed and longed to die. Two nurses took care of her, working in shifts of three around the clock. Circulatory problems meant she could no longer use her hands or feet and she had to be carried everywhere. She spent most of the time in a wheelchair and was now spoon-fed by a nurse; her weight dropped to eighty-five pounds. Soon she would lose the power of speech, be blind and on an intravenous drip. To keep her entertained, a pianist was brought in to play medleys of her favourite songs, such as 'Bye Bye Blackbird' and 'I Get a Kick out of You'.

Blum had dismissed most of her staff, including her secretary, Joanna Schultz – John Utter had left in the autumn of 1975 with neither pension nor severance pay, after she accused him of colluding with Mountbatten for the return of the Duke's papers. By 1980, the thirty-two staff had been reduced to the butler, Georges Sanègre, his wife Ophelia the housekeeper, Martin the gardener-cum-chauffeur, the laundress, and the Duchess's Portuguese maid Maria. Several of the pugs had also gone – given away after the Duchess could no longer bear their barking.

Aline, Countess of Romanones, one of the few allowed past the gatekeepers, Maître Blum and Doctor Jean Thin, was shocked by the change in her friend when visiting her in 1984:

> This time Georges directed me through the boudoir to her bedroom, where she was seated in the wheelchair, with her back to the door, looking out at the trees and garden. A nurse was with her. Her hearing was excellent, and she turned her head and smiled. Our eyes held for a moment before she turned back for want of something to say, and I was choked by the great difference in her. The hair around her face was

white, due to not having been dyed in a long time. The hair was still long and thick, done in a braid pulled down and folded under at the nape of her neck.

She wore a blue wool jacket, and on the sofa behind her were her favourite pillows, one stitched with the words 'You can never be too rich or too thin', the other with 'Don't worry. It never happens'. Her bed had been replaced with an adjustable hospital one. Although she looked neat and seemed not to be in pain or unhappy, I could see that this fastidious woman would certainly not want to receive her friends any longer. No fancy dress, no makeup, no nail polish – and grey hair!

I pulled up the chair she used at her dressing table and sat down beside her. She was looking at me, and her face had a sweet, almost timid expression. Placing her hand on mine, she asked, 'Who are you, my dear?'

I saw that it embarrassed her that she did not know. I said, 'I'm Aline.'

'Oh, Aline dear, forgive me.' She patted my hand. 'Look at the way the sun is lighting the trees. You can see so many different colours. Tell David to come in. He wouldn't want to miss this.'[21]

On 24 April 1986 Wallis died, aged eighty-nine, of heart failure brought on by pneumonia. Three days later, the Lord Chamberlain flew to collect her body to make the same journey that her husband had made almost exactly fourteen years earlier.

From RAF Benson it was taken to St George's Chapel at Windsor for a thirty-minute private funeral attended by the Queen, Prince Philip, the Queen Mother, the Prince and Princess of Wales, the prime minister Margaret Thatcher, Baba Metcalfe, Diana Mosley,

---

[21] 'A Bold Romance', *Vanity Fair*, June 1986.

Lady Dudley and the Countess of Romanones. A bearer party of Welsh Guards carried her coffin to the quire and at the conclusion of the service it was carried out to Elgar's 'Enigma Variations'.

'The service, with much processional pageantry, is beautiful, but deliberately excludes emotion,' wrote Kenneth Rose in his diary:

> After the service, when talking to Robert Runcie in the Cloisters, I ask him when he last attended the funeral of a person whose name was nowhere mentioned from beginning to end. He says: 'No never.' . . . Overall it was an odd occasion: all the grandeur and pageantry of a Royal funeral, yet with a cold heartlessness. No hospitality whatever was offered to the mourners: not so much as a glass of sherry or a cup of tea.[22]

Laura, Duchess of Marlborough added to the invitation in her scrapbook: 'A sad day, the Queen looked furious, the Queen Mother almost danced behind the coffin.'[23]

Wallis was buried beside her husband, but set apart from the other royal graves. Her gravestone simply reads: 'Wallis, Duchess of Windsor'. She would not be designated HRH even in death.

Almost immediately Mohamed Al Fayed took over the lease of the Bois de Boulogne home at a nominal cost, on condition he restore it to its Windsor heyday.

Some jewellery was left to Princess Alexandra, the Duchess of Kent and Princess Michael of Kent and some friends, but most was sold to benefit the Pasteur Institute's research into AIDS. Some 230 lots were sold at Sotheby's in Geneva within a year of her death, raising seven times the estimate – $50,281,887. Amongst those who bid were Elizabeth Taylor, who bought a diamond and platinum

---

[22] Rose, Vol. 2, p. 138.
[23] Thanks to Amy Ripley for supplying this.

brooch in the shape of Prince of Wales feathers for $567,000, and Calvin Klein.

In February 1998, Sotheby's auctioned off the rest of the Windsor possessions, including a slice of their wedding cake – neatly wrapped in a white silk box with their signatures – for $29,000, his wedding morning suit for $27,000, the Brockhurst portrait of Wallis was purchased by the National Portrait Gallery for $107,000, the Munnings painting for $2,312,000, two Cecil Beaton sketches of Wallis that had hung in her bathroom for $310,000, and the abdication desk for $415,000.[24] Designer Tommy Hilfiger bought many of the furnishings for a new house in Connecticut.

It was the end of an era.

[24] In today's prices, $29K is worth $47K; $27K is worth $44K; $107K is now $175K; $2,312,000 is $3,820,000; $310K is $512K and $415K is $680K.

CHAPTER 24

Relationships

'The Duchess rather baffled me,' remembered her wartime PR spokesman, René MacColl. 'I was never at my ease with her. What causes one human being to fall madly in love with another is occasionally clear to third persons. More often it remains a mystery to the onlooker. So far as I was concerned, it was emphatically a mystery in this case.'[1]

It is a question that has continued to intrigue. Was the Windsors' relationship totally harmonious or did the couple feel they had to pretend to live out the love story that everyone wanted, even if it was not true?

'I am well aware that there are still some people in the world who go on hoping our marriage will break up. And to them I say, Give up hope, because David and I are happy and have been happy for twenty-four years, and that's the way it will continue to be,' Wallis told *McCall's* magazine in 1961:

For my part, I have given my husband every ounce of my affection, something he never had a great deal of in his bachelor's life. Notice, I use the word 'affection'. I believe it is an element apart from love, the deep bond one assumes as a part of marriage. You may know the phrase 'tender loving care'; it

---

[1] MacColl, pp. 123–4.

means much the same thing. It means doing the things that uphold a man's confidence in himself, creating an atmosphere of warmth and interest, of taking his mind off his worries.[2]

Is that true? Certainly the Duke remained besotted with her all his life. Walter Monckton was later to write:

No one will ever really understand the story of the King's life . . . who does not appreciate . . . the intensity and depth of his devotion to Mrs Simpson. To him she was the perfect woman. She insisted that he be at his best and do his best at all times, and he regarded her as his inspiration. It is a great mistake to imagine that he was merely in love with her in the ordinary physical sense of the term. There was an intellectual companionship, and there is no doubt that his lonely nature found in her a spiritual comradeship . . . He felt that he and Mrs Simpson were made for each other and that there was no other honest way of meeting the situation than marrying her.[3]

Winston Churchill noticed how:

He delighted in her company, and found in her qualities as necessary to his happiness as the air he breathed. Those who knew him well and watched him closely noticed that many little tricks and fidgetings of nervousness fell away from him. He was a completed being instead of a sick and harassed soul. This experience which happens to a great many people in the

[2] *McCall's* magazine, June 1961.
[3] Birkenhead, pp. 125–6.

flower of youth came late in life to him, and was all the more precious and compulsive for that fact.[4]

The evidence for her affection for him is less apparent. Wallis had enjoyed the status and social contact that her relationship with the Prince of Wales brought, but it is doubtful that she was ever in love with him, or she fully considered the implications of the relationship. After George V died, she suddenly found herself involved in events she could not control. This included a relationship with a man so obsessed with her that he was prepared to commit suicide if she would not stay with him, and even to forsake the throne. By the time she wished to extricate herself from the relationship, she was stuck.

As far back as the cruise on the *Nahlin* in August 1936, Diana Cooper had noticed that Wallis did not want to be left alone with the King. She wrote in her diary: 'The truth is she's bored stiff with him, and her picking on him and her coldness towards him far from policy are irritation and boredom.'[5]

One area of hurt throughout their relationship was her status and how she was treated. It began as soon as he abdicated, with long telephone calls to Austria about finances and status, and continued throughout the thirty-five years they were married, much of her venom directed against his family.

'But of course her great mischief was that she went at him morning, noon and night and right up to one o'clock in the morning, two o'clock in the morning, steaming up against his family,' remembered Kenneth de Courcy. 'She went on and on and on and on.'[6]

---

[4] Martin Gilbert (ed.), *Winston Churchill: Prophet of Truth*, Vol. 5 (Heinemann, 1976), p. 810.

[5] 'The *Nahlin*', p. 30, DUFC 2/17, Churchill College Archives.

[6] Kenneth de Courcy, p. 6, BREN 2/2/5, Churchill College Archives.

'The duchess was a complicated person – cold, mean-spirited, a bully and a sadist,' observed Dr Gaea Leinhardt, stepdaughter of Wallis's ghost writer, Cleveland Amory. 'My parents found the duke not very bright, a wimp, and basically a very sad man. He had made an appalling choice and knew that he had taken the wrong path and now had to live with the consequences. They found him pathetic.'[7]

Yet it some ways it was Wallis's very dominant manner that most appealed to the Duke. Writing to his mistress Freda Dudley Ward in January 1920, he had told her:

> You know you ought to be really foul to me sometimes swerties & curse & be cruel; it would do me worlds of good & bring me to my right senses!! I think I'm the kind of man who needs a certain amount of cruelty without which he gets abominably spoilt & soft. I feel that's what's the matter with me.[8]

There was certainly a strong masochist and Dom/sub aspect to the couple's relationship, both sexually and in everyday life. 'She was harsh, dominating, often abominably rude,' wrote Philip Ziegler in the official life. 'She treated the Prince at the best like a child who needed keeping in order, at the worst with contempt. But he invited it and begged for more.'[9] 'She dominated the Duke but he did not just put up with it, he actually liked it,' remembered Cleveland Amory.[10]

Mona Eldridge, who met the Windsors on numerous occasions whilst working for the Woolworth heiress and socialite Barbara Hutton, later wrote:

[7] Morton, *Wallis in Love*, pp. 318–19.

[8] Rupert Godfrey, *Letters from a Prince* (Little, Brown, 1998), p. 245.

[9] Ziegler, *Shore to Shore*, p. 237.

[10] Amory, *Best Cat Ever*, p. 142.

Barbara also believed that Wallis had a sense of having been cheated by life. At times she would sound bitter and implied that her husband had failed her, that he had not kept his promise. She had a way of denigrating him by reminding him that he had let her down *again*. People on her staff told me how she would reprimand the Duke like a harsh mother with a naughty child, not infrequently reducing him to tears. Paradoxically, this only caused him to cling more tightly to her.[11]

Charles Murphy remembered on one occasion a journalist called on their Paris home to collect a manuscript from the Duke:

to hear the Duchess rant at him for littering the dinner table with his papers: 'I've got twenty guests dining here in two hours! Why didn't you make this mess somewhere else?' The dining room was his only office and he had no other choice, replying, and the journalist never forgot his exact words, 'Darling, are you going to send me to bed in tears again tonight?'[12]

'He was like a child in her hands,' Lady Alexandra Metcalfe told Cleveland Amory. 'Poor little man, he was given hell; it was a stranglehold she had over him.'[13] 'He never had any real mothering, she never had any children,' remembered Kenneth de Courcy. 'Both needed each other.'[14]

Weak and below average intelligence, the Duke needed a woman to dominate him with that abjectness which former girlfriends

[11] Eldridge, pp. 86–7.
[12] Bryan and Murphy, p. 478.
[13] 'TV Tale of Two Windsors', *New York Times Magazine*, 18 March 1979.
[14] 'The Windsor Papers', Kenneth de Courcy, Box 3, Folder 5, Hoover Institute.

had found so disconcerting. The result was that he was completely dependent on his wife.

In many ways the Duke had never properly grown up physically or emotionally. Childhood mumps may have led to a hormonal imbalance. Alan Lascelles wrote in his diary:

> Wise old Dawson of Penn told me several times that he was convinced that EP's moral development (not physical) had for some reason been arrested in his adolescence, and that wld (*sic*) account for this limitation. An outward symptom of such arrestation, D of P wold (*sic*) say, was the absence of hair on the face of the subject. EP only had to shave about once a week.[15]

Frank Giles, showering with the Duke in 1940 after a game of golf, noticed that 'he had absolutely no hair on his body, even in the places where one would most expect it to be.'[16]

The Duke worshipped his wife, trusted her, felt secure with her and was restless when she was not there. 'When she was present, he watched her every movement, listened to her every word and responded to every inflection in her voice,' remembered Mona Eldridge. 'He often said that nothing was too good for her.'[17]

'His wife was constantly in his thoughts,' later wrote Dina Hood. 'If he went out alone he looked for her the moment he returned home. If she went out without him and remained away for any length of time, he became nervous and preoccupied.'[18] She added,

---

[15] LASL 8/8, Churchill College Archives. Before coming to the throne, the Duke signed himself 'Edward Princeps', or EP. His property in Alberta was known as the EP ranch.

[16] *Sundry Times,* p. 24, and Frank Giles, p. 26, BREN 2/2/7, Churchill College Archives.

[17] Eldridge, p. 89.

[18] Hood, p. 35.

'I have seen him in the middle of a haircut in his dressing room get up and run to his wife, leaving his astonished hairdresser agape.'[19] 'If he was in a room and she came in, the moment she came in the room he became vivacious, he became happy, he became full of life, it was just amazing,' recollected Dudley Forwood.[20]

'I have rarely seen an ascendancy established over one partner in a marriage by the other to so remarkable a degree,' Frank Giles remembered. 'He seemed to revel in being with the Duchess, in sunning himself in her smile, in admiring her appearance, in listening to her conversation.'[21]

'I have never known any person so totally possessed by the personality of another,' wrote Kenneth de Courcy:

> He seemed to me to retain no individuality at all whenever she was present and when we were alone he constantly jumps up looking for her or asking on the house telephone where she was. If she was away he was restless and unhappy. Once in the South of France, when I was staying with my mother and the Duchess was in Paris, the Duke was at a total loss and I was asked to dinner on three successive evenings . . . Did she love the Duke of Windsor? I am afraid the sad answer is that she did not. She admires him, she likes him, but it never went further and I think he knew it and it was that which made him restless and induced him to concede his very innermost person to her authority in the hope that love would come . . . She never learnt to love the Duke and, in my opinion, she never ever experienced love at all for anyone.[22]

[19] Hood, p. 36.
[20] Forwood, p. 5, BREN 2/2/7, Churchill College Archives.
[21] Martin, p. 424.
[22] 'The Windsor Papers', de Courcy, Box 3, Folder 5, Hoover Institute.

Given the speculation over their relationship, what was the nature of the couple's sex life? The FBI reported, after interviewing Father Odo, that Wallis had:

> told certain individuals that the Duke is impotent and that although he had tried sexual intercourse with numerous women, they had been unsuccessful in satisfying his passions. According to the story related by Father Odo, the Duchess in her own inimitable and unique manner has been the only woman who had been able to satisfactorily gratify the Duke's sexual desires.[23]

Count Edward 'Eddie' Bismarck told Gore Vidal 'that Wallis's sexual hold over the duke was that only she knew how to control his premature ejaculation.'[24]

'The Prince had sexual problems. He was unable to perform,' Lady Gladwyn, wife of the former British ambassador in Paris, told Hugo Vickers:

> 'It was all over before it began – she called it a hairpin reaction.' She said that the Duchess coped with it. I commented, 'She was meant to have learned special ways in China.' 'There was nothing Chinese about it,' said Lady Gladwyn. 'It was what they call oral sex.'[25]

What hung over Wallis was the supposed existence of 'The China Dossier' relating to her activities in China, mainly sexual but also

---

[23] FBI file, HQ 65-31113.

[24] Vidal, p. 208.

[25] Hugo Vickers unpublished diary, 2 June 1982, Vickers, *Behind Closed Doors*, p. 310.

political, one of three reports supposedly gathered by the British Intelligence Services and shown to King George V in 1935. It was said that members of the Government and Royal Household had seen it, but its details remain vague. Tommy Dugdale, then parliamentary private secretary to the prime minister Stanley Baldwin, told Kenneth de Courcy that the 'Intelligence Service had a case against Mrs Simpson which, if we could but read it, would entirely change our attitude.'[26]

Kenneth de Courcy was told about it by Sir John Coke, Queen Mary's equerry, in the 1950s. He noted in a memo that:

> he has read the secret dossier on the Duchess of Windsor, some details of which he told me and said he had recommended Churchill. He says that her personal record is so shocking that no English gentleman could properly advise Queen Mary ever to receive her or in any way relent. He assures me of such facts and challenges me to say whether, having heard such facts, I could tell him that he should advise Queen Mary to relent. I replied that if the allegations were true, I could not.[27]

De Courcy remembered parts of the dossier including – 'that she'd got power over Count Charlot amongst other people in that way, and had an illegitimate child by Charlot,[28] and abortion . . . that's why she had this internal problem all her life.'[29]

---

[26] Kenneth de Courcy to Duke of Windsor, 27 September 1951, de Courcy Papers, Hoover Institute.

[27] 10 March 1951, Box 3, Folder 4, de Courcy Papers, Hoover Institute.

[28] Philip Ziegler is quoted that she 'had a child by Count Ciano (later Mussolini's son-in-law)', James Fox, *Vanity Fair*, September 2003.

[29] Kenneth de Courcy, p. 56, BREN 2/2/5, Churchill College Archives.

The existence of the China dossier has never been proven. Even so, Dudley Forwood told Charles Higham in 1987:

> The techniques Wallis discovered in China did not entirely overcome the Prince's extreme lack of virility. It is doubtful whether he and Wallis ever actually had sexual intercourse in the normal sense of the word. However, she did manage to give him relief. He had always been a repressed foot fetishist, and she discovered this and indulged the perversity completely. They also, at his request, became involved in elaborate erotic games. These included nanny-child scenes: he wore diapers; she was the master. She was dominant, he happily submissive.[30]

Nicky Haslam agrees about the infantilism. 'I mean nappies,' he says. 'They were all sexually screwed up by Queen Mary. Potty Gloucester [the Duke's brother] liked wearing Queen Mary's clothes, though he wasn't gay. The Duke was certainly gay. I know that for a fact.'[31]

Queen Mary, the last royal to believe in the divine right of kings, had never intervened in the callous bullying that George V meted out to his children. 'Of course, none of them came up to George V for horrors,' says Diana Mosley. 'There's a ghastly photograph in my book where they're being drilled by their father and they're all in floods. Oh, I mean, too awful.' 'Being treated as a little boy, given orders, and punished when naughty,' Michael Bloch gathered from his sources, were to the Duke's taste.[32]

---

[30] Higham, *Wallis* (Sidgwick & Jackson, 1988), p. 72.

[31] 'The Oddest Couple', James Fox, *Vanity Fair*, September 2003. Confirmed in email by Nicky Haslam to author, 11 April 2021.

[32] James Fox, *Vanity Fair*, September 2003.

Relationships

Charles Wilson, whose mother was married to Ulick Alexander, Keeper of the Privy Purse, was told by her that:

> Edward gained pleasure from being beaten by Wallis who delivered the strokes with her own small whip . . . He needed the stimulus, I think in order to perform in the normal manner – something with which he had great difficulty in earlier relationships . . . It was at a country house party where the then Prince of Wales and Mrs Simpson were guests that the Prince's private detective came to Ulick one morning with some worrying discoveries. He produced a pair of the Prince's underpants striped with caked blood and a small whip that he found in Mrs Simpson's underwear drawer . . . There is no doubt that Edward loved Wallis, but he was frightened of her – this she was quick to exploit.[33]

In 2012, Scotty Bowers, a Hollywood barman, published his memoirs, *Full Service: My Adventures in Hollywood and the Secret Sex Lives of the Stars,* in which he claimed he had sexually procured men and women for numerous Hollywood stars from 1946. Amongst his clients were Sir Cecil Beaton, who wrote of Bowers in his published diaries, Noël Coward, and the Duke and Duchess of Windsor.

Chapter Fourteen in the book, 'A Royal Affair', is devoted to the couple, claiming that 'during the late forties and early fifties' Cecil Beaton had introduced them to Bowers, saying the Duke was 'a classic example of a bisexual man', that 'Wallis Simpson shared similar bisexual urges . . . but essentially, he was gay and she was a dyke'. According to Bowers, 'he and I slipped into the guesthouse at

[33] 'Dark Side of the Great Love Story', *Sunday Express*, January 1994, quoted Gwynne Thomas, *King, Pawn or Black Knight* (Mainstream, 1995), pp. 38–9.

the bottom end of the large garden, stripped off, and began making out. Eddy was good. *Really* good. He sucked me off like a pro.'[34]

Over the next few days, Bowers writes that he supplied 'a nice young guy for Eddy and a pretty dark-haired girl for Wally. Each time I sent somebody different. The royal couple enjoyed variety . . .' Bowers wrote that Wallis 'was not in any way inhibited. She was very fond of dark-haired women, usually those with hair colour similar to her own . . . Wally really knew what she was doing. She did it in style and with intense passion.'[35]

Amongst those who confirmed that Bowers' stories were true were Gore Vidal, who spoke at the book launch, film director John Schlesinger, and the novelist Dominick Dunne. The film director, Lionel Friedberg, who ghosted *Full Service*, spent 150 hours with Scotty over several months, constantly testing him for accuracy. 'Not once did he deviate from what he had said before. He had a photographic memory down to remembering number plates from years before . . . I don't think he could tell a lie . . . I don't doubt that everything he said about the Windsors was true.'[36]

A documentary, *Scotty and the Secret History of Hollywood*, directed by Matt Tyrnauer, was released in 2017. Tyrnauer, who told me he interviewed Bowers on and off camera over a three-year period, confirms that his independent reporting lined up with the information in Friedburg's earlier interviews. Additionally, Tyrnauer interviewed more than forty friends and associates of Bowers, including men who were sex workers at Bowers' gas station in the 1950s, all of whom corroborated Bowers. Friedberg's view about Bowers' veracity:

[34] Scotty Bowers, 'A Royal Affair', *Full Service* (Grove Press, 2013).

[35] Bowers, 'A Royal Affair', *Full Service*.

[36] Interview with Lionel Friedberg, 13 April 2021.

Everything I put in the movie checks out – either in printed documents, books, manuscripts, diaries, newspaper clips, etc. It all matches up. Details regarding homes and home addresses and architectural features of homes he was in that he could not have possibly have known unless he was in the houses. Also sources who were with him at the time who confirmed events. Obviously I could not prove everything he told me, but that would have been beyond the scope of my project. Whenever I went to check something, it panned out, however.[37]

* * *

'My husband gave up everything for me; if everyone looks at me when I enter a room, my husband can feel proud of me,' Wallis told Elsa Maxwell. 'That's my chief responsibility.'[38] The result was that Wallis spent a fortune on her appearance and clothes.

The Duchess was not conventionally good-looking with a prominent jaw and outsized hands, but she ate carefully – under the guidance of the nutritionist Gayelord Hauser – with the result at 5 foot 4 inches, she rarely weighed over 100 lbs, with measurements of 34 inch bust, 22 inch waist and 34 inch hips.[39]

Aline Romanones remembered how her shoes were always shined underneath, on the instep and inside the heel, as they could be seen when the legs were crossed, and that she always carried an extra pair of white gloves in her bag: 'One pair to go, one pair to come back.'[40]

In the 1930s, her favourite designers were Mainbocher and Schiaparelli, by the 1950s she had switched to Dior, Balenciaga and Chanel, and she even experimented with pants suits in the 1950s and

[37] Matt Tyrnauer, emails to author, 1 and 2 May 2020.

[38] Elsa Maxwell, *RSVP: Elsa Maxwell's Own Story* (Little, Brown, 1954), p. 301.

[39] Mosley, *Duchess of Windsor,* p. 188.

[40] Countess of Romanones, 'The Dear Romance', *Vanity Fair,* June 1986.

miniskirts in the 1960s. She made the short evening dress fashionable as well as, because of her flat chest, high-necked evening gowns.

This all came at a great cost. 'The Duchess bought clothes from several couturiers and she would beat the prices down on the pretext that she would advertise the clothes she wore,' remembered Mona Eldridge. 'Both she and the Duke were notorious for their stinginess, resorting to all sorts of shameless deceits to avoid paying bills. In the case of the Duke, it was pathological.'[41]

During the 1950s, staff were used to increasingly angry letters and calls from unpaid suppliers, not least the jewellery houses Cartier and Van Cleef. The result was that a deal was struck that Wallis would borrow jewels for public events as long as the name of the designer was leaked to the Press and they were returned promptly.

The Windsors only kept to the first part of the bargain – they borrowed, but didn't return. Unfortunately, it is no longer possible to identify which items in the collection were paid for and which were not. A wholesale clear-out of all correspondence at the time of the Duchess's death in 1986 ensured that we shall never know the full extent of this dishonesty. However, one former servant told me grimly: 'Rarely was anything ever handed back.[42]

Courtney de Espil, married to Wallis's former lover Felipe de Espil, had presciently written at the time of the Abdication:

Today in my humble opinion, England must feel luckier to be rid of a man so weak, this Jekyll and Hyde king of so little inner stability and yet such outward charm . . . They have

[41] Eldridge, p. 86.
[42] Christopher Wilson, *Daily Mail*, 2 December 2010.

ahead of them years in which to decide where to live. They will have no country and he 'no job'. Can any love exist or be nourished on this slender fare? . . . For Edward is no longer a king. In her eyes he can only be a poor weak man who depends on her now, who has given away his all. Can they dance every night at a different cabaret to keep life gay?[43]

The problem for the Windsors was that they were superficial people with little sense of obligation and few interests. When pressed, a friend of Wallis's came up with 'gossip . . . and *marvellous* housekeeping'. Wallis herself said that her talent was 'getting people to talk'.

The art historian John Richardson says of her:

She was a society rattle, straight out of Thackeray, in a way. She must have been like one of those Regency ladies around George IV, prattling away in this hideous voice. Funny. A marvellous *maîtresse de maison*. The food was superb, and she got it right – it wasn't too overdone. The place always looked very attractive – wonderful flowers and modern American touches. You could be sure that cocktails were superb. But the conversation was idiotic.[44]

'The Duke and Duchess led totally self-centred lives; there was no consideration for anything but the gratification of their own needs,' according to Mona Eldridge. 'The life they led was borne out of disappointment, frustration and unfulfilled expectations.'[45]

[43] de Espil, p. 696, Box 9, Folders 1–3, Library of Congress.
[44] James Fox, *Vanity Fair*, September 2003.
[45] Eldridge, p. 87.

'It was a really empty life but it was what they enjoyed,' noted John Utter. 'She loved anything to do with a party. They were wretched personalities, completely egocentric.'[46]

Their ambitions were partially satisfied by creating beautiful homes and an extensive social life with equally shallow people, but there was a restlessness as they relentlessly entertained, partied, travelled as if escaping from something – each other, the past, responsibility. Certainly both were escaping from unhappy childhoods – his emotionally barren, hers in terms of wealth and status.

Contrary to a great love story, Wallis had been emotionally blackmailed into marriage and had stuck with it because she had no other option. She had been attracted to him as Prince of Wales and King, but that attraction had waned after he had given up his throne, leading to a mixture of guilt, pity, dissatisfaction, boredom and irritation. The affairs, the constant shopping, the travel and entertaining were an attempt to provide some stimulation in a life with little meaning and with a man she did not love.

[46] David Pryce-Jones, 'TV Tale of Two Windsors', *New York Times Magazine*, 18 March 1979.

CHAPTER 25

Traitor King

'It is a rare writer who has not tackled at least one book on the Duke and Duchess of Windsor,' asserts Craig Brown. 'Books have been written proving conclusively that they were a good thing and that they were a bad thing; that she loved him but he didn't love her; that he loved her but she didn't love him; that they loved one another and that they both hated one another.'[1]

Thirty-five years after her death and almost fifty years after his, the books – both fiction and non-fiction – documentaries, musicals, and films continue to appear and to adopt very different points of view towards the couple. Some still argue that this was one of the great love affairs of the twentieth century, others that Wallis felt trapped in a marriage that she had never wanted. No book before has started after the Abdication in 1936 and looked fully at what happened to the Windsors in their exile.

The accepted account is that they were rejected by the Royal Family because the former king had put private desire above public duty, that they could not be seen to support a man who had turned his back on his birthright, and there is some truth in that. The Monarch was Supreme Governor of the Church of England and he simply could not hold that role and marry a twice-divorced woman

---

[1] Craig Brown, *The Times*, 19 September 1990.

– but might the royal rejection also be because it was believed that the couple had behaved in a treacherous manner?

The conventional line is that the Duke, like the rest of his family and many politicians, financiers and aristocrats before September 1939, was determined that the carnage of the First World War must be avoided at all costs and that some form of accommodation with Hitler was possible, to allow him to focus on the real threat to the British Empire – communism.

It argues that in the summer of 1940, the couple became unwitting pawns in a Nazi plan to persuade the Duke to take on the role of a British Pétain. The German and Spanish officials involved then exaggerated what was happening to suit their own agendas and please their superiors. The Windsors were naïve and foolish and at worst, used German approaches to leverage their own interests.

Though the Windsors continued in their exile in the Bahamas to believe that Britain's best interests lay in a negotiated peace, the entry of America into the war in December 1941 put an end to their idealistic notions and they then served the Crown with loyalty. It is best summed up by the Duke's authorised biographer, Philip Ziegler:

> the Duke felt the war could and should have been avoided, that he was defeatist about the prospects of victory in 1940 and 1941, that he preached the virtues of a negotiated peace. He had been indiscreet and extravagant enough in what he said to give the Germans some grounds for believing that he might be ready to play an active part in securing such a peace and returning to the throne after it had been negotiated. That is bad enough. What they do not show, and cannot show since no evidence exists, is that the Duke

would ever have contemplated accepting such an invitation
if it had been issued.[2]

The argument of this book is that there is plenty of evidence, as
demonstrated in the previous pages, that the Windsors were not
foolish and naïve, but actively engaged with the German intrigues.

The Germans had long realised that King Edward VIII was a
potential ally and both he and Wallis were targeted before, during
and after his reign. One of the key figures in the German plan was
the Austrian princess, Stephanie von Hohenlohe, who was sent to
London, where she took an apartment in Bryanston Court next
to Wallis. According to a British Intelligence report, her role was
to select from amongst the British Establishment 'possible future
friends of Hitler and Nazi Germany'. Notes for an unpublished
memoir show the list was headed by the Prince of Wales and
Wallis Simpson.[3] This Stephanie von Hohenlohe did working
through social hostesses such as Emerald Cunard.

Countless sources speak of Wallis's closeness to the German
embassy and, in particular, Joachim von Ribbentrop, including
Philip Ziegler, who was writing with exclusive access to papers in
the Royal Archives. 'The Foreign Office is anxious less the (Foreign
Office) cypher be compromised,' wrote Sir Robert Vansittart to
Stanley Baldwin, 'as Ms S is said to be in the pocket of the German
Ambassador.'[4]

The Danish Ambassador told Ralph Wigram in the Foreign
Office that Mrs Simpson:

---

[2] Ziegler, p. 552.

[3] Box 3, Princess Stephanie zu Hohenlohe papers, Hoover Institute.

[4] Ziegler, *Edward VIII*, p. 274. This was Ribbentrop's predecessor, von Hoesch.

tried to mix herself up in politics. She endeavoured in every way to single out the German Embassy and to have everything German preferred at Court . . . Under the influence of these surroundings the King, at times, made statements which tended to show that his sympathies were coloured by Nazism and Fascism.[5]

Kenneth Rose, staying with the former MI5 officer Victor Rothschild in the 1980s, noted in his diary: 'Some talk of MI5. They had reason to think that Edward VIII when Prince of Wales was in too-close touch with Ribbentrop.'[6]

Another Nazi informer was Wallis's dressmaker Anna Wolkoff, imprisoned in 1940 as part of a spy ring centred around the American diplomat Tyler Kent. MI5 had first become aware of Wolkoff in 1935, 'when one of their agents reported that Wolkoff was using her position with Mrs Wallis Simpson (the future Duchess of Windsor) to provide the Nazis with confidential information derived from the Prince of Wales (the future Duke of Windsor). Lord Vansittart informed the (then) Prime Minister, Stanley Baldwin, but no action appears to have been taken.'[7]

After the Abdication, the Germans kept up the pressure and the Windsors were happy to play along, culminating in the October 1937 tour of Germany and the friendships with a series of Nazi sympathisers. It is perfectly clear that in the summer of 1940 the Duke, who reported none of his communications with the various Spanish emissaries to the British authorities, knew that he was

[5] Count Ahlefeldt Laurvig to Ralph Wigram, 16 October 1937, RA KEVIII, Ab. Box 4, quoted Ziegler, p. 269.

[6] 6 November 1982, Richard Thorpe (ed.), *Who Loses, Who Wins: The Journals of Kenneth Rose*, Vol. 1 1979–2014 (Weidenfeld & Nicolson, 2019), p. 66.

[7] *Searchlight*, October 1989, p. 9.

dealing with the Germans and not the Spanish – how else would his maid have been able to travel to Paris – and that his various attempts at delaying departure to the Bahamas had more to do with the international situation than his domestic affairs.

There is then the killer telegram of 15 August 1940, with him agreeing to stay in touch with the Germans using a special code should the situation change. This is backed up by plenty of evidence, including the diaries of the MI5 officer Guy Liddell and Alan Lascelles' correspondence.

A report from a British intelligence agent in Lisbon during the war related that the Germans had recently approached Charles Bedaux to determine if Windsor would be prepared to be King in the event of a German victory. The report contained a transcript of a supposed conversation between Mrs Bedaux and Wallis, in which the former referred to such a discussion between Bedaux and the Duke in 1937 and that the question then discussed was:

> very prominent in the minds of certain powers today. We have been asked seriously of the possibility, and we, continuing to believe that both of you are still of the same opinion, have given absolute assurance that it is not only possible but can be counted on. Are we right?[8]

Though vague, Sir Alexander Cadogan's response is revealing. 'The paragraph is certainly capable of the blackest interpretations. But it would be difficult to get a conviction on it.'[9]

David Eccles, who had been told to keep an eye on the Duke during July 1940, later admitted that the Germans 'were trying to get

[8] Notes by Thomas and Hardinge, RA KEVIII Ab. Box 3, quoted Ziegler, p. 459.
[9] *Ibid*, p. 459.

him to agree and he would sort of play the hand for a peace conference in which the Germans would see that he got the throne.'[10]

Matters had become so serious that MI5 had even opened a file
on the couple, an unprecedented occurrence for a member of the
Royal Family.[11]

Everyone from Churchill and the Royal Household to the Intelligence Services believed the Duke to be a traitor rather than a fool,
hence the desperate attempts to cover up, delay and minimise the
publication of the captured German communications.

And, of course, not all of the captured documents were made
public. John Wheeler-Bennett realised that the integrity of the
German Documents series depended on releasing the Windsor
material, but revealingly he wrote: 'we duly included *the bulk* of its
contents in the Series D, Vol. X (author's italics).'[12] Michael Bloch
in *Operation Willi* points out that twenty-eight telegrams relating
to the Windsors were not published.[13]

Donald Cameron Watt, later Professor of International History at
University of London, was the first British historian to see the Windsor section when some 400 tons of documents arrived at Whaddes-
don Hall. 'Everything was there which we thought should have been
there, with one exception. There was no record of the meeting at
Berchtesgaden.'[14] The question one has to ask is, why not?

Kenneth Rose wrote in his diary in 1979, after meeting Anthony
Eden's widow and Churchill's niece, 'Clarissa Avon tells me that
she has always hated the Windsors, and thought it "wicked" of

[10] Lord Eccles interview, p. 14, BREN 2/2/5, Churchill College Archives.

[11] It was destroyed in 1946. Interview Phil Tomacelli, 26 May 2020.

[12] John Wheeler-Bennett, *Friends, Enemies and Sovereigns* (Macmillan, 1976), pp.
81–2.

[13] Michael Bloch, *Operation Willi: The Plot to Kidnap the Duke of Windsor, July
1940* (Weidenfeld & Nicolson, 1984), p. 2.

[14] Donald Cameron Watt interview, John Costello, *Mask of Treachery*, p. 457.

Winston to destroy the evidence about the Duke's apparent readiness to become a German stooge in 1940.'[15]

Indeed, Churchill, who had done so much to support the King during the Abdication Crisis, refused in September 1958 to go on a cruise on Aristotle Onassis's yacht, *Christina*, because the Duke and Duchess of Windsor had been invited and 'since 1940 he had never felt the same about the Duke and thought that it would be wrong for him to associate with him too closely.'[16]

The Duke may have claimed in 1966:

> I acknowledge now that, along with too many other well-meaning people, I let my admiration for the good side of German character dim what was being done to it by the bad. I thought that . . . the immediate task . . . of my generation . . . was to prevent another conflict between Germany and the West that could bring down our civilisation . . . I thought that the rest of us could be fence-sitters while the Nazis and the reds slogged it out.[17]

But there is plenty of evidence that his views about the Nazis did not change after the war and that his choice of close friends, such as Robert Young and Oswald Mosley, was unfortunate.

'My parents were horrified by their dinner table talk, where they made it perfectly clear that the world would have been a better place if Jews were exterminated,' recalled Cleveland Amory's stepdaughter, Dr Gaea Leinhardt.'[18] On one occasion the Duke took a lady guest's hands in his and 'closing her fingers together, enclosed her

[15] 8 May 1979, Thorpe (ed.), *Who Loses, Who Wins*, p. 2.

[16] Anthony Montague Browne, *Long Sunset* (Cassell, 1995), p. 242.

[17] *New York Daily News*, 13 December 1966.

[18] Morton, *Wallis in Love*, p. 319.

hands over them. The Duke continued, "You just don't understand. The Jews had Germany in their tentacles. All Hitler tried to do was free the tentacles." With that, he released the lady's hands.'[19]

Patrick Kinross was shocked when the Duke claimed: 'I have never thought . . . Hitler was such a bad chap.'[20] Roy Strong writes in his diaries of playing canasta with the Duke – 'You have to be really dim to play that' – how the Duke 'eulogised Hitler. It confirmed all one had feared.'[21]

There can be little doubt that if the Duke of Windsor had not renounced the throne that he would have tried to use his influence to seek peace with Hitler in 1940. Without the support of the King, after Dunkirk, even Churchill might have been unable to resist the pressure from Lord Halifax and others to negotiate with the Germans. If so, the history of the world would have been very different.

Other 'what if' questions remain. What if the Prince of Wales had never met Mrs Simpson at that weekend house party in January 1931? How much did she encourage his pro-German and antisemitic beliefs? Without her by his side, would he have had the courage or the strength to pursue such a traitorous course?

The Abdication remains one of the most traumatic episodes in royal history and the tension between public obligations and private desires continues to be a significant trope in the story of the Royal Family. The country was lucky that in the crisis which Edward VIII generated, George VI and his daughter Elizabeth rose to the challenge.

Edward's refusal to discharge his duties as King as he would wish to do was ironically the making of the modern British royal family.

---

[19] Amory, *Best Cat Ever*, p. 141.

[20] *Ibid*, p. 141, and Lord Kinross, 'Love Conquers All', Books and Bookmen, Vol. 20, p. 50.

[21] 15 February 1984, Strong, pp. 358–9.

If Edward's renunciation of the throne threatened to destroy the monarchy, his brother and niece saved it.

Acknowledgements

I am grateful to the following for their help in researching the book:

Thank you to Her Majesty Queen Elizabeth ll for permission to quote material held in the Royal Archives.

Neil Adams and Lydia Dean at the Borthwick Institute, the University of York, for making Lord Halifax's papers available; Henric af Trolle and Neils af Trolle for help on Georg af Trolle; Nicole Allen at Churchill College; Peter Allen for research in French archives; Todd Allen for information on Frederick Evans; John Annersley and Clare Flemming at Marist College Archives and Special Collections; Stephanie Arias at the Huntington Library; Simone Baddeley at Lincolnshire Archives for copying a selection of 6th Baron Brownlow's Papers; Norman Baker for sharing some of his research; Carrie Balfour for checking the Sir John Balfour papers in her possession;

Lord Balniel for making available the private diary of the 27th Earl of Crawford; Bruce Barnes and Ken Fox for research on Oscar Solbert; Julian Beare for talking about his father Robin Beare; Jessica Becker at Yale University Library for the Dean Acheson/ John Balfour correspondence; Francis Beckett for sharing his father's autobiography showing how Oswald Mosley thought he might come to power during the Abdication; Robin Benson for information on his father Rex Benson; Simon Berthon for providing the scripts of his programme on the Windsors; Tony Biddle, who talked about his parents' friendship with the Windsors;

Michael Bloch for sharing his knowledge about the Windsors; Charlotte Breese for various leads, not least on one of the Duke's illegitimate children; Frank Bowles at Cambridge University Library for the Adolf Berle diaries; Elizabeth Burnes at NARA for Charles Wurtenberg's files; Jimmy Burns for various introductions; Teal Cannaday for help contacting Cornelia Guest; Anne Carmel for information on the Harry Oakes case; Amy Cary and Susan Stawicki-Vrobel at Marquette University for the Fulton Oursler papers; David Clark at the Harry S. Truman Library & Museum; Neil Cobbett, the Modern Overseas Records Specialist at the National Archives;

Rose Collis for sharing her research on Nancy Spain; David Columbia at New York Social Diary; Hannah Costelle at the Filson Historical Society; Tara Craig for some introductions; Lord Crathorne for access to his parents' diaries and letters; Candida Crewe and Bel Crewe for information on their grandfather Hugh Dodds; Julie Crocker at the Royal Archives; Vincent Curcio for information on Walter Chrysler Jr; Melissa Davis at the George C. Marshall Foundation for papers by Sir John Balfour; Rose Deakin for help with her mother Mary Donaldson's papers; Anne de Courcy for various introductions and sharing her research notes; Leshelle Delaney, the Director of Bahamas Archives;

Thomas W. Dixon, Jr at the Chesapeake & Ohio Historical Society; Stephen Dorril for various tips; Nicole Duncan and Jeremy Boraine for supplying a copy of *A Lion in the Bedroom;* Catherine Eccles for helping to trace papers relating to her grandfather David Eccles; Heidi Egginton at the National Library of Scotland for help with the Crawford papers; Hannah Elder at the Massachusetts Historical Society; Mona Eldridge, one of the few living people to have known the Windsors for talking to me; Allan Erskine-Lindop for information on Reginald Erskine-Lindop;

Patrick Fahy at the FDR Presidential Library & Museum for tracking down obscure correspondence with the Windsors; Cindy Farkas Glanzrock for arranging the interview with her mother Francine Sears; Adam Fergusson for allowing me to see his grandmother Blanche Dugdale's diary; Caryl Flinn for discussing Russell Nype; Catherine Flynn, the Penguin Random House archivist, for help in tracing publishing archives; John Fox the FBI historian for advice tracking FBI files; Lionel Friedberg, the ghost of *Full Service*, for talking to me; Glyn Gowans for his friendship and wise counsel;

Lavinia Graecen for the introduction to Patrick Skene Catling; Harlan Greene at the Addlestone Library for information on Laddie Sanford; Philip Greenacre for sharing his grandfather Douglas's papers; Cornelia Guest for talking to me about the Windsors; Matthew Guillen at the Virginia Museum of History and Culture for copying for free extensive references to the Windsors; Bethany Hamblen and Naomi Tiley at Balliol College, Oxford, for help with the Monckton papers; Anna Hampton for copying at Georgetown University Library; James Hanning for various introductions;

Carey Harrison with stories of the Windsors' encounters with his parents Lilli Palmer and Rex Harrison; Nicky Haslam for various introductions and insights; Mallory Herberger and Sandra Glascock at the Maryland Center for History and Culture; Louise Hilton for help with Guido Orlando's papers; Suzanne Hodgart for various introductions; Mark Hollingsworth for sharing the Axel Wenner-Gren diary, which he had paid to have translated; Tammy T. Horton at the Air Force Historical Research Agency for Mike Scanlon's diary; Oliver House at the Bodleian Libraries;

Carolyn Howes at the Information Commissioner's Office for help on FOI requests; Debbie Hughes for information on her grandmother Hildegarde Hamilton; Sarah Farnsworth Hunnewell & Theo Armour for information on Polly Howe; David Irving for some leads on the Windsors' activities in 1940; Patricia Jenkins for some tips on photographs; Rebecca Jewett for advice on the Clifton Webb papers; Peter Jordaan for helpful suggestions and contacts; Chris Jussel for information on Arthur Vernay; Rachel Kiddey for various introductions;

Jennifer Kawar for information on her grandfather Reggie Erskine-Lindop; Martin Kinna for talking about his uncle 'Peter' Kinna; Robert Lacey for various introductions; Celia Lee for contacts; Jenny Liddiard at Bloomsbury for access to the Churchill online archive; Neill and Emma Lochery for information on the Windsors in Lisbon; John Loftus for talking to me about the Windsor FBI files; David Lough for guidance on the Windsors' financial affairs; Anthony Luke for a copy of the Hola programme on the Windsors; Andrea E. Lynn for copies of the Grace Coolidge diaries;

Kelly McAnnaney at the National Archives at New York City; Desmond McCabe at PRONI for the Montgomery Hyde papers; David McClure; Sharon Messenger at the British Academy for Peter Russell research; Zara Metcalfe for trying to secure access to her grandparents' papers; María Isabel Molestinaat at the Pierpoint Morgan Library for information on Hank Walter; Marianna, Dowager Viscountess Monckton and Viscount Monckton for help with Walter Monckton's papers; Sara Morrison for talking to me about the Windsors; Andrew Morton for sharing some of his research;

Michael Murray on the Windsor friendship with Arthur Davis; Eve Neigerat at Boston Public Library for information on Cleveland

Acknowledgements

Amory; Alicia Nieva-Woodgate for talking to me about Alice Gordon; Cinda Nofziger at the Bentley Historical Library; Russell Nype for talking about his father; Christopher and Julie Oakes for talking about the Oakes family; Maria Ognjanovich at Monuments Men Foundation For the Preservation of Art for research on the Anthony Blunt mission to Germany; David Olson at Columbia University Library for the Hubert Pell memoir;

James Owen, the author of the standard book on the Oakes murder, for making his research notes available; Allen Packwood, Andrew Riley and Tom Davies at the Churchill College Archives, who are always unfailingly helpful; Jane Parr at Boston University Libraries for Stephen Birmingham's papers; Sarah Patton at the Hoover Institute; Jonathan Petropoulos for useful discussions; John Pickering for help tracing the Wachman family; Michael Pye, the author of an excellent book on the Windsors in the Bahamas; Heather Riser at the University of Virginia for the Stettinius correspondence;

Mike Rothmiller for research in LAPD files; Patrick Salmon, Chief Historian at the Foreign, Commonwealth and Development Office, for help locating various papers; Edith A. Sandler at the Library of Congress for Robert Bingham's papers; Charlie Scheips for help with Lady Mendl; Dorothy Schmidt-Spilos for talking about her grandfather Walter Foskett; Francine Sears for talking about her friendship with the Windsors; Anne Sebba for various leads; Lucy Smith-Ryland for an introduction; David Storrier for talking about his uncle David Storrier; Lara Szypszak at the Library of Congress for copying the papers of Courtney Letts de Espil and Clare Booth Luce;

John Tackett for guidance on Palm Beach Society; Jane Tatam, ghost writer of Anne Seagrim; Tim Tate; Bruce Taylor, Peter Russell's biographer, for details of Russell's activities in the summer of

1940; Taki Theodoracopulos for talking about the Windsors and their circle; Peter Thompson for lending a recorded phone call with Alfred de Marigny; Marcus Tian for copying in Columbia University Library; Charles Tilbury for lending the unpublished diaries and letters of Valentine Lawford; Phil Tomacelli for revealing that the Duke of Windsor's MI5 file was destroyed in 1946; Sibilla Tomacelli for talking about her friendship with the Windsors;

Stephen Trott for information on Pitsford Hall; Matt Tyrnauer; Vianca Victor at Columbia University Library; John Waddilove for talking about his father; Jehane Wake for help with Rex Benson; Lord and Lady Wakehurst for tracing the Dugdale diaries; Pat Wertheim for insights into the Oakes case; Nigel West for as always perceptive insights; Professor Douglas Wheeler for help on Portugal during the Second World War; Joan Wheeler-Bennett for talking about Sir John Wheeler-Bennett; Lord Wigram; Paul Willetts for help with Princess Dimitri; Craig Wright at the Herbert Hoover Presidential Library; and Irene Wright for introductions on David Storrier.

As ever, I am grateful to my agent Bill Hamilton for brilliant agenting and the very professional and friendly team at Bonnier – publisher Matt Phillips; editors Justine Taylor and Sophie Nevrkla, publicists Jena Petts, Lizzie Dorney-Kingdom, Karen Stretch, Nikki Mander and Izzy Smith; marketing manager Jess Tackie; production controller Ella Holden, picture researcher Fiona Greenway and audio editors Laura Makela and Alexandra Schmidt. For the third time, by special request, Barry Johnston has expertly and conscientiously copyedited the text. My wife Angela was the first person to read the book, and the book is dedicated with love to her and our two children, Robert and Alice.

Attempts have been made to clear all permissions but do contact me with any corrections or new information at Lownie@globalnet. co.uk

Fiction and Drama

SELECTED FICTION ABOUT THE WINDSORS

Gertrude Stein, *Ida*, Random House, 1941:
A novel, about a woman famous for being famous, based on the modernist Stein's former Baltimore neighbour, Wallis Simpson.

Henry Patterson, *To Catch a King*, Stein & Day, 1979:
Retelling of Operation Willi in which the Duke of Windsor pretends to cooperate with the Nazis, but instead sends their invasion plans to Churchill.

Clive Irving, *Axis*, Atheneum, 1980:
The exploits of Walter Schellenberg, including the attempted kidnapping of the Duke of Windsor in 1940.

Timothy Findley, *Famous Last Words*, Macmillan, 1981:
Reminiscences of American fascist Hugh Selwyn Mauberley, where the Windsors conspire with Ribbentrop to overthrow Hitler.

Pauline Glen, *The Windsor Plot*, Arlington Books, 1981:
Another take on Operation Willi involving foiled assassinations of King George VI and Churchill.

Michael Kilian, *Dance on a Sinking Ship*, **St Martin's, 1988:**
A 1935 cruise with various English aristocrats, including the Mountbattens, Charles Lindberg, and the Windsors, involving Soviet and Nazi agents.

Graham Fisher, *The Plot to Kill Wallis Simpson*, **St Martin's Press, 1989:**
A faction on a plot to murder Wallis Simpson.

Anne Edward, *Wallis*, **Rowman, 1991:**
Biographical novel up to the Abdication.

Peter MacAlan, *The Windsor Protocol*, **Severn House, 1993:**
Another variation on Hitler placing Windsor on the British throne.

Elizabeth Luard, *Emerald*, **Bantam, 1994:**
The story of the secret love-child of the Duke and Duchess of Windsor, Emerald Alexandra Mary Fitzwallace, born in May 1937, set in France, Mexico and New York.

Max Collins, *Carnal Hours*, **Dutton, 1994:**
Chicago detective Nathan Heller investigates the death of Sir Harry Oakes.

Eliot Roosevelt, *A Royal Murder*, **St Martin's Press, 1994:**
Crime novel featuring sleuth First Lady Eleanor Roosevelt investigating the murder of a wealthy Swedish businessman in 1940 Bahamas, involving the Windsors and Nazi plots to gain a foothold in the Americas.

Al & Joanna Lacy, *A Prince Among Them*, **Waterbrook, 2001:**
Kidnap attempt on the young Prince of Wales.

Robert Oldham, *Saving the King*, **Raven, 2001:**
Alternative history of Second World War Britain, in which Britain has been invaded by the Germans and the Duke and Duchess of Windsor are poised to take the throne.

Fiction and Drama

William Boyd, *Any Human Heart*, Hamish Hamilton, 2002:
In his journals Logan Mountstuart journeys through the twentieth century, where he becomes intimately involved with the Windsors in the Bahamas.

Guy Walters, *The Leader*, Headline, 2003:
An alternative history with Edward VIII on the throne with Wallis, Oswald Mosley as Prime Minister, and Winston Churchill imprisoned on the Isle of Man.

Rose Tremain, *The Darkness of Wallis Simpson*, Chatto, 2005:
Title story in a collection of short stories in which Wallis on her death bed looks back on her early life.

Javier Marias, *Your Face Tomorrow III: Poison, Shadow and Farewell*, New Directions, 2005:
Sir Peter Wheeler, based on Sir Peter Russell, is tasked to shepherd the Windsors to the Bahamas.

James Irwin, *Mokanshan: A Tale of Wallis Simpson's Naughty Shanghai Postcards*, iUniverse, 2005:
In 1936 the lost nude negatives of Wallis from her time in China become the target of the British Government, Nazi agents, Chiang Kai-shek, the media and crime syndicates.

Laurie Graham, *Gone with the Windsors*, Collins, 2005:
The fictional diary of Maybell Brumby, a wealthy American widow and social-climbing friend of Wallis Simpson, covering Wallis's life between 1932 and 1940.

Helen Batting, *Wallis Simpson's Diary*, Pen Press, 2006:
A satirical fictionalisation of Wallis's 1934 diary.

Mitch Silver, *In Secret Service*, Simon & Schuster, 2007:
An unpublished Ian Fleming memoir outlining, amongst much else, the Windsors' links to the Nazis.

Tom Gabbay, *The Lisbon Crossing*, William Morrow, 2007:
A spy thriller, partly based in wartime Lisbon, featuring the Duke and Duchess of Windsor.

Clive Fletcher, *The Duke of Windsor's Last Secrets*, Lulu, 2008:
The last secrets include the China Dossier, the Windsors' links with the Nazis, a jewellery scam, and the Windsors' links to Rudolf Hess.

Carlos Mundy, *The Toucan Lodge*, New Generation Publishing, 2009:
Novel based on the author's father's exploits as an MI6 agent, during which he met the Windsors.

Rebecca Dean, *The Golden Prince*, Broadway Books, 2010:
Romantic novel, set in 1912, with the seventeen-year-old Prince of Wales falling in love at a country house weekend.

Kate Auspitz, *The War Memoir of (HRH) the Duchess of Windsor*, Quartet, 2011:
A supposed memoir by the Duchess of Windsor, found after her death, suggesting the marriage was engineered to save Britain from a Nazi king.

Rebecca Dean, *The Shadow Queen*, Broadway, 2012:
An imaginative recreation of Wallis's early life until she meets the Prince of Wales.

Juliet Nicolson, *Abdication*, Bloomsbury, 2012:
The events of 1936 seen through the eyes of May Thomas, who has come from Barbados looking for her first job, and Evangeline Nettlefold, an old school friend of Wallis Simpson.

D.J. Taylor, *The Windsor Faction*, Chatto, 2013:
Edward succeeds to the throne after the sudden death of his mistress Wallis – was she murdered? – in a counter-factual story on what his reign might have been like.

Fiction and Drama

Liz Trenow, *The Forgotten Seamstress*, Avon, 2014:
A quilt produced in 1910 by a seamstress at Buckingham Palace, who falls in love with a young Prince of Wales, reveals its secrets to the seamstress's daughter.

Jose Goulao, *A King Up Hitler's Sleeve*, Author House, 2014:
The Nazi intrigues with the Duke of Windsor, 1937–1940.

Hugh Robertson, *The Fools' Crowns: King or Pawn*, Alresford Publishing, 2014:
The Abdication Crisis and was the world's most famous playboy prince a traitor?

Hugh Robertson, *The Fools' Crowns: Traitors' Games*, Alresford Publishing, 2014:
A mix of fact and fiction leading up to the wedding of the Duke of Windsor to Wallis Simpson and the events that followed.

Kate Auspitz, *Wallis's War: A Novel of Diplomacy and Intrigue*, University of Chicago Press, 2015:
Satirical fictional memoir, in which Wallis intrigues against Edward.

Harry Leavey, *The Duchess and the Soldier's Revenge: The Secret to the Royal Windsor Jewel Heist*, Create Space, 2016:
Fictionalised account of the 1946 Ednam robbery, interweaving the lives of the Windsors and the burglar Leslie Holmes, written by Holmes's granddaughter.

Beatriz Williams, *The Golden Hour*, Morrow, 2019:
Leonora 'Lulu' Randolph arrives in the Bahamas in 1941 to write about the Duke and Duchess of Windsor and discovers some uncomfortable truths.

Hugh Robertson, *The Fools' Crowns: The Court of Knaves*, Alresford Publishing, 2020:
The German tour in 1937.

C.J. Carey, *Widowland*, Quercus, 2021:
Dystopian novel set in 1953, thirteen years after the Grand Alliance between Great Britain and Germany was formalised and George VI and his family have been murdered, centring around the coronation of Edward VIII as King.

Wendy Holden, *The Duchess*, Welbeck, 2021:
Fictionalises the unknown London life of Wallis Simpson.

SELECTED DRAMAS ABOUT THE WINDSORS

George Bernard Shaw, *The King, the Constitution and the Lady*, 1936:
Short play about the Abdication.

Helen Tracy Lowe-Porter, *Abdication*, 1948:
Best known as the translator of Thomas Mann, *Abdication* had its premiere in Dublin in 1948.

Royce Royton, *Crown Matrimonial*, 1972:
Play about the Abdication.

Dan Sutherland, *The Woman I Love*, 1978:
Another Abdication play, it was filmed that year with Richard Chamberlain and Faye Dunaway in the central roles.

Simon Raven, *Edward and Mrs Simpson*, 1978:
Seven-part TV series based on Frances Donaldson's biography, with Edward Fox as Edward, Cynthia Harris as Wallis, and Peggy Ashcroft as Queen Mary.

Jack Higgins, *To Catch a King*, 1984:
Based on the 1979 Jack Higgins thriller about the wartime plot to kidnap the Duke of Windsor, the film starred Robert Wagner.

Fiction and Drama

William Luce, *The Woman He Loved*, **1988:**
Reverential film starring Anthony Andrews, Jane Seymour, and Olivia de Haviland as Aunt Bessie.

James Leasor, *Passion and Paradise*, **1989:**
Film of the murder of Harry Oakes – played by Rod Steiger – based on Leasor's book.

Elizabeth Proud, *The Life and Legends of Wallis Simpson*, **1996:**
A three-part BBC radio drama about Wallis Simpson.

William May, *Always*, **1997:**
Musical based on the Windsor love story.

Linda Grifiths, *The Duchess, aka Wallis Simpson*, **1998:**
A magical realist play on Wallis Simpson told with a little help from her friend Noël Coward and a host of 'society ghosties'.

Gary Kirkham, *Queen Milli of Galt*, **2005:**
A romantic comedy, based on a real episode, about a 1919 romance between the Prince of Wales and a Canadian woman, Millicent Milroy, who later claimed to have had a morganatic marriage with him.

Sarah Williams, *Wallis & Edward*, **2005:**
TV movie starring Joely Richardson.

Robin Glendinning, *The Windsor Jewels*, **2007:**
BBC Radio black comedy based on the 1946 Ednam jewellery robbery.

David Seidler, *The Kings Speech*, **2010:**
Film focusing on the relationship between George VI and speech therapist Lionel Logue, it has a cameo role for Edward VIII.

William Boyd, *Any Human Heart*, **2010:**
Four-part TV series based on William Boyd's novel of the same name.

Nicholas Wright, *The Last Duchess*, 2011:
Stage play based on Caroline Blackwood's book about the relationship between Maître Blum and Wallis.

Madonna, *WE*, 2011:
Film focused on Wallis Simpson, written, produced and directed by Madonna.

Bob Kingdom, *An Audience with the Duke of Windsor*, 2012:
One man show at Edinburgh Festival, starring Bob Kingdom.

Rose Tremain, *The Darkness of Wallis Simpson*, 2015:
Radio adaptation of Rose Tremain's story with Elizabeth McGovern in the title role.

Selected Bibliography

BOOKS

Airlie, Countess of, *Thatched with Gold* (Hutchinson, 1962).

Alford, Kenneth, *The Spoils of World War II: The American Military's Role in Stealing Europe's Treasures* (Birch Lane, 1994).

Allen, Martin, *Hidden Agenda: How the Duke of Windsor Betrayed the Allies* (Macmillan, 2000).

Allen, Martin, *The Hitler–Hess Deception* (Collins, 2003).

Allen, Peter, *The Crown and the Swastika* (Robert Hale, 1983).

Alsop, Susan, *To Marietta from Paris 1945–1960* (Weidenfeld & Nicolson, 1976).

Amory, Cleveland, *The Last Resorts* (Harper, 1948).

Amory, Cleveland, *Who Killed Society?* (Harper, 1960).

Amory, Cleveland, *The Best Cat Ever* (Little, Brown, 1993).

Baker, Norman, *And What Do You Do?* (Biteback, 2019).

Baldwin, Billy with Michael Gardine, *Billy Baldwin, An Autobiography* (Little, Brown, 1985).

Balfour, John, *Not Too Correct an Aureole* (Michael Russell, 1983).

Balfour, Neil and Sally Mackay, *Paul of Yugoslavia: Britain's Maligned Friend* (Hamish Hamilton, 1980).

Barber, Noel, *The Natives Were Friendly* (Macmillan, 1977).

Barnes, John and David Nicholson, *The Leo Amery Diaries, Vol, 2, 1929–1945* (Hutchinson, 1988).

Barrie, J.J., *The King's Son: The True Story of the Duke of Windsor's Only Son!* (Custom Book Publications, 2019).

Beaton, Cecil, *The Wandering Years* (Weidenfeld & Nicolson, 1961).

Beaton, Cecil, *Self Portrait with Friends: The Selected Diaries of Cecil Beaton 1926–1974* (Weidenfeld & Nicolson, 1970).

Beaton, Cecil, *The Parting Years* (Weidenfeld & Nicolson, 1978).

Beaverbrook, Max, *The Abdication of King Edward VIII* (Hamish Hamilton, 1966).

Beevor, Anthony and Artemis Cooper, *Paris After the Liberation* (Hamish Hamilton, 1994).

Bernays, Robert and Nick Smart (eds.), *The Diaries and Letters of Robert Bernays,1932–1939* (Edwin Mellen Press, 1996).

Birkenhead, Lord, *Walter Monckton*, (Weidenfeld & Nicolson, 1969).

Birmingham, Stephen, *Duchess* (Little, Brown, 1981).

Birmingham, Stephen, *The Right People: A Portrait of the American Social Establishment* (Little, Brown, 1958).

Blackwood, Caroline, *The Last of the Duchess* (Macmillan, 1995).

Bloch, Michael, *The Duke of Windsor's War* (Weidenfeld & Nicolson, 1982).

Bloch, Michael, *Operation Willi: The Plot to Kidnap the Duke of Windsor, July 1940* (Weidenfeld & Nicolson, 1984).

Bloch, Michael (ed.), *Wallis and Edward: Letters 1931–1937* (Weidenfeld & Nicolson, 1986).

Bloch, Michael, *The Secret File of the Duke of Windsor* (Bantam, 1988).

Bloch, Michael, *The Reign & Abdication of Edward VIII* (Bantam, 1990).

Bloch, Michael, *Ribbentrop* (Bantam, 1992).

Selected Bibliography

Bloch, Michael, *The Duchess of Windsor* (Weidenfeld & Nicolson, 1996).

Bloomenkranz, Sol, *Charles Bedaux: Deciphering an Enigma* (iUniverse, 2012).

Bocca, Geoffrey, *She Might Have Been Queen* (Express Books, 1955).

Bocca, Geoffrey, *The Life and Death of Harry Oakes* (Weidenfeld, 1959).

Boelcke, Willi A. (ed.), *The Secret Conferences of Dr Goebbels, October 1939–March 1943* (Weidenfeld & Nicolson, 1970).

Borkin, Joseph, *Robert R. Young* (Harper & Row, 1969).

Bowers, Scotty, *Full Service* (Grove Press, 2013).

Bradford, Sarah, *King George VI* (Weidenfeld & Nicolson, 1989).

Bragg, Melvyn, *Richard Burton: A Life* (Little, Brown, 1988).

Brendon, Piers and Philip Whitehead, *The Windsors: A Dynasty Revealed* (Hodder & Stoughton, 1994).

Brendon, Piers, *Edward VIII: The Uncrowned King* (Allen Lane, 2016).

Brody, Iles, *Gone with the Windsors* (John Winston Company, 1953).

Brown, Anthony Cave, *The Secret Servant: The Life of Sir Stewart Menzies* (Michael Joseph, 1988).

Browne, Anthony Montague, *Long Sunset* (Cassell, 1995).

Bryan III, J. and C.J.V. Murphy, *The Windsor Story* (Granada, 1979) .

Bullitt, Orville H. (ed.), *For the President Personal & Secret: Correspondence between Franklin D. Roosevelt and William C. Bullitt* (Deutsch, 1973).

Cadbury, Deborah, *Princes at War: The British Royal Family's Private Battle in the Second World War* (Bloomsbury, 2015).

Camp, Anthony, *Royal Mistresses and Bastards: Fact and Fiction 1714–1936* (Society of Genealogists, 2009).

Carter, Miranda, *Anthony Blunt: His Lives* (Macmillan, 2017).

Catling, Patrick Skene, *Better Than Working* (Liberties Press, 2004).

Chase, Edna Woolman and Ilka Chase, *Always in Vogue* (Gollancz, 1954).

Christy, Jim, *The Price of Power: A Biography of Charles Eugene Bedaux* (Doubleday, 1984).

Coats, Peter, *Of Generals and Gardens* (Weidenfeld & Nicolson, 1976).

Cockett, Richard (ed.), *My Dear Max: The Letters of Brendan Bracken to Lord Beaverbrook 1925–1958* (Historians Press, 1990).

Colville, John, *The Fringes of Power: Downing Street Diaries 1939–1955* (Hodder & Stoughton, 1985).

Cooke, Alistair, *Six Men* (Bodley Head, 1977).

Costello, John, *Mask of Treachery* (Collins, 1988).

Costello, John, *Ten Days That Saved the West* (Bantam, 1991).

Cowan, Bob, *Sir Harry Oakes, 1874–1943: An Accumulation of Notes* (Highway Bookshop, 2000).

Craton, Michael, *A History of the Bahamas* (Collins, 1962).

Crosby, Ken and Nigel West, *Crosby's Luck: An FBI Special Agent in Latin America* (Independently published, 2020).

Crowson, N.J. (ed.), *Fleet Street, Press Barons and Politics: The Journals of Collin Brooks* (CUP, 1998).

Culme, John and Nicholas Rayner, *The Jewels of the Duchess of Windsor* (Thames & Hudson, 1987).

Curtis, Charlotte, *The Rich and Other Atrocities* (Harper & Row, 1976).

Dahlerus, Birger, *The Last Attempt* (Hutchinson, 1948).

Deacon, Richard, *The British Connection* (Hamish Hamilton, 1979).

Selected Bibliography

de Bousingen, Denis Durand, *The Duke of Windsor* (Robert Hale, 1972).

de Courcy, Anne, *The Viceroy's Daughters* (Weidenfeld & Nicolson, 2000).

de Marigny, Alfred, *More Devil than Saint* (Beechhurst Press, 1946).

de Marigny, Alfred with Mickey Herskowitz, *A Conspiracy of Crowns: The True Story of the Duke of Windsor and the Murder of Sir Harry Oakes* (Bantam, 1990).

de Vries, Susanna, *Royal Mistresses of the House of Hanover-Windsor: Secrets, Scandals and Betrayals* (Pirgos Press, 2012).

Dennis, Geoffrey, *Coronation Commentary* (Heinemann, 1937).

Diliberto, Gioia, *Debutante: The Story of Brenda Frazier* (Knopf, 1987).

Dilks, David (ed.), *The Diaries of Sir Alexander Cadogan* (Cassell, 1971).

Dimbleby, Jonathan, *The Prince of Wales* (Little, Brown, 1994).

Ditzen, Eleanor Davies Tydings, *My Golden Spoon* (Madison Books, 1997).

Documents on German Foreign Policy 1918–1945, series D (1937–1945), Vol. X: The War Years 23 June–31 August 1940, HMSO, 1957.

Doerries, R.R. (ed.), *Hitler's Last Chief of Foreign Intelligence: Allied Interrogations of Walter Schellenberg* (Routledge, 2003).

Döhring, Herbert, *Living with Hitler: Accounts of Hitler's Household Staff* (Greenhill Books, 2018).

Donaldson, Frances, *King Edward VIII* (Weidenfeld & Nicolson, 1974).

Dorril, Stephen, *Blackshirt* (Penguin, 2006).

Duff, David, *Queen Mary* (Collins, 1985).

Dupuch, Eugene, *Tribune Story* (Benn, 1967).

Dupuch, Eugene, *The Murder of Sir Harry Oakes* (Nassau Daily Tribune, 1959).

Earle, Peggy, *Legacy: Walter Chrysler Jr and the Untold Story of Norfolk's Chrysler Museum of Art* (University of Virginia Press, 2008).

Eccles, Sybil and David, *By Safe Hand: Letters of Sybil and David Eccles 1939–42* (Bodley Head, 1983).

Eckert, Astrid, *The Struggle for the Files: The Western Allies and the Return of German Archives after the Second World War* (Cambridge University Press, 2012).

Eldridge, Mona, *In Search of a Prince* (Sidgwick, 1988).

Evans, Simon, *Prince Charming Goes West: The Story of the E.P. Ranch* (University of Calgary Press, 1993).

Flinn, Caryl, *Brass Diva: The Life and Legends of Ethel Merman* (University of California Press, 2007).

Forbes, Rosita, *Appointment with Destiny* (Cassell, 1946).

Fremantle, Anne, *Three-Cornered Heart* (Collins, 1971).

Gade, John A., *All My Born Days* (Charles Scribner, 1942).

Garrett, Richard, *Mrs Simpson* (Arthur Barker, 1979).

Getty, J. Paul, *As I See It* (WH Allen, 1976).

Giles, Frank, *Sundry Times* (John Murray, 1986).

Glass, Charles, *Americans in Paris: Life and Death Under Nazi Occupation 1940–1944* (Harper Collins, 2009).

Godfrey, Rupert, *Letters from a Prince* (Little, Brown, 1998).

Goering, Emmy, *My Life With Goering* (David, Bruce & Watson, 1972).

Graham-Murray, James, *The Sword and the Umbrella* (Times Press, 1964).

Gray, Charlotte, *Murdered Midas: A Millionaire, His Gold Mine, and a Strange Death on an Island Paradise* (Collins, 2019).

Selected Bibliography

Hagen, Lewis (ed.), *The Schellenberg Memoirs* (Deutsch, 1956).

Hardwick, C.M., *Time Study in Treason: Charles E. Bedaux, Patriot or Collaborator* (Peter Horsnell, 1990).

Harris, Kenneth, *Talking To: Best of the Kenneth Harris Interviews* (Weidenfeld & Nicolson, 1968).

Harris, Kenneth, *The Queen* (Weidenfeld & Nicolson, 1994).

Hart-Davis, Duff (ed.), *In Royal Service: The Letters and Journals of Sir Alan Lascelles 1920–1936* (Hamish Hamilton, 1989).

Hart-Davis, Duff (ed.), *King's Counsellor: Abdication and War* (Weidenfeld & Nicolson, 2006).

Harvey, John (ed.), *(Oliver Harvey, Diplomatic Diaries 1937–1940* (Collins, 1970).

Haslam, Nicholas, *Redeeming Features: A Memoir* (Jonathan Cape, 2009).

Heffer, Simon (ed.), *Henry 'Chips' Channon: The Diaries 1918–38* (Hutchinson, 2021).

Hesse, Fritz, *Hitler and the English* (Wingate, 1954).

Heymann, C. David, *Poor Little Rich Girl: The Life and Legend of Barbara Hutton* (Random House, 1983).

Hibbert, Christopher, *Edward: The Uncrowned King* (Macdonald, 1972).

Hichens, Mark, *Abdication, The Rise and Fall of Edward VIII* (Book Guild, 2016).

Higham, Charles, *Trading with the Enemy* (Delacorte, 1983).

Higham, Charles, *Wallis: Secret Lives of the Duchess of Windsor* (Sidgwick & Jackson, 1988).

Higham, Charles, *Mrs Simpson: Secret Lives of the Duchess of Windsor* (Sidgwick & Jackson, 2004).

Higham, Charles, *In and Out of Hollywood* (University of Wisconsin Press, 2009).

Hood, Dina Wells, *Working for the Windsors* (Wingate, 1957).

Houts, Marshall, *Who Murdered Sir Harry Oakes?* (Robert Hale, 1976).

Hyde, H. Montgomery, *The Quiet Canadian* (Hamish Hamilton, 1962).

Hyde, H. Montgomery, *Baldwin* (Hart-Davis, 1973).

Hyde, H. Montgomery, *Crime Has Its Heroes* (Constable, 1976).

Hyde, H. Montgomery, *Secret Intelligence Agent* (Constable, 1982).

Irving, David, *Churchill's War,* Vol. 1 (Veritas, 1987).

James, Robert Rhodes (ed.), *Memoirs of a Conservative* (Weidenfeld & Nicolson, 1969).

James, Robert Rhodes, *Victor Cazalet: A Portrait* (Hamish Hamilton, 1976).

Jardine, R. Anderson, *At Long Last* (Murray & Gee, 1943).

Jebb, Miles (ed.), *The Diaries of Cynthia Gladwyn* (Constable, 1995).

Jelke, Ferdinand Frazier, *An American at Large* (Duell, Sloan and Pearce, 1947).

Jones, Thomas, *A Diary with Letters 1931–1950* (Oxford, 1954).

King, Greg, *The Duchess of Windsor* (Aurum, 1999).

Kinross, Patrick, *The Windsor Years* (Collins, 1967).

Larman, Alexander, *The Crown in Crisis* (Weidenfeld & Nicolson, 2020).

Leifland, Leif, *The Blacklisting of Axel Wenner-Gren* (Askelin & Hägglund, 1989).

Lindbergh, Anne Morrow, *The Flower and the Nettle* (Harcourt Brace Jovanovich, 1976).

Lindroth, Orjan, *The True Story of Axel Wenner-Gren* (The Swedish Press, 2006).

Lochery, Neill, *Lisbon: War in the Shadows of the City of Light 1939–45* (Public Affairs, 2011).

Selected Bibliography

Lockridge, Norman, *Lese Majesty: The Private Lives of the Duke and Duchess of Windsor* (Boar's Head Books, 1952).

Lynn, Andrea, *Shadow Lovers* (Perseus Press, 2001).

MacColl, Rene, *Deadline and Dateline* (Oldbourne Press, 1956).

Macintosh, Alistair, *No Alibi: The Memoirs of Captain Alastair Mackintosh* (Muller, 1961).

McKinstry, Leo, *Operation Sealion* (John Murray, 2015).

McLeod, Kirsty, *Battle Royal: Edward VIII & George VI* (Constable, 1999).

Malinowski, Stephan and Jonathan Andrews, *Nazis and Nobles: The History of a Misalliance* (Oxford University Press, 2020).

Marlborough, Laura, Duchess of, *Laughter from a Cloud*, (Weidenfeld & Nicolson, 1980).

Marquis, John, *Blood and Fire: The Duke of Windsor and the Strange Murder of Sir Harry Oakes* (LMH Publishing, 2006).

Martin, Ralph, *The Woman He Loved* (WH Allen, 1974).

Maxwell, Elsa, *RSVP: Elsa Maxwell's Own Story* (Little, Brown and Company, 1954).

Menkes, Suzy, *The Windsor Style* (Grafton, 1987).

Middlemas, Keith and John Barnes, *Baldwin: A Biography* (Weidenfeld & Nicolson, 1969).

Minney, R.J. (ed.), *The Private Papers of Hore-Belisha* (Collins, 1960).

Moorehead, Lucy (ed.), *Freya Stark, Letters Vol. III* (Compton Russell, 1989).

Moran, Lord, *Churchill: The Struggle for Survival* (Constable, 1966).

Morton, Andrew, *17 Carnations: The Windsors, the Nazis and the Cover-Up* (O'Mara, 2015).

Morton, Andrew, *Wallis in Love: The Untold True Passion of the Duchess of Windsor* (O'Mara, 2018).

Mosley, Charlotte (ed.), *The Letters of Nancy Mitford and Evelyn Waugh* (Hodder & Stoughton, 1996).

Mosley, Diana, *Duchess of Windsor: A Memoir* (Sidgwick & Jackson, 1980).

Mosely, Diana, *A Life of Contrasts* (Hamish Hamilton, 1977).

Nicolson, Nigel (ed.), *Harold Nicolson: Letters and Diaries 1930–1939* (William Collins, 1966).

Nicolson, Nigel (ed.), *Harold Nicolson: Letters and Diaries 1939–1945* (William Collins, 1967).

Nicolson, Nigel (ed.), *Harold Nicolson: Letters and Diaries 1945–1962* (William Collins, 1968).

Norwich, John Julius (ed.), *The Duff Cooper Diaries: 1915–1951* (Weidenfeld & Nicolson, 2005).

Norwich, John Julius (ed.), *Darling Monster: The Letters of Lady Diana Cooper to Her Son John Julius Norwich 1939–1952* (Chatto & Windus, 2013).

O'Neil, Patricia Cavendish, *A Lion in the Bedroom* (Park St Press, Sydney, 2005).

Owen, James, *A Serpent in Eden: The Greatest Murder Mystery of All Time* (Little, Brown, 2005).

Palmer, Dean, *Tea with Hitler* (The History Press, 2021).

Palmer, Lilli, *Change Lobsters and Dance: An Autobiography* (Macmillan, 1975).

Parker, John, *King of Fools* (St Martins, 1988).

Pasternak, Anna, *The American Duchess: The Real Wallis Simpson* (William Collins, 2019).

Payn, Graham and Sheridan Morley (ed.), *The Noël Coward Diaries* (Weidenfeld & Nicolson, 1982).

Perry, Roland, *The Queen, Her Lover and the Most Notorious Spy in History* (Allen & Unwin, 2014).

Selected Bibliography

Picknett, Lynn and Clive Prince and Stephen Prior, *War of the Windsors: A Century of Unconstitutional Monarchy* (Mainstream, 2002).

Petropoulos, Jonathan, *Royals and the Reich: The Princes von Hessen in Nazi Germany* (Oxford University Press, 2006).

Phillips, Adrian, *The King Who Had to Go: Edward VIII, Mrs Simpson and the Hidden Politics of the Abdication Crisis* (Biteback, 2016).

Pimlott, Ben, *The Queen: A Biography of Queen Elizabeth II* (Collins, 1996).

Platt, Owen, *The Royal Governor . . . and The Duchess: The Duke and Duchess of Windsor in The Bahamas 1940–1945* (iUniverse, 2003).

Pope-Hennessy, James, *Queen Mary* (Allen & Unwin, 1959).

Powell, Ted, *King Edward VIII: An American Life* (OUP, 2018).

Pye, Michael, *The King Over the Water: The Scandalous Truth About the Windsors' War Years* (Hutchinson, 1981).

Quennell, Peter (ed.), *A Lonely Business* (Weidenfeld & Nicolson, 1981).

Ravensdale, Baroness, *In Many Rhythms* (Weidenfeld & Nicolson, 1953).

Roberts, Andrew, *Eminent Churchillians* (Weidenfeld & Nicolson, 1994).

Roberts, Cecil, *The Pleasant Years* (Hodder & Stoughton, 1974).

Rogers St Johns, Adela, *The Honeycomb* (Harper & Row, 1969).

Romanones, Aline, Countess of, *The Spy Went Dancing* (Putnam, 1990).

Rose, Norman (ed.), *Baffy, The Diaries of Blanche Dugdale 1936–47* (Valentine Mitchell, 1973).

Schad, Martha, *Hitler's Spy Princess: The Extraordinary Life of Princess Stephanie von Hohenlohe* (Sutton, 2004).

Scheips, Charlie, *Elsie de Wolfe's Paris: Frivolity Before the Storm* (Abrams, 2014).

Schofield, Victoria, *Witness to History: The Life of John Wheeler-Bennett* (Yale, 2012).

Schwarz, Paul, *This Man Ribbentrop: His Life and Times* (Julian Messner, 1943).

Seagrim, Anne, *An Improbable Career* (privately published).

Sebba, Anne, *That Woman* (Weidenfeld & Nicolson, 2011).

Selby, Sir Walford, *Diplomatic Twilight* (John Murray, 1953).

Shakespeare, Nicholas, *The Men Who Would be King* (Sidgwick, 1984).

Shanley-Toffolo, Oonagh, *The Voice of Silence* (Rider, 2002).

Shaughnessy, Alfred, *Both Ends of the Candle* (Peter Owen, 1978).

Shawcross, William, *Queen Elizabeth, the Queen Mother* (Macmillan, 2009).

Smith, Amanda (ed.), *Hostage to Fortune: The Letters of Joseph P. Kennedy* (Viking, 2001).

Smith, Jane, *Elsie de Wolfe: A Life in the High Style* (Atheneum, 1982).

Spooner, Doreen, *Camera Girl* (Mirror Books, 2016).

Spoto, Donald, *Dynasty: The Turbulent Saga of the Royal Family from Victoria to Diana* (Simon & Schuster, 1995).

Steed, R.H.C. (ed.), *Hitler's Interpreter* (Heinemann, 1951).

Stowell, Sean, *Dr Alexander Cannon: The King's Psychic* (Great Northern Books, 2014).

Strobl, Gerwin, *The Germanic Isle: Nazi Perceptions of Britain* (Cambridge University Press, 2000).

Strong, Roy, *Splendours and Miseries: The Roy Strong Diaries 1967–87* (Weidenfeld & Nicolson, 1997).

Sulzberger, Cyrus, *A Long Row of Candles* (Macdonald, 1969).

Sulzberger, Cyrus, *An Age of Mediocrity* (Macmillan, 1973).

Selected Bibliography

Taylor, Fred (ed.), *The Goebbels Diaries 1939–1941*(Hamish Hamilton, 1982).

Templewood, Viscount, *Ambassador on Special Mission* (Collins, 1946).

Templewood, Viscount, *Nine Troubled Years* (Collins, 1954).

Thomas, Gwynne, *King Pawn or Black Knight* (Mainstream, 1995).

Thornton, Michael, *Royal Feud: The Queen Mother and the Duchess of Windsor* (Macmillan, 1985).

Thorpe, Richard (ed.), *Who's In, Who's Out: The Journals of Kenneth Rose, Vol. 1 1944–1979* (Weidenfeld & Nicolson, 2018).

Thorpe, Richard (ed.), *Who Loses, Who Wins: The Journals of Kenneth Rose, Vol. 2 1979–2014* (Weidenfeld & Nicolson, 2019).

Trevor-Roper, Hugh (ed.), *Hitler's Table Talk* (Weidenfeld & Nicolson, 1953).

Turner, Henry Ashby, *General Motors and the Nazis* (Yale, 2005).

Turnquest, Orville, *What Manner of Man Is This?: The Duke of Windsor's Years in The Bahamas* (Grant's Town Press, 2016).

Urbach, Karina, *Go-Betweens for Hitler* (Oxford University Press, 2015).

Vickers, Hugo, *Cecil Beaton* (Weidenfeld & Nicolson, 1985).

Vickers, Hugo, *The Private World of the Duke and Duchess of Windsor* (Harrods Publishing, 1995).

Vickers, Hugo (ed.), *The Unexpurgated Beaton* (Weidenfeld & Nicolson, 2002).

Vickers, Hugo, *Behind Closed Doors* (Hutchinson, 2011).

Vickers, Hugo (ed.), *The Windsors I Knew: An American Private Secretary's Memoir of the Duke and Duchess of Windsor, Nassau, Bahamas 1940–1944* (Independently published, 2018).

Vidal, Gore, *Palimpsest: A Memoir* (Deutsch, 1995).

Vincent, John (ed.), *The Crawford Papers: The Journals of David Lindsay 1892–1940* (Manchester University Press, 1984).

Vreeland, Diana, *DV* (Knopf, 1984).

Wainwright, Robert, *Sheila: The Australian Ingenue Who Bewitched British Society* (Allen & Unwin, 2014).

Wainwright, Robert, *Enid: The Scandalous High-Society Life of the Formidable 'Lady Killmore'* (Allen & Unwin, 2020).

Waller, John, *The Unseen War in Europe: Espionage and Conspiracy in the Second World War* (I.B. Tauris, 1996).

Warwick, Christopher, *Abdication* (Sidgwick & Jackson, 1986).

Watt, Donald Cameron (ed.), *Contemporary History in Europe: Problems and Perspectives* (Allen & Unwin, 1969).

Webb, Clifton, *Sitting Pretty: The Life and Times of Clifton Webb* (University Press of Mississippi, 2011).

Weinberg, Gerhard, *A World at Arms* (Cambridge University Press, 2005).

Weitz, John, *Hitler's Diplomat: The Life and Times of Joachim von Ribbentrop* (Weidenfeld & Nicolson, 1992).

West, Nigel, *The Guy Liddell Diaries, Vol. 1: 1939–1942* (Routledge, 2005).

West, Nigel, *The Guy Liddell Diaries, Vol. 2: 1942–1945* (Routledge, 2005).

West, Nigel, *Cold War Spymaster: The Legacy of Guy Liddell, Deputy Director of MI5* (Frontline, 2018).

Wheeler-Bennett, John, *King George VI: His Life and Reign* (Macmillan, 1958).

Wheeler-Bennett, John, *Friends, Enemies and Sovereigns* (Macmillan, 1976).

Williams, Chris (ed.), *The Richard Burton Diaries* (Yale, 2012).

Williamson, Philip and Edward Baldwin (ed.), *The Baldwin Papers* (Cambridge University Press, 2004).

Wilson, Christopher, *Dancing With the Devil: The Windsors and Jimmy Donahue* (Collins, 2000).

Selected Bibliography

Wilson, Jim, *Nazi Princess: Hitler, Lord Rothermere and Princess Stephanie von Hohenlohe* (History Press, 2011).

Windsor, Duchess of, *The Heart Has Its Reasons* (Michael Joseph, 1956).

Windsor, Duke of, *A King's Story* (Cassell, 1951).

Windsor, Duke of, *The Crown and the People 1902–1953* (Cassell, 1953).

Windsor, Duke of, *A Family Album* (Cassell, 1960).

Windsor, Duke of, *Windsor Revisited* (Houghton Mifflin, 1960).

Wright, Peter, *Spycatcher* (Viking, 1987).

Wright, William, *Heiress: The Rich Life of Marjorie Merriweather Post* (New Republic Books, 1978).

Young, Kenneth (ed.), *The Diaries of Sir Robert Bruce Lockhart 1915–1938, Vol. 1* (Macmillan, 1973).

Young, Kenneth (ed.), *The Diaries of Sir Robert Bruce Lockhart 1939–1965, Vol. 2* (Macmillan, 1980).

Ziegler, Philip, *Mountbatten* (Collins, 1985).

Ziegler, Philip, *King Edward VIII* (Collins, 1990).

Ziegler, Philip (ed.), *From Shore to Shore: The Final Years* (Collins, 1989).

ARTICLES

Bates, Stephen, 'Edward Forced to Stay in Exile or Risk Income', *Guardian,* 30 January 2003.

Bowcott, Owen and Stephen Bates, 'Fear that Windsors Would "Flit" to Germany', *Guardian*, 30 January 2003.

Boyd, William, 'The Real-life Murder Case Behind Any Human Heart', *Guardian*, 13 November 2010.

Bry, Charlotte, 'End of an Era', *People Magazine*, 22 December 1986.

Cornforth, John, 'The Duke and Duchess's House in Paris', *Country Life*, Vol. 181(26), 25 June 1987, pp. 120, 123–5.

Dawson, Elizabeth, 'Comfort and Freedom: The Duke of Windsor's Wardrobe', *Costume: The Journal of the Costume Society*, 1 June 2013, Vol, 47, No. 2, pp. 198–215.

Edwards, Anne, 'For Belvedere: Inside the Private Realm of Edward VIII and Wallis Simpson', *Architectural Digest*, December 1991.

Evans, Rob and David Hencke, 'Wallis Simpson, the Nazi Minister, the Telltale Monk and an FBI Plot', *Guardian*, 29 June 2002.

Evans, Rob and David Hencke, 'Hitler Saw Duke of Windsor as "No Enemy" US File Reveals', *Guardian,* 24 January 2003.

Flanner, Janet, 'Department of Amplification: Annals of Collaboration', *New Yorker*, 22 September, 6 and 13 October 1945.

Hussey, Christopher, 'Fort Belvedere, Surrey', *Country Life*, 19 and 26 November 1959.

Fox, James, 'The Oddest Couple', *Vanity Fair*, September 2003.

Kinross, Lord, 'Love Conquers All', *Books and Bookmen*, Vol. 20, 1974, p. 50.

Legrand, Cathy, 'Another Look at a Bahamian Mystery: The Murder of Sir Harry Oakes', *International Journal of Bahamian Studies*, Vol. 16, 1 January 2010, pp. 92–101.

Oursler Jr, Fulton, 'Secret Treason', *American Heritage* 42, No. 8, December 1991.

Palmer, Lilli, 'Garbo and the Duke', *Esquire*, September 1975.

Paul, J.B., 'The Duke of Windsor and the Nazis', *Quadrant* 49, pp. 70–5.

Pigeon, Rene, 'Royal Renunciation: Edward VIII and the Problems of Representation', *Film & History,* Vol. 45(2), Winter 2015, pp. 13–23.

Selected Bibliography

Prochaska, Frank, 'Edward VIII: A Prince in the Promised Land', *History Today* 58, No. 12, 2008.

Pryce-Jones, David, 'TV Tale of Two Windsors', *New York Times Magazine*, 18 March 1979.

Rogers St John, Adela, 'Windsors' Own Story', *King Features Syndicate*, November 1940.

Romanones, Countess of, 'The Dear Romance', *Vanity Fair*, June 1986.

Sweet, Paul, 'The Attempts to Officially Influence the Edition of the Documents on German Foreign Policy, 1933–1941', *Quarterly Journals for Contemporary History*, Vol. 39, 1 April 1991, pp. 265–303.

Sweet, Paul, 'The Windsor File', *The Historian*, Winter 1997.

Wheeler, Douglas, 'In the Service of Order: The Portuguese Political Police and the British, German and Spanish Intelligence, 1932–1945', *Journal of Contemporary History*, Vol. 18, No. 1, January 1983, pp. 1–25.

Wilson, Christopher, 'The Night That Edward Confronted Wallis Over Her Gay Lover', *Mail on Sunday,* 20 September 2014.

Windsor, Duchess of, 'Our First Real Home', *Woman's Home Companion*, October and November 1954.

Index

Index

Index

Index

Index